0919

MW00810369

# The Utah Gold Rush

## The Lost Rhoades Mine and the Hathenbruck Legacy

by

Kerry Ross Boren
& Lisa Lee Boren
with
Randy W. Lewis

COUNCIL·PRESS ™
Springville, Utah

Copyright © 2002 by Kerry Ross Boren & Lisa Lee Boren

All Rights Reserved.

No part of this book may be reproduced in any form whatsoever, whether by graphic, visual, electronic, film, microfilm, tape recording, or any other means, without prior written permission of the author, except in the case of brief passages embodied in critical reviews and articles.

ISBN:  1-55517-614-3
v.1

Published by Council Press
Imprint of Cedar Fort Inc.
www.cedarfort.com

Distributed by:

Typeset by Kristin Nelson
Cover design by Adam Ford
Cover design © 2002 by Lyle Mortimer

Printed in the United States of America
10 9 8 7 6 5 4 3 2 1

Printed on acid-free paper

Library of Congress Cataloging-in-Publication Data

Boren, Kerry Ross.
 The Utah Gold Rush : the lost Rhoades mine and the Hathenbruck legacy
/ by Kerry Ross Boren, Lisa Lee Boren, with Randy W. Lewis.
    p. cm.
 ISBN 1-55517-614-3 (pbk. : alk. paper)
1.  Uintah Mountains (Utah and Wyo.)--Gold discoveries. 2.  Uintah
Mountains (Utah and Wyo.)--Biography. 3.  Hathenbruck, F. W. C. 4.
Rhodes family. 5.  Gold mines and mining--Uintah Mountains (Utah and
Wyo.)--History. 6.  Treasure-trove--Uintah Mountains (Utah and Wyo.) 7.
Uintah Mountains (Utah and Wyo.)--History. 8.  Frontier and pioneer
life--Uintah Mountains (Utah and Wyo.) I. Boren, Lisa Lee. II. Lewis,
Randy W. III. Title.
 F832.U39 B67 2002
 979.2'14--dc21
                        2002002562

In memory of Gale R. Rhoades,
beloved cousin and friend,
who died on Hoyt Peak while searching for the Rhoades-Hathenbruck Mine.
He left his footprints in the wilderness and his heart in the mountains he loved.

# Acknowledgments

The authors gratefully acknowledge the following individuals for their contributions to this work

Bill Bleazard, who has forgotten more about the mountains and mines than most men will know

William "Bill" Mangum, grandfather of Randy Lewis and grandson of FWC Hathenbruck

Gary Young, who is a living tribute to his illustrious ancestors

Marva Loy Eggett, who strives to preserve the heritage of the Ute People

Patsy Christensen, who's personal belief in our effort has been heartfelt

Harold & Bette Hathenbruck, for providing access to the Hathenbruck papers

Jerry and Kathy Woolsey, fellow travelers on old trails

Paul Tabbee, great-grandson of Chief Tabby

C. Jan Bodily, grandson of Iowa J. Hall, an unsung westerner

Evan Dee Warner, for preserving the rare history of his renowned grandfather, Matt Warner

the late George Thompson, historian and loyal friend, who will be missed

the late Mel Fisher, who came, who saw, who conquered

and Lee Nelson, whose constant support and encouragement made this book possible

# Table of Contents

# A NOTE TO THE READERS

Following the publication of our book, *The Gold of Carre-Shinob*, in 1998, there was a renewal of interest in the Lost Rhoades Mines. Treasure hunters and prospectors flooded onto the reservation and into the mountains in record numbers. Unfortunately, many of them entered the Uintah-Ouray Indian Reservation without permission, leaving behind a trail of destruction, cutting down trees and digging holes with reckless abandon.

An attempt was made in *The Gold of Carre-Shinob* to discourage treasure hunters and prospectors from searching for the gold, but the lure of riches too often closes ears and minds to reason. The gold of the Uintah Mountains belongs exclusively to the Ute people, for whom it is secured. Too long have they suffered from the encroachment of the white man upon their land and upon their sacred traditions.

It is our hope that the readers of this book will learn the lesson of history from its pages. Illicit searches for the sacred gold of the Uintahs have brought about no greater reward than death and destruction, desolation and desecration.

At the same time, we realize that any attempt to discourage treasure hunters and prospectors will be an excuse in futility. The lure of riches far surpasses any benefit of advice, and will more than likely only encourage the search further.

Nevertheless, in the firm belief that most treasure hunters and prospectors are basically professional, we encourage all readers of this book with intentions to search for the Lost Rhoades Mines to seek permission of the Ute people before entering the reservation. Respect their rights and traditions, and leave the land as you found it—the most beautiful and sacred ground on earth.

The Authors

# INTRODUCTION

This is where it all began—with Bill Mangum.

When I was about eight or nine years old my grandfather Bill Mangum, of Heber City, Utah, often told us stories about his grandfather, F.W.C. Hathenbruck, and his gold mines. He said there were seven mines, but that his grandfather Hathenbruck had one in particular that he tried to develop.

Hathenbruck had built a cabin in Grandaddy Basin, in the vicinity of the mine, which fell into disrepair over the years, and a pine tree grew on top of the cabin, out of the old collapsed dirt roof.

The mine may not be close to the cabin, my grandfather Mangum said, but if you follow up the small stream nearby until it disappears into the mountain, you will find yourself in a bowl; you go around the bowl about two-thirds of the way and there you will find a hole. There are steps inside, going down into the entrance of the mine. Inside the entrance the mine opens up and there is a gold vein running through the wall of the mine. The vein, he said, ran from one-half inch thick to three-feet thick.

There is a sacred Indian burial ground near the mine and the Indians watch this place very closely.

My grandfather Mangum knew a great deal about his grandfather Hathenbruck's mine, and when I was a boy he talked a lot about it. Then suddenly that changed. Bill said he was awakened from his sleep one night to discover an Indian standing in his room. He was in full dress, like a chieftain, with a headdress as pure and white as a brilliant snow. The Indian spoke to him and said, "Bill, do not go to the place of the mines, for you and your family will be in danger." After this experience, it was hard to get my grandfather to talk about the mines anymore. He became very close-mouthed and would never say anything of value again concerning the mines.

On one occasion I was with my grandfather Mangum up near the Yellowstone River, and not far from the Uintah River. He looked up toward a nearby hill and said, "This is the location of one of the mines." Then he drove on and said no more about it.

All of my life I have heard stories of the Lost Rhoades Mines and of the part my ancestor, F.W.C. Hathenbruck, played in their history. It has stimulated a life-long interest in the lost mines. I have spent many years in the mountains, searching out old trails, Spanish symbols carved into trees and ledges, and other remnants of early mining activity. I have been to the ruins of Hathenbruck's old cabin, and I have managed to collect many family photos and papers relating to Hathenbruck and the mines.

There have been a number of books written on the subject of the Lost Rhoades Mines, but to date, the only book to detail the history of F.W.C. Hathenbruck has been *Footprints in the Wilderness: A History of the Lost Rhoades Mines*, by Gale R. Rhoades and Kerry Ross Boren. However, there has been no definitive history of F.W.C. Hathenbruck, and so it was I decided to collaborate with Kerry Ross Boren and his co-author, Lisa Lee Boren, to present the complete account of the remarkable life of F.W.C. Hathenbruck and his connection to the Lost Rhoades Mines.

The new information, together with previously unpublished maps, affords many new clues to treasure hunters, but perhaps even more importantly, it serves to protect the heretofore unknown history of one of the most remarkable men of his age.

Randy W. Lewis

# FOREWORD

The seventy-six year old man had fallen on hard times. In 1928 he was selling sewing machines and insurance policies door-to door in order to eke out a meager living. He was a familiar sight on the tree-lined streets of Provo, Utah. It was hard not to notice him. He wore an old tweed suit with matching vest, mended by one of his sewing machines to patch the holes where moths had made a recent meal. Where once he had an arm, his right sleeve hung limp and vacant. His neatly-trimmed and carefully-groomed goatee was white with age. He carried his paperwork in a tattered old carpetbag with his only arm, and knocked on doors with the toe of his shoe. He would set his bag down in order to take off his hat to the lady of the house. He exhibited the refined manners and decorum of an aristocrat, and spoke softly with a slight German accent. The distinguished-looking old gentleman was renowned for his gentle nature and benevolent largesse, in spite of his recent poverty. It was quite a come-down from the lofty pinnacle of success and prestige he had once achieved, and a paradox—because F.W.C. Hathenbruck had the potential to be the wealthiest man in the world!

F.W.C. Hathenbruck was a man of mystery. He carried in his breast two secrets of immense propor-tions, either of which, if made known, could alter the history of the world. The first of these secrets concerned his birth and parentage. The second of these secrets concerned the Lost Rhoades Mine. Hathenbruck seldom discussed either, with good reason—for many years his life depended on it. He had been forced into exile because of his illegitimacy. His birth became a threat to one great nation and an embarrassment to another. His knowledge of the Rhoades mine and his partnership with Caleb Rhoades made him a liability to both, and in the end prevented him from claiming it.

In 1971, I co-authored the landmark book *Footprints in the Wilderness: A History of the Lost Rhoades Mines* with my cousin Gale R. "Dusty" Rhoades, great-grandson of Thomas Rhoades, original discoverer of the mine. It was the first history written about the now famous lost gold mines. At that time, very little was known about the legendary mines, which were then better known as the "Lost Brigham Young Mines." Since that time, a number of accounts of the mines have been written, including a posthumous account by my late cousin Gale Rhoades, who lost his life searching for the mines in 1988.

In 1998, after nearly thirty years of silence concerning the Lost Rhoades Mines, I wrote *The Gold of Carre-Shinob*, co-authored with my wife Lisa Lee Boren. This book revealed for the first time the asso-ciation of Montezuma's treasure with the Rhoades Mines. It also presented for the first time the much neglected perspective of the Ute Indians on dealing with the mines.

When I wrote *The Gold of Carre-Shinob* I never intended to write another book about the mines, believing not only that another book on the topic would be redundant, but because my life has been liter-ally cursed by association with the mines. However, in the interim, a great deal of new information presented itself, offering not only new insight into the history of the legendary mines, but many new clues to their location.

I also determined to include with the text some pertinent information and clues withheld from my previous works, together with the reproduction of numerous maps which have long been kept from public scrutiny. But the basis of the book revolves around the history of the very remarkable character

F.W.C. Hathenbruck, together with his many notes, letters and papers gathered into one place for easy reference, for those who wish to search them for clues to the location of the famous mine.

There are a number of mines connected with Thomas and Caleb Rhoades. This book deals primarily with one of them, the Spanish mine which was the focus of interest by Rhoades and Hathenbruck, ostensibly rich enough, according to Caleb Rhoades, to pay off the national debt with enough surplus to pave the streets of New York City with gold! This mine is definitely located in the upper Rock Creek-Grandaddy Lakes Basin area, and the clues offered herein are specific. This volume completes the series of informative books about the Lost Rhoades Mines. Every attempt has been made to frankly present the evidence connected with this particular mine as completely as possible.

No complete account of the mines can be made in one volume. I have attempted to include as much pertinent information as possible, in the limited space. However, there are some things I will never tell, some clues I will never give, in deference to oaths taken and promises made to certain parties.

I am neither a treasure hunter nor a prospector. I have perhaps a peculiar overview. My interests are primarily concerned with history. It might surprise the reader to hear that I would prefer the mines remain forever hidden and undiscovered. To my mind, the greatest treasure that can be found in the Uintah Mountains are the mountains themselves. Having been born and raised there, I am adamantly opposed to any destruction and desecration of their natural beauty and splendor by mining or "progress."

Moreover, I believe unequivocally that the gold of the Uintah Mountains belongs exclusively to the Ute Indians for whom it is sacred. I intend to forever honor the sacred trust they have placed in me.

I have had the rare privilege of seeing some marvelous things connected to the Lost Rhoades Mines; for me it is enough.

Someone once asked me, "If these mines are so famous and so rich, why hasn't anyone ever found one?" The answer is simple: Someone did—F.W.C. Hathenbruck.

Kerry Ross Boren

# Chapter 1

## The Hathenbruck Legacy

The family tree of F.W.C. Hathenbruck begins, for our purposes, with Count Heinrich the Rich of Nassau (1180-1250), who was married to the Dutch Machteld of Guelders. Their eldest son, Walram II (1220-1276), was the father of the German King Adolf (1255-1298). Count Heinrich and Machteld were the ancestors of the Nassau-Weilburg line and the present Grand Duke of Luxenburg. A younger son, Otto I (ancestor of F.W.C. Hathenbruck), was the ancestor of the Nassau-Dillenburg line and the present Queen of the Netherlands.

The Nassau-Dillenburg family acquired vast possessions in the Netherlands by careful inter-marriage, beginning with Engelbert I (1370-1442), son of Otto I, who married the rich Dutch heiress Johanna van Polanen. They acquired the principality of Orange through the marriage of Hendrik III (great-grandson of Heinrich and Machteld) of Nassau (1483-1538) to Claudia of Chalon.

Johann V (1455-1516), Count of Nassau, Lord of Dillenburg, Siegen and Breda, stadholder of Guelders and Zutphen (1504-1505), grandson of Engelgert I, married in 1482 to Elizabeth of Hesse (1466-1523).

William I the Rich (1489-1555), son of Johann V and Elisabeth, was Count of Nassau, Vainden and Dietz, and married (1506) Waldurgis of Egmont (1489-1529). He married secondly in 1531 to Juliana of Stolberg-Wenigerode (1506-1580), widow of Philip II of Hanau-Munzenberg (1501-1529).

William I the Silent (1533-1584), son of William the Rich and Juliana, was also known as William of Orange. He was Prince of Orange (1544), Count of Nassau, Vianden and Dietz, Viscount of Antwerp, Baron of Breda, stadholder of Holland, Zealand and Utrecht (1559), Brabant (1577) and Friesland (1580). His first wife was Anna of Egmont (1533-1559), Countess of Buren, whom he married in 1551. After the death of his first wife, William of Orange had an affair with Eva Elix and fathered a son, Justinus of Nassau (1559-1631). He married secondly in 1561 Anna of Saxeny (1544-1577), which was annulled. His third wife, whom he married in 1575, was Charlotte de Bourbon-Montpensier (1546/47-1582). His fourth wife was Louise de Coligny (1555-1620), in 1583, widow of Charles de Teligny and daughter of Gaspard de Coligny.

Frederick Henry of Orange-Nassau (1584-1647), was Prince of Orange (1625), Count of Nassau, stadholder of Holland, Zealand, Uttrecht, Overijssel and Guelders (1625), Groningen and Drenthe (1640). Frederick Henry recognized one illegitimate child, Frederick of Nassau-Zuylenstein (1623/24-1672), whose eldest son Willem (1649-1708), became Count of Rochford and Viscount of Tunbridge. The last known descendant of the line of Nassau-Zuylenstein died in 1990. In 1625 Prince Frederick Henry married Amalia of Solms-Braunfels (1602-1675).

Louis Henriette (1627-1667), daughter of Frederick Henry and Amalia, was the aunt of William III, King of England, Scotland and Ireland (1688). Louise married (1646) Frederick William, The Elector of Brandenburg (1620-1688).

Frederick I (1657-1713), son of Frederick

William and Louise Henriette, was the first King of Prussia (1701). He married first in 1679 Elisabeth Henriette of Hesse-Cassel (1661-1683), secondly in 1684 Sophia Charlotte of Great Britain and Hannover (1668-1705). In 1708 he married thirdly to Sophia Louise of Mecklenburg (1685-1735).

Frederick William I (1688-1740), son of Frederick I and Sophia Charlotte, was King of Prussia (1713). He married in 1706 his cousin, Sophia Dorothea of Great Britain and Hannover (1687-1757). They had 14 children including:

August William (1722-1758) who married (1742) Luise of Brunswick-Wolffenbuttel (1722-1780). They had three children, including:

Frederick William II (1744-1797), King of Prussia (1786). He married first in 1765, divorced in 1769 his cousin, Elisabeth of Brunswick-Wolffenbuttel (1746-1840), and second in 1769 Frederike of Hesse-Darmstadt (1751-1805). He contracted a third bigamous and morganatic marriage in 1787 to Julie von Voss (1766-1789) and a fourth in 1790 to Juliane von Donhoff (1768-1834). In addition he recognized and enabled the children of his liaison with Wilhelmina Enke (1753-1820). He had nine legitimate children by his first two marriages, including:

Frederick William III (1770-1840), son of Frederick William II and Frederike. His sister, also called Frederike, married in 1791 Frederick August of Great Britain and Hannover, second son of mad King George III. Frederick William III was King of Prussia (1797). He married first in 1793 the famous Louise of Mecklenburg (1776-1810), and secondly in 1824 Augusta von Harrach (1800-1873). He had 5 sons and 5 daughters by his first wife, including:

William I (Wilhelm I) of Germany (1797-1888), King of Prussia (1861), Emperor of Germany (1871). He married in 1829 Augusta of Saxe-Weimar (1811-1890).

William I was grandfather of F.W.C. Hathenbruck. He was born 22 of March 1797 and died 9 March 1888. As King of Prussia and later the first German Emperor (Kaiserreick), he was a cautious ruler who presided over the rise of the Prussian Hohenzollern dynasty to official predominance over most of the other German states. His military career earned him a reputation as a reactionary, and he commanded Prussian troops in suppressing a revolt in Baden in 1849. He succeeded his ill elder brother, Frederick William IV, first as regent in 1858 and then as King of Prussia in 1861.

Initially, William's devotion to the constitution of 1848 seemed to herald a new era. His insistence, however, upon reorganizing the army to increase efficiency and political reliability brought on a constitutional conflict in 1862 with the Chamber of Deputies. Rejecting the compromise suggested by Otto von Bismarck, whom he appointed as prime minister, William strengthened both his ascendancy over the army and his opposition to parliamentary control. (William's correspondence with Bismarck was published in English translation in 1903). He commanded the army with the advice of his other chief advisor, Helmuth K. B. von Moltke.

William was content to stay out of the limelight in favor of the able men he retained in office. Although favoring German unity, he resisted his proclamation as German Emperor at Versailles in 18 January 1871, considering it a diminution of Prussian power. Honest, straightforward, and equipped with extraordinary common sense, William was innately conservative, desiring slow internal development to strengthen the monarchy and favoring strong ties with Russia. (His sister, Charlotte "Alexandra Feodorovna," married in 1817 Czar Nicholas l of Russia.) His conscientiousness and his modest, direct manner won him great popularity with the German people in his last years. He was succeeded briefly by his son, Frederick William III.

Frederick William III was born 18 October 1831 and died 15 June 1888. He reigned as

Emperor of Germany for only 99 days following the death of his father, when he himself died of cancer. Frederick III married in 1858 to Victoria, eldest daughter of Queen Victoria of Britain. As crown prince he served in the Franco-Prussian War (1870-1871) and was a patron of the arts. Frederick was considered a liberal, and his death disappointed many who had looked forward to his rule. He was succeeded by his son William II, who is better known as Kaiser Wilhelm II.

In 1851, at the age of twenty, Prince Frederick III had an affair with a palace maid, Fraulein Louisa Hudinburgh. When it was discovered that Louisa was pregnant with his child, Frederick's father William I, fearing the scandal that would disrupt the political aspirations of the Hohenzollern family, arranged to have the maid sent out of the country to deliver her bastard child.

William had already arranged a marriage of his son Frederick III with the daughter of Queen Victoria, as soon as the girl came of age. Victoria, whose own plans for the marriage alliance with the Hohenzollerns were threatened by the affair, was used to dealing with scandals among the nobility. She offered to take Fraulein Hudinburgh into her service as a Lady-in-Waiting at Buckingham Palace until after her delivery, and to take on the responsibility of the child's birth and primary education, until such time as her young daughter, also named Victoria, married the child's father.

When the time neared that Louisa was to deliver, she was transferred from the palace to one of the Queen's townhouses in Middlesex, London. Here, attended by the Queen's maids and a charity midwife, the child of the future Emperor of Germany, Frederick III, and the maid Louisa Hudinburgh, was born on 30 November 1852. The child, a boy, was given the anglicized name of Frederick William Claudius Hathenbruck. As an illegitimate child, he could

neither be confirmed in the Anglican Church nor carry his father's surname. Hathenbruck was the anglicized version of his mother's name—Hudinburgh.

After receiving his fundamental education in England, young Hathenbruck was summoned back to Germany when his grandfather became King of Prussia in 1861. He was placed with an aunt to be raised at Homburg, Toralansicht, with emphasis placed on his religious development. He was confirmed in the local church on 20 May 1866 at the age of fourteen. His confirmation certificate lists his name as "Frederick Wilhelm Claude," with no surname. The fate of his mother is unknown.

He was frequently brought to the palace, where his old grandfather now reigned as King of Prussia. His father, Frederick III, who was Crown Prince, and a patron of the arts, introduced him to the world of music, literature, and painting, and this cultural stimulation remained with him for the rest of his life. In later years his letters to friends were replete with references to the classics and fine music. His father took him to see performances of the famous Lippizaner (Lippenzaner) Stallions, and there he met a youth near his own age, Karl von Esterhazy, who would become his closest friend and companion. Esterhazy was himself the scion of a noble family; for generations the Counts of Esterhazy had been the official keepers and trainers of the Lippizaner Stallions, and Karl von Esterhazy was also an excellent horse trainer. Karl's grandfather had been a close friend and fellow Mason with the great composer Wolfgang Amadeus Mozart.

Hathenbruck's military training was not neglected. He attended military school for several years, and when the Franco-Prussian war threatened to explode he entered the army at the direction of his grandfather. But he found military life and regimen distasteful. He much preferred intellectual pursuits.

If Hathenbruck was less than enthusiastic

about a military career, his half brother, William II, was not. William was born 27 January 1859, was thus fully seven years younger than his brother, and jealous of his seniority. From his birth, William had a withered arm and under-developed left hand, which some have credited to his unstable and restless personality. He was early alienated from his liberal-minded parents by his belief in the divine nature of Kingship, his love of military display, and his impulsiveness. After studying at the University of Bonn, he entered the army.

William developed a strong antagonism toward England, the country of his strong-willed mother, Victoria, the daughter of the British Queen. His mother was the dominant parent, and her son's vociferous views toward her native land contributed to her display of favoritism toward her stepson Hathenbruck, who had been raised with her in England. Hathenbruck found himself embroiled unwillingly in the political intrigue.

For political purposes, young Hathenbruck was sworn to secrecy concerning his noble birth. As far as the populace knew his name was Hathenbruck, and he was simply one of the many young men of the palace who were sponsored by the royal family. Then one day, just before the outbreak of the Franco-Prussia War, just before William I was crowned Emperor of Germany at Versailles, Karl von Esterhazy made a major indiscretion: at a palace gathering he violated protocol by revealing that his good friend F.W.C. Hathenbruck was the true son of Crown Prince Frederick!

Such political furor was hardly ever known before in the Kingdom. Karl von Esterhazy was declared a demagogue, a political agitator, and his life could be forfeit. To save himself, he fled Germany and emigrated to the United States. Uncertain of his own fate, F.W.C. Hathenbruck went with him.

# Chapter 2

## PRINCE OF THE WEST

There is an oft-repeated story that F.W.C. Hathenbruck came West in 1857 in the Utah Expedition as physician for the army of Col. Albert Sidney Johnston, who had been sent by President Buchanan to subdue a supposed Mormon insurrection. It makes an interesting tale, but its tellers fail to realize that in 1857 Hathenbruck was only five years old!

In fact, Hathenbruck came West about the year 1869, when he was seventeen, in the company of his friend Esterhazy. They were part of an expedition generated by Hathenbruck's cousin, Wilhelm of Wied (1854-1907). Wilhelm was the second generation of his family to visit the American West. His father, Hermann of Wied (1814-1864), had also visited. Hermann married in 1842 to Marie of Nassau (1825-1902) who, like Hathenbruck, was a descendant of William of Orange. In the early 1830's while still Prince of Wied and in the throes of adventurous youth, Hermann had made an expedition into the headwaters of the Upper Missouri River. He explored and lived among the Mandan Indians, writing an account of his adventures.

Hermann's expedition inspired his son Wilhelm of Wied, who inherited his father's title and estates in 1864, to make his own trip to the American West, before his proposed marriage in 1871 to Marie of the Netherlands. Wilhelm's expedition started by hunting buffalo on the Kansas prairie, and indeed went hunting big horn sheep in the mountains of Wyoming, guided by the old mountaineer Jim Bridger.

When the expedition arrived at Fort Bridger, Wilhelm of Wied returned to Germany, but Hathenbruck remained in the West. Fort Bridger had been sold to the Mormons, who used it as a supply station for immigrating wagon trains. Fascinated by the stories he had heard about the Mormon people, Hathenbruck decided to continue on to Utah Territory and see for himself whether or not they were true.

Hathenbruck settled briefly in Utah Valley, at Provo, a place he came to like enough to make it his permanent home—eventually. For the time being, however, the main attraction of Utah Valley came in the shape of pretty sloe-eyed fourteen year-old Rozilla Rebecca Saunsecie. Rozilla was born 17 October 1855 at Provo, a daughter of Louis and Narcissa Rebecca (Fausett) Saunsecie. Her father was from Nebraska Territory, her mother from Tennessee, and the Saunsecies were converts to the Mormon Church. They fell in love beneath the perpetual snows of Mount Timpanogos and were married on 8 June 1871 at Provo; he was not quite 19, she was not quite 16.

While Hathenbruck was ascending to the institution of marriage in the American West, in Germany his grandfather, William I, was ascending to the position of Emperor. It was to have a profound impact upon the future of Hathenbruck. The old Emperor sent a delegation to Utah to meet with his grandson and induce him to come home. The emissaries assured Hathenbruck that he was in no danger now that his grandfather reigned, and that he was being offered the fulfillment of his dreams—a state-sponsored university education.

The offer was inducement enough for Hathenbruck to return to Germany. As promised, he was enrolled at the University of Heidelberg. He graduated with honors and degrees in medicine and mineralogy. But he was soon to learn that his recall had not been altogether for his education.

Hathenbruck's ostentatious half-brother, William II, was still lashing out against England, his mother's native land. To complicate issues, William's youth, inexperience, and desire to rule on his own brought a decisive clash with Chancellor Otto von Bismarck. Bismark had controlled German affairs for nearly 30 years, and he could see the writing on the wall if William were to succeed as German Emperor.

Ultimately, William would succeed to the throne in 1888, and he would force Chancellor Bismarck to resign in 1890; but for the time being, Bismarck was in power and with Victoria's help he devised a scheme which he hoped would prevent William's rise to power. That scheme was to involve legitimizing F.W.C. Hathenbruck, which would make him the eldest son and heir, and displacing William II as the next Emperor of Germany. There was already precedent: Hathenbruck's second great-grandfather, Frederick William II, King of Prussia, recognized and ennobled the children of his liaison with Wilhelmina Enke. There were numerous examples in the family tree.

If ennobled and legitimized, F.W.C. Hathenbruck would become "Fredrich Wilhelm Claud Hohenzollern," King of Prussia and Emperor of Germany! But Hathenbruck had other designs for his future. When the intrigue was plotted, he was enrolled in the University of Heidelberg. Though he might have been ambivalent about striving for the throne, his relatives were not; and he had some very impressive relations: Victoria, daughter of the British Queen, was his step-mother; Czar Nicholas II of Russia was his cousin; King Edward VII of England was his step-uncle; King George V of England was a cousin; in addition to a myriad of high-born aunts and uncles of the Hohenzollern dynasty. Most of these relatives, especially the English ones, would do most anything to prevent William II from becoming German Emperor. His hatred of the English and his love of military might could incite war. Their dread proved prophetic when William II, as Kaiser Wilhelm, Emperor of Germany, led the factions which brought about the First World War.

F.W.C. Hathenbruck was caught between the feuding factions. William II had surrounded himself with powerful political allies who were opposed to Chancellor Otto von Bismark and fearful that Hathenbruck might be ennobled and, as the eldest son, be placed on the throne. Intrigues were conspired against his life. If he remained in Germany, one of two scenarios would be played out: he would become German Emperor, or he would be assassinated.

But there was a third option: with his university degrees in medicine and mineralogy in hand, he could return to voluntary exile in the United States. He had a wife and children waiting for him in Utah. At last he turned his back upon his heritage and fled Germany forever. When both his grandfather and father died within months of one another in 1888, and with his half-brother Kaiser Wilhelm securely in power, he felt no more ties with his homeland.

The next decade of Hathenbruck's life is unmapped, though some things are known. Shortly after his return to the States, he signed on as post-physician for the U.S. Cavalry at Fort Sedgwick, Kansas. In later years he spoke of the hundreds of soldiers he patched up and attended as a result of Indian attacks, gunfights, wagon accidents, and mule-kicks. It might have been these experiences that inspired the story of his service with Johnston's Army.

Hathenbruck became enamored of the various native tribes he encountered. He kept notes on their languages, customs, and traditions, and sent them to his old professor in Germany; today they repose in the special collections of the University at Heidelberg. Even at this early date his notebooks are filled with notations on mineral deposits and topographical maps of his discoveries during his travels.

In 1876 Hathenbruck was attached to an army unit stationed near Deadwood, South Dakota. He spent his leisure hours prospecting in the Black Hills, filling his notebooks with notations which predicted the bonanza that was soon to be unearthed there. The discovery of Black Hills gold had the unfortunate side effect of displacing the Sioux Indians from their homelands, resulting in the Custer Massacre on the Little Big Horn, just across the border in Montana. When the official burial party arrived at the massacre site, Hathenbruck was one of the several attending doctors who examined the remains and identified the body of Gen. George Armstrong Custer. Later, when Custer's widow, Libby, applied for her husband's insurance, among the witnesses verifying the death of Custer is the prominent signature of "F.W.C. Hathenbruck, M.D."

During the mid-1880s, Hathenbruck opened a medical practice and assay office in the Colorado boomtown of Telluride. His old friend Karl von Esterhazy joined him there, still afraid for his life. Esterhazy was thoroughly convinced that a hit-squad had been commissioned to hunt him down and kill him. He was probably correct. During ensuing years, several mysterious attempts were made upon his life.

While they resided at Telluride, both Esterhazy and Hathenbruck became acquainted with a young renegade Utah boy named Robert Leroy Parker. Parker and his associates robbed the San Miguel Valley Bank at Telluride in the summer of 1889. Parker later became better known as Butch Cassidy, leader of the outlaw gang known as the Wild Bunch. During the 1890s, Esterhazy trained horses for the Wild Bunch in the Robbers Roost country of Utah.

Still fearing for his life, he felt protected among the outlaws. He was known among them only as "The Dutchman."

During the 1880s, David Moffat, wealthy president of both the First National Bank of Denver and the Denver & Rio Grande Railroad Company, pushed his railroad through Colorado westward into Utah. In order to accomplish this, the great Moffat Tunnel was driven through the barrier of the Colorado Rockies. F.W.C. Hathenbruck was the topographical engineer.

Afterwards, Hathenbruck returned to Provo. As the Denver & Rio Grande Railroad crossed Utah, once again Moffat called upon Hathenbruck to serve as topographical engineer building the railroad over the difficult Soldier Summit, through the Wasatch Mountains, between the towns of Price and Springville.

In the early seventies, two major discoveries were made at Park City, Utah, near the summit of the Wasatch Mountains: the Silver King and the Ontario. The former had been discovered by an Indian prospector named Supickett, (better known to the whites as Pick Murdock), and developed by Senator Thomas Kearns. The Silver King made Kearns rich: rich enough to build a mansion in Salt Lake City, rich enough to establish the Salt Lake Tribune newspaper, and rich enough to succeed in politics. The Ontario, on the other hand, was developed by a man already rich, another senator—George Hearst of California. Both mines made Park City a boomtown, and people flocked there in droves. One of them was F.W.C. Hathenbruck.

Hathenbruck opened an office in Park City where he practiced medicine and assayed ore. He made money enough at both to do some prospecting of his own, and the assays that he performed afforded him clues to prime locations. His expertise in mineralogy made his services in demand for many mine-related jobs, including the inspection of the large ore mills. During one inspection at the Kearns Mining & Milling Company property, he was asked to unclog large augers which had become stuck with ore. As Hathenbruck was digging between the augers up to the elbow of his right arm, the generator suddenly engaged the augers, mangling his arm and trapping him in the machine. All efforts to extract him proved futile. A runner was sent to retrieve Dr. Hathenbruck's medical bag from his office in town. The amazing doctor then commenced to amputate his own arm!

The loss of his right arm did not deter him. He practiced the use of his left hand until he was sufficiently adept to return to his medical practice. He opened an office in Provo and eventually built and operated the "F.W.C. Hathenbruck & Company Store" which specialized in fine furnishings, dry goods and notions for the residents of Utah Valley.

Hathenbruck soon gained the reputation of a kind, gentle, honest and generous physician and merchant who held no malice or prejudice toward anyone, regardless of race, color or creed. He treated and traded with the poor and minorities whether or not they could afford his services. He became known to one and all as "The Doctor."

Among the Doctor's many admirers were the Ute Indians from the Uintah-Ouray Reservation in the Uintah Basin. Even though the reservation was a hundred miles distant, the Utes would often travel to Provo to deal with the Doctor, rather than with the military personnel on the reservation, because he treated them with greater respect and honored their customs.

Hathenbruck discovered that he could do a lucrative business by trading directly with the Indians in the Uintah Basin. He was forbidden by law to trade on the reservation itself, so he had constructed a makeshift store just outside the reservation boundary near the present town of Roosevelt, Utah. Once or twice a year he would transport goods to the Basin by freight wagon, and his Indian friend, Tim Johnson, who lived and worked at the Indian Agency at White Rocks (a.k.a. Whiterocks), would lead a large contingent of Indians to the reservation boundary to trade. More often then not, he gave away a fourth as much as he traded. Eventually he sold out his interest in the operation to Al Murdock, who established a permanent mercantile at the location, around which grew the town of Roosevelt. Still, the Indians continued to make the long trip to Provo to deal directly with the Doctor.

Thus matters stood until one day late in the year 1894 when Hathenbruck received a mysterious telegram:

*Dr. F.W.C. Hathenbruck*
*243 East 5th North*
*Provo, Utah*

*Will be in Provo on Thursday next 2PM your residence—stop—would like to meet with you re matters of utmost importance—stop—by recommendation of WM H Dodge—stop*

*Caleb B. Rhoades*
*Price, Utah*

# Chapter 3

## THE RHOADES MINES

In 1894, the Rhoades Mines were only an unfounded rumor. No one could be certain they even existed, though it was universally believed that they did. The residents of Castle Valley and the town of Price were especially convinced of it. Caleb Rhoades, the source of the rumors, was a resident of their community. More than that, he was a pioneer founder of the settlement of Castle Valley, and was highly respected by all who knew him. But he was also a very private and secretive man.

Caleb Baldwin Rhoades was born in Illinois in 1836, in the midst of the religious insurrections between the Mormons and non-Mormon factions. In 1846, at ten years of age, he accompanied his father, Thomas Rhoades, and other family members, in a wagon train that arrived in Utah a full year before Brigham Young and the main body of Mormon pioneers. His life had been filled with adventure from early youth. The Rhoades wagon train had traveled across the plains with the Donner-Reed wagon company, and they had parted just before reaching Fort Bridger. The Rhoades company took the longer, more established northern route, while the Donner-Reed group took the unproven southern "Hastings Cut-off", put forth in a booklet published by Lanford W. Hastings, who had never traveled it. The fate of the Donners is patent history—stranded in heavy snows in the Sierra Nevada Mountains of California, they resorted to cannibalism to survive. The Rhoades family, who had arrived safely in California by the northern route, were in the rescue party which saved the survivors of the Donner-Reed company. [For a full account see: *Footprints in*

*the Wilderness: A History of the Lost Rhoades Mines*, Kerry Ross Boren & Gale R. Rhoades, Publishers Press, Salt Lake City, 1971.]

The Rhoades family had long been associated with gold. Thomas Rhoades was among the discoverers of gold at Sutter's Mill in the American River in California, and when he returned to Utah, he paid a tithe of ten percent of his findings, which amounted to $17,000 — which means that he recovered $170,000 worth of gold in California, no small sum in those days.

After settling in Rhoades Valley, near Kamas, and at Salem, Utah, Caleb Rhoades explored Castle Valley in 1877, and in the following year settled there, establishing a ranch some five miles from the town of Price. Almost from the beginning the rumors began to circulate that Caleb Rhoades had a gold producing source somewhere in the Uintah Mountains north of Price.

Rhoades frequently left Price with his pack mule and would set out toward the Uintah Mountains. When he returned, some ten to fourteen days later, he would immediately catch the first scheduled train to Salt Lake City, refusing to tell anyone where he had been. On his return from Salt Lake City he had new clothes, new furniture, new seed and improvements for his farm, an expensive gift or two for friends, and frequently a doctor or lawyer whom he had induced to move to Price at considerable monetary expense to himself.

Caleb's mysterious behavior and resolute secrecy was the cause of much controversy among his friends and neighbors, many of them envious of his great wealth. But the knowledge of such richness had not come as a blessing to Caleb Rhoades. It was, instead, the source of great consternation. He could not reveal to anyone the reason why he could not work the gold source openly, nor even confirm the existence of such a gold source.

In fact, whatever knowledge Rhoades may have had of gold in the high Uintahs must be kept secret by virtue of the presidential and congressional order which had revoked any mining rights he may have had upon these lands prior to 1864, by the creation of the Uintah-Ouray Indian Reservation.

Nevertheless, Caleb revealed to his brother that he did indeed have knowledge of a gold source in the Uintah Mountains, but he could do nothing about it due to an oath he had taken to Brigham Young and to Chief Aropene of the Utes. The mine was called the Sacred Mine, and it was protected by the Indians. But he admitted that he knew of seven other rich gold and silver mine locations in the Uintah Mountains—old Spanish mines, he called them—which were not affected by his oath.

In 1884, Caleb's younger brother, Enock Rhoades, who was engaged to be married to a young lady in Salt Lake City, pestered his brother to reveal to him the location of just one of the mines. He promised to take out only enough gold to give him a start in his new married life, and never to return. Against his better judgment, Caleb finally agreed. He provided his brother Enock with a map and instructions to a Spanish gold mine located somewhere in the Upper Rock Creek area of the Uintahs.

Enock departed from Price one day, telling his family and friends only that he was on his way to Salt Lake City to retrieve his bride-to-be. If anyone noticed that he left Price leading a pack-mule, instead of taking the train, no one made much if it. In fact, he headed north through Nine Mile Canyon (where writer Lee Nelson has found Enock's name carved on a ledge) toward the

snow-capped Uintah Mountains.

Enock Rhoades found the old Spanish mine on Rock Creek and filled his packs with as much of the rich ore as he could conveniently carry. Elated, he started off the mountain toward Salt Lake City; but he didn't get far. The Indians were waiting for him. He was forced to abandon his pack animal with all of the gold and to flee on horseback, but not before he took an arrow in the back. He made it as far as the Strawberry Valley when weakness overwhelmed him and he was forced to make camp and attempt to remove the arrow. Before the dawn of the following day the Indians caught up to him again and killed him. Caleb had to retrieve his younger brother's mutilated body, and it made him even more resolute to keep his secret.

Then, on 24 May 1888, the Congress of the United States passed the first of a series of laws which made it possible for him to develop his mines. This Act (25 STAT. 157) "provided that a designated portion of the Uintah Valley Indian Reservation should be restored to the public domain and sold upon ratification by three fourths of the adult male Indians residing on the reservation"; and, further "That all moneys [sic] arising from the sales of this land shall belong to said Indians and be paid into the Treasury of the United States and held or added to any trust funds of said tribes now there." [In the United States Court of Claims, No. 47569, The Uintah and White River Bands of Ute Indians, Plaintiff v. The United States of America, page 7.] Caleb Rhoades once again began to think seriously about developing his mines.

On a certain evening in 1893, Caleb invited three of his closest friends—John A. Powell and the Horsley brothers, A.W. and Ernest—to his home near Price. Ernest Horsley was the local Mormon bishop. He told them he had something to reveal to them, but before doing so he swore them to absolute secrecy. He spoke to them throughout most of that night, and because one of the Horsley brothers recorded the conversation in his diary, we have a record of it.

Caleb revealed to them that he did in fact have a gold mine in the Uintah Mountains, and to prove it he showed them samples of the rich ore. They asked him why he did not open his mine and work it. He explained the circumstances, and his friends listened intently.

He said that there was enough gold in the mine he worked to pay off the national debt if only he could get governmental permission to develop it, but inasmuch as it was on the Ute Indian reservation he was stymied. The recent attempts by Congress to reopen the reservation were too slow in coming to fruition, and he began to express his bitterness and frustration. He mentioned the irony of how he had settled Castle Valley with dreams of making it a farmland, only to have coal discovered and the coming of the railroad, turning the valley from agriculture to industry; and yet he couldn't develop his own mine. "At that time," he said bitterly, "both my father and myself were perfectly content with the agreement, but times have changed." He continued by saying that even though the Indians were his friends, his bitter past experience, resulting in the death of his brother Enock, taught him that it would not be safe to let anyone else in on the fabulous secret unless he could obtain permission from the Utes. He swore that while he had taken gold from the Spanish mines, he had never revealed the location of the Sacred Mine to any man, nor would he do so as long as he lived. He had sworn an oath to Brigham Young and to Chief Aropene, and he felt bound to that oath.

The genesis of the "Lost Rhoades Mines" lies in the tale of an ancient source of gold predating even the Ute Indians, stemming from their ancestors whom the Utes called the "Old Ones." The Old Ones were undoubtedly the Aztecs, because the Utes owe their origin to the Uto-Aztecan ethnology.

The Aztecs mined the gold in ancient times and utilized it for sacred masks and statuettes used in their religious ceremonies, and in jewelry worn by the Kings and priests. When the Aztecs left the Utah region circa 1169 A.D. (according to their own calendar sources), they carried away the gold they had already mined, and left the Utes in charge of protecting the Sacred Mines.

The Aztecs settled en masse in central Mexico and built the great city of Tenochtitlan and made it the center of a great empire. Then, in 1519, when Montezuma reigned as emperor, Hernan Cortes and his Spanish army invaded Mexico, conquered the Aztecs, and confiscated their gold. Montezuma was killed, but before he died, he dispatched more than 1500 royal bearers north along the "Trail of the Old Ones," loaded with the bulk of the great Aztec treasure—boxes of pearls and precious gems, gold and silver masks and statuettes, and disks the size of cartwheels, made of gold and silver and inscribed with glyphs and sacred writings—and they deposited the treasure in a sacred cave in the bowels of the Uintah Mountains. The Utes, who called the place Carre-Shinob ("where the Great Spirit dwells"), were made the caretakers of the treasure, as well as the mines from whence the gold had derived. [For more information, see: *The Gold of Carre-Shinob*, Kerry Ross Boren and Lisa Lee Boren, Bonneville Books, Springville, Utah, 1998.]

For more than 600 years the sacred treasure of Carre-Shinob, and the Sacred Mines from whence the gold derived, were left in the care of the medicine men (shamans) of the Ute Nation. Then, not long before the arrival of the Mormons in 1847, the guardianship of the sacred gold was given to a Ute chieftain—a man the whites called Chief Walker.

Chief Walker was born about 1808, a son of Moonch, a Ute war-chief, and Tishuem Igh, a Paiute woman. His Indian name was Pan-a-

Carre Quinker ("Iron Twister"). As a young man, Pan-a-Carre Quinker questioned his destiny and so went off alone into the Uintah Mountains to fast and pray to Towats for an answer. [For more details, see *The Gold of Carre-Shinob*, op. cit; also: *Following the Ark of the Covenant*, Kerry Ross Boren & Lisa Lee Boren, Council Press Books, Springville, Utah, 2000.]

Pan-a-Carre Quinker claimed to have seen a vision of Towats in which the Great Spirit showed him Carre-Shinob and the Sacred Mines, and told him that he would now be the guardian of the sacred gold. Towats changed his name from Pan-a-Carre Quinker to "Yah-Keerah," which means "Keeper of the Yellow Metal." The whites, unable to pronounce his name correctly, called him Walker.

Towats also told Walker that he was to reveal the secret of the sacred gold to no man, except the "High Hats," when they came. At first Walker thought the High Hats must be the O'uatz (Mexicans), for they had once mined the region and took out much gold; but they were cruel to his people, and he knew it could not be them, for Towats had said the gold could only be used for good. When Jim Bridger, Kit Carson, Peg Leg Smith and other mountain men came into the region, he thought it might be them, but they laughed that he thought they could be miners.

Then, in 1843, Chief Walker was at Fort Uintah in the Uintah Basin to trade with the whites, when he lapsed into a coma. Antoine Robidoux, the post trader, thought he was dead, but he eventually revived, to tell a strange tale. He said that Towats had changed him into a spirit, and he had flown like an eagle over the Uintah Mountains and beyond, to the plains of Wyoming. Towats had shown him the High Hats in another vision, crossing the prairie and the mountains in their "rolling wickiups." More than this, Towats showed him one great man among them to whom he must give the secret of the sacred gold. "When will this man come?" Walker asked.

"Soon," Towats replied.

On 14 June 1849, Chief Walker rode into Salt Lake Valley at the head of a contingent of his warriors, to speak with Brigham Young about the intentions of the Mormons toward his people. As the pipe of peace was passed between them, Walker's eyes fell upon Isaac Morley, one of the Mormon authorities.

"I have seen you before," the chief told Morley. "I have seen you in a vision. You will come and live among my people. We will be brothers."

On 23 October 1849, Isaac Morley set out for the Sanpete Valley with 244 colonists to settle in the midst of the Ute Indians. He founded the town of Manti and came to be revered by both Mormons and Utes. The friendship between Isaac Morley and Chief Walker deepened until, on 13 March 1850, Morley baptized Walker and his brother Aropene [Aropeen, Aropine, etc.] by immersion in the ice-choked waters of City Creek near Manti.

# Chapter 4

## CHIEF WALKER
## AND THE MONEY-ROCK

The bond of friendship and trust between Isaac Morley and Chief Walker was at its apex at the time of Walker's baptism. Shortly after his baptism, Chief Walker came alone to Morley's home and asked to speak to him in private. Morley described the event in his journal:

*...Walker appeared to be very nervous and uncertain. He never seemed comfortable indoors, and at first I attributed it to this, but there was something different in his demeanor that I could not discern the meaning of. "I will show you something," he said, removing a small buckskin pouch tied on a long leather thong about his neck. He dumped the contents onto the table-top. Even in the dim light I could see that the pile of thumb-sized rocks were gleaming with yellow color, and I recognized it immediately as being as pure gold as I had ever seen. Walker called it "money-rock," and I was quite surprised at his casual attitude towards the great fortune before him.*

Walker recited the long history of the gold, informed Morley that Towats had shown him in a vision that Morley was to be the man to whom he should reveal the secret, and then said, "I will show you where is money-rock." But Morley convinced the chief that the gold should be given to the Mormon Chief, Brigham Young, for the benefit of all the Mormons.

Walker reluctantly agreed to provide the gold to Brigham Young, under certain conditions, but first he must take Morley to Carre-Shinob, because Towats had commanded it. They would go, he said, as soon as the snow melted in the high country. Isaac Morley wrote

promptly to Brigham Young, and the letter reached the Mormon President on 23 March 1850:

*...Thinking this to be a matter of the utmost urgency, and for your eyes only, I remit this letter among those sealed as matters of intelligence concerning the Natives of this place. Walker has this day come to see me, bringing with him a pouch of what appears to be the purest gold, in the form of nuggets uniformly the size of the nail of the thumb or larger. He reports these to have come from an ancient mine somewhere high in the mountains to the east of this place, and has offered to take me there, and to give me the gold on the basis of our friendship. He tells a marvelous story of a vision, in which the spirit of Towats appeared to him, making him the keeper of the "money-rock," as he calls it, until the Mormons came, at which time he was told to give it to them. He perceives, somehow, that I am the man that Towats chose to have the gold, but I have managed to convince him that you, as the great Mormon Chief, should have it, and he is willing that it should be so...*

*I firmly believe in the truth of Walker's statement that such a mine does exist somewhere in the mountains, and I am willing to go with him there to verify it, if you see it in your wisdom for me to do so. Walker says the trip will take two or three weeks, as soon as the snow melts in the mountain passes. The snow goes daily here in the valleys, and should be gone in the high country before a month or two has passed...*

*The door is opened for a marvelous work in these last days, and an expression of good feelings from Walker has given us the prospect of filling the bellies of the Saints with food and our temples with decorations befitting the Lord of Solomon. If the mine is as rich as Walker purposes it to be, then might our temple rival even that of Solomon's in its richness...*

*I would never permit others to enrich themselves, nor would I enrich myself, at the expense of the Natives who daily perish from cold and hunger and disease. It is my fervent hope that the Lord of Hosts has chosen me as a means to bring forth this wealth for His purposes, that His people, red and white alike, may be relieved of their suffering...*

*Walker will do nothing until hearing from you, which I pray will be by return messenger, for it is the nature of the uncivilized mind to forever change...*

On 13 May 1850, Isaac Morley wrote in his journal: "This morning before sunrise, I left Sanpete [Valley] in the company of Walker, Ungas-ton-igats, Poonch, and Arropine for the sacred mine of the Indians." He records the route taken out of Sanpete Valley as being through Salt Creek Canyon and eastward over Sanpete Mountain. His journal offers some interesting descriptions of the route:

*...[from Sanpete Mountain] we turned northeasterly, traveling all of one day and into part of one night, so that after dark I saw but little in the way of landmarks. On the morning of the third day, leaving our night camp in a grove of aspen, we emerged from a large ravine which wound like a snake for several miles onto a dry plateau. Here, for the first time I beheld the snow-crested peaks of the Uintah mountains (which Walker calls—"Winty") to the north, which I had observed several years since to our south while crossing the Plains near Bridger's Fort...*

*On the evening of the fifth day we camped near a cold stream which tumbles off the mountains in levels, like stairs, where Poonch made a willow trap and caught us several trout for supper. Next to our camp was an old trail between trees with curious markings on them, which Walker said were carved there by the Mexicans in the time of his grandfather, who the Mexicans called Saint Peter or Pedro...*

*Walker recounted an interesting story of a party of these Mexicans who brought gold from the Indian mine on burros into the valley south of Sanpete some three years since—about the time the Mormons first arrived in Zion. The Mexicans were all killed in their camp and the gold returned to the Indian mine along this very trail. After the gold was thrown back into the bowels of the mine, the Indians took the burros away and slew them, in order to keep their spirits from divulging the mine's location. As I was told this story, I could not refrain from wondering, or at least pondering, that if they would dispose of a burro for any uncivilized reason, how easy would it be to do the same to a white man like myself, worth much less to them than a burro? At night my prayers reflect my fears, and I am always surprised when in the morning I awaken alive and well...*

*On the sixth day we arrived at a large alpine lake, after meandering through timber for many hours. We skirted the south shore and climbed a low pass between two large buttes protruding above the timber line, and covered, as is most of this high country, with layers of rocks. Beyond the pass we traveled all day through alternating meadows and trees, the meadows being deep and wet from melting snow...*

*On the seventh day we crossed the largest crest and dropped swiftly down the northern slope, past some vermillion cliffs to our right (east), then through heavy timber for two hours. We emerged at the foot of a large formation which I named "The Two Sisters," where a fault has rended the cliffs, leaving a huge crack between two large formations resembling, I thought, women, but Walker prefers to think of them as bears, guardians of the entrance to the sacred Indian mine...*

*Entering between the Two Sisters, we left our horses in a lush meadow, and ascended what appears to be an ancient trail, which climbs abruptly to a promontory whereby one can see the country both north and south for many miles with unobstructed view...*

*The entrance to the Indian mine lies just beyond this place, but Un-gas-ton-igats, and Poonch would go no further, having a superstitious aversion to the mine itself; and so, following close behind Walker, who alone dared to go further, I found myself soon ascending the steepest trail of our journey, where no horse could ascend or descend, but which might have been negotiated by a burro or mule...*

By the first week of June 1850, Isaac Morley had returned to Sanpete Valley, in possession of 58 pounds of almost pure gold. On June 9th he ordained Chief Walker an Elder in the Melchizedek Priesthood, the first of his tribe to be so honored.

Brigham Young put the gold to good use. Late in the fall of 1849, at about the same time Isaac Morley led the colonizers to Sanpete Valley, Thomas Rhoades arrived from California and paid a tithing of $17,000 in gold dust gleaned from Sutter's Mill. Rhoades's gold, together with Morley's gold, formed the basis of the coinage of gold coins, so-called "Mormon Money." John M. Kay and Willard Richards, under the supervision of Thomas Bullock, established the "Deseret Mint" in the home of Dr. William Sharp, dentist. The gold coins were cast in the values of $2.50 to $20.00, and were engraved on one side with an emblem of "clasped hands," surrounded by the official

engraving title and value amount, while the obverse was engraved with the "all-seeing eye," surrounded by the logo, "Holiness to the Lord."

Brigham Young left Salt Lake City on 31 July 1850 for a personal visit to Sanpete, where he arrived on Sunday, 4 August, averaging 27 miles a day with a meeting at Fort Utah enroute. To welcome the Church leader, Manti's only cannon was fired in salute from atop Temple Hill. On the day following his arrival, Brigham Young met secretly with Chief Walker, under the guise of going trout fishing with Isaac Morley. William Potter served as interpreter (though Walker spoke good English, he preferred to negotiate in his own language for the benefit of his sub-chiefs.) They discussed the possibility of bringing more gold out of the mountains for the use of the Mormons.

Chief Walker was happy to please the great chief Brigham, but he imposed specific conditions on further retrieval of the gold from the Sacred Mine. The location of the gold would be revealed to only one man, mutually trusted by Brigham Young and Chief Walker— not even Brigham Young was to know the location of the mine. The penalty of death would be imposed upon the man chosen to retrieve the gold should he reveal the location to any other person without permission from the Utes; any white man who attempted to follow the chosen man would also suffer death. Finally, the Indians would at no time assist in the removal of the gold, and the man chosen must take only as much as was needed on one trip at a time— no mining operation would be allowed.

About one month after the April conference of the Church in 1852, Brigham Young came to Manti accompanied by Thomas Rhoades, who had been appointed to the office of Church Treasurer the preceding March, prior to general conference at which time he was sustained in that office.

On 13 May 1852, when Brigham Young left

Manti, he invited Isaac Morley to travel with his company, ostensibly to familiarize him with conditions existing in that part of Mormon country. Morley returned on June 9th.

Brigham Young's purpose was to bring together Isaac Morley, the only white man who had actually been to the mine, and Thomas Rhoades, who had been selected as the man to bring gold from the Sacred Mine—subject to the approval of Chief Walker. Walker, being pleased with the negotiations, granted his consent for Thomas Rhoades to retrieve the gold. Brigham insisted that all parties involved swear an oath on the Book of Mormon that the agreement would not be rescinded and that no other party would be made privy to the secret. The oaths were performed in July, in the Endowment House, all of them dressed appropriately in temple garments—including Walker. Morley makes it clear in his journal that it was a "blood oath," i.e. the person who violated it would forfeit his life.

Thomas Rhoades made his first trip to the Sacred Mine shortly thereafter. All that is known about this initial trip of Rhoades' was that it took 14 days and that the first load of gold "was pure; and weighing about 62 pounds."

Thus matters stood for the next few years. Then, following the April 1854 General Conference of the Church, Isaac Morley paid a visit to his old friend, Chief Walker, who was camped on Meadow Creek. Morley wrote in his journal:

*There were tears in Walker's eyes. He was ill, and thought we might never see one another again. I told him that Towats would never allow brothers to be parted, and that should either of us die, or us both, we would meet again in the Lord's Heaven. He seemed pleased and comforted at that. "When Walker die," he said, "my brother Morley will speak to Towats when I am buried?" I told him I would. We parted with an embrace, which thing is not customary with Walker. He is the most unforgettable man I have ever known.*

On 29 January 1855, after a prolonged illness, Chief Walker died at his camp on Meadow Creek in Millard County. His body was tied to the back of his favorite horse and was escorted by a long procession of mourning, wailing, gourd-rattling Utes to the top of the mountain above Meadow Creek. A day or two later, several Ute Indians rode into Salt Lake City looking for Isaac Morley. They informed him of Chief Walker's death, saying, "You come." Several of the brethren, including Heber C. Kimball, cautioned Morley that Walker had often expressed the desire to have several Mormons killed and buried with him, to accompany him on his journey to the land of medicine dreams. Nevertheless, without hesitation, Morley hastily departed with the Indians, saying that he had given his promise to Walker to consecrate his grave and commend his soul to God.

It was early in February when Isaac Morley set out up Meadow Creek accompanied by Aropene and a few of the sub-chiefs. Even though it had been a relatively mild winter, the snow lay deep near the summit of the mountains, and their progress was slow. According to Indian custom, they traveled in absolute silence.

Even before they reached the crevice in the mountain rim where Chief Walker's body lay entombed, Morley heard the sound of crying. At first he thought it was someone mourning for the dead chief, but the mourners had long since departed, and as they neared the place he realized that the crying was emanating from the burial crevice, which had been walled up with rocks. The sounds came from two Piede slave children—a boy and a girl—who were placed there to accompany Walker on his journey to the spirit world. They were left alive, entombed within the grave, to slowly starve to death, their crying calculated to scare away evil spirits which might try to steal Walker's spirit on its three-day journey to the great beyond.

Aropene, who had succeeded his brother as chief, suddenly revealed that the burial was only temporary; Walker had requested to be buried with his ancestors at Carre-Shinob! His body had been packed in snow to preserve it until the snows melted in the high country. It was still expected that Isaac Morley would accompany the second burial party to perform last rites according to his promise.

Thomas Rhoades, the only other white man now permitted near the Sacred Mine, was indisposed by illness during 1855, and could make no trips into the mountains. His nineteen-year-old son, Caleb Baldwin Rhoades, was chosen to accompany Morley and the Ute tribal burial party on the pilgrimage to Carre-Shinob to inter the body of the chief. Caleb Rhoades was required to take the same oath his father and Morley had taken, and had to meet the approval of Chief Aropene. All things in readiness, with utmost secrecy being enforced, Isaac Morley and Caleb Rhoades departed Salt Lake City sometime late in April, and by the first week of May arrived at Meadow Creek.

At Meadow Creek the two white men joined Chief Aropene, his brother Tabby, and five other Utes—Un-gas-ton-igats, Cessapoonch, Fuchawana, Un-gaco-choop, and Rabbit—and repaired quietly to the crevice tomb on upper Meadow Creek and removed the body of Chief Walker. The body, still frozen, was strapped to the back of one of his favorite mounts for his last trip to Carre-Shinob.

This was Caleb Rhoades' first view of the Sacred Mine. A distinction must here be made between *Carre-Shinob* and the *Sacred Mine*. Carre-Shinob is a series of nine great caverns in which reposes the treasure of the Aztecs, as well as other ancient artifacts, and the remains of numerous "Old Ones," former leaders of the Uto-Aztecan nation. The Sacred Mine is one of seven ancient caves from which the sacred gold

was mined, and from which, according to Indian belief, their ancient race emerged from the underworld.

Chief Walker was interred—in a sitting position— within a chamber of Carre-Shinob, where also reposed the bones of his grandfather Sanpete, and many other of his ancestors. Like Sanpete, Walker was adorned with golden Aztecan artifacts—masks, breastplate, anklets, bracelets, necklaces and rings. Because of the superstition prevalent among the Utes, only Fuchawana, a Shaman, entered the burial chamber with the two white men.

When the final ceremony concluded and the two white men stepped outside into the bright sunlight only Aropene and Tabby were to be seen. Aropene instructed the two men to go to the Sacred Mine itself, collect the gold needed for Brigham Young, and return by themselves to Salt Lake City; the Indians were going south, he said. Then, to Morley, Aropene said, "You no come here any more." "Don't worry," Morley replied. "I am too old." He was nearly seventy.

Isaac Morley died at North Bend, Utah, on 24 June 1865 at the age of seventy-nine. His part in the saga of the Rhoades Mines was never known before the release of our book, *The Gold of Carre-Shinob*, in 1998.

Caleb Rhoades replaced his father as the delegated person to bring gold out of the Sacred Mine for Brigham Young and the Church. Moreover, he continued to work the Spanish mines for his own use for fifty years!

One evening in 1897, at a gathering of friends in a home at Price, Utah, everyone present was called upon to dance, recite, play music, or in some way contribute to the evening's entertainment. When it came the turn of Caleb Rhoades, he rose slowly from his chair and surprised everyone by telling the story of the mines for the first time publicly. His speech was recorded by Lester Eklund, who was present, in his journal. Caleb said:

*Folks, I must confess that I'm one of those unfortunate beings that nature, in bestowing her gifts, overlooked. I can neither sing, dance, nor recite. However, and inasmuch as there has been so much speculation about the Rhoades Mine, I'll tell you facts concerning the same, hoping you will let me off at that.*

*One day, shortly after my father had returned from the gold fields of California, he met President Young on a street in Salt Lake City. "Brother Rhoades," President Young began, "you are the very man I've been looking for. I've a little mission for you. I want you to go into the Uintah Mountains to an old mine, with a guide that Chief Walker is going to appoint, and bring back as much gold ore as you can."*

*On the appointed day, true to his promise, Chief Walker met President Young. With him he brought several hundred warriors, all gaily attired, a gesture which bespoke the importance that the noted war chief regarded the occasion...That was in the beginning. Father made many trips, both to and from the old mine, without incident.*

*Then, one summer, father was ill and couldn't go, and for some time Chief Aropene,*

*who was then chief of the Utes, seemed to be mentally wrestling with the problem. Then his dark eyes snapped as if an answer had come. Pointing to me he asked, "What about Boy?" To which President Young nodded approval. At that, Chief Aropene ordered my guide to come forward, and in the presence of all assembled, he gave final instructions to my new guardian; "You go Uintah, get plenty money rock, bring to great White Chief." He pointed to President Young, then pointing to me, he added, "If boy get hurt, lost or no come back," at that he drew his hunting knife across his own throat, the meaning of which no one doubted. Of me he requested that I hold up my right hand and vow before all present that I never would disclose the location of the mine to anyone as long as I lived. That oath I have never broken.*

*We went, and in due time returned with the ore. Thus, I fulfilled father's mission. I've been back since, and as long as President Young was alive the Indians proved friendly enough, but since, they have shown a very ugly disposition. Going back into the Uintahs has become very dangerous. [Journal of Lester Eklund, courtesy his widow, Pears S. Eklund, Manti, Utah.]*

# Chapter 5

## THE RHOADES-HATHENBRUCK CONNECTION

The 1888 Act of Congress had very little effect in reopening the Uintah Reservation, so the Congress of the United States, on 15 August 1894, enacted still another law. This Act, (28 Stat. 286&337), "directed the appointment of a commission (1) to make allotments in severalty to the Uncompahgre Indians within the reservation... and (2) to negotiate and treat with the Indian properly residing upon the Uintah Indian Reservation, in the Territory of Utah, for the relinquishment to the United States of the interest of said Indians in all lands within said reservation not needed for allotment in severalty to said Indians." [In the United States Court of Claims, No. 47569. The Uintah and White River Bands of Ute Indians, Plaintiffs v. The United States of America, Defendant, pp. 8-9.]

Caleb Rhoades could at last see the possibility of working some of his mines. He fired off letters to some of the more prominent congressmen, seeking confirmation and clarification of the new law. Jointly they replied, explaining that "...a commission would be appointed, with the interests of the Ute Indians in mind, for the cession to the United States of all lands within the Uintah Reservation not needed for Indian allotment for the purpose of sale to private citizens of the United States. Said lands, with the exception of forest reserve, reclamation withdrawals and certain mineral entries which may later be determined, were to be restored to public domain and opened for disposition under the public land and the homestead laws for the benefit of the Indians; Provided, that the amounts thus received shall, in the aggregate be sufficient to pay said Indians in full the amount agreed upon for said lands as determined by the commission and the Indians."

In regard to Rhoades' inquiries about mineral leases the congressmen replied: "Nothing shall impair the rights of an individual or any private company to negotiate with said Indians for a mineral lease, or for that matter, the rights of any mineral lease which bears the approval of the Secretary of the Interior."

The commission to be appointed under the Act of 1894 was delayed due to improper wording, and the time lapse gave Caleb Rhoades time to begin negotiations with the Indians and to begin courting the federal government for permission to open a mineral lease on the reservation lands. During the subsequent months of political delays, Caleb traveled to Salt Lake City, Provo, and Colorado Springs to seek the advice of professionals who could help him secure the lease.

At Salt Lake City he met with his brother-in-law, William H. Dodge (who married his sister Lucinda Rhoades Clawson), who had developed the famous Silver King Mine and most of Park City, Utah. Acting upon Dodge's advice, Caleb went to Provo where he secured legal counsel from Dodge's friend and attorney John T. Clark. He then went to Colorado Springs to enlist the aid of L. O. Wight, manager of the Strowger Automatic Telephone Exchange, in superintending all mineral surveys he hoped to acquire from the Ute Indians.

Rhoades was on friendly terms with the Utes, but his acquaintance among them had been of necessity limited to those members of the tribe associated with the sacred gold. The majority of the tribe were unfamiliar with him, and vice versa, and he would require the full support of the entire Ute tribe to secure a lease. He needed the cooperation of a man well-respected by the Utes, a man well-qualified to conduct business, a man of sterling reputation capable of dealing with government officials. He found such a man residing at Provo, a man who could handle the Utes better than he, a man of considerable influence and a man with a prestigious degree in mineralogy. That man was F.W.C. Hathenbruck.

Caleb sent a telegram to Hathenbruck to announce his arrival. They met at Hathenbruck's home, 243 East 5th North, Provo, and they spoke at considerable length. They were frank and open with one another. Hathenbruck revealed his royal heritage and Rhoades spoke freely of his long-held secrets. He showed the Doctor some of the rich ore he had taken from one of his mines—wire gold in gray ore paralleling quartz and rose silver veins. They both professed their satisfaction with one another and agreed that they had the foundation for a mutually beneficial partnership. Hathenbruck proved to be an adept negotiator, a fact which Rhoades secretly admired. He demanded a full partnership of one-half interest in all mining properties in return for his services in dealing with the Indians and government officials. Moreover, he would not simply rely on Caleb's word alone that such a gold mine existed, he wanted to be taken to see it for himself. Caleb Rhoades agreed without hesitation.

In later years, Hathenbruck recalled that first visit to the mine. Caleb had led him out to the reservation and into the mountains by a devious route, through canyons and along stream beds while under cover of darkness, to avoid detection by the Indians. He entered the mine with Rhoades and examined it with the trained eye of a geologist. He obtained ore samples which veri-

fied that the mine had once been worked by the Spaniards. Hathenbruck later told another business partner, George A. Storrs:

*On one wall of the mine tunnel, perhaps 75 meters from the entrance, a vein of pure gold ran diagonally from floor to ceiling for another 10 meters. The vein was six inches wide at the narrowest point, and widened to almost two feet at the widest place, following a parallel vein of quartz about four inches thick, the whole coursing through a gray ore which proved to be tellurium. Caleb was fearful, and rightfully so, that to reveal the existence of the solid vein would cause a stampede to the reservation, so I took ore samples only from an exterior vein. Even so, the ore assayed between $20,000 to $150,000 to the ton.*

The evidence clearly proved the existence of the Spanish mine, and further showed that its great wealth had not been over-exaggerated. Rhoades and Hathenbruck had agreements drawn up by attorney John T. Clark of Provo, and both parties signed and a new partnership was formed. It is a further testimony to Hathenbruck's negotiating skills that he took top billing: The company was titled "Hathenbruck and Rhoades." Nevertheless, the partnership was sound, and would weather the worst of storms that unscrupulous politicians and shady corporations, backed by huge sums of money, could throw at them in subsequent years.

Throughout the 1890s, Rhoades and Hathenbruck became so involved in the mining development that they neglected their other obligations. Hathenbruck was almost constantly away from home conducting business in Washington, D.C., and Rhoades spent most of his time in the mountains in preparation for impending survey work. The Doctor had so neglected his regular business affairs that the

F.W.C. Hathenbruck & Company Store was on the verge of going under. His wife called him away from business in Washington to return home and put things in order at the store. He hired George A. Richards as a partner to manage the store in his absence, and rushed hurriedly back to Washington.

Caleb Rhoades was similarly self-involved. His farm near Price, where he was renowned for raising fine honey bees and cattle, was left in the care of his wife Sidsie. While Caleb was away in the mountains, she often had a young neighbor girl named Ellen stay with her for companionship. Ellen was the niece of Frederick E. Grames, one of Caleb's close friends, and later became Mrs. Ellen Gourley of Lakeport, California, from whom much of this information was obtained. Sidsie was also frequently visited by Caleb's two daughters, Linda and Martha Ellen (by his previous marriage to Malinda Powell), who lived at nearby Price with their husbands on land deeded to them by Caleb in former years.

Both men were racing against time. The news of their endeavor to obtain a mining lease from the Indians would be made public in a matter of months. To make matters worse, a rumor was already being circulated that Rhoades was attempting to open up the Sacred Mine. His attempts to explain to both his friends and the Indians that he was not seeking the lease to work the Sacred Mine, but instead a Spanish mine, failed miserably. As a consequence, he dispatched Hathenbruck to the reservation in an attempt to bring the Indians together in an open council meeting. Such a meeting was required by law to obtain the mineral lease. For a time it looked as though he would not succeed, as one obstacle after another blocked his way. Hathenbruck gave an account of his experiences to a reporter, which was published in the *Salt Lake Herald*, 3 February 1905, as follows:

*I have been in the reservation more or less for the last sixteen years... I knew of the original Caleb Rhoades [sic] mineral location, and back in the days when Colonel Randelet [sic] was Indian agent at White Rocks I began trying to get a lease from the Indians for 480,000 acres of valuable mineral land in the Uintah reservation. I went to Colonel Randelet and told him what I wanted him to do. He said he favored it and permitted me to go among the Indians to explain my proposition to them. I camped with them; went from tepee to tepee, sometimes with an interpreter and sometimes without because I could speak the Indian language myself [In fact, Hathenbruck spoke six languages and several Indian dialects fluently.] Before I was ready to call the Indians in open council in the matter Colonel Randelet told me he had resigned and that he did not wish to do anything to embarrass his successor; that he desired to leave him free to act in this matter.*

*Captain William H. Beck succeeded Randelet and I went to him. He said his predecessor had explained the whole situation to him and that he favored my proposition. He permitted me to go ahead with my negotiations with the Indians.*

*At this same time there was an allotment commission in the reservation to induce the Uintah Indians to give the Uncompahgre Indians a portion of their land. They had been moved in from Meeker, Colorado, and were on the Uncompahgre reservation temporarily. The government wished to settle them on a portion of the Uintah Reservation and a commission composed of Jeffries, Harper and H. P. Myton was there for that purpose. These men worked for two years without success. Finally they asked me to use my influence with the Indians to induce them to accept the offer of the government. In three weeks I secured the agreement of every Indian in the reservation allotment.*

*While all of this was going on, another special commission headed by Inspector Bartch, visited the reservation and investigated all that was to be done. Special Indian Inspector Reynolds was on the ground also, so that if there had been anything wrong about my dealing it would have been known.*

*There was dirty work enough to prevent me from securing my lease. I was shot at a number of times. I held my life to be in danger all the time. An attempt was made to bribe Captain Beck through his son to have him kill me; but in spite of all this I won. I got the consent individually of every one of the 980 Indians in the reservation to my lease, and then I called the Indians together in open council at White Rocks. This open council was required by the law to make the lease legal.*

*All of the Indians on the reservation gathered except old Chief Tabby, and none of them would sign my lease or the allotment to the Uncompahgres without Chief Tabby. The commissioners were at their wits ends and it looked as though the whole matter would fall through. I suggested that we send for Chief Tabby and bring him in. None of the commissioners would go; none of the Indians would go; I could get no white man to make the trip.*

*Finally I said, "I will go myself." I took with me my nephew, Henry Nuttall. We went forty-five miles into the mountains in the dead of winter to Chief Tabby's camp in the creek country. We found the chief sick and it did not seem as though he could live. He was over eighty years old at the time and might have been ninety. I doctored him in his camp for a week and then told him he was well enough to go to the council. He consented to make the trip. We put him into a lumber wagon and started. We would travel three or four miles in the warmest part of the day. Then we would stop for the*

*night, build up a great fire and fill Chief Tabby with herbs and coffee to thaw him out. The weather was bitter cold and the snow was deep. We were in danger of being frozen to death all the time, and of being buried in an avalanche many times.*

*I sent runners on ahead to notify the others that we were coming, so that they could keep the Indians from straying off. I sent word to have a place prepared for all the Indians for the day of our arrival. When we reached White Rocks and every Indian was enjoying a good hot meal old Chief Tabby got up on the spring seat of the wagon and made them a speech telling them to sign my lease and the allotment of the Uncompahgres.*

*This was December 18, 1897. Later in the day I called the twenty-one chiefs, including Chief Tabby, into a council and we talked the whole matter over. Everything was open and above board. Chief Tabby said he was very old and would not live to get the benefits of the lease. He was poor, he needed food, clothes and a team to get back to his camp. He thought the other chiefs should concede him this much. They did, and I gave my own team to the old fellow together with a supply of food and clothing.*

*My lease was signed by every Indian present at the council including the twenty-one chiefs. It gave me a lease on the 480,000 for ten years with the option of renewing at the end of that time. I was to give the Indians 10 per cent of the net proceeds of all the mines opened under the lease. My lease was signed at two o'clock in the afternoon and the allotment of the land to the Uncompahgres was agreed to at four o'clock of the same day. The council closed with a barbecue.*

Unfortunately, two and one-half months prior to the signing of the lease the story was leaked to the press. Bold headlines announced "Utah's Klondike" and told of Caleb Rhoades and

F.W.C. Hathenbruck obtaining a mineral lease for the Indians. Caleb's friends and neighbors, all faithful Mormons, feared that he had broken his oath and expressed concern for his soul. Here follows several more examples of the publicity taken from the files of the *Salt Lake Herald* (Sept. & Dec. 1897):

*White Rocks, Utah, Sept. 30— Many years ago a man by the name of Rhoades discovered what he claimed and supposed to be a great gold mine of the Wasatch Mountains. This discovery antedated the declaration of the Uintah Reservation by the President of the United States Abraham Lincoln (1861). Through and by the direction of Brigham Young, Rhoades discontinued his operations on the mine and left there, after a lapse of many years. The mine having become located within the boundaries of the Uintah Reservation by the act of the President above referred to, no work upon it could be accomplished unless consent of the Indians could be obtained, and the approval of the Secretary of the Interior thereto.*

*During the time since the discovery, Rhoades (Thomas) died and left his equity to this mine in the hands of his son (Caleb), who has associated with himself in his endeavors to obtain the lease of this property, Mr. F.W.C. Hathenbruck, under the firm title of Hathenbruck and Rhoades. These gentlemen, it would seem, have some rights in equity, and if the mine can be leased and the consent of the Indians obtained they are apparently entitled to all the benefits which might accrue for such a lease. They have been endeavoring for years to interest the department through the agents to have their desired lease to the mine accomplished. They have, however, been unable through unknown causes until recently to obtain official hearing to which they are undoubtedly entitled.*

*It goes without saying in this part of the country that the discoverer of any mineral has a claim in equity. Messrs. Hathenbruck and Rhoades appealed to the present Indian agent, Captain W.H. Beck, United States Army, for a lease upon the property. After listening to their statement they were notified that the consent of the Indians must be obtained in open council and that the matter would have to be submitted to the Commissioner of Indians Affairs for his recommendation, then to the Secretary of the Interior for his approval.*

*The Uintah and White Rivers, the Indians interested, met together today in concert for the purpose of reaching a decision which, whatever it may be, will probably be given in open council tomorrow. The action of the Indians in making or refusing to make a lease of the mine is of vital importance to them and if they consent it will open a great revenue for them and the Klondike of the United States.*

*Specimens for the Rhoades mine have assayed at $1,000 to the ton and a two-foot vein of quartz which has been traced for half a mile assays $35. The gold on the more valuable specimens of free wire. It is stated that influential men of Denver, Salt Lake City and Washington are associated with Hathenbruck and Rhoades in their scheme and that capitol [sic] to work and build a railroad to the mine has been guaranteed. There is no way to predict the action of the Indians, but Tabby, the Uintah chief, is thought to be in favor of the lease. Sowawick, chief of the White Rivers, is doubtful.*

*White Rocks, Utah, Oct. 1— In spite of a steady down pouring rain, the open council of Uintah and White River Indians assembled here today to promulgate their decision reached in joint session yesterday, relative to the reservation lease...*

*There were present Chief Tabby and head-*

in men Charlie Mack and John Duncan of the Uintahs, and Chief Sowawick and head-on men Marcisco and Caloomp of the White Rivers, together with about fifty others of less importance in the tribe. Mr. Hathenbruck presented the case for his firm.

At 3 o'clock Capt. Beck called the council to order, and said, "You understand the proposition; what do you want to do regarding the lease?"

Here several said that they were not thoroughly conversant with the terms, and the following was stated: The Indians are to receive $2500 a year, whether the company makes or loses, and after $25,000 have been made by the company 10 per cent of all profits accruing goes to the two tribes, the lease to be for ten years.

After... Tabby declared himself as voting for the lease, and told the rest of the Indians to speak their minds fully and withhold nothing. Following Tabby, Sowawick spoke, and after twenty minutes palaver upon subjects foreign to the question he ended by voting against the lease.

From the time of Sowawick's vote it grew hot. Everyone wanted to talk at once. When finally Sowawick got the floor he spoke directly to Mr. Hathenbruck, and said: "I do not want any of the Indian lands leased to whites. We have but a small piece of ground and it is too narrow. If you come in, others will follow, and we will be despoiled of our lands and set down on some ant-heap."

...Mr. Hathenbruck explained that the mine had been discovered previous to the act declaring this reservation, and that the dimensions of the property leased are small, only four miles square, and that they would be smaller were it not that there were no plats by which to describe it, hence meridian and parallels must be employed.

Sowawick said that he knew nothing about the reservation before he came here, and that he

knew nothing about description of lands. He only knew that he was opposed to a lease.

Here, Tabby took the floor and exhorted his followers to stand by the lease, and old Sowawick left the room without adieu, taking Caloomp with him. The council was fast assuming the appearance of a political caucus, then Tabby said: "I am strongly in favor of this lease. Our agent says it will benefit us, and I believe him. When I suggest anything the White Rivers always oppose it, and if you, my own people, do not come out and support me, I can't carry this lease alone. I need help, and I want you to give it to me."

This vigorous speech produced its effect, and a great strife was created, but still no one volunteered his verbal support to Tabby. Then after a pause David Copperfield arose and voted with Tabby. The rest followed rapidly, and the meeting was adjourned. Another attempt to bring the White Rivers in to line will be made in a day or two. The lease can be passed over their heads, they being the minority. The prospects tonight are that the lease will get the approval of the Indians.

"CALEB RHOADES MINE"
THE MYSTERIOUS BONANZA OF THE
UINTAH RESERVATION
WIRE GOLD AND SILVER
FABULOUS VALUES IN THE WHITE
AND YELLOW METAL

Mineral brought in by F.W.C. Hathenbruck... Application made for a strip four miles square.

F.W.C. Hathenbruck of Provo is at the Cullen.

Mr. Hathenbruck is just in from the Uintah Indian Reservation, in the northeast portion of Utah, where the Herald readers will know he is interested in the resurrection and rehabilitation of the famous old Caleb Rhoades gold mine, *concerning which so much has been written and said during the past few years.*

*The Rhoades mine is accounted as being one of the richest propositions in the state of Utah, and while the reports regarding it[s] fabulous wealth have probably been added to with each succeeding year, there is no doubt but that it is a bonanza, and better than a Klondike, at least Mr. Hathenbruck thinks so, and he is straining every nerve to acquire a foothold in this ancient producer of the precious metals, for its exact location, although clothed in mystery for many years, is now known...*

*A Herald representative had a pleasant interview with Mr. Hathenbruck yesterday... According to Mr. Hathenbruck... "The ledge is well defined, and the pay spread is from three inches to three feet in width. There is what we call barren rock in the ledge, but even this assays 35 ounces in silver and $4 in gold, while the pay streak goes as high as $150,000 in gold and silver to the ton, the gold contents of the mineral predominating." Mr. Hathenbruck then got his grip and showed the Herald man a number of samples of ore from the mine and they were magnificent, the mineral being almost solid tellurium, and was covered and streaked through and through with wire silver and gold that was beautiful to look at. Mr. Hathenbruck also stated that the Caleb Rhoades ledge was full of just such mineral as this, and he produced an assay certificate showing the results obtained from half an ounce of ore, the values of which were 1,800 ounces of silver and $17,000 in gold to the ton.*

*As has already been stated, Mr. Hathenbruck has succeeded in obtaining permission form the Indians to work the old Caleb Rhoades mine, but before he can strike a pick in the development of the property or ship*

*a pound of ore he will be obliged to also secure permission of the government to mine there, and it is this that has brought him to Salt Lake, as, with his associated, he has made application to the department of the interior for a Grant of Four Miles Square in the desired locality, and if he is successful he will inaugurate a mining enterprise on a gigantic scale.*

Shortly after Caleb Rhoades' new mining ventures were made public and controversy over whether or not he had broken his sacred oath was at a peak, a party was held at the Price Town Hall in celebration of the fiftieth anniversary of the arrival of the Mormon pioneers to Utah, and to honor the early settlers of Castle Valley. Caleb Rhoades, an original pioneer to Utah and one of the earlier settlers of the valley, was asked to speak to the congregation.

In a moving oration that lasted for ninety minutes, Caleb recounted how he had come to Utah in 1846, a full year before Brigham Young and the first pioneer arrived. He talked at length about pioneer days, and he ended by recounting how he had made his sacred covenant to God, and about his oath to Brigham Young and Chief Aropene. This was only the second occasion he had spoken about the mines, and as far as is known, it was the last. In the course of this speech he revealed a knowledge of at least five other mines on the reservation, apart from the Sacred Mine of the Utes.

He took this occasion to vindicate himself and to squelch the rumors that he was going to violate his oath and openly work the Sacred Mine. He ended his speech by saying, with emphasized conviction: "Until this day, I have kept my covenant that I made with God....I have never shown any man and I never intend to do so as long as I live!"

# Chapter 6

## GOD, GOLD & GOVERNMENT

The news of the Rhoades bonanza spread rapidly. Even before Hathenbruck arrived in Washington, D.C. to submit the Utah lease to Secretary of the Interior Cornelius N. Bliss for approval, special interest groups backed by eastern money had organized to defeat the measure. These men, many of them elected government officials, had formed "dummy" corporations with the sole purpose of defeating the Utah lease and obtaining for themselves the famous and fabulous Rhoades Mine.

In Utah, Mormon interests coalesced to protect what they considered their entitlement to the mines. In their view, Chief Walker had given the Sacred Mine, at least, to Brigham Young and the Church. This was not true, of course; Brigham Young had never been given the mine, only some of the gold from it, but in the view of Young's successors, it was a valid claim. There were even a number of alleged prophecies, prominent among which was that the gold had been "hidden up" by angels to come forth at some future time of calamitous events for the saving of the Church and the Mormon people.

Utah had achieved statehood in 1896, while Rhoades and Hathenbruck were in the midst of seeking their lease, and now there were Mormon senators and congressmen in Washington, prominent among them being Reed Smoot and George Q. Cannon. These Mormon officials were busy organizing their own coalition against the Rhoades-Hathenbruck lease. F.W.C. Hathenbruck later recalled the circumstances arising from these machinations by the special interest groups:

*I went at once to Washington to secure a ratification of my treaty by Secretary of the Interior Cornelius N. Bliss. I found that my troubles were by no means over; that I had people to deal with more uncertain than the Indians. I had won on the reservation, but that was only part of the battle. Secretary Bliss showed me a letter to him from George Q. Cannon [Reed Smoot's companion politician for Utah, and an Apostle of the Mormon Church] in which that gentleman said that the men at the head of my scheme were poor and ignorant and unable to swing a proposition worth from $50,000,000 to $100,000,000. Mr Bliss said he would recognize my claim before any other on the reservation but he said he was going to resign, that he did not like the work.*

*Bliss resigned and Hitchcock came in and my lease was pigeon-holed. One of the hardest workers against me was (Major) Dick, who is now United States Senator from Ohio. He was a lobbyist then and a particular friend of H.P. Myton.*

*I had not been long in Washington before I discovered that I must have help if I expected to win. The pressure was too strong against me unless I could secure the influence of men high up in Washington. A meeting of a number of prominent men from New York was arranged to be held in the Manhattan Hotel in New York City and I went over from Washington to attend that meeting. The result of it was that I agreed to turn over a portion of my interest in exchange for help in getting my lease ratified by Secretary Hitchcock. Jesse S. Sherman, Warren Hooker, Judge H.C. Henderson and William Ward were to give their assistance. They were all congressmen from New York at the time. Sherman was the chairman of the committee on Indian affairs, and for that reason had much influence. Others became interested later. Among these were Judge Thomas of Chicago, Postmaster General Henry C. Payne and Colonel George F. Timms. The New York parties [later] organized the Florence Mining Company.*

*The upshot of the whole matter was that my lease was never ratified by the Secretary of the interior; but when the law passed providing for the opening of the Uintah reservation, 640 acres of consecutive mineral ground in the reservation was to be given the Florence Mining Company before the opening. It is not easy for me to recognize the justice of this arrangement. If the matter is ever opened up for investigation there will be some disgraceful revelations.*

Disgraceful indeed. The Florence Mining Company was given special privileges to enter the reservation and explore for minerals without obtaining permission from the Indians. The Utah firm of Hathenbruck & Rhoades was denied entry to the reservation by threat of arrest if they should be caught upon Indian Lands. Judge J.T. McConnel was permitted upon these lands to secure a lease on a tract of land fifteen miles square east of Strawberry and south of the Duchesne River in what was known as the Indian Creek country. Judge McConnel was unable to hold onto his lease for lack of capital and was bought out by the American Asphalt Company.

The American Asphalt Company soon found itself in financial straits and began experimenting exclusively with gilsonite, and sold the McConnel lease interests to private people who formed the Raven Mining Company. Their right to locate was confined to the fifteen square miles of the original lease, but they were noticed prospecting over the entire reservation.

There were strong suspicions that the Raven people and the Florence people were the same. While the Florence Company had no right to locate hydrocarbon ground and the Raven Company had no right to locate precious ore claims, they were so situated that they could exchange if any locations were contested. When Hathenbruck's public complaints against this chicanery brought about questions of legality, inasmuch as the Florence and Raven companies had never acquired permission from the Indians in council, they countered by inducing seven Indians to accompany them to Washington and sign their lease; their lease was ratified by the Secretary of the Interior even though the law required the Indians to sign in open council, in majority, on the reservation.

The end result was that there was never a congressional investigation into the illegal practices of the Florence and Raven companies, whose ruthless greed raped the reservation lands without respect for the Indians. They failed to find any significant mineral, in spite of their professional geologists, and failed even more miserably to locate the famous Rhoades Mine. At one point, as the government geologists scoured the reservation, someone asked Caleb Rhoades if he was not concerned that these professionals might find his mine. He laughed and replied, "Not in the least; it is in the least likely place they would ever expect to find it. Besides, they could stand on top of it and never see it."

While eastern political interests were conspiring against the Hathenbruck & Rhoades Lease, in Utah similar efforts were underway by parties affiliated with the Mormon Church. As mentioned earlier, there were unofficial Mormon prophecies which maintained that the Uintah Mountain gold belonged to the Church, and had been hidden up until such a day as it would be needed to save the Church from destruction. That day seemed to have arrived in 1896, even while efforts were underway to obtain the gold by other interests, and the Mormon faction was not about to let it happen.

The Edmunds-Tucker Act of 1887, enacted against polygamy, formally dissolved the corporation of the Church of Jesus Christ of Latter-day Saints, the entity holding title to most Church-owned businesses and properties, such as their banks, their cooperative mercantile, their industries and land holdings.

By the 1890s, the Mormons were making trade-offs with the federal government, and agreed to abandon polygamy and to dissolve its political arm, the People's Party. In return, they requested statehood for Utah in 1896, amnesty for previously persecuted Mormon polygamists, and most importantly, the restoration of the Church property. Church historian Leonard Arrington wrote:

*The Raid had finally culminated in the long-sought goal of statehood, but had produced capitulation in many areas of Mormon uniqueness, not the least of which was the decline in economic power and influence of the church. The temporal Kingdom, for all practical purposes, was dead—slain by the dragon Edmunds-Tucker.*

Church President Heber J. Grant had gone to Wall Street in the 1890s to seek financial aid, arranging loans from New York banks; in so doing he, in effect, mortgaged the Church. Therefore, the above account of Mormon intervention in the Hathenbruck-Rhoades Lease was an effort to secure gold and save the Church from financial ruin. It is not idle speculation. There is considerable evidence, not the least of which was a visit by Heber J. Grant to speak personally about obtaining a "loan" from none other than Caleb Rhoades!

It is a convoluted story that begins with a letter by Jesse William Knight, son of Utah mining magnate Jesse Knight, to his mother, reminiscing about family history. The letter can be found in the book *The Jesse Knight Family* by Jesse William Knight, at the Utah Historical Society [see also: *The Gold of Carre-Shinob,* op.cit.]

*April 2, 1930*

*Dear Mother:*

*In the spring of 1896, just prior to discovering ore in the Humbug Mine, Father said to me one day as we were walking up the mountainside that he felt sure that he was going to find ore in the ground and we would have all the money we wanted and that some day we would save the credit of the Church.*

*This remark did not meet with my judgment at that time and I had some little argument with Father about it, saying that he did not know how much we would want, nor did it look possible for us to save the credit of the Church when it was owing a million dollars or more. Our own ranch was mortgaged and we did not know how to meet that obligation. But notwithstanding this, Father said he hoped I would remember what he said; he said he did not wish to quarrel or argue with me about it and only wanted me to remember what he had said...*

*Money accumulated very rapidly, and as I had heard father say that he had received a letter from President Woodruff at a certain time regarding help given the Church to save its credit, Leon Newren and I put in a part of a day trying to find among the old papers this letter from President Woodruff to father, but we were unable to find it. [This letter was subsequently found and is reproduced on page 30.]*

*I had just left the building after the search when I met President Joseph B. Keeler on the street, who said to me before I had time to tell him what was on my mind, that he wished to tell me the details about father making a certain loan to the Church; and strange as it may seem, his story, which he subsequently wrote in the form of a letter, answered the very question that was in my mind, and which I had hoped would be answered in the letter from President Woodruff, for which we had searched. I am enclosing you herewith a copy of the letter from President Keeler which goes to confirm very positively the statement which father made to me about saving the credit of the Church.*

*Your son,*
*J. Wm. Knight*


*March 31, 1930*
*President J. Wm. Knight*
*Provo, Utah*


*My Dear Brother Knight:*

*I was very much interested in our conversation in regard to an unusual occurrence that transpired November 22 and 23, 1896, in which your father, President Woodruff, Trustee-in-trust for the Church, and myself participated. The details of the event, which I here briefly relate originated in a request made by President Wilford Woodruff at a special Priesthood Meeting following the general October semi-annual Conference of the above named year. As you know such meetings are composed of General Authorities of the Church, Presidencies of the Stakes, Bishops of Wards, and other officials. At that time I was Bishop of the Fourth Ward, Provo, and your father and his family resided there.*

*In the Priesthood meeting above noted, many topics were presented, discussed and disposed of in the usual way. Just before adjournment, however, President Woodruff arose and made a special request, namely: That when the Bishops present returned to the respective wards they would visit members who were possessed of means and who might be able to lend money to the Church for a short period, in any sum large or small, on which interest would be paid as well as the principal. He explained that the Church was in very straightened circumstances financially. This condition was brought about in part, he said, on account of the Federal Government confiscating Church property and through other oppressing anti-Mormon laws passed by Congress by which the peace of the people had been greatly disturbed, property of the Church wasted, and the industries of the then Territory depressed and hindered. He presented this matter, he said, because right now there were some very pressing demands on the Trustee-in-trust, and the credit of the Church was at stake.*

*This particular request went entirely out of my mind until the afternoon of Sunday, November 22, 1896. I was returning home from our Tabernacle services; and when within a short distance of my home a voice said to me—a voice as audible as that of a person— "Jesse Knight will lend the Church $10,000.00." That was all. Then it was that I distinctly remembered the remarks of President Woodruff bearing on this subject. I immediately changed my course and went to the home of "Uncle Jesse," and found him in his parlor reading. After a few preliminary greetings, I rehearsed to him what had transpired in the meeting, and what President Woodruff had said about the Church being financially embarrassed. But* before I could ask him whether he would make the loan, he said instantly, "Yes, I'll lend the Church $10,000.00 and I'll see the Cashier this afternoon and have a check ready for you tomorrow morning, and you may take it down to Salt Lake." That was at a time when there was but one train a day to Salt Lake. So, early in the morning, he met me at the station and handed me an envelope containing the check.

As it happened, President Woodruff, with his counselors, George Q. Cannon and Joseph F. Smith, and several of the Twelve were present in the President's office when I arrived. After viewing the contents of the letter, President Woodruff was very much pleased; and it appeared to me that a great weight was lifted off his mind. At the request of President Woodruff, I spent several hours there and took lunch in the office with him and several of the brethren.

A letter was formulated to Brother Knight and was given to me to hand to him. When I arrived at Provo he was at the depot to meet me. I did not know the full contents of President Woodruff's letter, but Brother Knight remarked to me a few days later that President Woodruff had said that the check was the means of saving the credit of the Church. Brother Knight also remarked to me some months later that was one of the best loans he had ever made.

> Very sincerely your brother,
> Joseph B. Keeler

[Note: The actual letter from President Wilford Woodruff to Jesse Knight is found as follows:]

*Office of*
*The First Presidency*
*of the*
*Church of Jesus Christ of Latter-day Saints*
*Box B*

Elder Jesse Knight,
Provo,

Dear Brother:

I am just in receipt of your check for $7,000, per hand of Bishop Keeler, which makes $10,000 in all which you have kindly advanced to me as trustee in trust for the Church. I feel that this kindly act on your part is in answer to my prayers to the Lord to open some door of relief whereby we may be enabled to meet pressing demands upon us. I feel very thankful to you, and feel with every sentiment of my heart to say, God bless you and prosper you.

> With kind regard,
> Your Brother,
> Wilford Woodruff.

P.S. My note in your favor for $10,000, at 8 percent in hereby enclosed.

The foregoing letter addresses only part of the story. Heber J. Grant, who was at the time a member of the Quorum of Twelve Apostles and later President of the Church, asked Jesse Knight for $5,000 to assist some Church member who had gotten financially involved in a failing venture. Jesse declined to loan any money to the men, stating that it was a private venture on the part of the men and was their responsibility, having little to do with the Church.

Apostle Grant then turned to Caleb Rhoades and asked him for the same donation, adding that he should pray about it. Jesse Knight overheard the request and asked Grant why he had not asked him to pray about it. "Because you refused altogether to do anything," Grant replied. Jesse was somewhat offended, declaring that he, too, believed in prayer, and he said he would go straight home and pray about it. After praying,

Jesse felt inspired to do so, and he sent his check for $10,000, together with a check for $1,000 from Reed Smoot, Jesse's close friend.

When Jesse Knight next encountered Heber J. Grant, he said with a smile, "When you ask me for another contribution, I'll pay it without stopping to pray." Shortly thereafter the first President sent the following telegram:

*Salt Lake. September 3rd, 1898*
*To Jesse Knight and Reed Smoot,*
*Provo.*

*God bless you and yours forever. May you and all your loved ones have a great abundance of peace, prosperity and happiness in this life and may you all enjoy an eternity of bliss in the life to come is the profound and heartfelt prayer of your brethren in the Gospel.*

*Lorenzo Snow*
*Joseph F. Smith*
*Heber J. Grant*

All of the above makes an interesting account about Jesse Knight having saved the credit of the Church, but his $10,000 and Reed Smoot's $1,000 could in no way be construed as "saving the credit of the Church." A mere $11,000 would not have even paid the interest on what the Church then owed. In fact, the money was intended to save the reputations of three of the general authorities, a fact confirmed later in a letter from Heber J. Grant to Jesse Knight's son, as follows:

*Church of Jesus Christ of Latter-day Saints*
*Heber J. Grant, President*
*Salt Lake City, Utah*
*February 15, 1923*
*Elder J. William Knight*
*Provo, Utah*

*My dear brother Knight:*

*One of the most remarkable and wonderful things, to my mind that ever happened to my life was when your father sent me $10,000 to assist in saving the honor and good names of President Joseph F. Smith, Frances M. Lyman and Abram H. Cannon, in connection with the Utah Loan & Trust Company of Ogden. Brother Reed Smoot sent $1,000.00 the same day...*

*Sincerely your friend and brother,*
*Heber J. Grant*

In reality, Jesse Knight had organized a group of his own to enter the reservation, and by all accounts he found gold and brought it out. It was ostensibly this gold that was contributed to the Church to save its credit. In fact, there are strong indications that Jesse Knight, together with Reed Smoot, was behind the formation of the Raven Mining Company, to counter the government's formation of the Florence Mining Company. The main goal of both groups was to force Hathenbruck & Rhoades out of business and off the reservation and to secure the mine for themselves.

Caleb Rhoades and Jesse Knight had been friends and both were acquainted with Senator Reed Smoot. Smoot was primarily allied to Knight's endeavors, to secure the gold for the Church, but pretended to be sympathetic to the interests of Hathenbruck & Rhoades in an effort to undermine their lease and secure it for Knight's interests. This is made clear in a letter from Caleb Rhoades to Reed Smoot, dated 23 October 1901:

*Reed Smoot,*
*Provo, Utah*

*My good Friend:*

*In my haste to write to you last time I neglected to enclose the information you requested regards to my present indignation of the actions of Bro. Jesse Knight and his interference in my efforts to secure the Indian lease.*

*...I do not need to inform you, since you were a party to the information at that time, that Bro. Jesse Knight brought out significant amounts of ore from that mine against the warnings to the contrary that he should do it. You will remember that these are the amounts he gave to Pres. Woodruff just before his [Woodruff's] death nearly six years ago, to save the credit of the church.*

*...Pres. Grant [Heber J. Grant] knew about these things as I am sure you will remember, and he could testify to them, if he would, but they, [i.e. the general authorities] are not about to do that while this thing is unsettled with the government. I don't blame them for not wanting to get involved, but on the other hand they are involved, and between them and Bro. Jesse Knight's recent efforts against me, I am left in a hard place.*

*...I do not worry that Bro. Jesse Knight will ever reveal the location of the mine or that he will use it for any purpose other than that which his conscience dictates. I am more concerned with his attitude towards me which our friendship has never merited in the past...I will not go near the sacred mine again because I know he has agents everywhere and in the government. I say these things to you not to accuse because you have been a friend to both of us but instead to permit you to understand my feelings about*

*Bro. Jesse Knight's recent bid to overcome the mining lease. I hope you are still a friend and in support of our efforts for which we keep you in mind always...*

*...I might talk to Bro. Jesse if the opportunity arises and it might occur when I visit at Diamond [probably Diamond City at Tintic] within the month...*

*Yours truly,*
*Caleb B. Rhoades*

Reed Smoot was the most powerful U.S. Senator that Utah ever sent to Washington. It is notable that he was, at the same time, a member of the Council of Twelve Apostles of the Mormon Church. He was, consequently, romanced by many different persons seeking the benefit of his considerable influence. Ironically, it was Smoot's high tariff in the trade bill—the highest in U.S. history—that is said by many to have been the cause of the Great Depression of 1929-1930, after which he was never again re-elected to office.

It is apparent that Reed Smoot was part of a swiftly developing plot. Hathenbruck needed his aid so badly he was willing to sign over his interest in the Rhoades mine as collateral for securing his influence. That document is as follows:

*FOR VALUE RECEIVED, I hereby sell, assign, transfer, and set over, to Reed Smoot, all my right, title, and interest in and to that certain lease between the Indians of the Uintah Indian Reservation, in Utah, and myself and Caleb B. Rhoades; and also my right, title and interest in the Capital [sic] stock subscribed by me in the articles of incorporation of the Rhoades Mining & Milling Company, and which articles, with my assignment, have been deposited with H. S. Young, Cashier of the Deseret National Bank, to be used and filed and said company incorpo-*

rated when the said lease is approved by the Secretary of the Interior of the United States, or prior thereto, if a majority of the parties interested therein so desire.

I hereby authorize the filing of said articles and the substitution of the name of Reed Smoot for my own whenever it appears in said articles, and hereby authorize and direct the officers of said corporation, when formed, to transfer and deliver to said Reed Smoot all stock to which I would have been entitled in said company if I had not made this assignment.

And I hereby authorize the said Reed Smoot, to sign all papers, documents, receipts and releases in my name, whenever the same is necessary, to perfect in him the interest hereby assigned by me to him in said lease and in said corporation.

Witness my signature this 24th day of April, A.D. 1901.

F.W.C. HATHENBRUCK

Signed in the presence of :
ELIAS A. GEE

Even while Smoot gave every indication that he had the Hathenbruck & Rhoades interests at heart, he was even then providing J.H. Moyle, attorney for the Mormon Church, with copies of the information attained from Hathenbruck. This is evidenced by the following letter:

Salt Lake City, Utah, June 12, 1901
Hon. Reed Smoot
Provo, Utah

Dear Friend:

I believe you have the Articles of Incorporation of the Rhoades Mining Company, which I would be very glad to have at your earliest convenience.
The lease has not yet been approved but there seems to be every prospects of its being approved, at an early day.
With kind regards, I am,

Very respectfully yours,
J.H. Moyle

Hathenbruck continued to depend on Smoot, believing that the Senator was his advocate, and all the while Smoot was dealing behind the scenes with the Church and with Jesse Knight to overthrow the Hathenbruck & Rhoades lease. An example of Hathenbruck's continued trust in Smoot is evidenced in the following letter:

Salt Lake City, Jan. 20th 1902
Mr. G. Taylor

Dear Sir:

I just learned that you have served papers to vacate—(I just returned from the Las Vegas Desert)—I am surprised at that, and have written [illeg.] Smoot to see you at once, for [illeg.] to your satisfaction. I am regrettably detained here a few days, hence I ask a few days delay from you. Hoping this will meet your approval, I remain

Respectfully,
F.W.C. HATHENBRUCK

F.W.C. Hathenbruck and Caleb Rhoades had weathered political storms, and they both believed Reed Smoot was their loyal friend; but Smoot was working hand-in-glove with Jesse Knight behind the scenes. When Jesse Knight went onto the reservation, without benefit of a lease or Indian approval, surrounded by a small army of gunmen for protection, Hathenbruck and Rhoades decided to take measures to protect their own interests. They hired their own gunfighters. A clash was inevitable.

# Chapter 7

## GOLD & GUNFIGHTERS

In July 1896, Jesse Knight struck his bonanza at the Humbug Mine at Tintic. It was the first of many such major discoveries that eventually made him extremely wealthy. But earlier in the same year, before the strike, Jesse Knight was anything other than wealthy; in fact, he was barley paying his debts.

The Mormon Church was also nearing bankruptcy and the general authorities had approached Jesse Knight seeking financial aid. But Knight had not yet struck the bonanza at Tintic, and so the question must be posed why the Church authorities would seek out Jesse Knight for aid. If Knight had access to wealth at that point, where did it come from?

Jesse Knight was born at Nauvoo, Illinois, 6 September 1845, a son of Newell Knight and Lydia Goldthwaite. He came west to Utah with his parents in the original wagon company of Brigham Young in 1847, when he was two.

Knight's family was long associated with gold mines and buried treasure, and Jesse was steeped in esoteric lore. His grandfather, Joseph Knight, had been involved with Joseph Smith in the translation of the "Gold Plates" to the Book of Mormon, and in digging for buried treasure in Pennsylvania. [see; *The Gold of Carre-Shinob*, op. cit. at Chapter Seven.] His father, Newell Knight, had received a manifestation which was the first recorded "miracle" in the Church when he was possessed by a demon and levitated off his bed to the rafters of his bedroom.

Jesse Knight became involved in prospecting and mining very early in his life. He apparently had an early interest in the Sacred Mine, long before it became common knowledge. The Twitchell family intermarried with the Knights in Utah. In an unpublished history of the Twitchell family (*The History of James Twitchell, Sr.)* is recorded an account of "Uncle Jesse's" association with the mines that is worth reproducing:

*Uncle Jesse Knight often told us the story of his Dream Mine, which he said was located somewhere northwest of Vernal in the Uintah Mountains. He said that one day in about 1885 he was standing on a hilltop overlooking the Uintah-Ouray Indian Reservation where he had gone to build an irrigation canal, when he was overcome with a tremendous weakness which caused him to sink to the ground to his knees. While he was in this position he experienced a dream or a vision of an old mine, filled with treasure and with a vein of gold three to four feet in width and running the extent of the cavern. He said he felt as if he had been transported to the place in the spirit, and when he looked up, he saw the Angel Moroni standing in the air above him, and Moroni told him the history of the mine.*

*Moroni said that the mine was worked many years ago by an ancient people who used the gold for decoration and to make gold plates to keep their records and history on. The angel revealed to Uncle Jesse Knight that the plates which Joseph Smith had translated into the Book of Mormon had been made from that same gold source. When Moroni was alive and walked the earth, he obtained the gold for the plates from the cavern and wrote his history on them, carrying them to where Joseph Smith found them in the Hill Cumorah in New York State.*

*Uncle Jesse Knight said the room or the cavern was filled with gold plates and many kinds of gold artifacts and that the walls had been plated with pounded gold and there were hieroglyphics written on the walls. Uncle Jesse Knight had seen some of the characters from the original plates of the Book of Mormon, and he said these characters were identical in every fashion.*

*Moroni told Uncle Jesse Knight that sometime in the future, the Church of Jesus Christ of Latter-day Saints would be facing financial ruin, and that when that day came, Uncle Jesse Knight would be called to get gold from the mine and save the credit of the Church.*

*...When Uncle Jesse Knight awoke from his dream or his vision, he was too weak to move for a long time. Finally he made it back to Salt Lake City and he told members of his family about the experience, and he told them that someday his Dream Mine would help save the credit of the Church... In 1896, about the time that James Twitchell left Beaver [Utah] for northeastern Utah to settle, Uncle Jesse Knight was called to bring gold from the mine to save the Church from going bankrupt, and so his dream was fulfilled.*

The mention of caverns paved with gold, the presence of gold plates, and hieroglyphics, makes one wonder if Jesse Knight found Carre-Shinob itself. In 1896, Caleb Rhoades told a reporter for the *Uintah Papoose* newspaper of Vernal that the mine contained not only gold ore, but "worked gold, bullion, and artifacts of gold of fine workmanship and quality."

Whether or not Jesse Knight found the many things attributed to him, one fact is certain: he was on the reservation in 1896 with a group of gunmen, representing the Raven Mining Company. Both Hathenbruck and Rhoades were restricted from the reservation under threat of arrest, and so they needed someone with special qualifications to protect their interests. This man would need to be a tough gunfighter of some

reputation with a thorough knowledge of the reservation and the Indians. During 1896 a number of important events were transpiring simultaneously: the Mormon Church was facing bankruptcy; F.W.C. Hathenbruck and Caleb Rhoades were negotiating for a mining lease on the reservation; Jesse Knight and the Raven Mining Company were on the reservation attempting to circumvent the Hathenbruck-Rhoades enterprise; and Butch Cassidy, recently released from the Wyoming State Prison, was at Vernal organizing the Wild Bunch gang of outlaws. All of these events were seminally connected.

One of the members of Cassidy's gang was the bank and train robber Matt Warner. Warner, who was born Willard Erastus Christiansen at Levan, Utah, on 12 April 1864, ran away from home at the age of fourteen after hitting another boy over the head during an argument over a girl. Believing that he had killed the boy, Willard ran away to Brown's Park, an outlaw refuge in the Uintah Mountains, changed his name to Matt Warner, and rode the Outlaw Trail.

Matt was suffering financial reverses. He had promised his wife Rosa that he would go straight, so he hadn't pulled a robbery in some time. Rosa was terminally ill with a cancer on her hip, and her leg was eventually amputated in the military hospital at Fort Duchesne on the reservation. Medical bills had eaten up his savings. Butch and the boys had passed the hat and given him some slack, but he had succumbed to the pressure, got drunk, and "shot pool" with his six-shooter at a Vernal saloon and had to pay a hefty fine.

When Hathenbruck and Rhoades showed up in Vernal looking for a gunman to protect their interests on the reservation, Matt saw a golden opportunity. He was an avid prospector already, and he was well acquainted with the reservation and on friendly terms with the Ute Indians. There is also some evidence that Matt knew Caleb Rhoades and possibly Hathenbruck prior to that time.

On 23 June 1896, the following agreement was entered into between Rhoades and Hathenbruck on the first part, and W.E. Christiansen on the second part:

*This agreement, made and entered into this 23rd day of June in the year one thousand eight hundred and ninety six, by and between F.W.C. Hathenbruck of Provo City, Utah County, and Caleb Rhoades of Price, Carbon County, in the State of Utah, parties of the first part; and W.E. Christiansen of Vernal, Uintah County, in the State of Utah, party of the second part. Witnesseth, that:*

*Whereas the parties of the first part have certain knowledge of the existence and location of certain mines, placer, veins or lodes, bearing precious minerals, on the Uintah Reservation, and desire to enter into a contract or lease, with the tribe of Indians occupying the Uintah Reservation, for the development and working of said placers, veins or lodes, the contract or lease to be on the terms and of the nature and character of the copy which is attached hereto and made a part of the agreement.*

*Now therefore, the parties of the first part, at the request of the party of the second part, and in consideration of the covenants herein expressed to be performed by the party of the second part, do hereby agree to transfer, set over, and convey to the party of the second part, a One Twentieth part interest in the aforesaid contract or lease, when the legal title in the same shall have been procured and apportioned, as in the said proposed agreement specified.*

*And the party of the second part, in consideration of the promises, and for certain expenses paid in hand from time to time as they are merited, hereby agrees to act as guide and liaison and help to negotiate with the Indians of whom he has particular knowledge and understanding, and to serve on such capacity as is needed to complete the safe and certain consummation of the aforesaid contract or lease between the parties of the first part and the tribe of Indians occupying the Uintah Reservation.*

*And it is further mutually covenanted and agreed, if, in any manner, the party of the second part to the said proposed agreement shall fail or neglect to procure or help to secure the lease or title to, and the working of said mines, the parties of the first part therein shall be fully and completely exonerated and released from the covenants and provisions of this agreement.*

*IN WITNESS WHEREOF, the said parties have hereunto set their hands and seals, the day and year first above written.*

*F.W.C. HATHENBRUCK*
*CALEB B. RHOADES*
*SIGNED, SEALED AND DELIVERED*
*IN THE PRESENCE OF*

*W.E. CHRISTIANSEN*
*ROBERT D. SWIFT*

Two opposing forces were converging on the Uintah Reservation, bringing with them all the elements of an impending war. On the one side were gunmen hired by the secret investors of the Florence and Raven companies—one of whom was Jesse Knight—and on the other side were the gunmen hired by Hathenbruck and Rhoades to protect their interests. The force of hired guns running around in the mountains of the reservation country was bound to end in an encounter, and it did so, in August of 1896.

By the middle of summer 1896, gunfighters from around the region were converging on the town of Vernal, all hoping to be hired by one side or the other in the impending feud, or share in some way the profits derived from the possible opening of the fabulous gold mine.

The intrigue began seriously when Caleb

Rhoades hired one Henry B. Coleman, a mining promoter of dubious character and reputation, to proceed to a location somewhere in the back reaches of upper Dry Fork Canyon northwest of Vernal. Coleman was to meet there with Robert David Swift, another mining promoter, saloon owner, and some-time member of Cassidy's Wild Bunch. Swift, a Missourian, had also ridden at one time with the James and Younger gangs. On 23 June 1896, he had been a witness to the agreement between Hathenbruck and Rhoades with Matt Warner, the latter of whom was his particular friend.

Swift made a camp in the mountains and settled down in a tent awaiting the arrival of Matt Warner, whom Hathenbruck and Rhoades had hired to help them move the camp. Warner had agreed to go up the mountain to protect their interest according to their agreement, but was delayed because he demanded $500 in expenses. Hathenbruck and Rhoades wired Salt Lake City to get approval of the money. Warner set out the same day, accompanied by his friend Bill Wall, a gambler who once worked in the mines at Telluride, Colorado, (and may have known Hathenbruck from that time), who went along "just for the ride." They arrived at the camp, which was situated in a grove of trees, just at sunrise. As Warner and Wall rode across a clearing toward the tent, Swift was in the process of cooking breakfast.

As Warner and Wall reached the middle of the clearing, gunfire suddenly erupted from behind nearby trees. At the first shot, Warner instinctively pulled his rifle from his saddle boot and leaped from his horse, almost firing simultaneously while he pulled his startled friend Bill Wall to the ground.

The two men took refuge behind some quaking aspen trees where Matt began to return a deadly fire at his ambushers. Protected by a tree, he took a heavy toll on his attackers, even though one of the men kept firing at a single spot

on the tree, trying to force a slug through the trunk to kill him.

The tree ambushers proved to be the Stanton brothers—Ike and Dick—and one Dave Milton. When the gunfight ended a brief few minutes after it began, Dick Stanton and Dave Milton were dead or dying, and Ike Stanton was seriously wounded (he later had his leg amputated.) Matt Warner and his companions were untouched.

Warner was arrested for the murders of Stanton and Milton and lodged in the jail at Vernal. Butch Cassidy, Charles Crouse, Elza Lay and a few other members of the Wild Bunch (including William C. Boren, grandfather of author Kerry Ross Boren) gathered in the streets and threatened to take Matt out of jail by force, to save him from a lynch mob which had organized to "string him up." Sheriff John T. Pope took Warner and Wall out of the jail secretly at night and transported them over the Uintah Mountains via the old Carter Military Road to the railroad station at Carter Station, Wyoming, and from there by train to the Weber County jail at Ogden, Utah.

Cassidy and his gang converged on Ogden with a force nearly 75 strong, threatening to remove him from the jail, but Warner talked them out of bloodshed. He said he would rather have a good attorney, and so Cassidy hired Douglas A. Preston of Wyoming. But Preston was expensive, so on 13 August 1896 Butch Cassidy, Elza Lay and Henry Rhodes "Bub" Meeks held up the bank at Montpelier, Idaho.

Matt Warner was tried in Ogden and sentenced to five years in Utah State Prison on 21 September 1896. He was released in January 1900 by Governor Heber M. Wells, and settled in Price, Utah, on the farm owned by Caleb Rhoades. He prospected with Caleb until the latter's death in 1905, at which time Warner purchased Rhoades' property from his widow, Sidsie.

\* \* \*

Matt Warner was in jail during the remainder of the year 1896. Hathenbruck and Rhoades were compelled to look elsewhere for someone to defend their claim. In early September they made an attempt to secure the services of Butch Cassidy and Elza Lay, offering them the same terms as Matt Warner. The original letter to Butch and Elza has not been found, but the response is found among Hathenbruck's papers:

*Ashley, Utah, Oct. 5th, 1896*
*Mr. F.W.C. Hathenbruck*
*Provo, Utah*

*Dear Will,*

*We found your letter of September 17th waiting with Mrs. D\_\_\_[probably Mathilda Davis, Cassidy's good friend] when we returned from looking after Matt's interests. We have been very popular lately and much sought after by those who wish to make our acquaintance, and so the nature of our business requires frequent travel. Your letter says you will be in Vernal on Oct 11th but we regret that we can't meet with you as planned because we are about to go south where the weather fits our clothes. It don't look as though Matt will be out anytime soon, but we can recommend our friend Matt Thomas who can be reached through Charley Crouse at the Antler saloon. He knows the reservation and speaks Ute as good as any of the tribe. You met him not long ago at his brother's saloon in Price. Maybe you will remember him. He was the sober one. If the weather holds Mac [Elza Lay] will be back this way by the end of Oct. to settle some personal business. You can reach him at the Antler saloon. We both hope you*

*secure the Indian lease, and that when your [sic] rich uptown you will not forget your old friends.*

*GEORGE CASADY*
*BILL MACGINNIS*

Unable to secure the services of Butch Cassidy and Elza Lay, Hathenbruck and Rhoades were compelled to look elsewhere for someone to defend their claim. On 19 November 1896 they entered into an almost identical agreement with Matt Thomas of Vernal as they had made with Matt Warner.

J. Matthew "Matt" Thomas was a gunfighter of some reputation and a close friend and associate of Matt Warner and Butch Cassidy. In addition, Thomas was well acquainted with the Indians and spoke the Ute language fluently. Thomas chose a carefully selected circle of associates to go with him into the mountains in the late fall, to clean up the camp area that had been vacated by Henry Coleman and Bob Swift after the Dry Fork ambush. Among those who accompanied Thomas were Mid Nichols (another of Matt Warner's close friends and a renowned gunman in his own right), Bob Swift, George A. Storrs and Elza Lay. The latter had apparently returned to "settle some personal business" in time to join the Thomas venture; shortly thereafter, Lay left for his honeymoon at Robber Roost, having recently married Maude Davis of Vernal.

All of these men—with the exception of Storrs—had ridden with Cassidy to Ogden in the month of August in the attempt to break Matt Warner out of jail, and all of them—including Matt Warner—would again later be connected with the mines.

George Alfred Storrs was born 5 July 1863, at Springville, Utah, a son of George Storrs, Sr., and Lydia Mary Kindred. He died 3 May 1937, in Salt Lake City, and was buried in Forest Lawn Cemetery, Glendale, California, very near the grave of Elza Lay who had been buried there three years earlier. Storrs had been a somewhat renowned lawman and one-time warden of Utah State Prison. At the same time, he was heavily involved in mining and construction. As we will see, he later became associated in partnerships with both F.W.C. Hathenbruck and Jesse Knight. He appears to have been sympathetic to Caleb Rhoades until the time of Rhoades' death in 1905.

# Chapter 8

## INDIANS AND INCIDENTS

Between the years 1894 and 1905, when F.W.C. Hathenbruck first entered into a partnership with Caleb Rhoades, and after Rhoades' death, Hathenbruck's life was beset with trials, tribulations and intrigues. From early 1896 until the signing of the lease on 18 Dec. 1897, he had lived on the reservation among the Indians, gaining their trust and support for the Indian lease. He had organized a band of gunfighters and desperadoes to counter the moves of the Florence and Raven mining companies on the reservation. He had haunted the halls of Congress courting politicians, dignitaries, and government officials, seeking their influence for the ratification of the lease, only to have most of them work against him behind the scenes.

Strangely, Caleb Rhoades maintained a low profile throughout most of the negotiations, generally to leave everything in the capable hands of his partner. On 8 February 1898, for example, Rhoades gave Hathenbruck full power of attorney to act in his behalf in all matters of the lease.

They set about immediately to secure expense money and cooperation by selling off one-twentieth percentage parcels for amounts generally not exceeding $250 to $300. On 15 November 1896 they sold one-twentieth part to Hathenbruck's fellow Germans, John Beck, Gottlieb Beck, Eberhard Bauer for $300, for their promise to "use all diligent means, influence and exertions to consummate and help to bring to a successful issue and termination and execution fulfillment of said proposed agreement between [Hathenbruck and Rhoades] and the tribe of Indians occupying the Uintah

Reservation, Utah." Four days later they gave one-twentieth part to Matt Thomas for his services as "interpreter and help to negotiate with the proper Chiefs."

On 10 December 1896, they secured the services of James S. Clarkson of Philadelphia, and Hirum B. Clawson, a noted Salt Lake City attorney, for nine-twentieths part of the mine, for $1,000, "to be used to pay the expenses incident to procuring the lease from the Indians, as well as to pay off and discharge the obligations already incurred in that behalf..." Other similar agreements were made with attorneys to handle the paperwork and legal matters, individuals who had influence with the White River (Uncompahgre) Utes, politicians, mining engineers, and others [see Appendix: Indians Lease, Agreements and Mining Deeds].

On 8 February 1898, Hathenbruck sold one-twentieth part interest in the mine to Thomas H. Cavanaugh of Olympia, Washington, for $1,000. It would prove to be the cause of an attempt to drive a wedge between the partners Hathenbruck and Rhoades. On 15 January 1900, Hathenbruck filed a "Complaint and Prayer for an Injunction and Restraining order" against C.B. Rhoades and T.H. Cavanaugh, alleging, among other things, that:

*...machinations, misrepresentations and fraudulent practices of defendant Cavanaugh the Said T.H. Cavanaugh has been and now is secretly... destroying the partnership existing between Hathenbruck and Rhoades...and thereby jeopardizing and injuring the interest of the ...lease...The plaintiff further avers, that he is informed and believes... That the said*

*Thomas H. Cavanaugh defendant with the consent of defendant C.B. Rhoades obtained by...fraud and misrepresentations, is now endeavoring to organize a Stock Company for the handling [sic] and managing of said lease to the detriment and injury of plaintiff... and... that said claims of T.H. Cavanaugh are false and without right and are made for the purpose of defrauding and injuring plaintiff...*

Believing Reed Smoot to be his friend, on 24 April 1901, Hathenbruck signed over all of his interests in the lease to Smoot in order to protect his interests from the machinations of Cavanaugh. He was yet unaware that Smoot was working in alliance with Jesse Knight and the Florence and Raven companies. Hathenbruck was being constantly surrounded by unseen and unknown enemies, greedy for a portion of the mine. On 25 April 1902 Hathenbruck filed an affidavit stating that during the spring or early summer of 1897 he had met N.C. Myton, Indian Agent and member of the Allotment Commission of the Uncompahgre Indian reservation at Duchesne, on the reservation, and that they had engaged in conversation. Myton told him that if Hathenbruck would allow him to come in on the ground floor of the lease, he could virtually guarantee to secure the approval of the lease, but that if he did not, Myton would see to it that the lease was never approved. Hathenbruck stalled by stating that he would have to submit the proposition to his partner Rhoades before he could commit himself.

In about the month of July 1897, Hathenbruck and Rhoades met Myton on Second Street, between Main and State, in Salt Lake City. Myton asked Hathenbruck if he had conferred with Rhoades about the proposition he had made. Hathenbruck said that he had.

"What are you going to do about it?" Myton queried.

"I'm afraid that we can't accept your proposition," Rhoades told him.

"You will never get your lease approved," Myton said, shoving his hat down on his head and walking away in a huff.

Indian Agent Myton was already playing both sides. In an undated letter to "Mr. Smith" of Washington, D.C., Myton made it clear that his intentions were to protect the interests of the Florence and Raven companies against Hathenbruck and Rhoades on the reservation:

*Department of the Interior,*
*U.S. Indian Service,*

*Mr. Smith,*

*You must not allow the Indians to bother Mr. Bassant and his party, he has authority from Washington to be on the Reservation. You and Mr. McAndrews must see that they are protected, regardless of what the Indians say.*
*Rspt-*
*N.C. Myton*
*Agent*

With so many enemies, known and unknown, seen and unseen, it is no small wonder that several attempts were made upon Hathenbruck's life. In an interview with a reporter for the Salt Lake Herald on 3 February 1905, the Doctor had stated: "There was dirty work enough to prevent me from securing my lease. I was shot at a number of times. I hold my life to be in danger all the time. An attempt was made to bribe Captain Beck through his son to have him kill me..."

The details of the numerous attempts at Hathenbruck's life are sparse, but several are known, at least one of which is recorded by Hathenbruck himself. Hathenbruck wrote the following letter to Senator Thomas Kearns, whose aid he sought after learning of the many plots levied against him.

*Salt Lake City, Utah, Aug. 27, 1904.*
*Senator Thos. Kearns,*

*Honored Sir:*

*In our conversation this morning we touched upon a point in which I am deeply interested, viz: Uintah Reservation. It appears strange to me, that after complying with the Laws and also the ruling of the Interior Department government governing Indian reservation, as regard [to] leasing mineral, agricultural and grazing lands, and receiving encouragements and acknowledgments from the Interior Department and the entire sanction (obtained in open council meeting) by all the, then interested Indians residing upon said Uintah Indian reservation lands, that I should be treated as a criminal when venturing upon said reservation lands, in any capacity. To qualify the foregoing, I desire to state that I in 1903 was employed as Topographer & Guide by F.M. Lyman, C.R. [Caleb Rhoades] having a contract to survey several townships on the Uintah Reservation, and I was prevented from pursuing my labors with said Mr. Lyman, through certain parties inciting the Indians against me, in jeopardy of my life, caused by one F.C. Timms misrepresenting my intentions toward the aforesaid Indian tribe, and again this present year 1904, the same Colonel F.G. [sic] Timms claiming to represent the Florence Mining Co., makes public assertions that I am entirely tabooed from the Reservation and in addition, that I neither had nor could get any justice, to repeat his words, "from here to Washington," also that he would get his friends to pass a law, whereby I should be debarred from locating any mineral claims on said reservation, for two years after its opening...[the complete letter is reproduced in the Appendix.]*

Tabauche (pronounced Tab-Wash), better known as Wash, was a son of Nauhnan and a grandson of old Chief Tabby. He was signer number 112 in the Indian lease. In his old age, Wash became a particular friend of author Kerry Ross Boren, to whom he related the following story:

*One day not long after we met in council and signed the Indian lease, I rode with the Doctor [Hathenbruck] from Fort Duchesne up the mountain to Towanta Flat. Apporah, Wanrodes, Cut Lip Jim and Frank Doctor rode with us. The Doctor wanted talk with Mountain Sheep, Bridger Jim, and Johnson [Tim Johnson, an Indian] who had camp at Towanta.*

*Maybe ten mile from Towanta, Johnson come down and meet with the Doctor. Johnson say, "Better you no come up. Bad whites say to me at White Rocks if you come up, they shoot you." Doctor, he say, "I go up anyway," and we go.*

*At Mountain Sheep Pass, somebody up on ridge shoot at us like hell, and we ride for cover of trees. Apporah was shot in leg, but he stay on his horse and in the trees we all help him down and the Doctor tie his belt around Apporah's leg to stop the blood.*

*I go with Wanrodes and Frank Doctor on foot through trees, and climb the hill, find place where two, maybe three men left signs. On ground we find empty 30-30 cartridges, but men they gone. Never know if men was whites or Indians, but I say whites; horse tracks wore metal shoes [Indians seldom shoed their horses.]*

*The Doctor give Apporah medicine for hurt in leg [i.e. the pain] and take him off mountain to house of John Patterson [an Indian, signer number 82 on the Indian lease], where we load him in back of wagon and take him to [military] hospital at Fort Duchesne. Apporah was all right, but he was mad as hell for long time and always walked bad [i.e. limped].*

# Chapter 9

## "THANK GOD, NOT CONGRESS..."

Matt Warner was released from prison in 1900, having served less than four years of his sentence for the so-called "Dry Fork Murders." He was unexplainably pardoned by Utah Governor Heber M. Wells. The popular version of the story was that Orlando Powers, one of the lawyers who had represented Warner at trial, negotiated Matt's release. Powers ostensibly had urged Union Pacific Railroad officials to offer amnesty to Butch Cassidy, then convinced Governor Wells to issue a pardon to Matt Warner on the condition that Matt would find Cassidy and urge him to turn himself in. Warner was given $175 for travel expenses, and during the last week of August 1900, he boarded a train at Salt Lake City bound for Rock Springs, Wyoming, hoping to locate his friend Butch either at Powder Springs or Brown's Park. However, when the train stopped at Bridger Station, just east of Evanston, Wyoming, the conductor handed Warner a telegram from Governor Wells: "All agreements off. Cassidy just held up a train at Tipton."

The story is romantic but more than likely is a red herring for something even more compelling. For example, Matt was pardoned in January; the Tipton train robbery did not occur until 31 August 1900, fully eight months later. What was Warner doing in the interim?

While the story about Matt Warner's search for his friend Butch may have some basis in fact, Matt's pardon seems to have come about in an entirely different manner. There is strong evidence that his release may have been as a result of his promise to Governor Wells and others to use his influence with Hathenbruck and Rhoades to obtain for them interest in the Rhoades mine.

"I have heard dad tell the story a hundred times," Matt's son, Boyo Warner, told author Kerry Ross Boren in 1972. "Dad said that one day he was called down to Warden Dow's office at the prison and there sat George Dern, a friend of his. Dern said, 'Matt, how would you like to get out of prison?'"

George Dern was a brother of one of Utah's popular governors, and the Derns were understandably good friends of Governor Heber M. Wells. The Derns were very prominent in Utah affairs. Ira Dern, World's Champion wrestler, was a good friend of Matt Warner (Matt performed an exhibition bout with Ira Dern at Salt Lake City), and modern-day actor Bruce Dern is a descendant of this family.

George H. Dern was president of the Consolidated Mercur Gold Mines Company, for whom Matt Warner had once worked as a union strike-breaker. He had formulated a deal with Governor Wells for Warner to be pardoned in return for Matt's promise to help secure an interest in the Rhoades mine. Governor Wells could not participate directly due to a conflict of interest, however, politics being as corrupt then as now, Wells could still profit from the scheme as a major stockholder in the Consolidated Mercur Company.

Apparently Matt did his part, for Dern's company obtained an undivided seven-fifteenths interest in Hathenbruck's rights on the reservation and a like amount for any locations made by Hathenbruck. Dern also used his influence to get Hathenbruck safely onto the reservation, as noted in the following letter of recommendation written by Dern to his associate, Arthur Brown, on the reservation:

*SALT LAKE CITY, UTAH, August 24, 1903.*
*Mr. Arthur H. Brown,*
*Uintah Indian Reservation.*

*Dear Art:*

*This will introduce to you Mr. F.W.C. Hathenbruck, with whom I have made a business arrangement, regarding certain locations he has the right to make on the reservation, before it is opened. It you can be of any assistance to him, whatever you do will be greatly appreciated by me.*

*Your & c*
*G. H. Dern*

During his explorations and negotiations on the reservation, Hathenbruck was protected by Matt Warner as his bodyguard. Matt was aided in his travels and access on the reservation by a handwritten pass given to him by the Governor. The pass, which Matt packed in his wallet for the rest of his life, read: "This man is OK. Heber M. Wells."

Between the years 1900 and 1905, the date of his pardon and Caleb Rhoades' death, Matt Warner worked alternately with Hathenbruck and Rhoades, and sometimes both together. Matt served as bodyguard, guide, camp-tender, interpreter (though both Hathenbruck and Rhoades spoke fluent Ute), and sometimes claim partner for the two men. He had helped in the construction of a cabin for Hathenbruck and Rhoades in the Grandaddy Lakes Basin in the vicinity of their mine, and guarded it against encroachment by the Florence and Raven Company speculators. After a few years, Matt named two of the small adjoining lakes "Boyo Lake" and "Joyce Lake", in honor of his two children.

While Hathenbruck worked diligently toward securing the Indian lease on the reservation, Rhoades did something quite curious.

Accompanied by Matt Warner, he explored and filed claims south of the reservation in Utah, and north of the reservation in Wyoming. These claims apparently had nothing to do with the Indian lease, and may have been locations brought to his attention by Matt Warner.

Sam Gilson (a deputy U.S. marshal who discovered Gilsonite, which is named for him) had found some horn silver (ceragyrite, a silver chloride) on the San Rafael Swell sometime prior to 1880. The horn silver was lying on the ground in the form of Desert Roses, which are simply incrustations which have accumulated on the ground following the erosion and weathering of overlaying formations.

Prior to 1883 the Rio Grande Western Railroad built a spur line, with Chinese labor, through the San Rafael Swell, then abandoned it. Here, five miles east of the tracks, Caleb Rhoades claimed the Silver Valley Mine. It is located precisely 9 miles from desert Switch, 16 miles from Green River Station, and 4 miles from the Violet Mine.

Why Caleb Rhoades should have shown such interest in a remote claim while in the middle of negotiations for the Indian lease is unknown, except that he must have believed it to be valuable. Perhaps it is something Matt Warner had first discovered while riding to Outlaw Trail, which passes through the San Rafael Swell on the way to nearby Robbers Roost. This seems to be borne out by the fact that, while Rhoades was claiming the Silver Valley Mine, Matt Warner and his brother-in-law (and fellow outlaw) Tom McCarty, were laying claim to tracts of land surrounding Rhoades' claim, and continued to do so for four years, even after Rhoades' death. The claims on the San Rafael are as follows:

Matt Warner, et al, Luzon Claim, below RR bridge and opposite old Fort Bottoms, October 1904.

Matt Warner and Tom McCarty, Building

45

Claim, March 10, 1906 Book K-329.

Matt Warner and Tom McCarty, Dragon Claim, March 10, 1906, Book K-329.

Matt Warner, et al, Roosevelt Claim, and

Matt Warner, et al, Old Summerville Claim, March 16, 1908 Book I-171,174.

Matt Warner, et al, Old Copperboy Claim, April 13, 1908, Book I-183.

Caleb Rhoades also filed claims in Wyoming, on the north slope of the Uintah Mountains, only a few miles from the area he proposed to secure by the Indian lease, just across the border in Utah. Either the claims were intended to secure extended veins from the Rhoades mine, or it was an effort by Rhoades to isolate as much of the surrounding area as possible from encroachment.

* * *

As early as 1902, Caleb Rhoades, who was then 66 years of age, was in failing health. He was no longer the robust mountaineer he once was, and his illness took a toll even on his physical appearance. Though 66 was not particularly old, with his long and bushy grey beard and hoary head, he is often referred to in letters as "The Old Gentleman." In a letter to Hathenbruck from H.C. Henderson, dated 19 May 1902, he states, "...I anticipated that Rhoades will cooperate with us and go to the Reservation if he is physically able to do so." It was becoming more and more difficult for Caleb to get out into the mountains. Yet he continued to do so another three years, hoping to live to see the opening of the reservation, his last hope to at last openly work his mine. But time was running out for him.

Caleb might have made it, had there not been a heavy snowfall which, by the spring of 1903, had weakened the beams of his cabin and the roof fell in on him, injuring him severely. Dr. Hathenbruck nursed him to recovery, but his health, already labored, declined even more.

On 2 Jan. 1905, while sitting before his fire-place in his cabin at Price, Caleb Rhoades suddenly died. He was sixty-nine. He was buried in the Price City Cemetery and his widow, Sidsie, planted a pine tree next to his grave. She devotedly drove to the grave every day in a buggy with her good friend, Mary Jane Grames, with five one-gallon cans of water to nurture the tree.

Sidsie was well provided for in her husband's will. He left her his huge ranch, a large herd of well-bred livestock, numerous commercial properties, a large share of stock in a local business, and $38,000 in cash. She made a trip to Denmark to visit relatives and recover from her loss, and gave power of attorney in her absence to F.W.C. Hathenbruck to look after her interests.

Matt Warner, who had recently married Elma Zufelt, was determined to put his outlaw past behind him and pursue his interests of ranching and mining. He purchased part of Caleb's ranch on which to live, from Sidsie, and in the meantime continued to work as a bodyguard for Hathenbruck who, now on his own, needed one more than ever.

Caleb's death came just three months prior to the opening of the Uintah-Ouray Reservation and his partner Hathenbruck was left with the task of pursuing their quest to open the mines to exploration. Numerous attempts were being made near the time of the reservation opening to beat Hathenbruck to the prize. But Hathenbruck did not immediately give up the quest.

"Thank God, not congress, the Florence Company was limited to 640 acres contiguous, instead of a reservation blanket, as was the Raven Company in the Hydro-carbon line. Their 640 acres takes but a small piece from the center of the belt, leaving a great many claims with the ore already in sight for the citizen and prospector, who are deserving of the ground."

These were the sentiments of F.W.C. Hathenbruck on 8 June 1905, only six days after the untimely death of his partner, Caleb Rhoades. By Act of Congress, 27 May 1902,

Hathenbruck and Rhoades had been granted the right to locate and possess 640 acres of reservation lands in lieu of their original lease of 1897, providing they could obtain permission of the Indians. The death of Caleb Rhoades had not altered that right, but the task of dealing with the Indians would be considerably more difficult because of it, and so it became imperative that Hathenbruck return to the reservation to insure success.

The one obstacle remaining was the "restraining Order" issued by the authorities then under the control of special interest groups, which had prevented Hathenbruck from entering the reservation. Uncertain as to whether or not it was safe to return, Hathenbruck wrote a letter to his old Indian friend, Tim Johnson, who lived and worked at the Indian Agency at White Rocks. He inquired if it would now be safe for him to return without threat of arrest, impressed upon his friend the importance of his new mineral lease, stated that he felt he could gain support for this lease from his Indian friends only if he were present among them. He also cautioned them to be wary of signing other leases which he had no doubt would be placed before them during the remaining few weeks prior to the opening of the reservation. On 6 August 1905, his friend Johnson replied:

*Dear Sir,*

*I have good opportunity to tell you what your friends say about your letter. They all glad to hear from you. The White Ute take your advice. They said you are alright & the Ouray Indians too take your advice.*
*I think the [white] people are coming in [on the reservation] now—just start to come in. I think that is not right...*
*You are fine man and all the Indians over the world know.*
*Please don't write again, wait until we write*

*you. The soldares [soldiers] are all [over the] country now.*
*This is all to you friend, From you friend.*
> *Tim Johnson*
> *W.R. Utah*
*P.S. Please do not come until we write again.*

Unable to immediately return to the reservation, Hathenbruck devised a plan for future use whereby he could have built water storage facilities and a power plant on the Rock Creek drainage. He would try to induce others to finance the project to further their own gain, while he would benefit personally by having a water and power source for the machinery necessary for working his claims. He completed the plan on 14 September 1905, which in pertinent part are as follows:

*The Headwaters of Rock Creek have their principal source of supply from two basins at an elevation of 10,500 feet surrounded by a watershed the elevation of which is from 11 to 13,000 feet. Basin No-1 has an area of about 3,850 acres with 15 natural reservoirs or lakes with a total area of 900 acres with an average depth of 10 feet. These lakes can be raised from 2 to 12 feet by an expenditure of about $25,000 in building dams. Each lake has only one outlet and dams need not average over 50 feet long to accomplish desired result—abundance of timber and other material contiguous to work—the whole basin thickly covered with timber. Basin No-2-Area about 6,000 acres with 8 reservoirs or lakes, elevation about the same as basin #1 with same facilities for dams... at the confluence of the streams emulating from these two basins the elevation is about 8,700 feet... at this place... natural facilities suggests the building of a power plant...The fall of the water into the plant will be about 1,000 feet—and if permissible by law the storage of water, insuring an even and* *steady flow at all time could be sold for agricultural purposes—There being a bench of excellent land comprising about 75,000 acres that must look for water from this stream...Distance from Heber (as the Crow flies) 32 miles, from Park City 37 miles to the plant—approximate water power generated at plant between 5 & 10,000 horse power, proximate cost of whole plant $400,000... a wagon road exists to within 5 miles of the site, from there the natural contour of the country would require no more than 3 short dugways to be built—The estimated cost [of road] would be no more than about $2,000...*

The plan never achieved fruition, meeting stiff opposition from some unexpected sources. The first to reject the scheme, on 23 November 1905, was George H. Dern, general manager of the Consolidated Mercur Gold Mine Company. In 1907, Hathenbruck was able to resurrect the plan with the support of the popular Utah Governor Simon Bamburger and financial backing from the Boston Consolidated Mining Company of Salt Lake City. Applications for water rights were filed and an extensive survey of the region was made at the cost of $10,000. But again the project was abandoned in 1908. Another attempt to revive it in 1915 also failed, but Hathenbruck's vision was ultimately proven sound when, in more recent times, a similar project developed the Moon Lake Basin, providing both water storage and hydroelectric power.

# Chapter 10

## GUNFIGHTER'S GOLD

Shortly after the death of Caleb Rhoades—apparently in the same month—F.W.C. Hathenbruck allied himself with the Sylvanite Mining Company. Time was of the essence, for the mountains were already filled with anxious prospectors. On 24 September 1905, Hathenbruck wrote the following letter to the President and Board of Directors of the Sylvanite Mining Company:

*Gentlemen;*

*Through unforeseen circumstances not being able to be present at the stockholder meeting, I herewith take pleasure to submit a report of my doings and locating since July 21st, 1905—for the Sylvanite Co—*
*On August 2nd 1905 I located the Sylvanite #1 and 2 a fissure vein breaking through the country rock—commonly known as Quartzite (but which I term a course Gueis). This mine—the nature and location of which has been described to me, over 20 years ago by Mr. C.B. Rhoades— and at a time before there was only talk over the fabulous Mines on the Reserve—and is what is termed the Rhoades Mine... These mines are— in the second left hand fork—going up stream from the narrows of Rock Creek— about 4 miles above the confluence of this fork with the main stream—*
*Another very important location was made on August 24th for our Company—via the Alice which is situated in the left hand fork of the second left hand fork in which the Sylvanite #1 and 2 are located and shows better values than any— on the surface—and is best approached*
*from the Plateau on the west and can readily be seen from one part of Plateau directly above the mine—but hard of access from the Forks—The A.C. Mine at the mouth of 2nd left hand fork of Rock Creek—going upstream—is a continuation of Sylv: 1 and 2 and low grate [sic:grade] Gold proposition in contact or Quartzite and Lime shale—located August 3rd, 1905...*

*Respectfully Yours,*
*F.W.C. Hathenbruck*

Some interesting statements are made in this letter. To begin with, Hathenbruck states that this mine was described to him more than 20 years earlier by Caleb Rhoades, which means he must have known Rhoades as early as 1885, a decade before their 1894 partnership. Secondly, this is obviously not the Rhoades mine, because he mentions locating it as late as August 1905. It does indicate, however, that Hathenbruck was working on the reservation prior to the opening, in spite of the restraining order forbidding him from doing so.

Hathenbruck's directions are somewhat vague, but he seems to be inferring that the Sylvanite #1 and 2 claims are on the second left hand fork of the West Fork of Rock Creek in his statement "about 4 miles above the confluence of this fork with the main stream." This places it in the Lodgepole Lake area, where Rhoades and Hathenbruck had a cabin while working the area earlier. Caleb Rhoades filed a mining claim in 1901 (Wasatch County Recorder's book O. p.133) in the same area, which he called

"Shipwreck #4." Gale Rhoades discovered a rock formation in Red Cliff Lake which resembles a shipwreck, which might well denote the area.

It should be kept in mind that while the Rhoades mine was in this general area, it was never filed on by Rhoades or Hathenbruck. To have made any official record of its precise location would have been the cause of a rush to the place by their special interest enemies.

Throughout the year 1906, Hathenbruck, in conjunction with other individuals (M.P. Trotter, E.E. Horn, John Christenson, Mamie C. Singleton), filed on numerous claims in this area: "Castle Rock Mine #1 and 2, "9 July 1906, "#1—on south side of Hades Canyon and west of what is known as Castle Rock on North Fork of Duchesne River"; and, "#2—easterly of Castle Rock #1." "Little Gulch," 14 July 1906, located "3 miles north of Stockmore on east side of the North Fork of the Duchesne River, in a box canyon running in a easterly direction." "Surprise #1 thru 4." 17 July 1906, located "in Dry Spring Canyon, on the west side, about 5 miles easterly from Stockmore." "Bertram Gold Placer Claim," 1 August 1906, located "_ mile easterly of Grand Dad (Grandaddy) Lake, in Little creek and Little creek Spring, on Rock Creek Slope." This latter was very near Lodgepole Lake. On 22 September 1906, they filed an annex to this claim following the contour of the nearby high plateau.

\* \* \*

Hathenbruck and Rhoades may not have succeeded in opening their mine, but they did inadvertently cause the opening of the reservation, to the detriment of the Indians. To their credit, neither man wanted that to happen, and whatever they did was with the consent of the Utes. The same could not be said for the federal government and the special interest groups.

As soon as the reservation lands were opened for white settlement (and mining) in 1905, President Theodore Roosevelt withdrew 1,100,000 acres from the Ute lands to create the Uintah National Forest Reserve. Then followed the opening of the reservation to white settlement.

It began with a political dispute between certain Mormon Church officials, Mormon Senator Reed Smoot, the Republican Party, and Thomas Kearns and his newspaper, the *Salt Lake Tribune.*

In 1901 Kearns—who was Catholic—had been elected to the United States Senate, but in 1905 the Republican Party (composed primarily of Mormons in Utah) withdrew its support from Kearns and elected George Sutherland. Kearns was outraged when he learned that the Church, under the leadership of Joseph F. Smith and Reed Smoot, were working to gain political and economic control of the state.

At the center of the controversy was William H. Smart, president of the Wasatch Stake, with ecclesiastical jurisdiction prior to its opening to identify suitable land with water resources for homesteading. He organized the Wasatch Development Company to assist Church members in locating Indian lands. Kearns blasted the move, accusing the Mormons of a "most insolent attempt to thwart by underhand means" efforts of the government to open the reservation, blaming "The present odious presidency of Joseph F. Smith."

However, in spite of the opposition, the Mormon Church was successful, and nearly 37,000 individuals from all over the country registered for Indian land during the first two weeks of August 1905. The drawing of names took place at the Proctor Academy in Provo on 16 August 1905. During the next few days over 5772 names were drawn from a barrel, each recipient gaining 160 acres of the choicest land. The Indians were understandably outraged. In 1906 a great number of them left the reservation in protest, going to the Pine Ridge, South Dakota, reservation of the Sioux, but after two years of starvation and death, they were at last compelled to return to the much-diminished Uintah Reservation in 1908 [see *The Gold of Carre-Shinob*, op.cit., chap 10, "The Red Exodus."]

\* \* \*

As noted earlier, Hathenbruck had been working the upper Rock Creek-Grandaddy Lakes Basin even prior to the opening of the reservation, in spite of the restraining order and threats against his life. But he dare not venture into the reservation alone, and surrounded himself with a bevy of gunfighters as bodyguards, as many as ten or more at times. Among them are the names of men who were, only a few years earlier, associated with Butch Cassidy and the Wild Bunch: Matt Warner, Elza Lay, Henry "Hen" Lee—and, a little later, even the notorious Sundance Kid.

Some years ago, the late Art Davidson of Lyman, Wyoming, discovered a telegram inserted in the pages of an old account book belonging to storekeeper T.C. Hilliard. The account book contains the record of purchasers who maintained accounts at Hilliard's store, including Butch Cassidy, who frequently bought supplies there.

The telegram, dated 3 July 1901, Washington, D.C., was from President Theodore Roosevelt to "Lt. Col. Jack Leroy Dempsey" and signed familiarly "Teddy." It dealt with "Teddy's Terrors" in the Spanish American War, offering amnesty and pardon for their participation on the War. Those to whom President Roosevelt offered amnesty were as follows:

Lt. Col. Jack Leroy Dempsey
Pvt Harv. J. Cassidy
Capt. Geo. C. Irwin
Pvt. Hiram Benson
Sgt. Richard Angel
Pvt. _____Jones

Pvt. Jeffery Mereaith
Pvt. William Meeks
Pvt. William Madden
Pvt. George Sullivan

It has been established that Robert Leroy Parker, alias Butch Cassidy, and a number of his gang formed a detachment of Teddy's Rough Riders during the Spanish American War. The telegram from Teddy Roosevelt, offering amnesty to the members of "Teddy's Terrors," seems clearly to allude to Cassidy and his outlaw regiment. The names given are obviously pseudonyms, but they correspond with the identities of the hierarchy of the Wild Bunch. Two prominent names are conspicuous by their absence— Matt Warner and Elza Lay, both of whom were in prison during the war. This telegram was to have ironic implications in connection with Hathenbruck and the Rhoades mine.

When the Florence and Raven mining companies dissolved upon the opening of the reservation in 1905, a new company was immediately formed, combining the two defunct companies into one, calling itself the Florence and Raven Mining Company. The stockholders of the newly organized company are the same names which appear on Teddy Roosevelt's 1901 Telegram! The Florence and Raven Mining Company stockholders are as follows:

Robert Leroy
Bill Phelps
George Parker
Frank Harris Sullivan
Richard Angel
Bill Meeks
Harv Logan
Harry Parker

Robert Leroy, a.k.a. Jack Leroy Dempsey, was a man known in later years as "Old Bob" Parker, a near relative of Butch Cassidy (for information concerning this man's true identity, see: *The Unholy Trinity-Butch Cassidy, The Sundance Kid, and Etta Place-The Untold Story*, Kerry Ross Boren and Lisa Lee Boren, unpub. ms.). Geo. C. Irwin (George Capel Irwin) was the sometime alias of Butch Cassidy. Frank Harris Sullivan, son of Florence Sullivan and Emily Jane Place, was half-brother of Etta Place, who was married at different times to both Butch Cassidy and the Sundance Kid. Frank and Etta's father was George Capel, alias George Ingerfield, was a mining partner of the great bonanza King, Senator George Hearst, developer of the fabulous silver mines at Park City. Harvey Logan was better known to history as Kid Curry. Hiram Benson was one of many aliases known to have been used by Harry A. Longabaugh, a.k.a. the Sundance Kid. Bill Madden participated with Cassidy in a number of major robberies. Bub Meeks participated with Cassidy and Lay in the Castle Gate Payroll Robbery (Utah) in 1897, and the Montpelier (Idaho) Bank Robbery the following year. Bub Meeks also participated with Henry Lee in the robbery of the Charles Guild store near Fort Bridger, Wyoming. Bill Meeks was Bub's brother. Richard Angel is believed to have been a brother of Truman O. Angel, architect of the Salt Lake Temple, who utilized the gold from the Rhoades mines as decoration. Jeff Mereaith (Murdock) remains an enigma. Jones was one of the brothers of Lovina Jones Boren, grandmother of Kerry Ross Boren; Lovina was raised with Butch Cassidy. Jones was also the adoptive father of the Indian "Happy Jack," friend of Caleb Rhoades.

The names, aliases all, are confusing, but the Florence and Raven Mining Company was a "dummy"corporation, formed merely to give Hathenbruck control of a region formerly dominated by the special interest groups. The real movers behind the company were two men whose names do not even appear as stockholders: Matt Warner and Elza Lay. How this came about is worth recounting.

* * *

Several days before his death, Caleb Rhoades drew two nearly identical maps on pages ripped from a notebook. He gave one copy to his wife Sidsie (since known as the "Mystery Map") and gave the second copy to his Indian friend Happy Jack with instructions to deliver it to Matt Warner (since known as the "Dangerous Country" map). Caleb told his wife that the map gave directions to the same mine which his brother, Enock Rhoades, had retrieved gold from shortly before being killed by the Indians in 1884. It becomes obvious from later evidence that Caleb gave the map to Matt Warner under some agreement that Matt should help Sidsie locate the mine. Matt's copy of the map, according to his own account, became an important tool in securing the release of Elza Lay from prison.

William Ellsworth "Elza" Lay, a.k.a. William Macginnis, was born 25 November 1868, in MacArthur, Vinton County, Ohio, and came West in his teens. He first foray into outlawry took place with Harry Longabaugh and Matt Warner, and he eventually became one of the leading members of the Wild Bunch. In 1896, Lay was one of the gunfighters hired by Hathenbruck and Rhoades to defend their mining interests on the reservation.

Following a train robbery near Folsom, New Mexico, in 1899, Lay and his companions shot and killed Sheriff Farr and several members of a pursuing posse. He was sentenced to life imprisonment in the New Mexico State Penitentiary for murder and armed robbery on 10 October 1899, under his alias William McGinnis (MacGinnis, etc.), #PNM 1348.

Lay was a model prisoner, at one point even helping to quell a prison riot. He was able to influence the Warden, who had an avid interest in mining, by recounting some of his experiences as a hired gun for Caleb Rhoades in protecting the fabulous gold source on the Ute Indian Reservation in Utah.

According to Matt Warner, he provided Lay with a copy of Caleb Rhoades' "Mystery Map" or

"Dangerous Country" map, which Lay effectively used to impress the warden. The warden became passionately interested in the Rhoades mine and even induced Governor Miguel Otero of New Mexico to become involved. Through Otero's intervention, Lay was pardoned on 10 January 1906 (though he was released before Christmas 1905), with a promise that he would go immediately to Utah and attempt to locate the mine, with the Warden and Governor as financial backers and silent partners. Lay teamed up in 1906 with his old cronies to form the Florence and Raven Mining Company.

There is a fact needing explanation. Harvey Murdock, grandson of Elza Lay, correctly pointed out to Kerry Ross Boren, during the compilation of this book, that his grandfather Elza Lay detested Matt Warner. Harvey expressed surprise that Elza would have been involved with Matt, considering his opinion of him, but the facts speak for themselves. They had a long history together, and outlawry—like politics—makes strange bedfellows. Matt was a brusque, egotistical braggart, and in point of fact few of the members of the Wild Bunch liked him; but he was a proficient gunman and a good man to have in one's corner. The evidence is strong that Matt Warner and Elza Lay were indeed involved in the search for the Rhoades mine.

Matt Warner's son, Boyo Warner, provided me with copies of the "Mystery Map" and the "Dangerous Country" map in 1971, and Marvel Lay Murdock, daughter of Elza Lay, provided me with a copy of the map her father sketched for Governor Otero, which is evidence that Matt Warner's claim was at least partially correct. [see: Appendix -Maps]

Elza Lay became involved in mining shortly after his release from prison. In 1908, Elza Lay and Butch Cassidy were employed as mine guards at Goldfield, Nevada, with mining magnate Mervin J. Monnette. Monnette, owner of Bankers Oil Company of California, took a liking to Lay and financed his education in geology and mineralogy.

Lay's first discovery of importance was an oil field beneath the old outlaw hideout of Powder Springs, and another in Clay Basin, both on the northern rim of Brown's Park, in Wyoming. He also discovered the natural gas deposits near Ogden, Utah, which he developed between the years 1910 and 1920 for the Provo Slate Company, Inc. This company was owned by Hathenbruck and George A. Storrs!

It should be remembered that Storrs, former warden of the Utah State Prison, was employed as a gunman by Hathenbruck and Rhoades during 1896-97 in securing their gold prospects on the reservation. On 7 September 1910, Hathenbruck entered into an agreement with Storrs, who owned a small quarry in Slate Canyon, adjacent to certain granite, slate and lime deposits recently purchased by Hathenbruck through the Timber & Stone Act of 3 June 1878.

Hathenbruck and Storrs developed the Provo Slate Company, Inc., which primarily produced purple, green and red roofing slate, and also included a granite quarry. But friction developed between the partners when Storrs became involved with the Doctor's old rival, Jesse Knight. As early as 1912, George Storrs was made a general manager of Knight's Spring Canyon Coal Company in Carbon County, one of Utah's largest coal producing claims. The town of Storrs, Utah, which belonged to Knight, was named for George Storrs, and Matt Warner—also employed by Hathenbruck—worked for Knight and Storrs as a lawman to keep order in the town. Hathenbruck, disgruntled with Storrs for his association with Knight, attempted to bring in other businessmen to the Provo Slate Company, with no success. By 1920, the partnership between Hathenbruck and Storrs had been dissolved.

# Chapter 11

## THE DEADLY SEARCH

In 1912, another group descended on the Rock Creek / Grandaddy Lake region and filed several groups of claims. On 14 July 1912, Edward Hartzell, D.C. Miles, L.M. Miles, James Hartzell, W.E. Cox, Parley and Frank Warren, J.C. Fergeson, and a Mr. Summers, filed on a group of claims called the "Eldorado." On 17 July they filed on a second group of claims called the "Klondike #1 and 2."

Their Eldorado claims were located "on the West Fork of Rock Creek and 3 forks, second left hand fork, 1/4 mile above cabin." It was, in fact, in the meadows adjacent to Lodgepole Lake just east of Grandaddy Lake, one-fourth mile west of the original Rhoades-Hathenbruck cabin. Their two Klondike claims were described as being "2 miles up the West Fork of Rock Creek, 4 miles from the big lake [Grandaddy Lake] in Rock Creek Basin, 8 miles above the [Upper] Stillwaters and 1 mile above the ranger or government cabin [located near the mouth of Cabin Creek], on the Left Hand Fork."

A new cabin with a corrugated tin roof was constructed for this group by William Davies, owner of the Rock Creek Ranch, and they began operations on two of the lower grade deposits at Lodgepole Lake. Wooden water troughs and ditches were constructed, and metal sluice boxes installed. But the operation eventually went defunct, and today only the collapsed cabin and some remnants of the sluices bear witness to their attempt. The Rhoades-Hathenbruck cabin, located in the timber one-fourth mile east, has been practically destroyed by a dynamite blast.

This group had worked only the low grade ore mentioned by Hathenbruck in his letters to the Sylvanite Company. The Rhoades mine was never found by them, though they were extremely close to the site. The reason, according to the Indians, was that this particular mine was situated in a large crack or crevice approachable only by being lowered by ropes. This was probably the mysterious "A.C. Mine" mentioned by Hathenbruck, who was never able to develop it for reasons soon to be made apparent.

Hathenbruck was not dismayed by this group's encroachment in "his" territory; in fact, they were there with his blessing. Edward Hartzell, originally from Pennsylvania, had married Sidsie Jensen Rhoades, the widow of Caleb Rhoades, and she had provided him with maps by Caleb, drawn shortly before his death on 2 June 1905.

James E. Hartzell was the son of Edward Hartzell by his first wife, Viola, and had been born in Scranton, Pennsylvania, on 15 October 1888. James Hartzell lost his life by heart attack while searching for this mine in the vicinity of the Bobby Duke Trail in August 1961.

Parley and Frank Warren lived at Vernal, Utah, and later at Price, where they had been acquainted with Caleb Rhoades. The history of D.C. and L.M Miles, J.C. Ferguson and Summers is vague, but W.E. Cox was none other than W.E. Christiansen, a.k.a. Matt Warner! It was in this same year that Matt Warner applied to have his name legally changed from Willard Erastus Christiansen to Matt Warner to facilitate his election as town marshal of Price, and it appears that his use of the alias "W.E. Cox" in his mining partnership claims was calculated to avoid notoriety. It is believed that the "John Christenson," who was involved with Hathenbruck in claims in the same area in 1906 was actually Matt Warner's brother, John Christiansen.

\* \* \*

Tom Dilly was a wild Texas cowboy. He had been "sparking" pretty Annie Marie Thayne, a young schoolteacher from Wellington, Utah, a small town near Price. Annie liked the wild life and the wild men it attracted. She had run around with Joe Walker, Bub Meeks, and Harvey Logan, and in 1900 she married Harry Longabaugh, alias the Sundance Kid, and bore him a son in 1901.

Sanford "Sang" Thompson, another member of the Wild Bunch, was staying on the ranch of William C. Boren (grandfather of Kerry Ross Boren) near Cleveland, in Emery County. When Annie Thayne turned her attentions to Thompson, Tom Dilly became insanely jealous. He laid up in the rocks of Thompson Canyon and killed Sang as he rode by. To avoid detection, Dilly decapitated the body and buried it in a box, where it was not discovered until some time later. Dilly then found work with Dan Kinney, foreman of the Webster Cattle Company.

When a man named Fullerton took over management of the Webster company, on his first day on the job he took it upon himself to give Dilly advice on how to shoe a horse, and Tom commenced to pistol-whip him. When another cowboy, Sam Jenkins, tried to interfere, Dilly gave him the same treatment, and they ever after hated each other.

In 1899 the Webster company was taken over by Dr. Andrew Dowd and a man named Forester, and they took Dilly in as a partner, contingent upon his promise to rustle livestock to build up their herd. They reorganized as the Patmos Head Land and Cattle Company. During the winter of 1899-1900, Dilly was joined in his rustling enterprise by Flatnose George Currie.

In May, Sheriff Jesse Tyler returned to the Book Cliffs, accompanied by Dilly's old enemy Sam Jenkins, whom Tyler had deputized in the hopes of bringing Dilly in. Instead they encountered three men sitting by a fire, wrapped in Indian blankets. Not knowing who they were, Tyler commenced to boast about having killed Flatnose Currie. The men proved to be Kid Curry and two companions. The Kid, a close friend and namesake of Flatnose George, fired from beneath his blanket and killed both Tyler and Jenkins.

Tom Dilly was believed responsible for the murders, but was eventually cleared at a preliminary hearing at Provo. Nevertheless, it cost the Patmos Head Land and Cattle Company $40,000 to get an acquittal. Tom promised to work something out to pay them back.

That fall Dowd and Forrester shipped a trainload of cattle to Kansas City in Dilly's care. Tom promised to ship some registered Hereford bulls to Dowd and Forrester, but instead absconded with the proceeds of the cattle sale and hastily fled to South America. He proposed to buy a ranch there, but soon joined Butch Cassidy and the Sundance Kid in robberies, only to be shot to death a few years later, in August 1911, at Mercedes, Uruguay.

In an attempt to recoup his losses, Dr. Andrew Dowd solicited a partnership with a man named Ketchum and Joseph R. Sharp to obtain possession of the Big Spring Ranch near Sunnyside, Utah. In June of 1905, within days of the death of Caleb Rhoades, F.W.C. Hathenbruck wrote the following letter (in pertinent part) to Mr. J.R. Sharp of Carbon County:

*The terms are now $10,000.00 in cash on signing of contracts... I only give you until July 1st to meet the deal at the price of 9 P.M. June 2nd 1905 [the time of Rhoades' death]... I have* *no fear of any trouble over our claims on the reservation in a physical form and legally. I am also loaded—because there are some things I did not feel called upon to explain or in other words "I have a card up my sleeve." ... Kindly give me your P.O. address that I may return your means advanced in expenses for Mrs. Rhoades & myself—and oblige.*

The letter clearly indicates some prior dealings between Sharp and Hathenbruck and Rhoades, but upon the death of Rhoades, the Doctor was holding out for more money for some planned efforts with Caleb's widow Sidsie.

In the fall of 1905, Sidsie approached Dr. Andrew Dowd and Joseph Sharp with a proposition. She offered them a limited partnership if they would help her locate the mine indicated on a map left to her by her husband. This is confirmed by the journal entries of Mr. Lester Eklund.

Sidsie and her new partners, Dowd and Sharp, searched for the mine for more than two years, from 1906 until 1907, with no success. On his death bed, Caleb had told her that "the mine was located below Low Pass," but Low Pass could never be located, and without that starting place, the mine could not be found.

While associated with Dowd and Sharp, Sidsie met Edward Hartzell, whom she married in 1911. In July of 1912, Edward Hartzell, his son James, Matt Warner, the Warrens and others filed on the Eldorado and Klondike claims in the Rock Creek/ Grandaddy Lake region. [For additional information on Joseph Sharp and his later search in 1928-30, and for a full account of the death of James Hartzell, see: *The Gold of Carre-Shinob*, op.cit., at Chap. 14.]

\* \* \*

In 1920, Hathenbruck dissolved his partnership with George Storrs, who had shifted his alliance toward the Doctor's old adversary, Jesse Knight. The Doctor had difficulty keeping part-

ners. The primary reason was that he knew the location of the Rhoades mine; he had been taken there by Caleb Rhoades—but he couldn't show anyone where it was because he had never secured a ratification of the Indian lease. If he showed the site to anyone, it could be stolen out from under him, especially because Jesse Knight's people were still avid to secure it, at any cost. Past attempts on the Doctor's life had proven that much.

Hathenbruck was growing older and the prospects for securing the mine were growing ever dimmer. He began to question whether or not he would live to see the mine opened. Desperate times called for desperate measures. If he couldn't obtain it openly, perhaps he could locate and secure it by force—and deception. What happened next is the stuff legends are made of.

Near the time of the fourth of July holiday, 1920, a man by the name of Caleb Landreth arrived in Bridger Valley, Wyoming, from Pittsburgh, Pennsylvania. After stepping off the train, Landreth stayed several days at a nearby ranch before setting up his own camp. He was soon joined by a 21 year-old cowboy named Harold Moslander, who had a local reputation as a "fast draw,"—able to draw and shoot either of his pistols with equal speed and accuracy.

A few days later, these two men were joined by another youth, a well-mannered fellow named Ernest Roberts, who joined them as a camp cook. He had a special talent for concocting a delicious Mulligan Stew.

There next appeared two parties consisting of eight men: "Old Man" Warren and his twin sons, Thursday and Friday Warren (so called because they were born before and after midnight on those two days of the week)— "Old Man" Warren was either Parley or Frank Warren, who had filed on the Eldorado and Klondike claims with Matt Warner and others in 1912; Matt Warner and Edmund Hartzell of Price; and Rock M. Pope,

Tom Welch and William Macginnis from Vernal. It was rumored that most of these men were the remnant of Cassidy's Wild Bunch. All of them were well armed and expert marksmen. They brought with them two pack horses loaded with supplies and camp equipment as they made camp with Landreth, Moslander and Roberts. Landreth, who seemed to have plenty of cash, paid for all supplies.

In the meantime, Amasa Alonzo Davidson and his wife arrived at a nearby ranch by buckboard. On the morning following their arrival, the men from the camp rode en masse to the ranch with their horses packed and an extra mount for Davidson. When Davidson saw the group of rough-looking characters, he refused to go with them. Davidson was not a gunman; he was a rancher from nearby Urie, Wyoming. His only qualification was that he had taught chemistry at a local school, and could assay gold. He was acquainted with young Ernest Roberts, but knew none of the others in the group. Beyond that fact, his only other connection was that he had at one time been a good friend of Butch Cassidy.

The men were sent back to their camp, and Landreth remained at the ranch with Moslander to attempt to convince Davidson to accompany them into the mountains. Landreth, a self-proclaimed prophet, hypnotist and spiritualist, said that he could prove by the "fates" of the cards that there would be no danger if Davidson went along with them.

Landreth produced a new deck of cards and had Davidson break the seal. Without touching the deck himself, Landreth instructed Davidson to shuffle them, as he explained that spades were bad luck cards, clubs signified trouble, hearts represented love and diamonds meant riches.

Mrs. Davidson then cut the deck and drew one card. The card was the king of hearts and Landreth told her it represented her husband. The cards were again shuffled—Landreth never touching them— and Davidson drew a card, the queen of hearts, which he was told represented his wife. The cards were again shuffled, and Mrs Davidson was told to draw five cards from any place in the deck and leave them face down. When these cards were turned over, they were found to be the ace, king, queen, jack and ten of diamonds—riches untold, Landreth indicated.

Davidson remained skeptical and even examined the deck, but found them to be regular cards. Mrs. Davidson, on the other hand, was thoroughly convinced and urged her husband to go. Davidson reluctantly consented, but only on the condition that he leave his rifle with his wife and go unarmed. He borrowed a gentle horse from his brother and rode unarmed into the camp the next morning, bringing along his acids, his blow pipe and camera.

# Chapter 12

## THE GUNFIGHT

F.W.C. Hathenbruck had a strong desire to locate and secure the Rhoades mine, and he financed an expedition to approach the mine from the Wyoming side of the Uintah Mountains, where they would be undetected. He employed some of the best gunmen available, men with proven reputations and abilities, to carry it out.

William Macginnis was, of course, Elza Lay, who had recently been employed by Hathenbruck and Storrs to develop the natural gas deposits near Ogden. These fields, among the largest producers in the West, were assimilated by the Knight Investment Company, through the machinations of George Storrs, and both Hathenbruck and Lay were "let out to dry." We have recounted Lay's history previously, as also Matt Warner, with whom Lay was involved in the 1920 expedition.

Ernest Roberts, the young camp cook, was the son-in-law of "Old Man" Warren, and thus brother-in-law to the twins, Thursday and Friday Warren. Not much is known about the Warrens prior to their involvement in the mining claims in 1912 and the 1920 expedition, except that they had some early connection with Caleb Rhoades or his wife Sidsie.

Harold Maughan Moslander was born 6 November 1898 at Aspen, Uinta County, Wyoming, son of Charles Humes Moslander (1856-1938) and Margaret Ann Maughan (1861-1930). Harold, born too late to participate in the Wild West era, fancied himself nonetheless a gunfighter, and was an avid fan of Butch Cassidy. He hung around with remnants of the Wild Bunch and became proficient with his two guns under the expert tutelage of none other than the

Sundance Kid. Following the 1920 adventure, Harold Moslander operated a ranch on the Bear River, near Evanston, Wyoming, where he died 1 July 1976, at the age of seventy-eight.

Rock M. Pope was the brother of Uintah County Sheriff John T. Pope. On 26 December 1895, Matt Warner, Rock M. Pope and John T. Pope had staked mining claims in Red Creek Canyon in Brown's Park, hoping to discover the Lost Ewing Mine. Rock Pope was a tough customer who had often served as a deputy under his brother, but just as often favored friendships with outlaws.

Tom Welch was a rancher on Henry's Fork in Sweetwater County, Wyoming, but he had also ridden with the Wild Bunch, and Butch Cassidy was his long-time friend. Tom had come West from Illinois in a wagon train in 1878 with his mother and stepfather to the mining camps of South Pass and Atlantic City, Wyoming. Tom was a tough old cattleman who had helped Butch and Sundance rob a train at Tipton, Wyoming, in 1900, and had killed several men in his wilder days.

Shortly before the group left for the mountains, they were joined by Jim Chrisman, a Wyoming gunman and friend of Tom Welch.

The most startling information dealing with the group of gunfighters involves the enigmatic Caleb Landreth. When Kerry Ross Boren interviewed Tom Welch in the early 1960's, he readily admitted his part in the expedition, and identified their leader, Caleb Landreth, as none other than Harry Longabaugh, a.k.a. the Sundance Kid! A photograph of Caleb Landreth, provided by a grand-nephew of Harold Moslander, compared digitally with a photo of Longabaugh, dispels all doubt.

Harry Alonzo Longabaugh was born 19 April 1868 in Pennsylvania, a son of Josiah Longabaugh and Mary Ann Place. Inspired by dime novels, he left home and headed West at the age of 14. He earned his famous sobriquet "Sundance Kid" after serving 18 months in the Crook County jail at Sundance, Wyoming. He rode into infamy with Butch Cassidy and the Wild Bunch, robbing banks and trains throughout the West before leaving for South America in 1901.

Following a string of robberies in Argentina, Chile, and Bolivia, Longabaugh returned to the United States. He organized a group of disciples in Ohio and brought them to California. He operated a burglary ring in San Francisco, and served four years in San Quentin, afterwards coming to Utah. In 1945, at the age of 77, he killed the town marshal of Mount Pleasant, Utah, and spent the next decade in the Utah State Prison where he died in 1955, at the age of 87, under the alias Hiram Beebe.

Longabaugh (as Caleb Landreth) appeared in Bridger Valley, Wyoming, in 1920, shortly after his release from San Quentin, and organized the search for the Rhoades mine. He possessed a very dominant personality, and it was inferred by those who knew him that he "mesmerized" people. He was a voracious reader and frequently quoted passages from the writings of Omar Khayam. He was a health food advocate, lauding Ralston products as superior to most other foods, and he professed to have dreams and visions and was adept in the occult sciences. It should be remembered that Longabaugh, under the name Hiram Benson or Bennion, was one of the stockholders of the Florence and Raven Mining Company.

Thus it is clear that at least half of the 1920 group were former members of the Wild Bunch, or in some way associated. All were proficient gunmen, even Davidson, though he was unarmed.

Before the group left Bridger Valley, Landreth had himself blindfolded, then went into a trance and drew a rough map on a piece of paper. Drawing an "X" on the makeshift map, he indicated that this would be their camp, and pointed out certain landmarks, saying that just below the camp there would be a small lake or pond, and that the stream flowing into it would be filled with trout. There would be lush meadows on all sides, he predicted, providing ample feed for the horses and, "Just above us is what appears to me to be some ancient castles." Some of these landmarks and locations were familiar to some of the more experienced men present, and they were amazed at the precision of his knowledge, but Landreth attributed it to "The spirit of the departed Indian Princess Ravencamp." In fact, however, Landreth had likely been provided with a copy of the map by Hathenbruck prior to the expedition.

The group of thirteen men at last set out on their mysterious quest for the Lost Rhoades Mine. They camped the first night on Stillwater Fork of the Bear River and caught pan trout for supper. The next morning Landreth again asked to be blindfolded and charted out the course for the day ahead. He predicted that they would come to an old cabin with plenty of wood and water. "The spirit of the Princess assures me of this," he told them. At least several of the men must have known that Landreth's accuracy was enhanced by a secret map in his possession.

Just before reaching the place, Landreth left Old Man Warren and his two sons to watch their back trail, to make certain they were not being followed, and to watch for Indians. Warren was chosen for this mission because he spoke the Ute language fluently, having been an interpreter at Whiterocks for many years. Rock M. Pope took Landreth's "inspired" hand-written map and went ahead in search of the cabin.

Near sunset they arrived in the vicinity of Mirror Lake and found the cabin, just as Landreth had predicted. It was a dilapidated old structure situated on the edge of present-day Scout Lake (near the Boy Scout summer camp called Camp Steiner). A well-defined trail led from the cabin up the mountainside, and some of the men were anxious to follow it right then, but Landreth encouraged them to wait until morning when he would seek directions from the spirit.

After supper all of the men went off by themselves for about an hour, leaving Davidson, Moslander and Roberts alone at the cabin. Moslander watched the men closely as they returned and silently went to bed. He expressed an uneasiness to Davidson and Roberts about the strange behavior of their companions, but Roberts put their minds at ease by saying that Old Man Warren was his father-in-law and the twins were his brothers-in-law, and would never conspire against him. The other man from Price (i.e. Matt Warner) had been a close friend of Butch Cassidy, but was a man of good character, and one of the other men was a retired cattleman and widower. The Vernal group, however, consisting of four hard men, had never been introduced—not even to Moslander and Roberts—and it was this group, headed by the surly Rock M. Pope, that Davidson feared most.

The next morning after breakfast, all of the men were anxious to go to the gold mine, but Landreth called them together and delivered a sort of sermon. He informed them that he had had a dream or vision in which the Lord had showed him the location of the famous lost mine, and had told him that he would be the instrument by which it would be brought forth, and that one-half of the money obtained from the discovery was to go toward organizing a new church, of which Landreth had been chosen as prophet and leader.

The men murmured their protests at these claims, for they had assumed they would all share equally in the mine. Landreth confused the issue by having himself blindfolded again and tried to draw a map to the mine, but the spirit of the Princess Ravencamp had forsaken him, he said, so he would have to find the mine without her help, or without the help of God.

Rock Pope, seeing the confusion of the men, took command of the situation. He placed Matt Warner in charge of Davidson and Moslander, instructing him to not let them leave the camp that day, and ordered young Roberts to have a meal ready for their return about sunset. The men then paired off, Landreth accompanying Pope.

After the men departed, Matt Warner sat down with the three men and took them into his confidence, saying that during the conference of the night before, Ross Pope had made it plain that Moslander, Roberts and Davidson were to be killed as soon as the mine was found. He instructed Davidson to declare whatever kind of rock that was found by Landreth to be worthless and this might save their lives. He informed them that their horses had been unhobbled and started off down the back trail the night before. There had been a discussion about shooting the horses, he said, but it was decided the shots might attract the attention of the Indians. Warner handed Davidson one of his pistols and told him not to hesitate to use it if it became necessary.

Near sunset, Landreth and Pope returned, and were soon joined by the others, all of them somber and silent as they ate their supper. Just as darkness fell, the last two men returned.

"What did you find?" Pope asked them.

"Nothing," came the reply.

"It's a lie!" cried Landreth. "Search them!"

One of the men reached for his gun and Pope shot him in the back. The critically wounded man was dragged to the firelight and Landreth searched his pockets. They were crammed full of high-grade gold-bearing ore. Pope asked the dying man where he had found it, and was promptly told to go to hell; in a fit of rage Pope shot the man in the head and killed him instantly.

Pope then turned to Davidson and ordered him to get his acids and test the ore for gold. Davidson tested the samples with his chemicals, then glanced briefly at Matt Warner before saying, "This is nothing but iron pyrites, sometimes called 'fool's gold'—it's worthless."

Pope eyed Davidson with scorn, knowing that he lied. He started to draw his pistol, but before he could clear leather, a shot rang out; Matt Warner had shot him dead. Instantly, all of the men began shooting at one another in mass pandemonium. Davidson and Moslander fired as they ran away from the firelight. They ran along their back trail all night and by morning caught up to their horses somewhere near Hilliard Flat about 14 miles southwest of Evanston, Wyoming (where Moslander later established his ranch).

Ernest Roberts was shot in the groin and it took him more than a week to make it out of the mountains. His wounds ended his marriage to his wife, Violet Warren Roberts, and caused his untimely death two years later. The official records state that he died from the effects of a ruptured appendix—his close friends knew better.

Of the thirteen men who participated in the ill-fated expedition, five were either killed or disappeared. The Warrens were never seen again. [For a more complete account of this battle, see: *The Gold of Carre-Shinob,* op. cit. at chap. 11.] The known survivors were Amasa Davidson, Harold Moslander, Ernest Roberts (who died two years later), Matt Warner, Edward Hartzell, Caleb Landreth (Longabaugh), Bill Macginnis (Lay), and Tom Welch.

When Amasa Davidson had tested the gold ore at the campsite, he had slipped a piece of it into his pocket. That sample is now said to be in the University of Mines at Laramie, Wyoming.

Davidson had also taken a photograph of the old Hathenbruck-Rhoades cabin on the ill-fated trip of 1920. On Saturday, 28 July 1951, Amasa Davidson, accompanied by an attorney named Day, returned to the site of the old cabin at Scout Lake. Even after 31 years the old cabin was still standing, and Davidson found that it compared exactly to the old 1920 photograph. After exploring the area in search of the mine with no success, they returned home by way of Bear River.

In 1975, just a year before his death, Amasa Davidson, accompanied by two of his sons, made one last attempt to locate the elusive mine. The cabin was still standing, though the roof had caved in. Later, the cabin was burned to the ground by the U.S. Forest Service to prevent it being a danger to the many Boy and Girl Scouts who camp nearby during the summer months.

Matt Warner, who was eventually elected Justice of the Peace, town marshal and deputy sheriff at Price, returned to the Mirror Lake region several times before his death in 1938 to search for the mine. He brought out numerous gunny sacks of ore samples which, according to his son Boyo Warner, he stacked in his garage; but he never found the elusive mine.

\* \* \*

Since the 1920 gunfight in Grandaddy Lakes Basin, new information has emerged to explain it. F.W.C. Hathenbruck, who had been barred from the reservation for many years by the machinations of special interest groups, spearheaded in part by Jesse Knight and aided by Senator Smoot and other political allies, was desperate to secure the mine against all odds. He had been threatened, shot at, plotted against, and at last hired a bevy of gunfighters to protect him so he could visit the site in person. None of his efforts were effective because the Jesse Knight people had spies everywhere, following his every move. Hathenbruck once told his store manager, George Richards, "If I had ever gone directly to the mine, I have no doubt that my bones would have been left there to this day."

Having had so many attempts made on his life, Hathenbruck could no longer go safely anywhere in the mountains. The 1920 expedition was a last desperate effort on his part to locate and secure the mine. By hiring the best professional gunmen available, and bringing them into the mountains by way of Wyoming, he hoped to avoid the ever watchful minions of Jesse Knight and the Indians. The latter, while initially friendly, with the passing of time had become aggressive. Many of the old chiefs had died and the Indians, robbed of their lands and badly handled by greedy whites, made no distinction between friend and foe on their former lands.

The expedition might have succeeded but for the fact that some of the men, mostly the friends of Rock M. Pope, had been gotten to by Knight's special interest lobby, and tried to seize control of the mine from Hathenbruck's men. The result had been the disastrous gunfight.

But the 1920 expedition had been the result of an even grander scheme, a scheme which, had it been successful, might have changed the history of the world.

# Chapter 13

## THE KAISER GRANT

When F.W.C. Hathenbruck wrote a letter to Joseph R. Sharp in June of 1905, a few days after the death of Caleb Rhoades, he made a very enigmatic statement; "I have no fear of any trouble over our claims on the reservation in a physical form and legally. I am also loaded-because there are some things I did not feel called upon to explain or in other words 'I have a card up my sleeve.'"

Caleb Rhoades had been ill for some time and Dr. Hathenbruck, who had attended him from time to time, knew that he had not long to live. In that same year the reservation was to be opened. Hathenbruck had been prevented from entering the reservation by a restraining order, and every effort possible had been expended by the special interest groups to keep the Doctor from having access to Indian lands, including attempts on his life. Yet Hathenbruck conveyed to Sharp that he had no fear, either physically or legally, of securing his claims, because he had "a card up [his] sleeve."

Hathenbruck had spent years negotiating with the Indians and pounding on the doors of Congress, to no avail. He was circumvented by hypocrisy, greed, special interests, politics and red tape bureaucracy, and there seemed no end in sight to a ratification of the Indian lease and the securing of his claims. Instead, the reservation was being thrown open to land speculation from which he was excluded. With the death of Caleb Rhoades, Hathenbruck was free to pursue a very bold move, one which might have achieved success had it not been for an impending world war.

\* \* \*

Frederick Wilhelm Viktor Albert of Hohenzollern, better known as Kaiser Wilhelm II of Germany, son of Frederick III, Emperor of Germany, was the half-brother of Frederick Wilhelm Claud (F.W.C.) Hathenbruck.

Kaiser Wilhelm became Emperor in 1888 upon the death of his father. His first major action as Emperor was his dismissal in 1890 of the Chancellor Prince Otto von Bismarck, who had been largely responsible for the growth of the German Empire. Von Bismarck had once advocated legitimizing Hathenbruck and placing him on the throne, which had been the cause of young Hathenbruck's emigration to the United States.

Kaiser Wilhelm's administration of internal affairs was marked by the rapid transformation of Germany from an agricultural to a major industrial state. In foreign affairs he believed in the Triple Alliance of Germany with Austria-Hungary and Italy as a deterrent to war, but his contradictory and confused policies severely aggravated the international frictions that culminated in World War I.

As Emperor, Wilhelm endeavored to maintain and if possible extend the royal prerogative in order to make Germany a major naval, colonial, and commercial power. The conduct of foreign affairs was Wilhelm's major interest, but he had no basic policy and was greatly influenced by his ministers. Although he was a grandson of Queen Victoria, Wilhelm, by his naval program and his colonial and commercial aspirations, precluded an alliance between Germany and England and drove the latter into an *Entente Cordiale* with France. The already strained relations with France were further embittered by German interference in French colonial affairs in Africa, especially in Morocco.

The country of Morocco was located on a highly strategic position in the north of Africa overlooking the Straits of Gibraltar. While Germany did not have any real interest in what occurred in Morocco, they did see an opportunity to humiliate the French and possibly to weaken the *entente cordial* between France and England.

Chancellor von Bulow decided that the Kaiser should visit the Sultan in Tangier and pledge German support should the French become more aggressive in the Moroccan policy. A reluctant Kaiser was, more or less, tricked by von Bulow into making the visit on 31 March 1905. The visit did not go well for the Kaiser. In his own words to Chancellor von Bulow:

*I landed because you wanted me to in the interests of the Fatherland, mounted a strange horse in spite of the impediment my crippled left arm causes to my riding, and the horse was within an inch of costing me my life. I had to ride between Spanish anarchists because you wished it, and your policy was to profit by it.*

While the Kaiser may have been duped, others saw it as his own personal act of aggression. His uncle, King Edward VII of England, took the French side and described his nephew's Moroccan visit as "The most mischievous and uncalled for event which the German Empire has been engaged in since he came to the throne." As seen by the French, such radical diplomatic moves as this could well push Germany into a war with France.

This tension was followed by an even greater *faux pas*. The Kaiser granted an interview to British Colonel Stuart-Wortley who published it in the London *Daily Telegraph* on 8 October 1908. Among the Kaiser's implications were that the German people, in general, did not care for the British; that the French and the Russians had tried to persuade Germany to enter into the Boer War against the British; and that the German naval buildup was aimed more at Japan than the British. Thus he managed to successfully alienate the British, the Franco-Russo alliance, and Japan in one fell swoop. He further added insult to injury by stating, in the same interview, "You English are mad, mad as March hares." He was slowly driving Germany toward war with his acid tongue.

As early as 1897 or 1898, Hathenbruck realized the potential of his half-brother's political power to influence the U. S. government to ratify the Indian lease. It was a brilliant scheme, fraught with potential disaster. At that early date, Kaiser Wilhelm was still more or less in favor on the world scene. He had not yet rankled the sources of political power which later led to his downfall.

Hathenbruck had been working closely in Washington, D.C. with two men involved in promoting what was popularly known as "The Silver Question"; that is to say, enacting legislation which would back United States currency with silver and gold, and ultimately other nations on the world market. For Hathenbruck, the legislation would mean an increase in the value of gold from the Rhoades mine from an estimated value of $50 million or $100 million to as much as $1 billion!

The two men who were most influential in promoting the Silver Question were Senator James G. Blaine and an Englishman named Moreton Frewen. Senator Blaine became a candidate for the Presidency of the United States on the "Silver Ticket," i.e. a platform to promote legislation of the silver and gold act.

Morton Frewen was a Sussex gentleman who was a constant speculator in mining on a worldwide basis. He was involved with Cecil Rhodes in South Africa, as well as mining promotions in India, Australia, and the American West. He founded the famous 76 Ranch in Wyoming (which became the model for Owen Wister's classic novel "The Virginian") and invented a machine called "The Gold Crusher," a sluice-like device designed to extract even trace amounts of gold from marginal ore, and set up the first test models in Utah. More importantly, Moreton Frewen was the uncle of Winston Churchill, as well as the uncle of Laura Etta Capel, better known as Etta Place, who married both Butch Cassidy and the Sundance Kid.

While Senator Blaine and Moreton Frewen were in Washington, D.C., lobbying the Silver Question, they were approached by F.W.C. Hathenbruck with an unusual proposition. In return for their influence in helping to promote a land grant in Utah in behalf of Kaiser Wilhelm II of Germany, he would make them partners in the Rhoades mine, which would be secured by the grant. He assured them that even after the Kaiser acquired his share of the gold, there would be enough to pay off the national debt of the United States and to stock the treasury with enough gold to assure the passing of the Silver Act.

Apparently there were others made privy to the scheme, even though a shroud of secrecy was placed over the whole affair. It seems apparent that Hathenbruck's friend Harry Peyton, who was connected with the Department of Justice, was involved in the scheme, judging from a letter he wrote to Hathenbruck from his country home in Virginia on 31 July 1898. In a postscript, Peyton says: "Suppose you wire me about Wednesday to come to Washington...you can wire me that day simply to 'come, parties will be here,' and then I will come in Thursday evening, by that time I think I will long for just a little taste of *Washington High Life*. In the language of the lamented James G. Blaine *burn this letter*."

Stymied by government attempts to deny him not only the Indian lease but access to the land itself, Hathenbruck attempted to by-pass the government agents by securing a government grant in behalf of his half-brother, Kaiser Wilhelm. His "card up his sleeve" was the fact that no one in Washington, D.C.—or anywhere else, for that matter—knew of his relationship to the Kaiser. To keep this relationship secret, he employed Senator Blaine and Moreton Frewen to be his advocates under the guise of the Silver Question. Hathenbruck wrote to Blaine:

*Senator J.G. Blaine*
*Washington, D.C. May 14, 1898*

*Dear sir:*

*The only new development since writing you is a letter from Prince Hohenlohe-Schillingsfurst who gives a promising assessment of the Kaiser's support of our move to obtain the grant. The Prince [who was then Chancellor of Germany] has provided me with a diplomatic letter of recommendation permitting me to act in Wilhelm's best interests on the preliminary negotiations to obtain the grant. This is by no means an indication that I intend to abandon my efforts to obtain the Indian lease, for I believe that we will be successful in that endeavor, but the grant may serve as insurance in case of failure, so long as it remains undisclosed. I fully understand your present situation which, as you say, might limit your influence, however I would urge you to go forward, for if either the lease or the grant is obtained, your future will be assured. I have not yet received Mr. Rhoades' approval in writing but I see no reason why he would object, it being in his best interests, as well as my own. If it becomes necessary, I will return to Germany to seek written consent for the Kaiser to petition Congress for an act of grantorship in his behalf, at which time your*

65

*support will be crucial. Let me know immediately if this meets with your approval. I will of course be discreet in all correspondence concerning same.*

*Respectfully yours,*
*F.W.C. Hathenbruck*

The potential grant was for 100,000 acres of land encompassing most of the upper reservation— the same area proposed to be removed by Act of Congress for the opening of the reservation lands. Had Hathenbruck been successful in obtaining the grant prior to the opening of the reservation, history may have been far different than now. However, Caleb Rhoades adamantly refused to give his consent to the proposal, possibly believing such a move would be premature and hinder the success of the Indian lease.

As long as Caleb Rhoades was alive, the Kaiser grant would not be viable. Hathenbruck continued to promote the grant as a possibility behind the scenes, but unfortunately most of the correspondence concerning the grant between the years of 1898 and 1905 was lost, perhaps stolen along with many other papers in a burglary of the Hathenbruck family home in recent years. However, due to mention in other letters and documents we are able to discern the pattern of events.

Immediately following the death of Caleb Rhoades, Hathenbruck renewed his efforts to secure the Kaiser grant. By now it was apparent to him that the special interest groups were going to prevent a ratification of the lease. Desperate measures had to be taken to secure the Indian lands before the opening of the reservation. There were only about three months between the death of Caleb Rhoades in June 1905 and the opening. He listed his reasons in a letter to Moreton Frewen dated 21 June 1905: "Whatever influence you might have with the President, I implore you to use it immediately. Unless the petition for the grant is filed in congress prior to the opening of the Indian lands, we will have no redress in the courts thereafter."

It began to appear as though the deadline would not be met. Prince von Bulow had since succeeded Hohenlohe-Schillingsfurst as German Chancellor. He wrote to Hathenbruck conveying his regrets that the Kaiser could not respond personally due to "pressing foreign matters" (the Moroccan crisis), but assured him of the Kaiser's continued desire to acquire the grant. Hathenbruck, apparently frustrated by the delay, fired a letter to the German ambassador in Washington, D.C., and for the first time in writing called upon his relationship to Wilhelm as leverage, in the strongest words noticed in any of his correspondence:

*...The Kaiser should be reminded that it is in the best interests of the Fatherland for him to act promptly on the petition [for the grant], and to give it as much priority as his other foreign affairs. Time is of the essence and it is cumbersome to have to deal as I do with intermediaries. I need his prompt and personal attention to these matters on or before July 15th or risk losing the opportunity to file in Congress... I dare speak boldly to this issue on the basis of my kinship with the Kaiser which merits his personal response even above the protocol of nations, and I respectfully request that you should remind him of it. My station demands as prompt and personal recognition as the King of England or the Sultan of Morocco... The success of the grant depends upon my hearing personally from the Kaiser before July 15th. The economical success of the Fatherland could very well hinge upon his decision and for that cause I urge you to expedite this correspondence with all urgency...*

Hathenbruck touched a nerve by mentioning King Edward VII of England, who was the Kaiser's uncle, and with whom Hathenbruck was raised, for Wilhelm hated his uncle. It is probable that Hathenbruck capitalized on this fact to urge his half-brother to respond. It worked. While we do not have a copy of the Kaiser's response, we can gather from Hathenbruck's letter to Senator Thomas Kearns, whom the Doctor seems to have impressed to file the petition for grant, a sense of the Kaiser's reaction:

*Salt Lake City, Utah, July 17, 1905.*
*Senator Thos. Kearns,*

*Honored Sir:*

*...I am only in the city briefly, otherwise I would have come to see you in person, but I wanted to inform you of latest developments concerning the grant. Since the death of Mr. Rhoades I have worked diligently to renew the petition for re-submission to Congress before the opening of Indian lands which is now weeks away. The biggest hindrance to the outcome had been the delayed response from the Kaiser, but I am gratified to relate that I have recently received a personal communique from him, together with all of the requested paperwork needed for the filing. These documents will be delivered to you by this evening via special messenger and I hope I can depend upon your prompt attention to their filing. All of them have been certified by the Department of State to prevent any further delay...You must realize that I have not had formal communion with my family for many years and at one time there existed some rancor between my brother [the Kaiser] and myself, but his latest letter was filled with sentiments of brotherly love and support in behalf of obtaining the grant. He has assured me that the German ambassador will be on hand to act fully in his behalf and it might expedite matters if you can contact the ambassador as soon as you arrive in Washington... I am on my way back to the reservation today and can be contacted there at Col. Geo. F. Timms at Ft. Duchesne. If it becomes necessary for me to come to Washington, send me a telegram at that place and I will come immediately...*

> *Respectfully yours,*
> *F.W.C. Hathenbruck*

*[P.S.] I have shared a confidence with you concerning my relationship to the family of Kaiser Wilhelm; I depend upon your discretion, at least for the time being, as the revelation might hinder ratification of the grant.*

There was no love lost between the half-brothers, and Hathenbruck was likely well aware that Wilhelm's "brotherly love" was invented solely for the purpose of achieving the land grant which would include one of the wealthiest gold mines in the world. Wilhelm was anxious to make Germany a world power to be reckoned with, and Hathenbruck was the key. Hathenbruck knew where the gold was, and only Hathenbruck could retrieve it. The Kaiser grant would acquire and secure the land surrounding the Rhoades mine and keep it from the greedy hands of the political bureaucrats. Wilhelm had not forgotten that his half-brother once threatened to seize the throne, and Hathenbruck had not forgotten that his half-brother had forced his exile. But they could come together now in a common cause and feign whatever brotherly love was needed to cement the deal.

# Chapter 14

## THE GOLDEN TWILIGHT

In 1905, The Republican Party, comprised mostly of Mormons, withdrew their support from Senator Thomas Kearns, who was Catholic, and elected George Sutherland, a Mormon. Kearns blamed Church President Joseph F. Smith and Mormon Senator Reed Smoot for the cabal and sought an opportunity for retribution.

At the same time, F.W.C. Hathenbruck had finally arrived at the determination that Reed Smoot had been a Machiavellian, feigning friendship and support while unscrupulously working behind the scenes with Mormon interests to defeat the Hathenbruck-Rhoades Indian lease. He too held Smoot and the conspirators in utmost contempt.

The Kaiser grant gave both men an opportunity to strike back at those who had, like lice, infested and irritated their lives. Kearns managed to introduce the petition for grant before his term of office ended and prior to the opening of the reservation. Naturally the grant was vehemently opposed by the special interest faction who could see their plans for securing the Indian lands going out the window. But there was a greater lobby in Congress in favor of the grant. The United States had only recently emerged from the Spanish-American War. Already in Europe unrest threatened yet another war, and Kaiser Wilhelm, for better or worse, was in the middle of the controversy. At that early date, the United States courted the Kaiser as an ally. If Wilhelm wanted a grant of land in the American West, he would have it. The petition was granted, against the protests of the special interests lobbyists.

The grant, which gave the Kaiser 100,000 acres of the land being removed from the Indian reservation in the Uintah Basin, caused immediate conflict. It was promptly protested by special interest groups, by the LDS Church, by Utah politicians, and even by the Indians. Hathenbruck quickly appeased the Indians by promising them the grant would encompass acreage only in the mountain region and not take away more land than had already been removed by the 1894 Act of Congress (18 Stat. 286 & 337). It was small consolation for the Utes and an even greater setback for the Florence and Raven Companies, which went into dissolution.

Hathenbruck had won the first round, but it only bought him time, not results. The Indian lease, the grant, the reservation opening, and government reserves were all occurring simultaneously. Boundaries were confused and highly contested. The land allotment was the first to be resolved, gaining authority to open up lands on the reservation for white settlement. But the upper reservation, i.e. the high mountain region of the Uintah Basin, remained contested.

Hathenbruck found himself caught up in machinery of his own making. He had to continue lobbying for ratification of the Indian lease, while at the same time promoting ratification of the Kaiser grant which contested the same ground. Ultimately, however, the Kaiser grant held out the most promise for successfully acquiring ownership of the Rhoades mine, and it became his final hope.

Matters stood thus stalemated for the next nine years. The only positive progress was that the federal government established the 100,000 acre Kaiser grant out of the 1,100,000 acres set aside by President Theodore Roosevelt out of the Indian lands to create the Uintah National Forest Reserve. This finally gave Hathenbruck access to the lands, but the unsettled boundary disputes still prevented him from legally working the fabulous mine. He still held out hopes that things would change. They did... for the worst.

\* \* \*

The general misconception was that the Kaiser was a war monger solely responsible for the First World War. Wilhelm did not start the war; he didn't even want the war. The most that can be said is that the Kaiser did not do enough to try to control the actions of Austria-Hungary and prevent the outbreak of war. In the end he accepted war. He built up the German military machine and under the *Tirpitz Plan* built a naval fleet to rival that of Great Britain. He loved his numerous uniforms and surrounded himself with the elite of German military society. He was a "saber rattler" with an uninhibited tongue.

Wilhelm wavered between peace and war in July 1914. By removing himself to army headquarters during the war (1914-18), he lost contact with the German people and identified the monarchy with the war's outcome. He contributed to defeat by supporting far-reaching annexationist plans and unrestricted submarine warfare, which brought the intervention of the United States. The final blow came when his ministers and the public understood President Wilson's October 1918 armistice note to mean the Kaiser's very presence prevented peace. At the end, his generals told him his troops would march home to restore order, but not in his name. It was best, they said, that he abdicate, but while he temporized, the Majority Socialists declared a republic on the morning of 9 November 1918. After 300 years, the Hohenzollern dynasty was finished.

The Kaiser fled to the Netherlands on 10 November 1918. He purchased an estate at Doorn where he died 5 June 1941. He is buried on the grounds of his estate.

At the outbreak of the First World War in 1914, there was intervention by the United States, and the Kaiser fell from favor, but it took another two years to rescind the land grant in the Uintah Mountains of Utah. During those two years (1914-16), F.W.C. Hathenbruck worked feverishly in the mountains and elsewhere, trying to hold his crumbling dream together. It was not without cost. On 6 January 1916, his 32-year-old son, Wilford Reed Hathenbruck, died of mercury poisoning from too much exposure from gold assays.

By 1916, with the rescinding of the grant, the golden dream was—for all intents and purposes—essentially dead. The 100,000 acres reverted back into the Uintah National Forest. Since the mine was no longer on the reservation, the Indian lease was no longer valid. Hathenbruck's last great effort to secure the lease had been the 1920 expedition which had ended in a tragic gunfight. The loss of his son, the loss of life in the gunfight, the loss of his fortune, all contributed to the good Doctor's decline.

F.W.C. Hathenbruck and has beloved wife, Rozilla Rebecca Saunsecie, were the parents of thirteen children, all born between 1873 and 1896. Three or four of the children died in infancy. A daughter, Susan Alice, died at the age of 34, only two months before her brother Wilford died of mercury poisoning. The eldest daughter, Joanna Rebecca, died 11 April 1926, barely a year before her mother, who died 17 January 1927.

Most of Hathenbruck's income during the Kaiser land grant years came from investors in the mine who tapered off as the years progressed without success. He still owned his store in Provo and occasionally pursued his medical practice, though he had spent so much time away from home he had not built up much of a clientele. On 18 December 1915, an agreement had been reached between Hathenbruck's Provo Slate Company and the Lambert Manufacturing Company of Salt Lake City whereby the Lambert Company would purchase as much of the slate as he could produce for $3.50 per ton. It earned enough to keep the business solvent and turned a reasonable profit. But in 1920 the company faltered over disagreements between Hathenbruck and his partner Storrs. He ostensibly received an undisclosed annuity following the death of his father Emperor Frederick III, in 1888, but it did not endure long before the Kaiser stopped it. Likely he spent most of it on pursuing the Indian lease.

During the last few years of his life, Hathenbruck was relegated to accepting menial employment to support his family. He designed and promoted, without much success, a small gadget he called a "mechanical dictionary," a precursor to the modern computer. For a time he worked for the Wells Fargo Express Company at Provo, and at last he sold insurance and sewing machines door-to-door. In the mountains, only a few miles to the east of his home, was one of the world's most fabulous gold sources, but he existed in near poverty. The question begs to be asked: why didn't he visit the mine secretly and partake of its riches? Perhaps we will never know. What is known is that during his waning years, F.W.C. Hathenbruck grew weary of a world he had grown to distrust.

Following the death of his beloved Rozilla in 1927, Hathenbruck's health declined rapidly. His companion gone, his heritage shamed by a World War, and his dreams for obtaining the Rhoades mine shattered, Hathenbruck lived barely a year after the death of his wife. He died at Provo on 25 April 1928 and is buried in the Provo City Cemetery.

This nondescript one-armed man, with royal blood coursing through his veins, could have been a player on the world stage. For a time, in his youth, he was a contender for the throne as Emperor of Germany. He chose instead to spend his final years in search of an elusive golden dream. He had beheld with his own eyes one of the world's richest treasures, and he had visions of using it to change the world. Surrounded by avaricious and scheming men, he managed to remain scrupulously honest, so much so that in the end, when he eked out a living from door-to-door, he would not take any of the gold for himself. The greatest treasure F.W.C. Hathenbruck gave to the world was not gold, but—himself.

# Chapter 15

## THE HATHENBRUCK REPORT

In 1894, F.W.C. Hathenbruck and Caleb Baldwin Rhoades established the Hathenbruck & Rhoades Mining Company, which was organized to develop the fabulous Rhoades mine. Before Hathenbruck would finalize the agreement, he insisted that he be taken to the mine in order to assess it for himself.

Other than a few second and third-hand accounts, some of which we have mentioned, there has been little reference to what Hathenbruck saw and experienced of that signal excursion to the mine. However, after the company was formed, Hathenbruck, in his usual efficient manner, filed a company report which has never been previously published. It provides considerable important first-hand detail.

\* \* \*

A report of the Hathenbruck & Rhoades Mining Company made this 23rd day of July, Eighteen Hundred and Ninety-Five.

*On or about the 15th day of October, 1894, I left the vicinity of the Duchesne River in the company of Mr. Caleb B. Rhoades for an undisclosed location in the Uintah Mountains, county of Wasatch, Territory of Utah. Our purpose was to visit the Rhoades mine, which was originally located by Mr. Rhoades and his father in the year 1856, and appraise its mineral value.*

*We left under cover of darkness to avoid detection by Mr. Rhoades' rivals and Indians who might have taken exception to our presence in the region. We proceeded up the course of the Duchesne river, crossing that stream*

*numerous times and following the stream bed itself in many places, and following many winding and secluded canyons until we arrived in the vicinity of Lake Fork Mountain. After a long and sometimes difficult journey we made our camp on the southeast side of a major alpine lake...*

*The mine lies southeast of the southern edge of the lake basin, on the northeast side of a peak which became our beacon in locating the mine itself. The mine is near the base of an escarpment on the upper waters of the central left hand fork of Rock Creek, on the upper Stillwater drainage. Specific locations are withheld pending claim.*

*At the base of the escarpment, above a stand of timber, is the entrance to the mine, which is carefully hidden and unseen until entirely upon it. There is a second entrance on the opposite side of the escarpment about 1,000 feet distant, and at least two vertical air shafts extending to the surface of the escarpment. The surrounding area gives no evidence of any past mining activity; there are no apparent excavations, heaps, or tailings. Though not too distant from a watercourse, there are no indications of placer workings.*

*The entrance is small, showing signs of once having been much larger, but at one time someone had filled it with slag rock and dirt until the only access was by a small aperture at the top of the heap beneath the overhanging ledge of rock. Beyond the entrance are a number of rooms or caverns hewn from the solid rock of the mountain, which is composed primarily of a conglomerate limestone base* with a large vein of tellurium and quartzite that runs throughout at about a 22 degree gradient.

In the first room or cavern are to be found evidences that the mine was once worked by the Spaniards. At that early day, when the entrance was apparently full open accessible, this primary room was evidently a workshop of some kind, and by the evidence found there, it was a place where horses or mules had been kept. It was of considerable size sufficient to accommodate such an enterprise, perhaps 20 by 40 feet in dimensions with a high ceiling penetrated by a vertical air shaft about 9 by 9 inches which, as indicated by the soot-black on the ceiling, served as chimney or flue. Evidence of blacksmithing or farrier work could be seen with remnants of iron tools left behind, all apparently hand wrought. Also found remnants of Spanish uniforms and brought back a pocketful of buttons, buckles, and some brass and silver insignia pins, proving this to have been a mine worked by the Spaniards, as Mr. Rhoades had indicated...

From the primary room a narrow tunnel leads downward into the lower level of the mountain, past hand-hewn steps to a wooden door, hung on hand-forged iron hinges. In some places the door has been reinforced by leather straps nailed onto the wood. Behind the door are several more stone steps leading down into another room, somewhat smaller than the former. The secondary room is stacked with silver bars in several piles, to the number of 75 or more, covered over by animal hides, hardened and shriveled with time and very black in color. The bars too are somewhat blackened, either by age or by forging, and appear to have been forged elsewhere and brought to this place. Not a few of them are inscribed with forging symbols and some with dates ranging from the late 1700s to 1814, and the latter date seeming to be the last year in which the Spaniards worked this mine. According to Mr. Rhoades' agreement

with the Indians, we did not remove any of the silver bars...

Beyond the secondary room are a series of tunnels penetrating deeper into the mountain, all of them coursing downwards, apparently to intersect the meandering vein. Mr. Rhoades directed me into the main tunnel where the vein has been exposed. The vein follows a parallel vein of quartz through gray tellurium, emerging from the floor of the tunnel and coursing upward at an angle about 35 degrees to disappear into the ceiling after about 10 meters. At the narrowest point the vein is 6 inches in width and expands to more than 2 feet in width where it disappears into the roof of the tunnel. Presumably it expands to even greater width beyond where the Spaniards ceased their excavation. The vein is of the purest gold in such concentration as I have never before seen in my experience...

As per Mr. Rhoades' instructions I took assay samples only from an exterior vein but nothing from the main vein. His reasoning, in which I concurred, was that to reveal the existence and value of the main vein would be the cause of a Klondike rush to the region which could effectively destroy any plans for development of the mine.

The exterior vein, consisting of wire gold in crumbling gray ore and paralleling quartzite, had an assay value at $20,000 per ton at the surface and up to $150,000 per ton at a depth of two feet...

Several hundred meters from the outside entrance is a reddish colored ledge of what appears to be ferric oxide, perhaps hematite, indicating the presence of iron ore. This may have been the source of iron used by the Spaniards. Mr. Rhoades has assured me that there are several old rock kilns in the vicinity. He also pointed out an Indian burial ground about 250 meters northwest, on a plateau at the crest of the escarpment, and explained that *there are many dead Indians as well as Spaniards buried nearby, the result of a long-ago battle for the mine...*

*For these and other evidences I can and do authenticate the location as a Spanish mine of immense value, possibly as much as $50,000,000 or $100,000,000, in eventual profits. The site of the mine can be approached by a wagon road as near as a mile distant, and the entire basin is the potential source of hydraulics with which the mine can be developed. For an expenditure of no more than $20,000 the mine can be successfully opened and brought to a level of production, after which it will pay for itself in productivity...*

*The Indian lease must be pursued with haste and at any cost to open this region for exploration and development. I recommend that an area of Four Square Miles be acquired around the mine in order to secure all spurs, outcrops, or expansions of the vein, and to prevent competitors from encroaching upon lease rights. Mr Rhoades' claim for the value of the mine has not only been vindicated but surpassed...*

*(signed) F.W.C. Hathenbruck*

*Signed in the presence of :*

*Henry Nuttall*
*John T. Clark*

# Chapter 16

## THE BOREN—YOUNG CONNECTION

The Boren family originated in East Limerick and West Tipperary counties of Ireland as the clan O'Boran. Divested of their lands by the Cromwellian invasion, a number of O'Borans emigrated to America in the mid-1600s in search of a new future and fortune beyond the grasp of the hated British.

They settled first in Virginia and Maryland, but they resented the British domination there. William Boren was involved in Thomas Cresap's Rebellion against English rule in Maryland and fled south to Orange County, North Carolina, where he died in 1768. He was the father of two equally rebellious sons, Charles and Joseph.

Joseph Boren was a member of the North Carolina "Regulators," a group of dissidents who plagued the British with guerrilla warfare long before the American Revolution. He was captured and, it is believed, hanged by the British for treason against the crown. His brother Charles fled into the wilderness of the Cumberland Gap on the fringe of the Kentucky frontier.

Charles Boren had been born in Maryland in about 1718, where he married Mary Brashear, born 1720, a descendant of the famous French Huguenot, Benoni Brashear. Sometime prior to 1749 they migrated to Orange County, North Carolina, and eventually to the Cumberland Gap. Among their numerous children were the brothers, Bazel and John.

Bazel Boren was a Long Hunter, who explored the wilderness of Kentucky and Tennessee with Daniel Boone. In fact, Bazel Boren married Susannah Bryan, who was first cousin of Boone's wife, Rebecca Bryan. Bazel helped construct Boones Borough and Bryan's Station in Kentucky, and established his own fort, Boren's Fort, on Copper Creek, a branch of Clinch River, in the Cumberland Gap, in what is now Russell County, Virginia.

Bazel Boren was a lieutenant in the militia of Washington County, Virginia, and served in the American Revolution. He became a hero at the Battle of King's Mountain, Oct. 1780, when he killed the English leader Colonel Patrick Ferguson in single combat and ended the advance of the troops of Lord Cornwallis. For his distinguished service, Bazel Boren was given a grant of land in what became Robertson County, Tennessee.

Bazel became a justice of the court of Tennessee, and first register of Robertson County. He sat on the bench with his friend Andrew Jackson, who later became President of the United States. Bazel was a delegate to the Constitutional Convention which gave statehood to Tennessee in 1796. He died in Johnson County, Illinois, in 1812.

Coleman Boren, son of Bazel and Susannah, was born in Robertson County, Tennessee, on 14 October 1808. He converted to Mormonism in Southern Illinois and came to Utah in 1852, settling at Provo, where he died 13 May 1858. By his (polygamous) wife, Flora Maria Kingsley, he became the father of seven children, among whom were William Coleman Boren, Henry Kingsley Boren, and Albert Boone Boren.

Henry Kingsley Boren (1854-1942) discovered one of the old Spanish mines at the top of Daniels Canyon in 1896 (see: *The Gold of Carre-Shinob*, op. cit., at Chapter 15). Albert Boone

Boren joined Butch Cassidy's Wild Bunch and was killed in a gunfight in Nine Mile Canyon in the late 1890s.

William Coleman Boren (grandfather of Kerry Ross Boren) was born 17 January 1853 at Provo, Utah. He was only 5 years old when his father died under the most tragic of circumstances.

William's widowed mother, Flora Maria, only 31 when her husband died, remarried as a polygamous wife of Robert Broadhead of Heber City, with whom young William was raised. When still in his twenties, William "Will" Boren secured a contract to freight flour and other staples from the railroad to the Uintah-Ouray Indian Reservation, and thus began his lifelong association and friendship with the Ute Indians.

During the late seventies, Will turned his freight wagon to the more lucrative business of hauling ore for the newly developed Silver King Mine at Park City. It was here that he met the great Indian prospector, Supickett "Pick" Murdock, who first discovered the Silver King lode, before losing it to the machinations of Senator Thomas Kearns. Here too he met F.W.C. Hathenbruck, and was present at the Kearns Mining and Milling plant when the good Doctor amputated his own arm. Will Boren also knew Caleb Rhoades: in fact, the two families were related through intermarriage. Will spent a good portion of his life searching for the Rhoades mine.

On 18 March 1880, William C. Boren married pretty Lovina Jones at Heber City; he was 27 and she was 16. Lovina was born 8 February 1864 at Fairview, Sanpete County. She was a granddaughter of Joseph Smith, founder of Mormonism, and a great-granddaughter of Isaac Morley. Lovina's father died when she was only a year old, and as the youngest of a large family, she was "farmed out" to be raised by foster parents—Maximilian and Ann Campbell Gillies Parker. Thus she became the adopted

sister of Robert Leroy Parker, a.k.a. Butch Cassidy. After his marriage to Lovina, for the next twenty-odd years, Will's life was to be inextricably entwined with that of the amiable leader of the Wild Bunch, and even participated in several robberies. [see: *The Gold of Carre-Shinob*, op. cit. at Chapter 10.]

* * *

John Boren, brother of Bazel Boren, was an early settler of Madison and Gibson Counties, Tennessee. He had come from Washington County, Virginia, to Tennessee together with Jacob Young, and thus began a long and complex relationship between the Boren and Young Families.

Jacob Young was a frontiersman. He married Mary Boren, daughter of Bazel Boren and Susannah Bryan, and sister of Coleman Boren. Among their children was William Alma Young, born 28 August 1805 in Robertson County, Tennessee. He was a frontiersman, farmer, carpenter, and Indian missionary.

William Alma Young married (1) 11 November 1826 Leah Holland Smith; (2) 1848 Anna Reynolds; (3) 1849 Druscilla Boren. Druscilla Boren had been previously married to Nathan Keller, whose sister, Malinda, had been the first wife of Coleman Boren. Druscilla was the daughter of John Boren and Sally Alley. When William Alma Young's parents divorced, Druscilla's brother, Willis Boren, married William A. Young's mother, Mary Boren, who was a cousin of Willis and Drucilla. These complex intermarriages bonded the two families into one virtual family unit of extreme closeness.

William Alma Young was baptized into the Mormon Church on 1 May 1840 in Gibson County, Tennessee, and shortly thereafter went to Nauvoo, Illinois. Afterwards he migrated to Pottawattamie Indian territory in Iowa, and arrived in Utah in the summer of 1849. Among the children of William Alma Young and Leah

Holland Smith was Willis Smith Young, born 16 March 1829, in Trenton, Gibson County, Tennessee. He married Ann Cherry Willis an 28 September 1850, in Big Cottonwood, Great Salt Lake Valley, Utah Territory, and settled at Provo.

Willis Young's grandfather, Willis Boren, left Winter Quarters, Nebraska, to join his children in Utah in the summer of 1853. Willis Boren's cousin-wife, Mary Boren, died at Winter Quarters, and Willis married again to Mary Sampson. Their wagon company was organized under the direction of Daniel A. Miller and John W. Cooley on 8 June 1853, and arrived in the Valley of the Great Salt Lake on Friday, 9 September 1853. There was an interesting incident reported in camp on Sunday, 28 August 1853, taken from the minutes of Elijah Mayhew, company clerk:

*Came up Black's Fork 8 Miles, camped on Hams Fork. A difficulty having occurred yesterday morning between Brother Willis Boren and Brother Andrew Kilfoil. The matter was called up this evening and by consent of the parties, submitted to Brothers Miller, Cooley and Johnson— and the captains of tens. Brother Boren being charged with profane swearing, and also with threatening the life of Brother Kilfoil by shooting. And preparing his gun. Therefore, Brother Kilfoil, being charged with using abusive language towards Brother Boren, and the statements of both parties having been heard, and the testimonies of witnesses— It was considered by the said board that Brother Boren is guilty of the charges above specified and that he makes suitable acknowledgments to the camp and humbly asks for forgiveness of the same, which he accordingly did. And it was further considered that Brother Andrew Kilfoil is not guilty as specified above. All of which proceedings were approved by the camp, and agreed to by all the said parties.*

Willis Boren died near the age of 100 years. His death was noted in the Deseret Evening News of 30 November 1895 as follows:

*Obituary Notes, Tropic, Utah, 23 Nov 1895*

*On the 20th inst. Willis Boren departed this life after an illness of a little less than two hours, in which he suffered intense agony. According to Father Boren's veneration of his age he was ninety-nine years, eight months and nine days old. This, however, has been disputed by some of his old-time friends, they claiming that he was nearly 106 years old. Father Boren was born in Kentucky, March 11 1796. He was baptized into the Church of Jesus Christ of Latter-day Saints in 1840. He was personally acquainted with the Prophet Joseph Smith, and was with the Saints at the evacuation of Nauvoo. In 1852 he was Bishop of the Union branch on the Beyer. He crossed the Plains in 1853 and first settled in Provo. From there he moved to Provo Valley, then to Spring Valley. For the last twenty-five years he has resided at the home of his younger daughter, Mrs. Sarah A. Smith [wife of Thomas Washington Smith]. He died as he had lived, a true Latter-day Saint. editor.*

The families of William Alma Young and his son Willis Smith Young were pioneers, with Willis Boren and others, of Southern Utah, settling at Harmony and Toquerville. Willis Smith Young died 16 May 1910 in Escalante, Garfield County, Utah, and his wife Ann died six months later on November 19th. William Alma Young died in the town of Washington, Utah, in 1875. His first wife Leah moved to live with her handicapped daughter Rachel on her brother Thomas W. Smith's farm at Pahreah, Kane County, Utah. William's other wife, Druscilla, moved with her remaining children to San Bernardino, California, to be near her brother, Judge Alley Dennis Boren. On 2 December 1875 she married Benjamin Von Leuven, a member of the Reorganized Church of Latter-day Saints.

Willis Young and his family settled at

Escalante in 1876, at about the same time as Don Carlos "Carl" Shirts, who was a son-in-law of John D. Lee. John Wesley Young, born 26 November 1860 in Toquerville, Washington County, Utah, was son of Willis and Ann Young. He married Marcia Shirts in 1886 in Escalante. She was a daughter of Don Carlos Shirts and Elizabeth Williams. (Marcia's half-brother, Don Carlos Shirts, Jr., alias Carl "Mizoo" Schultz, was a member of the Wild Bunch.)

John Wesley Young (Jr.) was born 30 May 1888 in Escalante, the son of John Wesley Young (Sr.) and Marcia Ann Shirts. For the first seven years of his life, Wes lived with his parents at Escalante, where his father was in the sheep business. In about 1894 the family moved to isolated John's Valley, the closest settlement being Coyote near present-day Otter Creek Reservoir in Grass Valley, some 20 miles away. Wes Young married Minnie Irene Wilden on 13 December 1911, and died 8 June 1981 at Gunnison, Sanpete County, Utah.

Wes and Irene Young lived in various places over the years, including Kamas Valley, the old home of Thomas Rhoades and his son Caleb. Wes Young's final home was at Orem, Utah, down a long lane leading off State Street. It was distinguished by the statue of an Indian on a horse which Wes had made. He also made dinosaurs and other animals out of cement. He became renowned for his works, and for something else, as noted in the following article which appeared in the Thursday, 11 August 1966 *Orem-Geneva Times* newspaper:

*Treasure can be found in most unlikely places. A very unusual one is found at the end of an almost hidden dirt road going west at 1097 N. State in Orem. Hurry past the broken-down heaps of a neighboring repair yard and you'll suddenly find yourself surrounded by a forest of pines shielding life-size models of deer, sheep, horses and larger-than-life characters from the colorful past—all carved or*

*molded by the never idle, talented hands of Mr. John Young, retired, who lives there with his wife. Long retired as a pipe layer, Mr. Young spends his days whittling or molding creations from wood, or hydro-plastic cement. His inspiration is everywhere. The dog next door that always sits with head cocked, watching, or a statue in a park, or even a cartoon. Whatever catches his eye may be reproduced by his hands, and become part of his backyard museum. Mr. Young himself, is a colorful character; his face etched with lines and his mind filled with tales of adventure and history. His sense of humor and love of children are obvious in his choice of subjects. A large platform rocking horse has long been enjoyed by many youngsters, and the facial expressions of some of his characters are something to behold. Many of his animal creations are filled with genuine teeth or horns scavaged [sic] for the remains of some of them are wired so their eyes light up at night. Many of his miniature models are quite detailed, such as the delightful covered wagon, with moving parts and even wheel brakes. His tiny, carved hardwood saddles lined with sheepskin have brought many blue ribbons in local fairs. Mr. Young is also a miner and owns a quarry west of Great Salt Lake, Utah. Wonderstone secured from there has been used in abundance throughout his yard and home. He has combined many types of rock to create unusual mosaic designs on the outside wall of his home. A large bird bath, planters, and electrically wired towers are some of the projects made from the bright wonderstone. Self-taught and self-styled, Mr. Young is also a pioneer of tradition. It was his love of mountain lore, new frontiers, and the beckoning winds of adventure that caused him to rediscover the old "Lost Josephine Mine" 12 miles west of Mirror Lake between Provo River and Big Heber, 25 years ago. Actually, he stumbled upon the old mining site while* seeking shelter with his young son during a violent hail storm. Folklore says the mine was worked by Spaniards 400 years ago and yielded rich treasures of gold ore. The miners were ambushed by Indians at one time and the survivors camouflaged the entrance and returned to Spain. Mr. Young has claimed title to the mine and has built a road and cabin near the area using his old pioneer spirit of indepen-dence and hard work. The road has been named "Young's Road" by the Forest Service who obliged the miner by giving him a delayed permit to build the road and cabin. His hope now is to find the old hidden vault which is rumored to contain about $4 million in gold ore. He said the government offered to pay $35 an ounce for the gold if he is able to recover it. Treasures can be found in most unlikely places!

# Chapter 17

## THE LOST JOSEPHINE MINE

There are many legends concerning the famed Lost Josephine Mine. The only things known for certain about it are that it was located somewhere in the Great Basin, that it was worked by the Spaniards, sometimes by forced Indian labor—and it was fabulously rich. According to the most reliable accounts, the Josephine was worked from the mid-eighteenth century until about the year 1814 when the Spaniards were attacked by the Indians and forced to abandon the mine more or less permanently.

The Spaniards named the mine "El Mina de Josefina Empresa"—The Empress Josephine Mine—in honor of the consort of Napoleon. Why the Spaniards were disposed to honor the wife of the man who had invaded their homeland is uncertain. One account states that some of the men in the Spanish army who worked the Josephine were actually French defectors from Napoleon's army.

Over the years, many sites have been claimed as the Lost Josephine, and the true Josephine became lost in a plethora of claimants. In actual fact, the real Josephine appears to have been somewhere south of the Uintah Mountains, either in the Henry Mountains or the La Sals.

But there is another claimant for the Lost Josephine Mine that seems to have all the proper credentials, and it is located in the Uintah Mountains. Moreover, it appears to be identical to the Lost Rhoades Mine so diligently sought by F.W.C. Hathenbruck and Caleb Rhoades. The following story is recounted in the words of Gary D. Young, a grandson of John

Wesley "Wes" Young, with his gracious consent.

\* \* \*

It was the summer of 1939, while herding cattle for the Wilde Ranch located on the upper Weber River, above Oakley, Summit County, Utah, that John Wesley Young discovered the old Spanish Gold Mine. It was actually his son Keith, who had just that spring graduated from high school in Summit County, that first discovered the entrance. While riding along up a side canyon on the northeast side of Hoyt Peak, a sudden rain storm forced them to find shelter under a protruding bushy tree nestled against a small grey limestone ledge. After they had sat huddled up against the ledge and under the tree for a considerable amount of time, Keith crawled into a hole in the ledge and yelled, "Dad, there's a house down here!" Wes slid over and crawled into the small hole, if for no better reason than to get out of the cold rain.

As the storm subsided and their eyes became more adjusted to the dim light coming from the opening, they found themselves inside the entrance to a large room of approximately 25 to 40 feet in diameter with a ceiling height of about nine or ten feet, cut from solid rock. They rode back to their camp, obtained a good light and returned to the cave to inspect more closely. Inside, they soon discovered an array of ancient tools, all of which appeared to have been hand made— there was an old forge, an anvil resting upon a large block of black wood, an old shovel with rotted handle, a hammer and several chisels, a pair of what appeared to be prop-size logging tongs, a pair of blacksmith tongs and an old wood handle from a hand operated windless. And in addition to the very old tools, scattered upon the floor of the cave was much horse manure which indicated that these animals had been sheltered [there] many years before. Even the walls and the ceiling of the cave were caked with smoke and soot, suggesting that the room had once been used as a workroom or as living quarters by someone long before.

Further examination revealed at the southwest corner of the cave, an opening to a steep incline or shaft-like drift which had also been cut by hand from solid rock, extending on down into the mountain a distance of approximately 35 feet to that of a lower level and a tunnel. They immediately entered the narrow drift and carefully made their way to the bottom, climbed down on evenly-spaced steps which had been carved into the rock for easy access to and from the old mine. Also cut into the rock at elbow height along the course of the south wall of the drift was a trough-like shelf which looked like it had been used to transfer ore from the depths of the old mine up through the steep, narrow passageway. At the bottom of the 35-foot incline, they were surprised to [find] a large log door blocking the passageway of the old tunnel. Walking over to the door, they found it partially blocked open by a large slab of rock that had slipped down from the ceiling, resting on top of the door. They did not dare to pry the door open, but peered inside, as far as they could see, because it made a gentle curve to the west.

When they returned home to the Wilde Ranch, they related the experience to the rest of the family. Wes told them he believed they had found the lost "Rhoades Mine" of Mormon fame. When asked why he thought that, he replied, "Why else would they have a large wooden door in there?" Within a few days he had convinced his wife Irene and their children that if he had not found the Rhoades Mine, then it was another old Spanish mine of some kind.

He then took his 17-year-old-son Marion up to the mine to see it. They entered the large room and Wes directed his son down to the door. He then asked him if he thought there was any way to get it open. Marion looked up at the loose rocks over the door and replied that there was no way that he could see, without causing a cave-in. Any effort to crawl past the door could mean certain disaster. But they both agreed that the old mine could be valuable and they should at least try to excavate some of the rubble at the cave entrance. But an early snowfall forced them to return home for the winter.

Family responsibilities prevented their return to the old mine for some time. One of which was the Japanese shelling of Pearl Harbor on 7 Dec. 1941, where the oldest son, Jay Young, was killed on the USS battleship Arizona. Following that tragic event, Keith was drafted into the Army, Marion joined the Navy, and a younger son, Ted, joined the Marine Corps. The oldest son, Smith, had a deferment because of his family. During this time, Wes visited the old mine on several occasions during the summertime to explore the area in hopes of making further discoveries. He also filed claim on a mine out in the west desert on Cherry Creek in Eureka. He found out about it from a man who said he had "hit the mother lode," but he died of a heart attack. In 1980, Wes' grandson, Mike Young, went out to find the old claim. His grandfather had said there were tools and everything down at the bottom of a 45-degree incline, under a cave-in. Mike cleaned it all out and "found the tools and 'nuggets' all over the place— the only problem was they were pyrite."

On 23 Aug 1943, Wes Young located and filed a mining claim upon a large exposed vein, containing many pockets of fine-grained gold, silver and copper on the southeast slope of Hoyt Peak, calling his claim the Black Nugget Mine. He actually unearthed the vein while digging by hand with a pick and shovel through an outcropping of fractured shale and quartz. He hoped to recover high enough assay reports to finance his own mining operations. The original claim paper was located at the site by Stephen Shaffer in 1981, and photographed for his book [*La Mina del Yutas*, p.26].

Fearing that he might eventually be swallowed up by unscrupulous financial giants within the mining circle should the news of his discoveries leak out, Young decided to tell no one their discoveries, and as added insurance, they set out to confuse those who would question their activities by entering the region from various routes, always covering their trail as best they could. When they filed their claim with the Summit County Recorder, they made no mention of Township, Range or Section, stating only that the location was, "Near Polsin Basin in Summit County."

In working his discoveries of the Black Nugget vein Wes soon discovered that the ore was far more complex than it had first appeared, and profitable assays were not easily recognized. He had to send samples of rock to companies in Eureka, Utah, Colorado, and to a Frenchman whose office was located in San Pedro, California, who all revealed high values of gold and silver consistently in the range of thirty thousand dollars to the ton. This was a bonanza to be sure, especially when considering the value of precious metal during World War II. Later, in addition to the California, Colorado and Eureka assays, several very high assays were sent to Black & Deason, and the Crimson & Nichols assay offices in Salt Lake City, Utah.

Wes also carefully explored every aspect of the old mine on Hoyt Peak, which he and his son Keith had discovered prior to the War—from its entrance down to the old log door. He was evidently unaware of the Lost Josephine Mine tunnel works of the 1898-99 period, which were located just over the ridge and about 1,000 feet from his old mine entrance. A

drawing of the 1898 claim is reproduced on page 28 of Shaffer's book as reported in the 1898-99 issues of the *Wasatch Wave*, Heber City, *Park City Record*, and the *Mining Review*, Salt Lake City, Utah. The agreement between William Bird, Jr., Albert Bird, V.J. Avey, Isaac Hunter and Owen Bates, all parties of the first part, and Charles E. Hudson, party of the second part, called their claim the "Lost Mine Josephine." There were a total of twelve claims laid out and recorded. On 13 Oct 1898, a Township claim was laid, and some time in that same year four more claims were added to the original twelve. These added claims were named the "Eureka Mormon" claims. It is not clear why the locators thought that this was the location of the Lost Josephine Mine, or why their work on the claim was discontinued. [Note: Work was apparently discontinued when it was discovered that the site was on the Hathenbruck-Rhoades Indian Lease and later the Kaiser Grant.]

After locating what looked to be bars of pure silver in the old Spanish mine, the urge to explore beyond the thick log door became too great for Wes Young to resist, so he purchased some blasting powder early in the summer of 1944. Arriving at the mine site, he set a charge at a carefully selected location above the door. When the charge went off and the smoke and dust had cleared, he discovered to his dismay that most of the tunnel was now filled by rock and rubble and from the distance he could no longer see the door. The danger of further caving in was even more imminent. So at that point he decided to wait for his sons to return so they could help him remove the rubble and shore up the tunnel as they progressed.

Upon Marion's return in 1946, he went with his father up to examine the old mine and determine what they could do. Marion managed to crawl through the tunnel and across the rock rubble to where he could see the very top of the log door, still intact. But he dared go no further because of the loose rock above him. Together they agreed that excavation would be extensive and dangerous to say the least. Certainly they would need engineering advice on how to proceed. This required money they did not have, so for some time after that the original mining claim was abandoned. It wasn't until thirteen years later that Wes filed on his old claim again on 29 Aug 1959. He placed a group of seven claims, calling them the "Climax" for the benefit of himself, his wife Irene, and their sons, Smith, Keith, Marion, Ted, and Lynn.

During the summer of 1959, Marion Young took four boys, Gary age 12, Brent age 11, Randy age 10, and Mike age 9, up to Hoyt Peak for a camping trip. They pitched tents in a pine grove just east of where Wes later built his cabin. On the morning of the first day, they decided to hike down to Maxwell's Canyon to view a less ancient Yellow Jacket mine shaft. Sometime during the hike, Randy decided to leave his coat on a tree for the return trip since it was too hot and heavy to wear. He forgot that he had put a small piece of breakfast bacon in one of his pockets. About half way down the canyon, they passed what was called the big "Ice Cave," a vertical hole in the ground that opens up into a large cave with year-round ice in the bottom. The hike continued down Maxwell's Canyon to the mine before mentioned where two old cabins were located. Wes showed Marion and his boys inside the tunnel which he called the "Redman's Mine," because of the color of the rock. Metal rails were still laying on the floor where ore cars once ran. They explored to the back of the mine which was not very deep and came to an abrupt end.

After examining the area, Wes and his son Marion decided to hike up around the high flat white-rocked mountain to return to camp because they thought it would be less rigorous for the young boys. The coat left on their back trail could be retrieved later. Also Wes wanted to show his son Marion the old Indian burial ground on the same mountain where he had found some spear heads. Wes had kept the spear heads and was once offered several thousand dollars for them, but refused to sell. No one seems to know what eventually happened to them. Anthropologists from the University of Utah found out about it and tried to get Wes to show them the location of the graves, but he flatly refused. He always maintained great respect for the dead, and for the Indian beliefs and culture. As far as is known, he never did show anyone else the location of these graves except for his son Marion on this hike. But the walk turned out to be much further than expected and they ended up walking much of the night. The boys all remember the long hike in the mountains at night, with only the light of the stars to guide them. The men would stop every so often for a rest and the boys would immediately fall asleep, only to be awaken[ed] a short time later to continue their hike. Some time later Wes returned down [the] trail to retrieve the coat left by his grandson, only to discover it had been shredded by a bear who was doubtless searching for the piece of bacon left in the pocket!

That same summer of 1959, Wes struck up a friendship with John W. McBee, who had earlier claimed mineral properties to the west of his claims while in search of an old Spanish mine near the base of Hoyt Peak. They were near the same age and had similar interests, and became so trusting of each other they set up camp together in a tall stand of pines just below and southeast of the peak. During evening chats around the campfire each told stories known only to them. Wes learned from McBee that the Indians knew of an old Spanish mine on Hoyt Peak, and McBee learned from Young that he had indeed discovered such a mine in 1939. Wes did not tell McBee the exact location of the mine, however. Then one day, early in the summer of 1960, John McBee showed up in camp with an old Indian of the Ute tribe, believed to be 103 years old. McBee had brought him all the way from Ouray, Utah. He introduced him to Wes as Tommy Jewel (Tume-ju-all). The old Indian, according to McBee, knew the entire story of the rich Spanish mine at Hoyt Peak and McBee wanted his friend Wes to hear it. After a reasonable amount of time getting acquainted, the old Indian related the following story:

*"In about 1870, when I was only a small boy of about twelve years, I was brought out to this mountain by my father and a small band of warriors who were sent to kill a small group of Spaniards who were working an old gold mine. The leader of the Spaniards, known only as 'Black Whiskers' by my people, had come from California with a group of Mexicans which he had either bought or stolen for the purpose of working them in this mine, using slave labor. He had also managed to obtain a certain number of White River Reservation Indians which he, with the help of two other Spaniards, also forced to work the old mine. It was said that this Spaniard called Black Whiskers, had learned the location of the old mine by researching old records and had come with his Mexican and Indian slaves to work the mine for gold and silver. Prior to the presence of Black Whiskers, some of the reservation Indians had entered the old mine, peeled pure gold from its veins, and had taken the gold down to the Rhoades Valley Fort in Kamas where they had traded it for food, clothes and whatever they needed. But when Black Whiskers came, with two other Spaniards, they forced the Mexicans and Indians to work the mine, smelt the ore, and store up a large cache of gold and silver bars, which they stockpiled behind an old wooden door deep inside the mine. When me and my father, along with the other warriors, arrived at this mountain in about 1870, the miners were all down inside the mine working. A plan of attack was devised by the older men and I, being very young, was left a short distance behind, on the south side of a large rock, to hold the horses while my father and the others crept around the hillside and down through the timber to take positions less than 100 yards across from the old mine entrance to await the kill. All during the afternoon the Indians watched with anticipation, and when the miners finally began to emerge from a hard day's work from within the mine, the warriors steadied their rifles and took careful aim. Moments later, when Black Whiskers and his two Spanish companions were in clear view, the signal was given, shots rang out and the three Spaniards dropped to the ground in sudden death. The Mexicans and Indians were then released and sent on their way to freedom. However, before leaving the area, the Mexicans were allowed by the Indians to bury the dead Spaniards, as the Indians would not bury them after they had killed them. The Mexicans carried the three dead Spaniards up the hillside to a spot above the mine, on the north end of the rock near where the horses had been held by me, and there buried them alongside their personal belongings, erecting a wood cross as the gravestone. Following the massacre and the burial, the Indians told the band of Mexicans that they were free to leave and to return to their homes, but under no circumstances were they ever to return to the old mine. The Mexicans soon left the site of the mine, but they were for a time secretly watched by the Indians who feared that the Mexicans might try to return for the large cache of gold and silver bars stored deep within the old mine. And, true to the suspicions of the Indians, the Mexicans returned after only a few days, where they loaded as much of the gold and silver as they could carry on their pack animals and then rode off. As they rounded the hill, a short distance from the mine, they were*

*set upon by my people, and the Mexicans were made to bury the gold in the very place they stopped, in the side of the sloping hill, not far from the old mine. When all the gold and silver bars were buried, the Indians once again let the Mexicans go, but only with a stern warning that if they should ever return they would surely die. The Mexicans fled the area and they never did return."*

The old Indian died the following year at his home in Ouray, Utah. Wes Young located the old wooden cross which had been erected over the three slain Spaniards, exactly where the old Indian had reported it to be, but due to his superstitious nature, he refused to desecrate the graves, no matter what the value may have been of the objects buried there. He did, however, remove the old wooden cross from the graves, which he kept along with the Spanish tools found from the old mine. Finding the wooden cross was evidence that the Indian's story was valid.

Wes Young and his friend McBee as partners then filed claim on a ridge in the area they believed the cache of gold and silver bars may have been buried by the Mexicans on 29 Sept. 1960, calling it the "McBee Placer Claims." There were a total of two claims, which were later broadened by the addition of three more claims made 22 Aug 1961, called the "Climax Placer Claims," owned jointly by John Young, Irene Young, and their daughters Ila Esplin and Delsa Duncan (book 6, pp 245-247. Coalville, Summit Co. Utah court records). The men figured these claims would give them rightful ownership of the buried bars of gold and silver should they ever be found, since buried treasure could not be classified as a lode. However, nothing was ever located.

# Chapter 18

## THE SEARCH CONTINUES...

[Gary Young's account of his family's search for the
Lost Josephine Mine continues.]

During the summer of 1962, Wes showed his old Spanish mine to three of his neighbors in Orem by the names of Lyle Colledge, Darrell Osler and Dee Hatfield. He also showed them a vertical hole on the mountain above the old mine which he called the "Glory Hole, because you could throw a rock down it and never hear it stop falling." For many years, the cattlemen had placed logs over the hole to keep their animals from falling into it. But Wes figured it must have been an air shaft for the old Spanish Mine. Lyle Colledge climbed down into the hole on a rope at the time, but found nothing of interest. Lacking the proper equipment with which to explore its depths at the time of discovery, they could not determine whether the hole was man-made or whether it was a natural hypothermal blowout as the cattlemen had always assumed it to be. Their questions would go unanswered until they could explore the hole more fully.

In the fall of 1962, Wes struck up a conversation about the old Spanish mine with his coal delivery man in Orem, named Don Johnson. Johnson offered the use of heavy dirt-moving equipment, all at his expense, providing that he could get a lease agreement on the claims. Wes said he needed time to think it over. Johnson then contacted a man of considerable wealth, named Jack Olsen, and convinced him to try and obtain a lease from Wes Young, providing the funds were available for the purchase of whatever equipment and machinery would be necessary to open the old mine beyond the log door. Don Johnson and Jack Olsen would become the leasers of the Young claim. Another

possible partner was contacted, named Newell Carter. Carter had to convince Wes Young that the three were reliable men for the job, and that a lease of the property was the sensible thing to do, letting them do the job at their own expense while still retaining a large percentage of the profits for himself.

During Carter's many visits that winter to the home of Wes & Irene Young, the men learned that the mine was no longer under valid claim. Carter then convinced Wes that in order to reach a lease agreement he would first have to reclaim the old mine, otherwise the three men could put their own claim on it. But they wanted to take advantage of Wes Young's long-standing knowledge of the area. Wes agreed to reclaim the mine and then he would consider the terms of the lease. Carter advised him to obtain a good map from the State Highway Department before making his claim, and to file it accurately by township, range and section, as it was no longer legal to file the so-called 'floating claims' as he had done before.

Wes had to travel to the main office of the Highway Department on 13th South in Salt Lake City to obtain the proper map. By pure coincidence, he found himself standing in line in front of several University of Utah geology students. When he asked the clerk for a map of Hoyt Peak in Summit county, one of the students asked, "Are you acquainted with that area?" Wes replied, "Yeah, I've prospected the area," to which the student said, "While you were there, did you ever come across an old mine?" Young replied, "Why do you ask?" The student then remarked, "There's supposed to be an old Spanish mine up there somewhere. We've been going up there from the University for the last three years looking for it." Wes then said to them, "And what mine is that?" The student said it was called the Lost Josephine Mine. "We've got this journal which was written by the only survivor of a contingent of men who came out here from Spain to work the mine, and they would go there every year and work all summer, using Indians, as slaves, and then load up their shipment in pigskin bags and transport it by donkey train to the Gulf of Mexico where they would ship it back to Spain. But this one time the Indians got up in arms and massacred them all, except one who escaped death by hiding in the mine until the Indians were gone. He wrote the story in his journal, which was found in the archives of Spain, and he told of a six-million-dollar cache of gold and silver which was hidden in the old mine behind a large wooden door." Wes then asked the question, "What makes you think that the old mine is in the Hoyt Peak area?" The student answered, "We have the Spaniard's story and the maps. It's all recorded. We've followed the trail all the way from the Gulf of Mexico in Texas and right on through, and the map led us to Hoyt Peak. The mine had to be there somewhere on that peak." Wes jotted down the names and addresses of the students, saying that, "he would contact them if he found such a mine."

On 30-31 Oct 1962, Wes Young legally reclaimed the area of the old mine and the original Black Nugget diggings, placing five claims and calling it, "The Lucky John," and "Black Nugget" (book 6, pp 265-266, Coalville, Summit Co Utah court records). Later that same year, having recorded said claims legally with township, range, and section, he entered into a lease agreement of the property with Jack Olsen, Don Johnson and Newell Carter for the purpose of reopening the old Spanish mine. But unfortunately, by the time the lease was legally binding, winter had arrived in the high country, with no mining possible until the following spring. Meanwhile, Don Johnson made use of the money provided by Jack Olsen to purchase a D9 Caterpillar at auction for ten thousand dollars. This was mainly for the purpose of building a road to the mine. He also bought other equipment and stored it all until spring.

The following summer of 1963 was occupied mainly by the building of new roads to the old Spanish Mine which were necessary for the transfer of heavy mining equipment. Prior to this the only road in the vicinity of Hoyt Peak had been an old timber road which wound its way up Hoyt Canyon, across what was known as Muddy Bottom, and then to a tall stand of timber designated for logging. At that time there were no roads beyond Muddy Bottom to Hoyt Peak, which was to the north and nearly two miles away. Don Johnson brought the cat in, and graded the present road to the old mine beyond the point of Muddy Bottom. Marion Young loaded up his pickup truck with camping gear and took his family up to watch the road being made. To his surprise, the upper portion leading to the peak and mine was accomplished in one single evening with the use of the big cat. It is now designated as "Young's Road" on maps of the area.

Late in the fall of that same year, Don Johnson decided he would try to explore the Glory Hole. He had built a 24-foot ladder from two large green pine logs, spliced together by wooden slats for rungs, and lowered it down into the small hole. He let go of the ladder and it came to rest on a level inside the shaft about 22 feet from the surface. Johnson them had to lower himself into the hole by rope, using the crags of rock along the walls of the narrow shaft as footholds, until he reached the top of the ladder. He then crawled down the length of the 24-foot ladder to a floor, and moved into the darkness of a side tunnel. Eventually those at the surface lost any voice contact with him. Some anxious moments passed before he returned to report that on this first level, there was a very large room, and a maze of shafts and tunnels leading outward and honeycombed back through the mountain. More equipment would be needed before it could be properly explored. He made a list, which consisted of items such as lights, candles, rope, hard-hats and even cans of spray paint which he said they could use to mark their way back. But they would have to explore the tunnels more thoroughly at a later date.

The following summer of 1964, Marion Young sold his home in Murray, Utah, and moved his family to the town of Sterling in Sanpete Co. where his brother Keith Young had purchased a farm some years before. His oldest son Gary Young graduated from Murray High School that spring, and took over the work on the new farm in Sterling, while Marion continued his occupation of home construction in the area. Meanwhile up on Hoyt Peak, several brave men dared to slide down into the Glory Hole. Among them were Don Johnson again, Marion Young's son Mike, several cattlemen from Peoa or Oakley, and a University of Utah professor and students whom Wes Young had met back in 1962. The University professor and students merely descended to the first level of the shaft, and explored the shaft and large room. Mike Young explored the shaft to a greater depth, dropping down into the second level and into a side room before he returned. Don Johnson's route was easy to follow, marked with spray paint even further into the maze of tunnels.

The University professor is thought to have been Dr. Norman C. Williams, a geologist well known for his studies of the Wasatch Mountain range within the vicinity of Park City and the Uinta[h] Mountains on the vicinity of Hoyt Peak. Professor Williams and his students had, during the late 1950's and 1960's, set up a base camp on the south fork of the Weber River, where they explored, mapped and studied the mineral formations of such areas as Mahogany Ridge, Windy Point, the Smith & Morehouse drainage, Hoyt Peak and Park City areas. After exploring the Glory Hole, one student remarked to Wes Young, "Yep, this is an old Spanish mine, sure enough. It's the one we've been looking for!" Whether this conclusion was reached based upon findings in the Glory Hole and [the] old mine shaft which they also explored, or from knowledge gleaned from the old Spanish records, or a combination of all of the above is not clearly known.

The comments of those who went down into the Glory Hole were varied. Most of them held to the general consensus that the shaft was for the most part a natural fissure or fault, cut away by water and the forces of nature over thousands of years. Others had agreed in part, but also made mention that in many areas, particularly where ore belts were present, man at some time had chiseled and mined his own shafts, tunnels and rooms. In any case, whether this shaft was part of the Lost Josephine Mine or not, the possibility seemed to exist, based upon eyewitness reports that one of the many tunnels definitely lead in the direction of the old log door, allowing the removal of ore from the mine. Wes Young seemed to not be able to rest until every nook and cranny was explored down in the Glory Hole, but because of his advanced age, he had to let other people do it for him.

Excavation work continued at the old mine tunnel site during the summers of 1963 and 1964, but it was slow and dangerous. Newel Carter suggested running a new shaft or drift through the hillside to intersect with the old log door and supposed cache of riches. He knew of an old miner living in Gold Hill, Utah, who would come in and do the work for one dollar per running foot. Carter thought it would be best to leave the original mine entrance as it was, not only as a matter of historical preservation, but also to avoid further difficulty with falling rock from the already collapsing ceiling. It was a sound idea, based on all the directions, measurements, and locations pin-pointed by Wes Young.

Don Johnson on the other hand, figured the plan somewhat differently. He agreed that the making of a new drift would eliminate the danger of cave-ins, but he felt that it would be better to start inside the old entrance to avoid missing the exact location of the old log door at the northwest corner of the original large room. Not only would this save about 20 to 30 feet of drilling, blasting and mucking, but they could more accurately ensure a direct intersect. This too, seemed to be an excellent plan and in the end Don Johnson won his argument. However, this proved to be a costly mistake as the initial charges when set off, brought down a large portion of the old ceiling, completely filling the tunnel and covering all traces of the old wooden door. The second series of charges added to the destruction by filling a large portion of the old shaft with rubble, where the steps had been cut in solid rock in the southwest corner of the room, and also loosened large slabs of ceiling rock within the large room itself, to a point where it became too dangerous for men to work inside at all. With summer nearly over, and not really knowing what to do next, the miners decided to withdraw their equipment and machinery from the mountain and use the long winter months to devise a new plan. Unfortunately, however, due to the unexpected strain on available funds, coupled by the inability to agree on a new plan, a gradual loss of interest in the project set in, bringing to an end the lease agreement of Johnson, Olsen, and Carter. Wes Young was left with the old mine in worse shape than ever.

In spite of this, two major accomplishments had materialized from Young's venture with Olsen, Johnson and Carter. A road had been constructed to the mine site and a cabin had been erected upon the claims to serve as a shelter and a place for the men to rest after a hard day's work in the mine. This cabin (photograph on page 46 of Shaffer's book), was built for the most part by Wes and his son Marion, with some of the grandsons helping. Cement, sand and gravel was hauled in by Newell Carter. The cattlemen and Forest Service were upset over the building of the cabin on the south side of Hoyt Peak, near a spring that the cattle had used. Wes had cleaned the spring out to make a cement cooler which served as a refrigerator in the absence of electricity, and fenced it in to keep the cattle out. To appease the cattlemen, he built two water troughs down stream, but they didn't like what they viewed as his moving in on their summer range. Wes had the legal right to build the cabin and use the water from the spring. The Forest Service didn't like his road-building activities, and felt like their powers were being infringed upon. Wes told them he would do all he could to watch for possible poachers or whatever they wanted him to do, but it didn't seem to help. They sneaked in after everyone had left for the winter and burned it down. Destroyed in the illegal fire was Irene Young's antique treadle sewing machine and several of the old Spanish artifacts of Wes Young's. Roscoe Andrus told Wes that he had been riding with the cattlemen's association president when he bragged of burning the cabin down with the blessing of the Forest Service. Wes was enraged and filed a legal claim against the cattlemen and Forest Service. However, before the case came to court, Roscoe Andrus, the main witness against the cattlemen, had died. The Forest Service claimed it was a "controlled burn," but it was shown that the so-called controlled burn included no more than the cabin—only scorching a couple of trees near it. But the judge decided not to give a monetary award for Wes Young's losses, satisfied with a stern warning to the Forest Service and cattlemen that he had a legal claim to build a cabin and roads, and to leave him alone. The Forest Service officer was transferred out of the area by the U.S. Government.

In 1967, Wes Young along with his cousin LaVar Shurtz renewed the claim on Hoyt Peak. Shurtz was a construction worker from the Salt Lake City area. On 12 July 1967, they filed a series of claims across the south and southeast slopes of Hoyt Peak, encompassing the Climax and the Black Nugget properties by what they then called the "Little Fawn, Autumn Leaf and Bonanza" (books M8 page 109, M12 page 92, and m33 pages 30-31, Summit County Recorder's Office, Coalville, Utah). They transported a large rubber-tired backhoe, with bucket and blade, to the property and with Shurtz at the controls, excavated long, deep narrow trenches in the side of the sloping ridges to intersect with the massive ore veins of the original Climax and Black Nugget claims. This had never before been tried. Samples were then taken from depths of twelve to eighteen feet and sent to various assayers for analysis. These samples consistently showed values in the range of thirty thousand dollars per ton, which matched those taken years previously by Wes Young while excavation [was] only with a pick and shovel. Ore samples taken at deeper locations revealed rich ore pockets running as high as one to two hundred thousand dollars a ton in gold and silver. However, because of the ore complexity, extraction of the precious metals could only be obtained through chemical methods rather than the normal smelting techniques. This presented a problem, as chemical refineries at that time were nearly nonexistent. This made Wes wonder how the Spanish recovered their ore using their primitive methods of smelting alone.

During these backhoe excavations of Young and Shurtz in the summer of 1967-68, a second cabin was constructed upon the burned-out foundation of the first one. Like the first one, this cabin was used primarily for the mining of the properties. However the cattlemen and Forest Service complained that it was nothing more than "Wes Young's private hunting cabin," and continued to harass him contrary to what the federal judge had ruled. It afforded a comfortable living quarters for the miners and stood only a few yards from the crystal clear spring of water that the cattlemen claimed should only be used for their animals. One year there was an early snowstorm that trapped two men on the mountain. The local sheriff was contacted by the family and asked to go up in his snow cat to rescue them. He arrived to find the two men cozy and warm in their cabin, with a fire in the stove, and enough food to carry them through winter if necessary. They were preparing a meal when the sheriff arrived and Wes Young asked him if he would like to sit down and eat with them. When the sheriff asked them how they planned on getting off the mountain, they replied that if necessary, they had snow shoes and figured they could walk out if they had to. However, they obeyed the sheriff's request and rode down in the snow cat, after closing everything up.

Wes Young and LaVar Shurtz had been digging a long trench from north to south and were approaching the exposed part of a good vein, when they were approached by two men running electronic tests for the purpose of detecting mineralization for some large and well-known mining company. After inquiring as to the purpose of the long trench, the men set up their equipment out of curiosity and began sweeping the surface of the ridge, just south of the exposed vein and remarked, "If there's a vein of gold up here, it's got to be right there, only about 30 feet deep. Whatever it is, it's damn rich." Wes and LaVar thanked the two men, made mental notes of the location, planning to dig there after they finished with the exposed vein. It was later decided that to reach a depth of 30 feet with a back-hoe, they must continue their trench, followed by a short tunnel. To dig a 30-foot trench from directly above would be far too difficult and much too expensive. Unfortunately, they never finished the trench nor attempted the tunnel because a much more exciting possibility presented itself back at the old mine.

This change of plans had resulted from an unexpected visit by the uranium King Charlie Stein's [sic: Steen] mining engineer, who after viewing the old mine, suggested the possibility of yet another tunnel situated just south of the original entrance and said, "This old dump was not drug out of that hole up there—it had to be pulled from the mountain somewhere down lower at the base and about center of this ledge." Pointing to the location, he instructed Shurtz to use his backhoe to dig a trench through the old Spanish mine dump and clean off the face of the ledge base. If his theory was correct, they would find another old mine tunnel at that location. They followed the engineer's instructions and upon reaching the base of the ledge, the bucket crashed through the vertical wall of carefully stacked rocks, opening an entrance to yet another tunnel, just as the engineer had predicted.

After examining the old workings, Young and Shurtz concluded that there had once been a second entrance, typical of almost all Spanish mines, at the base of the ledge, where entry could be made by dropping vertically through a ten-foot shaft and to the four-foot wide, five-foot high tunnel. The tunnel itself was well-timbered with ancient stress points for an additional 100 to 150 feet, at which place they encountered a major collapse of ceiling and walls. They determined that at one time the two tunnels had been connected to each other by a walk-through passageway which had long since collapsed down to a small crawl space. Perhaps this collapse had been caused by Wes' blasting years before in the north tunnel.

This latest discovery still did not provide entry into the depths of the old mine, nor did it lead to the old log door or the presumed cache of gold and silver beyond. Nevertheless, it did reveal much more of the massive effort on the part of the old Spanish miners to extract mineral from the mountain, and it helped to boost the enthusiasm of Young and Shurtz. They were more certain that the old mine, when reopened, would eventually fulfill their dreams of untold riches. But winter was fast approaching, so all the work once again had to be discontinued. They had to take the back-hoe off the mountain with them. Then excavation of collapsed tunnels was as it had been in the past, more than they were prepared for, and so they accomplished very little work on the claims during the following summers of 1969 through 1971.

Their claims once again became invalid with the State of Utah and their cabin was, for the second time, torched and burned to the ground by the cattlemen and Forest Service. This time the vandals removed the smoldering bed frames and furniture, scattering them down the stream banks, leaving only the cement and rock footings and foundation. Years later, Pearl Lewis, mother-in-law to Marion Young and widow of Gilbert Lewis who had been bishop of Marion, Utah, for many years, noticed the inscription on the cattlemen's association president's gravestone which read in part that he was one of the most honest men of the valley. Pearl, a lady of impeccable integrity, laughed and said he was just the opposite, telling her once that he "would do anything for money." Ted Young accompanied his father Wes to confront the Regional Directors of the Forest Service in Ogden, Utah, concerning the second cabin burning, "and got nothing but a long run-around." Finally Ted told his father, "If you had a few thousand dollars to spend on a good attorney, and a lot of time, you could probably beat them, but if not, you've had it."

# Chapter 19

## WAYFARERS AND WAYBILLS

[The conclusion of Gary D. Young's account of his family's
search for the Lost Josephine Mine.]

In 1972, Irene Young suffered a stroke and required constant attention which could not be provided solely by Wes himself, so they decided to sell their home in Orem and move down to Sterling near the two boys, Keith and Marion. Here they settled first into a trailer behind Keith's home on his farm. Later a small wood frame home was built. By this time, Wes was 83 years old, with a slight loss of both hearing and eyesight due to cataracts. However, he was as physically strong and active as ever. He had never been to the hospital for himself in his entire life. But his wife Irene continued to suffer from a series of mild strokes and diabetes, the effects of which eventually caused her death. However, in spite of his advancing age and Irene's health problems, Wes remained optimistic about the possible reopening of his Spanish gold mine. He had learned the history, as well as the value of the old mine from the study of rare Spanish documents and from the story given him by Tommy Jewel, the 103-year-old Ute Indian. Copies of the old Spanish documents were believed to have been given him by Professor Norman C. Williams, consisting of a waybill, journal, map and shipping ledger. He obtained additional proof from the diary of a U.S. Marshall Kimball who had once arrested several Spaniards in the late 1800's who had been mining gold on Hoyt Peak with the use of Mexican and Indian slaves. Complete details of the arrest and of the Spanish mining operations were recorded in the diary. [Author's Note: This was probably William H. Kimball, son of LDS Apostle Heber C. Kimball, who, in addition to being a marshal, owned and operated a stage station at the top of Parley's Canyon, now called Kimball's Junction.]

A reproduction of the actual Spanish waybill was reproduced on page 93 of Shaffer's book. The translation of it is as follows: "Waybill-Year 1722-1814. This waybill pertains to the Mine of the Utes: called later the Josephine de Martinque, The Empress. This Mine can be found, West twelve leagues of the River Timpanogos headland and two leagues from the mouth of the River Santa Anna to the Southeast- to travel one league to the South through native land of valley grass to a canyon which enters the valley from the East. Follow this canyon East to a peak round and bare of growth, and from the peak measure 1600 varas to the Northeast. At the mouth of the Mine there are some small rocks and brush coverage at the base of a small dark ridge. The Mine of the Josephine de Martinique has 3 tunnels and 1 shaft- two tunnels of 400 (varas) run to the West and one tunnel of 350 varas runs to the Southeast. Tunnels and shaft be one mine. The Shaft runs 73 varas vertical and has four rooms and six tunnels. These rooms to be used as workshops for the transfer of the mineral silver and gold. Twenty-nine varas apart to the Sun at midday are these rooms. To the Percent of metal—of yellow metal which is half silver and one-fifth part of gold at one hundred and fifty varas. In this Mine we encountered slabs of virgin silver from one pound to five pounds. At this place in the Mine there is the Treasure of our comrades- 46 varas from the porthole of the Mine on the center of the tunnel, and 8 varas beyond one door of thick wood there is the Treasure: There are many slabs of virgin silver and 650 cargoes of bar silver and 240 cargoes of bar gold that are 6 millions. The Treasure abandoned for fear of death by hostile natives- of 42 comrades 8 survived. This Mine we worked (from) Year 1782 and covered 1814, as so written in the journal of work of expedition by me- Jose Joaquin Garcia, Captain- Mexico City, November Year 1814."

On 13 Oct 1982, a copy of the old Waybill was rediscovered by Gale Rhoades at the Brigham Young University Library in Provo, Utah. He showed it to Professor Jonathan Stowers and two teacher's assistants for the Spanish classes at the University of Utah, and also a Professor Hancock, who himself was from Mexico, having been born and raised there, and who knew a great deal about the subject matter. Each of them carefully read the old manuscript, analyzed it and then passed it on to the other, and then as a group, openly discussed it. Their findings, based upon their professional judgement, were that it was authentic in every way. At the close of the meeting Jonathan Stowers signed the following statement: "I have read the document. The language appears authentic, from the period, and there are mistakes that a native Spanish speaker would make. It appears authentic to me." Gale Rhoades afterward spent many hours exploring down in the Glory Hole and old mine, drawing diagrams of the maze of tunnels and rooms. Copies of these diagrams are found on page 97, 98 and 104 of Stephen Shaffer's book.

In September of 1973, Wes Young re-filed on all the old claims, naming them, "Autumn Leaf, Stewardship, Dedicated, and Heartrich." (Book M50 pages 426, 504-506, and 542-543, Summit County Recorder's Office, Coalville, Utah). During the summer of 1973, Wes offered two young men, by the names of Jim Nay and Lannie Seely, a percentage of his holding if they could locate another entrance to the cache of gold and

silver by entering the Glory Hole and exploring the tunnel leading toward the old mine. Being young men with minds set on adventure, they agreed. They descended by rope down through the narrow shaft opening and to the floor of the first level, where they found the old tree ladder still resting upon the wall of the large room. From that point, using flashlights and placing candles along the way, they slowly wound their way into the depth through the shafts, drifts and narrow passageways. At a point somewhere near the third level of the dark shaft, they discovered a small vertical hole or shaft that was obviously overlooked by Don Johnson back in 1964. It was so tight even, the little boys had to remove their coats to fit through. In the interest of safety, Seely agreed to enter the hole alone, while Nay remained behind for the purpose of summoning help if he ran into any trouble.

Alone, Seely carefully and slowly inched his way down through the small hole where at the bottom, it coursed its way horizontally, back through the mountain in the form of a long narrow passageway which appeared to be that of a natural crack or fault. And what he found at the end of that narrow fault was, to say the least, astonishing. In his own words, this is what Seely described: "I was going through this fissure (it was not a man made tunnel)—a real tight one, and it opened into a room about ten or eleven feet tall (natural, no digging) and 30 by 30 feet wide, and that's when I could see a door. The door was directly across the room from that small hole where I came in. The roof had caved in up against the door. About three-fourths of it was covered with overburden. It was wide, unbelievably wide, about four feet. The door was a good ten feet high. That's just guessing. I don't know if the floor elevated up or not, but the roof had come down and there was one rock up there that just a point was keeping it from sealing everything, and I was under that rock, and no way did I like that particular situation. It was just a big wood door. It wasn't plank or logs. The door I found was just a solid slab of wood, about four feet wide, with no breaks in it. I could see three feet of the top. It was wood like railroad tie wood. However, it wasn't treated with creosote or anything. I was sopping wet. I mean, everything was wet—that room in there was dripping all over. I bumped on it (the door) and it felt just as solid as solid, like you were hitting on railroad ties. I'll tell you one thing, I wanted to go on the other side of that door, but we didn't have any equipment, and we definitely planned to go back. But you know how life is, you never get back there."

Excited as Seely was during the exploration of the large room and his investigation of the huge door, he still made yet another discovery before leaving the old shaft, a discovery that even to this day cannot be explained. In the sandy floor of the large room, near the old door, he found a Roman coin. He later allowed Gale Rhoades and Stephen Shaffer to handle it and take photographs published on page 55 of Shaffer's book. Concerning the discoveries made within the Glory Hole tunnels, Lannie Seely remarked to Rhoades and Shaffer that, "My story up there is true and my buddy (Jim Nay) will back me up on it. There was a door and it was soaking wet. And I found the coin right down in that hole there by the door on the floor." Rhoades' and Shaffer's research found the coin to be an Antoninianus copper piece, coated with silver, minted under the rule of Gallienus Augustus of Rome, A.D. 259-268. This coin, about the size of a penny was minted under the rule of Publius Licinius Egnatius Gallienus, and shows the unlaureated head of Gallienus wearing a spiked battle helmet, around which is the inscription, "GALLIENVS AVG" (Gallienus Augustus). On the reverse is the symbol of a standing soldier wearing a full dress of armor and holding a spear, and the inscription, "VIRTVS AVG" (Virtus Augustus),

virtus being the Roman word for courage. The symbol and the inscription therefore being a tribute to the courage of Augustus Gallienus during previous war campaigns...

...One can only theorize on how this old coin got down inside the tunnels of the old Spanish mine on Hoyt Peak in Summit Co., Utah, but there is little doubt that it had been there for many years. Certainly the door found by Lanny Seely in 1973 was not the same door as was found by Wes and Keith Young in 1939. Although it appears to be the same tunnel, the distance separating them is approximately 200 yards, and the description of the two doors is radically different. Seely's door appeared to have been made of a large wooden slab, whereas Young's door was made of logs lashed together by rawhide. It is quite possible however, based on the compass and depth measurements, that one is the "front door" and the other a "back door" in the same tunnel.

Lannie Seely and Jim Nay's discovery of another possible entrance to the old mine has never been pursued. Safety and equipment factors are the probable reason. Seely's description of the condition of his door, blocked by rock boulders, has been enough to discourage most people, let alone the aged men Wes Young and LaVar Shurtz. By late fall of 1974, however, with the help of Mike Young they had completed the task of excavating the rubble from the entire length of the 35-foot incline, and they had done a fine job of restoring the drift. For shoring, they used squared, heavy duty timber which they purchased and hauled to the mine site. Only rubble which remained within the tunnel itself separated them from the old wooden door and from the treasure that they believed lay behind it. But LaVar Shurtz suffered a crippling accident that winter while working on a roof of a home in Salt Lake Valley, and Wes Young's age had caught up with him to the point where he could do little work on his

93

own. Gary Young, who was studying science in college, visited his aged grandfather shortly after the moon landing by U.S. astronauts. As they were sitting and viewing it on the TV, Wes exclaimed that it was a complete fake, fabricated by the Communists as part of a play to overtake the world, and that there was no way anyone could walk on the moon. Gary refrained from disagreeing, thinking only that here was a man who discovered possibly the most famous gold mine in the West—who had lived from the horse and carriage days through two world wars and the cold war of Communism, to the time that the first men landed on the moon. This old grandfather was a wonder indeed. He was entitled to his opinion—he had earned it.

His companion of nearly 70 years, Irene Young, died on 2 Jan 1979 in the hospital at Mount Pleasant, Utah, and was buried in the Sterling, Utah, Cemetery. John Wesley Young died on 8 Jun 1981 at the age of 93, none the richer for finding perhaps the richest mine in Utah history, known as the Lost Josephine. He had worked as a rancher all over the West, helped to build Geneva Steel, operated his own candy store, and was an employee of two railroads. The only time he had been confined to the hospital was the last week of his life. The day before he died, he asked the young nurse to marry him, saying "I'm just about getting so I can't do anything anymore, and I need someone to take care of me." In his final moments, he asked to see his sons to "tell them something important about the mine on Hoyt Peak." He was buried in the Sterling, Utah, Cemetery next to his wife Irene.

# Chapter 20

## THE MEL FISHER CONNECTION

Mel Fisher has been called "the World's Greatest Treasure Hunter," and the title is well deserved. He didn't earn the title solely because he spent more years than most in the search, but because he found and recovered the elusive "lost" treasure, giving hope to treasure hunters everywhere.

Mel had a dream and he was unrelenting in his pursuit of it. He was aware, through dedicated research, that as much as ten percent of all Spanish treasure secured in the New World is estimated to have ended up in "Neptune's Treasury"—the bottom of the ocean. He was determined to recover at least one shipload.

Of all the riches shipped from the New World to Europe during the era of the *conquistadores*, more than 85 percent was that of Spanish coins and bullion. In the year 1543 alone, more than half a million ducats worth was shipped to Spain, and this amount doubled each year thereafter until eventually some five billion ducats worth had been plundered for the greater glory of Spain. By today's standards this amount would exceed $60 billion and perhaps surpass $100 billion, considering the hundreds of ill-fated galleons which were lost at sea to storms and piracy. Mel Fisher went looking for one particular ship that had gone down in a storm in 1622 off the coast of Florida.

Mel's dreams of treasure began in childhood with the reading of Robert Louis Stevenson's *Treasure Island*, and stories about pirates of the "Spanish Main" fired his youthful imagination. He was fascinated by the exploits of deep sea divers in their cumbersome helmet suits who were just beginning the exploration of the sub-oceanic realms. There were no oceans in Hobart and Glen Park, Indiana, where Mel grew up, but at age eleven he made his own diving suit to use in a mud-bottomed lagoon. But it would be some years before Mel would be able to make his dream a reality.

Mel's father, Earl Fisher, taught him carpentry skills, and his mother, Grace Sprencel Fisher, taught him music and dance. Mel formed his first dance band while attending Lew Wallace High School in Glen Park, Indiana. He attended Purdue University, where he studied engineering and led his own 21-piece band. Mel entered the U.S. Army with the outbreak of World War II, and served with the U.S. Army Corps of Engineers. Prior to being shipped overseas to Europe he studied at the University of Alabama and was later awarded an honorary doctorate.

After the war, Mel roamed restlessly from Chicago to Denver, then to Florida where he renewed his primary interest in diving. In 1950 he accompanied his parents to Torrance, California, where they started a chicken ranch. While helping on the ranch and studying animal husbandry at El Camino College, he continued his interest in diving. He opened his first dive shop in a small feed shed on the family chicken ranch. He had a small compressor and sold "breathing" air and apparatus, as well as equipment and parts.

In 1953, Mel met the love of his life, a pretty, red-haired girl named Dolores Horton from Montana, whom he quickly dubbed his mermaid named "Deo." On their honeymoon, the couple went diving on shipwrecks in Florida and off the Florida Keys. They planned to open a store devoted exclusively to diving. They financed their dream by diving commercially for spiny lobster in the frigid California waters. They finally opened Mel's Aqua Shop in Redondo Beach; this was the first "dive shop" in the world.

Mel and Dolores Fisher became hugely successful in their pioneering business, training more than 65,000 novices in the new science of scuba diving. Mel made early underwater films and movies for training purposes, and soon branched into advertising and entertainment. He aired his own underwater adventure series weekly when television was still in its infancy. Dolores personally set a world underwater endurance record that continues to stand as a woman's record of more than 55 hours and 37 minutes [55:37:96]. Mel and Deo Fisher were the unofficial "king and queen" of the underwater world.

Mel and Dolores Fisher were the parents of five children: sons Terry, Dirk, Kim and Kane, and a daughter Taffi. The Fisher enterprise has always been a family affair, and Mel personally continued to develop new designs of wet suits, spear guns, gas guns, underwater cameras, housings, and other underwater equipment.

Together with other professional divers, the Fishers explored the California coast for shipwrecks. They also completed several treasure hunting expeditions into the Caribbean. While these ventures produced only limited results, each one added experience and unique training to Mel Fisher.

In 1962, while returning from the Caribbean through Florida, Mel encountered a treasure hunter named Kip Wagner. Wagner had been attempting to salvage the remains of ten shipwrecks of the 1715 Spanish Plate Fleet lost in a hurricane off Florida's East Coast. Ill-equipped and under-staffed, Wagner invited Mel to join him on a 50-50 basis.

Mel, together with a hand-picked crew of seven, agreed to move to Florida and work for one year without pay while searching for the treasure. After 360 days without success, the team was testing a device Mel invented called the "mailbox." It constitutes a tube which is lowered from the ship's stern over the propellers while the boat is securely anchored. The engines are then put in gear and the prop wash sends a layer of clear water from the surface downward to the bottom so the divers can see. But the "mail box" did something else too: it blew away the silt and sand and revealed 1,033 gold coins. Mel exclaimed: "Once you have seen the ocean bottom paved with gold, you'll never forget it!" Mel was hooked; he continued to salvage the 1715 Fleet for another decade.

About 1969, Mel shifted his focus from the 1715 sites to the tropical waters of the Florida Keys in search of the Spanish galleon *Nuestra Señora de Atocha*, which he had read about in *Potter's Treasure Diver's Guide*. The *Atocha* was a royal guard galleon with 40 tons of gold and silver aboard which sank in a hurricane along with other ships in 1622. Mel was now consumed by his passion.

In 1967, Mel searched throughout Europe until he found an old ship, purchased it, and brought it across the Atlantic Ocean to Florida. He converted it into a full size reproduction of a Spanish galleon which served as a floating museum and headquarters for Mel's operations.

In 1980, Mel Fisher made his first major discovery: more than 20 million dollars worth of gold and other riches of the *Santa Margarita*, a sister ship of the *Atocha* lost in the same storm of 1622. Mel developed his "Ship Museum" to exhibit, preserve, and study the artifacts he found. However, the "Ship Museum" sank in the early eighties, so Mel bought a former Key West Naval Station building to permanently house the non-profit Mel Fisher Maritime Heritage Society Museum. The building included a research center, education and conservation laboratories, and Mel's own private headquarters.

Mel's elusive dream, the *Atocha*, seemed always just out of his reach. The search took years, and cost lives (including one of Mel's own sons), but finally, on 20 July 1985, after more than 15 years, the *Atocha* mother lode was located. At 1:05 p.m. that day, the marine radio crackled to life in the Key West, Florida, office of Mel Fisher at Treasure Salvors, Inc. "AZG9605 Unit I, this is Unit II." From aboard the vessel *Dauntless*, Kane told his anxious father: "Put away the charts. We've got the 'Mother Lode!'"

They had recovered stacks of silver bars, chests of silver coins, gold, jewels, and thousands of other unique artifacts from the *Nuestra Señora de Atocha*. Mel Fisher had found what others only dreamed of finding. Besides the aforementioned items, they also recovered Spanish objects and wares, a variety of armaments and even seeds (which later sprouted!)

In 1990, Mel conceived the idea for the Mel Fisher Center, Inc., which was opened in Sebastian, Florida. The Center primarily serves to conserve and exhibit many of the new discoveries from wrecks of the 1715 Fleet which are still being discovered weekly. Many gorgeous emeralds and other precious items have been brought to the surface.

After the discovery of the *Atocha*, Mel continued to lead expeditions all over the world. Working with associate Pat Clyne and others, he conducted research and developed new treasure hunting techniques. Of particular significance is a high-resolution video remote-sensing package to assist in pinpointing and isolating possible underwater search targets from the air. "We're constantly doing state-of-the-art work to develop long-range density imagery systems for discriminating gold," said Mel. "We're way out ahead; we really are. We have always been on the leading edge of undersea technology and detection systems."

\* \* \*

I never had the pleasure of meeting Mel Fisher in person—but it nearly happened. Mel had read my book, *Footprints in the Wilderness: A History of the Lost Rhoades Mines*, which I co-authored with my cousin, Gale Rhoades, and he came to Utah to talk to us. Apparently he had discovered something of immense importance, and wanted to confirm some things with us. He was disappointed. Gale Rhoades had died while searching for the Lost Josephine Mine near Hoyt Peak in the Uintah Mountains...and I was incarcerated in Utah Sate Prison. Instead, Mel looked up my late good friend, writer and treasure hunter George A. Thompson.

For two summers during the 1990s, George guided Mel to various sites in the Uintah Mountains. In addition, they flew over the Uintahs from one end to the other, utilizing Mel's high-resolution video-sensing device in an attempt to pinpoint major lodes. Though designed for underwater exploration, Mel successfully adapted it for air-to-ground use. "The problem is," George Thompson wrote to me, "we are getting readings from one end of the Uintahs to the other!"

While traipsing the hills, Mel and George ran into a man named Jim Phillips, a rather mysterious fellow who had apparently uncovered a cache of gold bars. He allowed Mel to examine one or two of them, and Mel pronounced them to be of Spanish origin. Efforts to elicit a clue to the general area where the bars were found failed to shake Phillips from his secret.

Prior to the untimely and tragic death of George Thompson, together with his aged mother, in an automobile accident, Fisher had the good fortune to also be guided by one of the very best treasure hunters in Utah. (At the request of this prospector, his name and identity has been changed.) Together, Pard and George had guided Mel Fisher into the high

Uintahs and had taken him to the renowned Hathenbruck Crossing.

Pard learned Mel Fisher's interest in the Uintah Mountains: Mel had a map of the gold mines from whence had come the gold he found on the *Atocha*! He had spent countless hours over the years searching the dusty files of the archives of Spain, trying to find clues to the location of the *Atocha*. In the process, he stumbled across a map to the source of the *Atocha's* rich cargo, and that source was the Uintah Mountains!

While I can't be certain, it seems plausible that Mel's map must have come from the same bundle in which I located the Thomas Blake map, many years ago. The map, dated 1564, is titled: "Mapa de los Indios del Norte de la Rio Tizon en los Provincias Internas de la Nuevo España, de la exactitud de lo referido a Senor Tomás Blaque, acerca de aquel pais, en Julio, 1540." The map is signed "Archivo General de los Indias, 1564."

The English translation of the map: "Map of the Indians of the North of the River Tizon [Colorado] in the Internal Provinces of New Spain, exactly as referred to by Señor Thomas Blake, who was near this country in July, 1540." This map was discovered in the Archives at Madrid (Archivos de España) in a packet of documents transferred from the Archivos de los Indias at Seville, and thus overlooked by researchers for many years.

Thomas Blake was a Scotsman who accompanied the expedition of Cardenas to the Grand Canyon in 1540. Blake and seven Spaniards were sent out by Cardenas to explore the country northward in search of the source of Indian gold. The expedition camped near present day Vernal, Utah, and thus Blake became the first known European to visit what is now the State of Utah.

Inasmuch as the Council of the Indies was in charge of all documents pertaining to New Spain (i.e., America, especially the Mexican Provinces which then included Utah), it seems logical that the packets containing the map of Thomas Blake were also the source for Mel Fisher's discovery of the map showing the source of the gold shipped aboard the *Atocha*. Perhaps, had I the opportunity to compare notes with Mel, I might have found out.

According to Pard, the area of Mel Fisher's search was in the vicinity of the Upper Rock Creek-Grandaddy Lakes Basin, the same area embracing the Rhoades-Hathenbruck mine.

Among the maps which belonged to Happy Jack, one of the Ute tribal leaders and friend of Rhoades and Hathenbruck, was a map which apparently referred to the same location where Mel Fisher concentrated his search. Randy Lewis located the mine shown on the Happy Jack map, only to discover that the entrance to the mine had been blown up in recent years by the BLM. Apparently this government agency, with usual bureaucratic naivete, had sealed the entrance to protect visitors from entering unsafe environs, never knowing what the mine contained.

Mel Fisher, the greatest treasure hunter who ever lived, was close to the fulfillment of his greatest discovery yet: the source of all of the gold of the *Atocha*, and the source of most of the gold recovered by the Spaniards in the New World. Had fate not intervened, Mel Fisher might have made the greatest discovery of his career, and perhaps of all time. But fate did intervene, as it often does, at the most inopportune time. Mel Fisher died on 19 December 1998.

Among the many legacies he left to fellow treasure hunters was his motto: *"Today is the day."*

# Chapter 21

## BEN BULLOCK & BLACK HAWK

Ben II. Bullock holds the distinction of being the only man known to have located and filed upon one of the famous Lost Rhoades Mines. There has always been a mystery surrounding how he discovered his mine. The secret is revealed here for the first time; but first let us examine some background and recount the accepted version of events.

*On the 3rd of July (1835), Michael H. Chandler came to Kirtland (Ohio) to exhibit some Egyptian mummies. There were four human figures, together with some two or more rolls of papyrus covered with hiero-glyphic figures and devices. ...He was immediately told, while yet in the custom house, that there was no man in that city (New York City) who could translate his roll; but was referred, by the same gentleman, (a stranger) to Mr. Joseph Smith, Jun., who, continued he, possesses some kind of power or gifts, by which he had previously translated similar charac-ters. [Comprehensive History of the Church, Joseph Smith, Jun., 2:351]*

Thus wrote Joseph Smith of his purchase of a collection of Egyptian mummies and papyri from which he purportedly translated the *Book of Abraham*, one of the doctrinal scriptures of the Mormon Church. The "stranger" mentioned by Smith—who was certainly no stranger to the Mormon Prophet—was Benjamin Bullock II, son of Benjamin Bullock I and Sybil Drake, born 30 March 1792 at Grafton, New Hampshire, and who died 27 July 1852 on the North Platte River, Nebraska, en route to Utah. He married

24 January 1808, at Grafton, Dorothy Kimball, daughter of John Kimball and Polly Hoyt. The Bullocks resided at Mairie, New York, and according to the *Bullock Family History* [Clara Fullmer Bullock, Taber, Alberta, Canada, 1917], Benjamin Bullock happened to be at the customs house when Chandler arrived to collect his mummies.

According to this account, it was Bullock who instructed Chandler to take the artifacts to Joseph Smith and personally drove Chandler the 250 miles to Kirtland, Ohio, to meet the Prophet, with the mummies and papyri in the back of his wagon.

The same source informs us that it was a Mormon missionary, Dr. J.R. Riggs, who converted the Bullock family to Mormonism. On 8 October 1853, Dr. Riggs married Bullock's daughter, Jane Kilton Bullock (1819-1910). Riggs migrated with the pioneer exodus to Utah where he arrived on 5 September 1851 and settled at Provo to practice medicine. He remained that settlement's primary physician until the arrival of Dr. F.W.C. Hathenbruck.

Benjamin Bullock himself never joined the Mormon Church, although he moved to Kirtland, Ohio, and endured all the persecu-tions of the Saints in Missouri and Illinois giving as his reason that he could "do more good for the Church by staying out of the Church."

Bullock joined the pioneer wagon company of Coleman Boren (the author's great-grandfa-ther) but died of cholera on the North Platte River while crossing the plains. Coleman Boren took Bullock's widow Dorothy into his own home at Provo, Utah, where she died 23

September 1853. Benjamin Bullock's son, Benjamin Kimball Bullock (27 January 1821-22, March 1901) brother-in-law of Dr. John Riggs, married Martha Elizabeth Hart, whose mother was Mary Riggs, aunt of the good doctor.

Benjamin Bullock IV, who was for many years mayor of Provo, married Martha Hart on 26 January 1851. Their son was Benjamin Hart Bullock (Benjamin V) born 27 October 1878 at Provo, and who died at the same place on 12 July 1962. It is with Benjamin Hart Bullock that we note the first connection with the Rhoades mines.

Ben H. Bullock was a man who professed to possess gifts of the spirit. He claimed to have had a dream wherein he was visited by a heavenly messenger who revealed the location of a lost Nephite gold mine. Bullock worked his secret mine for many years and during this time he formed a close friendship with Bishop John Koyle who also had a "dream" mine revealed to him by the same heavenly messenger. Bullock often claimed that Koyle's Dream Mine was a "twin" to his own Nephite mine.

During the period when the Mormon Church threatened excommunication to anyone who worked Koyle's Dream Mine, that mine was closed down [see: *The Gold of Carre-Shinob*, Kerry Ross Boren & Lisa Lee Boren, Bonneville Books, Springville, Utah, 1998], and the assessment work necessary to be done in order to retain legal ownership of the property was neglected. When the deadline for the assessment work arrived, Ben H. Bullock was sitting in the lobby of the Kenyon Hotel in Salt Lake City, dozing in the early morning hours of the day. He later claimed that a clear voice spoke to him, interrupting his sleep, informing him to go immediately to the Dream Mine and take up the claims to save them for the stockholders of Koyle's company.

Bullock proceeded immediately to Spanish Fork where he obtained a horse and headed for Water Canyon. The deep January snow hindered his progress and he was forced to abandon the horse and proceed on foot, but even this was impossible, for he continually broke through the drifts up to his hips.

Bullock fell to his knees and prayed to the Lord to make the snow firm enough to support his weight so he could complete his mission. When he arose and tried again, the snow supported him easily and he proceeded to place notices on the main series of eight claims. Within three days he had recorded the claims and signed quit-claim deeds back to the Koyle Mining Company stockholders, thus securing it without losing their Church membership.

In the summer of 1958, Ben H. Bullock reported that he had discovered the Lost Rhoades Mines! *The Daily Record* newspaper of Salt Lake City, dated 23 June 1958, reported as follows:

### *LOST RHOADES GOLD MINE DISCOVERED RECENTLY BY BULLOCK MINES—METALS*

*Discovery of the lost Rhoades Gold Mine west of Moon Lake in Duchesne County, Utah, was announced this week by Mr. Ben H. Bullock of the Bullock Mine, Metals and Oil Corporation of Utah. Mr. Bullock stated that the mine was located by instrument test and through use of an old buckskin map drawn by Caleb Rhoades. The map is owned by Mrs. Mary Steele of Goshen, Utah. The mine was discovered by Mr. Bullock and his son, Vern Bullock, 100 W. 960 N., Provo.*

*In an interview with Mr. Bullock, he stated that the mine was originally discovered by Indians in that area. "Caleb Rhoades," he continued, "was liaison between the Indians and Brigham Young who was believed to have used the gold to mint money used by the settlers in the Salt Lake Valley."*

*"The gold vein," said Mr. Bullock, "is 600 feet*

*in width by 2,000 feet in length in a contact vein between porphyry and quartzite. Operation of the mine will begin soon," he continued.*

Though Bullock reported that he had found the mine with the aid of the buckskin map and by instrument test, it would appear that the story of the discovery is not so simple.

As early as 1940, Clark Powell, Sr., a relation of Caleb Rhoades through Caleb's marriage to his first wife, Melinda Powell, struck up a friendship with a young lady named Sadie who lived in Carbonville, a suburb of Price, Utah. As it happened, Sadie was the younger sister of Sidsie Adams Rhoades, Caleb's second wife.

Sadie supplied Clark Powell with a copy of a map showing the location of three rich gold mines, which map she said she had obtained from Sidsie Rhoades before her death, and that it was a copy of the original which Thomas Rhoades had taken from eight massacred Spaniards at Chicken Creek in 1857. By the use of the map, Caleb Rhoades had discovered at least two of the mines by 1859.

Sometime during the early 1950s, Powell came into contact with Carlos Foote who had discovered a vertical mine shaft in the area of one of the mines listed on the map. The two men decided to go to the mine and perhaps, by the use of the map, discover the location of the other two. They set out in the company of one other man, Roy Powell. On the way to the mine, however, an argument ensued between the parties and Foote became concerned for his life, and he silently departed from the camp one night and left the Powells on their own.

On his way off the mountains, Foote encountered Ben H. Bullock whom he told about the shaft. He also described a large pine tree which stood near the shaft of the mine, that had "Gold-1856" carved into the trunk. Foote had seen such a tree clearly marked on Powell's

Spanish map, and he was convinced that this was an authentic Spanish mine. He and Bullock thereby entered into some sort of agreement for Foote to show him the location of the shaft.

Foote placed three "x's" on Bullock's map which he had obtained from Mrs. Steele, but unfortunately his memory did not serve him correctly and the marks were not in the correct location, causing much confusion to this day for those who still search for the mines.

Though Bullock Mines, Metals and Oil Corporation did not find the other two mines, there is no doubt that what Ben H. Bullock did discover was Caleb Rhoades' famous "Pine Mine," clearly mentioned in Rhoades' mineral leases and other documents.

Bullock's exploration of the mine revealed some interesting circumstances. The shaft was barely large enough to permit a man to enter and Bullock improvised a "lift" by cutting a 55 gallon barrel in half and making a sling out of it by which he could be lowered into the vertical shaft.

At a depth of about 60 feet the vertical shaft ended and the tunnel continued horizontally into the bowels of the mountain. At this point the tunnel had been filled with fallen rock and all efforts to remove it from the confines of the barrel lift failed.

While Bullock returned out of the mountains to devise a new approach, claim jumpers entered the area with a bulldozer, hoping to scrape away the top layers and expose the vein, taking as much gold as they could and departing before Bullock returned. All they succeeded in doing, however, was to push the shaft full of rock and debris and to make it even more inaccessible.

A tragic side-note to this incursion was that the historic old pine tree with the inscription "Gold-1856" was pushed over the side of the mountain and permanently buried. Ben Bullock was blamed for this destruction, but the following letter, written by his son, Benjamin Vern Bullock (Benjamin VI), of Provo, to Gale Rhoades and Kerry Ross Boren (see: *Footprints in the Wilderness*, Gale R. Rhoades & Kerry Ross Boren, Publishers Press, Salt Lake City, 1971, p.396), dated 25 October 1971, indicates that Bullock had nothing to do with it.

*We hired a man by the name of John Munz, who lived on a ranch easterly of Duchesne, to haul two horses to our base camp site in his cattle truck. These we were unable to ride because of wind-fallen trees, so we tied them up, and I pulled my father up the mountain by him holding on to my belt—he was 80 years old at the time and crippled from a broken back and hip from a car wreck in 1950.*

*He and I found the location we wanted and when I located the claims [I] found an old logging road which made it possible for me to ride into the area on a tote gote; a little repair at the base of the mountain would [have] enabled me to drive all the way in my pickup...*

*We did not push over the tree with date & inscription on it. We did not have a bulldozer in the area and fill up No. 1 shaft, or any other shaft. At about the same time, an outfit from California operated out of Hanna with a bull- dozer but...no heavy equipment was even taken in by us... The heaviest piece of equipment we had, or caused to have, on the mountain was the 25th Tote Gote built by the Borham Co. of Provo, I rode and hauled out surveying equipment on it when staking our claims...*

Ben H. Bullock died 12 July 1962 at his home in Provo in his 84th year. He never opened the Pine Mine, although his son Vern maintained the claims on it. Before his death, Bullock intimated that the reason for his abandoning the project was not so much lack of accessibility or financing, but because of something he had either seen or experienced at that place.

Vern Bullock related in an interview in 1971 that after the article appeared on the discovery of the Pine Mine, his father received numerous letters, phone calls and visits from people inter- ested in promoting the discovery of the mine.

"I could have told great tales," Vern Bullock said, "but what we learned was our business."

Ben H. Bullock left a golden legacy. He may well have been one of the greatest prospectors in the West, even though his productivity may have been minimal. It is quite probable that Ben Bullock knew a great deal more about the lost mines than he was ever willing to reveal publicly.

Bullock's secret begins to unravel in a state- ment made to *The Mining Review*, published in Carson City, Nevada, under date of 21 June 1959:

*...The Nephite Mine—which is what I call the mine I discovered through a dream when I was in my youth—is located in the Uintah Mountains in Utah, northwest of the present-day town of Vernal....and there are at least a dozen other gold sources along those mountains just as rich in ore, but none which contain the relics I saw in my dream except the Nephite mine. ...Some forty years ago Uncle Jesse Knight approached me and wanted to invest in my Nephite mine, but I didn't then, nor do I now, wish to reveal the loca- tion of it. I am negotiating instead to open up several other mines which belonged to Caleb Rhoades, and which do not have the curse upon them that is contained with the Nephite mine....*

It is apparent from Bullock's statements that he did not claim that the Pine Mine was the same as his Lost Nephite Mine. The latter is clearly described as being northwest of Vernal; the Pine Mine is located in the Brown Duck Lakes region of the upper Rock Creek basin. According to Bullock, the Pine Mine was located by use of a map obtained from Mrs. Mary Steele of Goshen, Utah, a map originally drawn by Caleb Rhoades. In reality, however, the map was drawn by Joe

Sulser, copied from the description given to him by a fellow inmate in a Mexican jail cell. Sulser became Mary Steele's first husband.

Therefore we have at least three versions of Bullock's discovery: 1) he found it by use of a map drawn on buckskin belonging to Mrs. Mary Steele; 2) he found it by use of a map drawn by Joe Sulser in a Mexican jail cell; 3) he found it by use of a map which Clark Powell obtained from Sadie, younger sister of Sidsie Adams Rhoades, second wife of Caleb Rhoades. In fact, all three maps exist. The actual story of the discovery, however, is told here for the first time.

My family, on both the paternal and maternal sides, has long been closely associated with the Ute Indians, and especially to the two great chiefs, Walker and Black Hawk. My third great-grandfather, Isaac Morley, was the first white man to whom Chief Walker revealed the sacred gold of the Utes, and Morley baptized Walker and confirmed him as a member of the Mormon Church. They were close friends until Walker's death in 1855.

Both sides of my family had dealings with Chief Black Hawk, the most enigmatic war chief of the Utes, whose fame is eclipsed only by his more famous uncle, Chief Walker. Black Hawk, who was also called Antonguer or Antonga, was born circa 1824 at Spring Lake near the south end of the Utah Valley. His father Syn-nap-pitch (called Sanpitch, a.k.a. Tenacio) was a noted war chief and brother of Chief Walker. His mother was Taa-mar-oh-wich, whose name meant "mother of boys," for she was the mother of at least ten sons; she also had several daughters.

There are multiple differing descriptions of Black Hawk. The most accurate appears to be that of Captain James H. Simpson, a U.S. Army Corps of Topographical Engineers officer who led a team of artists, photographers, and scientists across Utah and Nevada on 8 May 1859. Simpson's trained eye gave us this description of Black Hawk:

*Just before dinner a Parvan [Pahvant] (Ute) Indian (Black Hawk) came into camp. This is the first Indian we have seen on our route. His squaw is a Go-shoot [Goshute] woman, and he lives among that people. Gave him his dinner and some tobacco. Had a sketch of him taken. He wears his hair tied up at the temples and behind; carries a buckskin pouch and powder-horn; a bow and quiver swung on his right side; wears a pink checked American shirt, buckskin leggins and moccasins, and a blanket around his loins; an old black silk handkerchief is tied about his neck. He has one huge iron spur on his right heel, and rides a sorrel pony. His height is 5 feet 7_ inches; has a stout square frame; age, probably 35; carries a rifle. His bow is 3 feet long, and is made of sheep's horn; arrow, 25 inches long, feathered, and barbed with iron. His countenance is ordinarily sardonic, but lights up in conversation, and shows as much intelligence as Indians do ordinarily. [Report of Explorations Across the Great Basin of the Territory of Utah for a Direct Wagon-Route from Camp Floyd to Genoa, in Carson Valley, in 1859, Capt. James H. Simpson, 1859; reprint Univ. of Nevada Press, Reno, 1983, pp.51-52.]*

Black Hawk was in his early twenties when the Mormons arrived in Utah in 1847, and was already a warrior of note. He lived with his cousins, the Timpanogos Utes, in Utah Valley, and preyed upon Mormon livestock.

On 1 March 1849 a Nauvoo Legion company was sent south with orders "to take such measures as would put a final end" to the Ute depredations upon Mormon stock. The Mormon troops surrounded the Indian lodges near dawn, and four Ute braves and their families took cover in a creek bottom and opened fire on the much larger Mormon force.

One by one the four Ute braves were killed, and thirteen women and children surrendered, including a young Ute brave who "looked to be about eighteen years of age." This was Black Hawk, who "had fought manfully" during the battle but when captured "shook with fright...expecting to be killed any minute." But he was not killed; he was taken with others to Salt Lake City where he was kept until spring.

Little Chief, who was in charge of the Timpanogos band, condemned the militiamen for "not killing the lad," predicting that he "would kill a white man yet for revenge." [*Diary of Hosea Stout*, Juanita Brooks, ed., 2 vols., Univ. of Utah Press, Salt Lake City, 1964, 2:344-47.] Black Hawk confirmed this account to Joshua Terry, the old Mormon mountain man. "It put bitterness in his heart; and though he lived for some time with the white people, his mind was ever set on avenging the wrong..." [*Autobiography of Pioneer John Brown*, 1820-1896, John Brown, ed. By John Zimmerman Brown, Stevens & Wallis, Inc., Salt Lake City, 1941, pp.103-105.]

On 10 March 1849, just four days after the militiamen brought young Black Hawk to Salt Lake City, Brigham Young appointed Dimick Huntington to lead a company of thirty men and their families to colonize Utah Valley. An-kar-tewets, who fifteen years later became "one of Black Hawk's most active raiders," boldly sat astride his horse and blocked the trail, telling the colonizers to go back where they came from. Huntington talked with An-kar-tewets and other angry Utes for over an hour, and finally the Indians relented but only after making Huntington "raise his right hand and swear by the sun that [the Mormons] would not drive the Indians from their lands, nor take away their rights." ["History of Provo City", *Tullidge's Quarterly Magazine*, July 1884, 3:234.]

The new colony built a fort of log cabins with twelve-foot pickets between the west of present Provo, and called it Fort Utah. Inside the enclosure they mounted a cannon on an elevated platform. Even before the fort was completed, however, they discovered that they had settled on a site that "was the great annual gathering place for all the Ute bands of the valleys for two hundred miles, east and south."

Tensions escalated. About the first of August 1849, an Indian the Mormons called "Bishop" was accused of stealing a shirt. Three Mormons, led by Richard Ivie, confronted Bishop and a struggle ensued in which Bishop was killed. Fearful of the reaction of the Utes should the deed be discovered, Ivie and his companions cut the dead man open, ripped out his entrails, filled his abdominal cavity with rocks, and sank the body in the Provo River. Ute fishermen subsequently found the body and soon learned that Ivie was one of the murderers. Bishop's family began taking shots at members of the Ivie family and wantonly killed cattle. [Isaac Higbee to Brigham Young, 15 Oct. 1849.]

The Mormons, weary of the constant cattle raids and related problems, were determined to attack the Indians before the Indians attacked them. Brigham Young was urged by Captain Howard Stansbury and Lieutenant George W. Howland, the only U.S. military officers in the area, that such a punitive strike was "not only of good policy, but one of absolute necessity [for] self-preservation." Young ordered out 150 militiamen, and Stansbury sent Howland along to indicate that the action was sanctioned by United States military authority. Howland's guide and scout was a Mormon, William Washington Potter, who was my maternal second great-grandfather.

Several days prior to the Mormon attack, "Antonguer, sometimes called Black Hawk, and several other Indians came into the fort asking peace for themselves and families, and offering service to aid the settlers." ["History of Provo," op.cit., p.239.] It was on this occasion that William Potter first met Black Hawk, for Black Hawk was in the fort when the Mormon troops from Salt Lake City arrived under the cover of darkness early on the morning of 8 February 1850.

Old Elk, leader of the Timpanogos Utes, set up fortifications for seventy warriors and their families not far from the fort. Later in the morning of their arrival the militia plodded through two feet of snow to confront the fortified Indians. Dimick Huntington tried to negotiate a surrender but Old Elk opened fire, beginning a week-long battle that was the bloodiest killing of Indians in Utah's history.

Black Hawk was an active participant in the campaign, assisting the Mormons. He had been living with the Mormons since his capture nearly a year earlier, and had apparently been convinced to lend his loyalty to the Mormon cause.

Old Elk's forces were well-armed and well-positioned below a river bank, and fought fiercely for two days, killing one Mormon and wounding eighteen others. The Mormons had brought up their cannon, using "chain shot," which had ripped off the legs of one Indian woman and killed and maimed others. Moreover, the Mormons contrived an ingenious portable barricade of logs in order to move their cannon into position.

During the night following the second day of fighting, Old Elk, suffering from a severe wound and a bad case of measles, deserted the stronghold with most of the survivors, leaving Stick-in-Head behind to delay the Mormons.

Early on the morning of the third day, Black Hawk was sent from the fort to scout out the Indian position. As he walked through the camp he found it deserted with the bodies of nine of his people lying grotesquely dead with "signs of many more being killed or wounded." [History of Provo," op.cit., p.239.]

After reporting back to the fort, Black Hawk agreed to guide one of the two groups of Mormons who went in pursuit of the fleeing Indians. One group, under Old Elk, had fled up Rock Canyon (above present-day Brigham Young University and the LDS Temple), while the other, led by Stick-in-Head, headed southwest toward the southern tip of Utah Lake. It was with the Rock Canyon group that Black Hawk went.

The Rock Canyon group consisted of, in addition to Black Hawk, William Potter, Peter W. Conover, William McBride, John McEwan, Samuel Ewing, Thomas Willis, Robert Egbert, Edward C. Holden, and Abram Conover. (Peter W. Conover was a son-in-law of Coleman Boren.)

By this time, William Potter had struck up a friendship with Black Hawk and the two of them proceeded up Rock Canyon ahead of the militia. Near the mouth of the canyon they found a few tepees and their arrival caused "a general scattering of the squaws and children." Inside the lodges they discovered the frozen corpses of Old Elk and about a dozen others, "including Squaws and children," some who had died of wounds, but most "through want, fatigue and exposure."

The militia gathered up twenty-three prisoners. Old Elk's wife, described as "the handsomest squaw in the Ute nation," tried to escape by scaling the nearly perpendicular cliffs and either fell or jumped to her death before the eyes of the militiamen.

Farther up the canyon more tepees were encountered and several more Indians killed in a skirmish. Black Hawk witnessed the single-handed capture of two Indians by William Potter, which impressed him greatly. One of the captured braves was later executed by the militia. Stick-in-Head escaped with the rest of the band but General Wells caught up to them on the ice of Utah Lake where 29 more Indians were killed and many more women and children were taken prisoner.

Following the Rock Creek fight the militiamen pillaged the dead Indians for souvenirs and Bill Hickman severed Old Elk's head from his body because Jim Bridger had offered a hundred dollars for it. [*Brigham's Destroying Angel*, William Hickman, Shepard Pub. Co., Salt Lake City, 1904, p.68.]

Hickman's action set a precedent. Dr. James Blake, an army surgeon accompanying the Stansbury expedition, commissioned two Mormons, Abner Blackburn and James Or, to return to the battlefields and decapitate all the corpses. Blake planned to send the heads "to Washington to a medical institution" for scientific examination. Some 40 or 50 heads were retrieved and boxed, but they were held for several weeks to be "held up as a warning to other Indians." The "weather turned warm" and "the Indian heads smelt loud" and turned "green with rot."

A number of braves, including An-kar-tewets and Black Hawk, together with 26 women and children, were held at the fort where their only shelter was beneath the cannon platform. They suffered from the snow and cold immensely. Here they sat huddled grieving the loss of their loved ones whose heads were exhibited before them.

Black Hawk's friendship with William Potter grew from Potter's compassion for the captured Utes. The Mormon guide and interpreter, seeing the suffering of the Indians from the cold, remonstrated with Lieutenant George W. Howland to supply the Ute captives with U.S. Army blankets. Howland would not give the blankets outright, but at last relented and let the suffering Indians "borrow" them while being held at the fort.

Potter then turned on the Mormon leaders, confronting General Daniel H. Wells. He told them that the women and children, some of whom were dying from exposure, should be taken to Salt Lake City and placed in homes where they could be cared for. Eventually, this was done, under the guise of being taught the "arts of civilization." [*Autobiography of George Washington Bean*, ed. Flora Diana Bean Horne, Utah Printing Co., Salt Lake City, 1945, p.62.]

Black Hawk, greatly impressed with Potter's courage and compassion toward his people, extended a most unusual gift to his new-found friend. Among the captives was Black Hawk's older sister, a young woman whom the whites called "Queen Victoria," presumably because of a resemblance. Black Hawk offered his sister to Potter as a wife. It may have been that she was then a widow of one of the murdered warriors, and that Black Hawk saw an opportunity to place her in a secure home and save her life. Whatever the reason, William Potter accepted the offer and Queen Victoria became one of his plural wives. [Queen Victoria was about thirty years of age, and thus was born circa 1820. After the death of William Potter in 1853 she never remarried and lived to a great age in southern Utah as a midwife. Victoria delivered my father, Edward Boren, and his twin brother Ezra, into the world at Clifton, Utah, in Bryce Canyon, on 9 November 1893, when she was about 73 years of age.]

The Potters remained closely allied to Blackhawk throughout his life. William Potter was killed in October 1853 in the Gunnison Massacre on the Sevier River, while serving as guide and scout for Captain John W. Gunnison. William Potter's nephew, Isaac Potter, who was a half-breed Pottowattamie Indian, rode with Black Hawk during the Black Hawk War, and Black Hawk often rode with Ike Potter's outlaw gang. Space does not permit a full recounting of these relationships and is mentioned here merely to broaden our knowledge of Black Hawk.

It is hardly more important to our purpose to list all of the reasons why Black Hawk went to war against the Mormons beginning in 1865. It was a combination of a broken treaty, the death of his father Sanpitch, and maltreatment by the

Mormons in general. But mostly it was the on-going feud with the Ivie family.

Richard Ivie, it will be remembered, murdered the Indian called Bishop, filled his abdominal cavity with rocks, and dumped his body in the Provo River, precipitating the Fort Utah War of 1850. Richard was the son of James R. Ivie who was credited with starting the Walker War in 1853 by killing an Indian by hitting him over the head with a gun barrel. He also participated in the killing of Black Hawk's comrade Squash-Head and in the wounding of his friend and ally Tintic, which precipitated the Tintic War of 1856. James R. Ivie was a relation by marriage to Coleman Boren.

Black Hawk got his revenge. In the summer of 1866, Black Hawk's band made a raid upon Ivie's poorly defended town of Scipio. The raiders found Ivie tending to "a favorite milk cow" in a pasture and filled the old man with arrows, and stripped him of all but his boots [*Our Pioneer Heritage*, DUP, 9:216.]

The Black Hawk War has been recounted in detail by other writers. Suffice it that for two years the war raged across the Territory, causing hundreds of deaths on both sides. It might have continued even longer except that Black Hawk was wounded.

On 11 June 1866, following the Scipio raid, Black Hawk led his warriors into a battle with Mormon militia led by Brigadier General William B. Pace at a place called Gravelly Ford near the present site of Vermillion. Riding a white stallion formerly owned by the slain James Ivie, Black Hawk boldly rode by the Mormon lines again and again, firing from behind his mount. Pace ordered his men to shoot the beautiful horse, and when it fell, Black Hawk continued to fire from behind the dead mount. At last a Mormon sharpshooter shot Black Hawk in the stomach, and the militiamen cheered as the chief retreated on foot "pressing his hands to his abdomen." [Other sources

maintain that it was Tamaritz, not Black Hawk, who rode the white horse that day; no matter—Black Hawk was wounded in the battle.]

The battles continued to rage on for another year, but Black Hawk's wound prevented his active participation and he had also contracted tuberculosis. Finally, in 1867, Black Hawk and a few followers appeared unexpectedly at the reservation in the Uintah Basin. Weary of war and bloodshed, Black Hawk agreed to a treaty of peace. He asked the superintendent of Indian Affairs to cut off his hair, that being shorn of his long war-braids was a token that he had abandoned the warpath. He signed a treaty in 1868 and peace was completely restored by 1869.

Realizing that he was dying, Black Hawk obtained permission from the superintendent of Indian Affairs to visit the Mormon settlements throughout Utah Territory to apologize for his depredations against them. Following this tour, Black Hawk returned to Spring Lake, near Payson, the place of his birth. He camped in the lower end of Payson Canyon where his two wives attended him until he died on 26 September 1870.

The Benjamin F. Johnson family watched as Black Hawk's wives strapped him to his horse and took him to the hills southeast of a lake made by the Mormons for irrigation purposes. Here, under an overhanging ledge of rock, he and his possessions were buried very near the place of his birth. *The Deseret News* published Benjamin F. Johnson's report as follows:

*Spring Lake Villa, Sept. 27, 1870*
*Editor, Deseret News*

*Dear Sir,*

*I hasten to tell you that Black Hawk, the Indian desperado, is dead. He has long been living here with his brother, "Mountain," together with "Joe" and his band for several days. We knew he was sick, but did not think of so sudden a demise. This morning, before sunup, the Indian wail was heard in their camp, and soon was seen one Indian squaw with two horses heavily packed, on the way towards the foot of the mountain. Stopping at a small ravine within sight of our door, they killed one of the horses and proceeded to put away the body of the great Black Hawk. This is the place of his birth. Here he commenced his depredations, and here he came back to die....*

The Hales family were related to the Potters by marriage. Thus the following affidavit is of considerable interest:

*Provo City,*
*Utah, July 7th, 1919.*

*To whom it may concern:*
*The latter part of September or first part of October about 1870 my parents and their family were living at Spring Lake Villa, Utah County, state of Utah.*
*Several of us young people would visit the Indian camp on the northwest of the little village and at this place "Old Black Hawk" was brought in a very sick condition. The Sunday before Black Hawk's death, several of us young people visited his camp and heard him moaning and saw him lying his bed. During the week he died, I, with others, stood on the main street of Spring Lake Villa, Utah, and saw old Black Hawk's body tied across his horse in the funeral procession, there being about eight horses rode by Indians, some in front of Black Hawk's horse and some following.*
*This procession followed a drag trail up the mountain a little east of south of Spring Lake Villa, to where his remains were buried. About nine weeks later, several of the Indians came to our home—two of the squaws had their heads*

*shaved, some of the Indians said they were Black Hawk's squaws and their "heap big chief" was dead.*

*(signed) CHANA E. HALES*

*Signed in the presence of Ben H. Bullock.*

That's right—Ben H. Bullock! The man who discovered one of the Lost Rhoades Mines is suddenly linked to Chief Black Hawk! And it goes even farther than that. The story begins to unfold in Madoline Cloward Dixon's book *These Were the Utes* (p.133):

*Some years ago Bishop B. H. Bullock of Provo and friends were in the vicinity of this old grave and felt impressed to secure if possible, the remains. After careful search they found the old resting place of Black Hawk: his remains were unearthed together with what remained of the old bridle, especially the rosettes which were so well known to the old settlers during the lifetime of this noted chief. The remains were carefully stored away for some time and later presented to the L.D.S. Church Museum on temple block.*

There followed a series of affidavits, all concerning Ben Bullock, all of which appear to be calculated to be convincing that Black Hawk was indeed dead and buried, found again and needed verification.

*Santaquin, Utah County, Utah*
*September 6th, 1919.*

*To Whom It May Concern:*
*During the year 1917 Bishop Ben Bullock was telling several men who were working at the Syndicate Mine on the mountain east of Santaquin, Utah, and a little east of south of Spring Lake Villa, Utah, that the remains of "Old Black Hawk," Indian, were buried some place near the tunnel that we were working in and one*

day while prospecting on the surface of the property I noticed in a slide of quartsite rock a piece that looked like the rock had been moved and a small mound built. I reported this to Bishop Bullock and then he, with Lars Olson and myself, started removing the rock and found the skeleton with beads, bridle, bridle bit silver rosettes, spurs, saddle, sleigh bells, ax, bucket, cup, parts of an old soldier coat with buttons and several trinkets, among them a china pipe. Later it was reported by those that knew the Indian that [these items] we had taken from the grave with the skeleton were Old Black Hawk's.

WILLIAM E. CROFT

Springville, Utah County, Utah, August 23, 1919.

To Whom It May Concern:

In the fall of the year 1870 I was in Spanish Fork, Utah County, Utah, this being my place of residence at that time and "Old Black Hawk" the noted war Indian came to my home and I cooked the last meal he ever ate in Spanish Fork, Utah, before he died at Spring Lake Villa, Utah County, Utah. I remember his looks very well, his head and face were shaped more like that of a white man than an Indian, and his teeth were in a very good condition.

I remember the silver rosettes, the bridle bit, his spurs, sleigh bells and things in general that he had when coming among the white settlers before his death and bear testimony that the silver rosettes, the bridle bit, bells and spurs that Bishop Ben H. Bullock had in his possession were what I saw in the possession of "Old Black Hawk" and also testify that the skull and the teeth in the jaws of the skull are "Black Hawk's."

LOUISE N. PACE

Provo City, Utah
August 26, 1919

To Whom It May Concern:

In 1911 I became interested in what is known as the "Syndicate Mine," located on the Santaquin mountain, a little southeast of Spring Lake Villa. Several of the old settlers of Spring Lake knew that old "Black Hawk" had been buried on the mountain near where we were working this property. At my leisure moments I would hunt for the spot where "Black Hawk" was buried, and one day, one of the miners, William E. Croft, reported that he had found what he supposed to be "Black Hawk's" grave. This started an investigation and Mr. Croft along with Lars L. Olsen and myself uncovered the remains of "Black Hawk," which were buried in a large quartsite slide. Three feet of rock were taken from the skeleton, and upon uncovering it, we found the remains in a sitting posture. The first article we saw was a china pipe, which was lieing [sic] on the top of his head. Then we discovered the saddle, the remains of the skeleton, portions of his horse's bridle that had been buried with him; sleigh bells, ax, bucket, beads, part of an old soldier coat with the buttons still intact. All of these we removed very carefully, and for safety deposited them with the Spanish Fork Co-op, where they were exhibited for several days. Subsequently at the suggestion of Commander J.M. Westwood, I secured these remains and conveyed them to the L.D.S. museum on temple block, suggesting that they should be placed on exhibition there and preserved.

BEN H. BULLOCK

* * *

Black Hawk's bones and possessions were displayed for decades in an LDS Church museum. In accordance with the Native American Graves Protection and Repatriation

Act of 1990, Black Hawk's remains were reinterred in a new grave at Spring Lake, Utah, on 4 May 1996, by his closest living relatives, the descendants of his brother Mountain. To all intents and purposes, the great Black Hawk was finally laid to rest in peace—or was he?

Why did Ben H. Bullock go to so much bother to document his discovery of Black Hawk's remains with affidavits? And why were the affidavits all worded as though Bullock had written them down to referring to "Old Black Hawk" in quotation marks, as though to emphasize some sort?

The answer lies in two letters written by Ben H. Bullock to F.W.C. Hathenbruck in the spring of 1920. Hathenbruck was the former partner of Caleb Rhoades, and had spent the last fifteen years following Caleb's death in 1905, in trying to open the reservation lands in an effort to work the Rhoades mine.

The letters are cryptic, but nonetheless revealing. Though dealing with several topics, we are concerned here only with references to Black Hawk.

Dr. F.W.C. Hathenbruck
Provo, Utah, March 13, 1920

Doctor:

...My father [Benjamin Kimball Bullock] who died about twenty years ago [22 March 1901] knew old Black Hawk very well. I believe I have related the story to you at some of our earlier meetings, but not in much detail, so I will elaborate a little here.

When my father arrived in Utah in 1851, Black Hawk was very friendly with the whites and lived around old Fort Utah where my father first met him. It wasn't until a few years later that Black Hawk became a desperado. ...

I have heard the story from my father's lips many times. One night while the family was at supper there came a knock at the door. This was,

I believe, near the time of the Fourth of July celebration at Provo in 1866. When my father opened the door, there stood a white man and Indian. My father recognized the white man immediately; it was the renegade desperado Ike Potter, and the Indian who was with him was Black Hawk's brother, a handsome Ute Indian named Mountain. (I believe you have mentioned that you know some of this man's family on the reservation.)

Needless to say, my father was very concerned to see these two men at his front door because the whole Territory was in the middle of the Black Hawk War. But Potter said they were only looking for Dr. Riggs who had not been at home. Dr. John Riggs had married my father's sister. ...

My father said he thought he knew where Dr. Riggs had gone but was reluctant to give this information to Potter without knowing the cause. Potter was known to ride with Black Hawk and participated in his raids against the Mormons. But Potter was heavily armed and insistent, so at last my father went with him, telling my mother not to be alarmed that he would be all right. Ike Potter told her that if she wanted to see her husband alive again, she should say nothing to anyone about their visit. ... [Having located Dr. John Riggs]...my father rode with the men [i.e. Potter, Mountain, and Riggs] to a place a few miles south of Provo where four or five other Indians were waiting, and in a group they rode well throughout the night to a canyon above Spanish Fork. There they found Black Hawk lieing [sic] in his tepee suffering from a bad wound in his lower intestines. He was in a great amount of pain and my father said they could hear him moaning before they even entered the tepee. ...

Dr. Riggs patched Black Hawk as best he could but he always said the wound was too deep and infected to heal without constant medical attention, which Old Black Hawk would have none of it. ....

When they came to get Dr. Riggs he was reluc-

*tant to go. He considered Black Hawk to be nothing but a murderer of Mormons and even when they arrived at Black Hawk's tepee he refused to treat his wound. The Indians threatened to kill him if he continued to refuse, but he told them "Go ahead and kill me and he will surely die."*

*Black Hawk knew my father quite well and begged him to intercede and convince Dr. Riggs to help him. My father said that Black Hawk was very weak, shaking and fearful of dieing [sic]. My father appealed to Dr. Riggs to remember his profession and his faith in the Lord and after much debate the doctor took care of Black Hawk's wound. He also treated another one of Black Hawk's war chiefs who had been wounded in the same battle [Tamaritz]. ...*

*Black Hawk was grateful [sic] to my father for coming to his aid and saving his life and told him that someday he would repay him for it. My father didn't think much of it at the time, being only too glad to make it back home in one piece.*

*The rest of the story you all ready know and the circumstances of how he was taken to the Black Hawk gold mine. He could have been a very rich man but he had only a mild interest in mining and was very much opposed to disobeying Brigham Young's dictates against mining and did nothing about it during his lifetime. ...*

*I have no doubt but that the Black Hawk gold mine shown to my father is the same that was shown to you by Mr. Rhodes or at least one of the several mines that he [Caleb Rhoades] knew about in that same area. Your description corresponds in every detail except your mention of the Spanish artifacts. ...*

*We were just about found out, as you well know, but my reported discovery of old Black Hawk's grave near Spring Lake should put to rest the rumors that Black Hawk was buried on the Uintah Reservation among his ances-*

*tors and provide you with an opportunity to proceed to the mine unmolested by them. I think the Knight Investment Company will not expend any more money in that behalf knowing that the grave of Black Hawk has been found. ...*
*As ever your friend,*

*BEN H. BULLOCK*

If taken verbatim, Bullock's statements seem to infer that the he actually found Black Hawk's grave, dispelling rumors that the great war chief had been buried on the reservation. But if that were the case, why did he go to so much trouble to document it? And why did he put the bones on public display? It would seem as though he was trying very hard to convince people that Black Hawk's remains had been found because there was some question about it.

The whole story is suspicious. Bullock and some of his friends were hanging around the old Syndicate Mine and having some leisure time just "happened" to decide to look for Black Hawk's grave and just "happened" to find it. After placing the remains in a window of the Spanish Fork Co-op, rumors began to circulate that Black Hawk was buried elsewhere. Bullock then transferred the remains to the L.D.S. Church museum, apparently to give them authenticity; but the museum curator, Benjamin Goddard, wanted proof that the remains were actually those of Black Hawk, so Bullock set out to obtain affidavits to support his claim. This is demonstrated by a newspaper article on the following page that appeared in the *Deseret Evening News*, Saturday, 20 September 1919:

*BONES OF BLACK HAWK
NOW ON EXHIBITION IN
L.D.S. MUSEUM*

*Benjamin Goddard Takes Precaution to Verify
Discovery of Grave of Indian Chief by
Affidavits
Before Placing Skeleton in Institution*

*A case on the northside of the L.D.S. Church museum is destined to become the center of interest to many a student of early-day Utah history. For resting peacefully in the midst of the very white settlers whom he loved to harass is all that remains of Chief Black Hawk who in the early sixties was dreaded and feared in many a town and settlement of Utah. What are declared to be the bones of the Indian desperado have been brought from their final resting place near Spring Lake Villa and now along with spurs, beads, sleighbells, ax, bucket, brass buttons and all such comforts which were supposed to accompany him to the Happy Hunting grounds are on display to the eyes of the White trespassers whom he so much resented.*

*Before placing the skeleton on exhibit Benjamin Goddard, in charge of the museum, has made every possible effort to prove their authenticity and has obtained a mass of evidence which seems to prove unquestionably that none other but the famous chief reposed in the museum. Mr. Goddard has not only secured the affidavits of the persons who exhumed the remains, but of early settlers near Spring Lake Villa who knew the chief and saw his funeral cortege pass up the mountain a little to the east of the Utah County town. There are also a number of interesting photographs showing the place where the body was found, and of the region where Black Hawk started on his last journey. ...*

\* \* \*

It seems as though Benjamin Goddard had

some serious concerns about the identity of the remains and wanted verification, which Bullock accommodated by providing affidavits. But there is that enigmatic statement in Bullock's letter to Hathenbruck that "We were just about found out,..." What was he hiding? Was it the fact that the remains he produced were not those of Black Hawk? That would seem to be the case if we take his statements seriously in his next letter to Hathenbruck:

*F.W.C. Hathenbruck
Provo, Utah, April 10, 1920*

*Doctor:*

*After our last meeting a few thoughts have occurred to me about your planned expedition to the mine. I have decided to deliver my father's map to the Black Hawk mine to you in person due to the uncertainty of the post. ...The remains of "Black Hawk" are now on display in the church museum to a pretty good audience and are generally accepted as authentic. Only you and I know the truth of the matter and I know you will be discreet with the information. My father never wanted anyone to know of his part in the burial of old Black Hawk among his ancestors or how he came about the mine. He never believed that Black Hawk was as bad a man as he was portrayed to be and he had an understanding of the Indians that reminds me very much of your own. If you were to find old Black Hawk buried in his mine I would not be surprised... [Ben H. Bullock to F.W.C. Hathenbruck, Hathenbruck Papers.]*

The story that seems to emerge from Bullock's statements and other supporting evidence is that the elder Bullock (Benjamin Kimball Bullock) had helped Black Hawk to recover from his wound in 1867 and out of gratitude had been shown one of the Indian mines. Because of religious scruples, the elder Bullock did not develop it. Moreover, the implications are strong that the elder Bullock had something to do with Black Hawk's burial "among his ancestors" on the reservation. Was Black Hawk buried with his uncle Wakara at Carre-Shinob? (see: *The Gold of Carre-Shinob*, Boren & Boren, op.cit). Is this the basis of Ben H. Bullock's claim to have knowledge of the "Lost Nephite Mine"?

It seems clear that Ben H. Bullock contrived the discovery of Black Hawk's grave at Spring Lake. Whose grave did he find? There are several candidates buried in the same area. For example, Benjamin F. Johnson, bishop of Spring Lake, wrote to the *Deseret News* on 5 October 1870:

*...Showone, a friendly Indian, the head of the camp about here, died at Goshen a few days since. Queant, another good Indian, lies in camp about ready to die. Really our Indian neighbors are fast passing away...*

Queant is known to have been buried in the vicinity where "Black Hawk's" bones were discovered. Was it Queant? Was it some other unknown chief? Or was it indeed Black Hawk? Because the Spring Lake burial site is on national forest land, Uintah National Forest Historical Archaeologist Charmaine Thompson headed an archaeological, anthropological and historical investigation that "identified" Black Hawk's remains, and supervised their reburial in Spring Lake on 4 May 1996. A number of eminent professionals assisted in the pursuit, including Native American consultant Clifford H. Duncan.

Yet, Uintah Basin Utes and other sources continue to maintain that Black Hawk was buried somewhere on the Uintah Reservation. (see: *Utah's Black Hawk War: Lore and Reminiscences of Participants*, Carlton Culmsee, Utah State Univ. Press, Logan, Utah, 1973, pp. 157-158.) Wash, grandson of Chief

Tabby (who was Black Hawk's uncle), who was born in 1865, the year the war broke out, and was five years old when Black Hawk died, told me personally that Black Hawk had indeed died at Spring Lake, but that he had been buried in the Uintah Mountains near his uncle, the great Chief Walker. Henry Harris, Indian interpreter, who married Mary Reed (whose nephew Bill Reed was my uncle), always maintained that Black Hawk had petitioned Uintah Agency Superintendent Franklin H. Head for permission to be buried on the reservation. This had taken place at peace talks in Strawberry Valley on 19 August 1868. Henry Harris and Dimick Huntington served as interpreters. Harris stated that Black Hawk had surrendered at the Uintah Agency only ten days after the murder of his old friend Ike Potter, which occurred on 1 August 1867. On 10 August Black Hawk and his family surrendered to Supt. Head at the Uintah Agency because he "feared Mormon treachery." [BVT. Col. O.E. Babcock to Maj. Gen. J.A. Rawlins, Chief of Staff, U.S. Army, 23 June 1866, AGO, M619, 454, #961A. Black Hawk requested to surrender to Supt. Head rather than Brigham Young and wanted "to be buried among his people on the reservation and not among the Mormons who had placed Sanpitch in jail....and killed him." Sanpitch had been Black Hawk's father.]

There seems to be little doubt that Ben H. Bullock publicly professed the discovery of Black Hawk's grave while privately stating otherwise. If he had indeed discovered Black Hawk's remains in 1911, why did he state nine years later in 1920 "If you were to find old Black Hawk buried in his mine I would not be surprised. ...."?

Perhaps we will never know exactly what occurred with Black Hawk's remains, but one thing is certain: in 1958 Ben H. Bullock announced the discovery of one of the Lost Rhoades Mines. Like his father before him, he had religious scruples about mining the sacred gold. Today, over 40 years later, the Bullock family maintains the annual improvements on the mine to secure ownership, but have never mined an ounce of gold. Does it have something to do with a promise made to Black Hawk? We are reminded of a statement made by Ben H. Bullock's son, Vern:

"I could have told great tales, but what we learned was our business."

# Chapter 22

## UTE GOLD & INDIAN TALES

All too frequently, when chroniclers write about the history of the Lost Rhoades Mines, they neglect or ignore the Indian quotient. Depending upon their particular bias, historians make claims for the Spaniards, or for the federal government, or for Brigham Young and the Mormon Church, or for F.W.C. Hathenbruck, or even for modern day prospectors. In point of fact however, the gold of the Uintah Mountains has always belonged to the Ute Indians, and it is still Ute gold.

The Utes were divested of their lands first by the Mormons and then by the federal government, both of whom violated important treaties. The 1864 Utah Legislature asked Congress for the removal of the Indians, from as far south as central Utah, to the Uintah Basin which had been set apart as a reservation by the executive order of President Abraham Lincoln in October 1861. [For additional details, see: *The Gold of Carre-Shinob*, op. cit. at Chapter Ten.]

The Rhoades-Hathenbruck lease became the cause of a large portion of the reservation being opened in 1905, to the great detriment of the Utes. With all due respect to both Rhoades and Hathenbruck, who compensated the Utes for their encroachment and did so with Indian consent, their efforts to secure the gold nevertheless had a detrimental effect on the tribe. They would never again have the freedom of their lands.

Historians have also overlooked a rich source of history and tradition. It seems passing strange that researchers should spend so much time and effort in gathering accounts of the mines from white men and totally ignore the Ute Indians, to whom the mines belonged. Part of the reason probably lies in the fact that the Utes are a vary taciturn people who do not divulge their secrets easily, and especially to the white race which has shown itself to be untrustworthy. Therefore, when we are fortunate enough to share their rare insights, it is valuable beyond measure.

My family has long been associated with the Ute people. My maternal second great-grandfather, William Washington Potter, was a renowned explorer and Indian interpreter. One of his several wives was a Ute woman whom the whites called "Queen Victoria," and who was a sister of the great war chief Black Hawk. William Potter was a guide and scout for the military expedition of Capt. John W. Gunnison. In October of 1853 the Gunnison party, including Potter, was killed by Indians on the Sevier River in central Utah; at least, that's the accepted version. In reality, the massacre was planned and executed by the Danites, led by Orrin Porter "Port" Rockwell, William H. Kimball, and others (essentially the same group who massacred the Mexicans at Chicken Creek in 1857), and assisted by a few renegade Indians from Chief Kanosh's band.

My third great-grandfather, Isaac Morley, pioneer settler of Sanpete Valley, was the closest white friend of Chief Walker of the Sanpete Utes, as recounted in a former chapter.

My paternal grandfather, William Coleman Boren, who freighted flour and other goods to the Uintah-Ouray Indian Reservation, lived most of his life in the midst of the Ute People, for whom he had the greatest admiration and respect. He had many Indian friends: Happy Jack, Mountain Sheep, Provo John, Inepegut, Cumpanees, Dick Wanrodes, Tim Johnson, to name only a few.

In 1901, Will Boren leased the ranch of Robert Marimon on Whiterocks River, on the reservation. In October 1902, Marimon became post trader at the Whiterocks Agency. Will Boren and his family lived on the reservation among his Ute friends. He organized a group of Utes to accompany him to Proctor Academy in Provo, Utah, where the allotments were being held, and they protested the removal of the lands, to no avail. In utter disgust, Will Boren packed up his family and encouraged friends and relatives to organize a wagon company and leave the reservation in protest; they crossed the high Uintahs and settled on the north slope.

My father, Edward Boren, was born at Clifton, Garfield County, Utah Territory, on 9 November 1893. An identical twin, he and his brother Ezra were delivered into the world by an Indian midwife— in fact, by "Queen Victoria," former wife of William Potter. My father had an Indian girlfriend living in the little town of Hayden. She bore him a child—and so I have a half-breed, half-brother or half-sister whom I have never met, The sobriquet "Hayden" stuck with him the remainder of his life.

My late uncle, Roy Boren, sowed his wild oats in his teens by buying liquor from Bill Macginnis' Saloon (Bill Macginnis, a.k.a. Elza Lay) on "The Strip," a sort of No-Man's Land in the middle of the reservation, and bootlegging it to the Indians living at Whiterocks. Because he made these illicit journeys late at night, the Utes called him "Wobanee"— the Night Hawk.

My aunt Verly Boren married a Ute, Bill Reed, whose father had been one of the signers of the Rhoades-Hathenbruck lease. My Uncle Bill was heavy-set who wore, his hair in braids, and with a wonderful singing voice he was reluctant to use in public. Bill's aunt, Mary Reed, was married to Henry Harris, interpreter at Whiterocks Agency, who had assisted in the lease negotiations between Hathenbruck and the Indians in 1897. [For a history of the Reeds, see: *The Gold of Carre-Shinob*, op. cit. at Chapter Eighteen.]

As a boy of fourteen I became a blood-brother to a young Ute named Danny Colorow. Danny's grandfather, an old man of 94 in 1955, was a son of Ute Chief Colorow, and was himself named Colorow. From old Colorow I learned a great many things about the Ute people and their history. Most of all I learned from him the great respect and dignity that his people have for their heritage and traditions.

My family's association with the Ute tribe afforded me a personal insight into the Indian traditions pertaining to the Lost Rhoades Mines. Their accounts add a significant and new dimension to the story of the Ute gold.

### TABUACHE (WASH)

Tabuache, or Tab-Wash— best known as "Wash"— son of Nauhnan, grandson of Chief Tabiona (Tabby), and great-nephew of the great Chief Walker, was one of the tribal elders privy to the secret of the location of the Sacred Mine. True to his trust, he never revealed that secret to any unauthorized person during his lifetime; which is not to say that he did not mention other things of consequence in relation to the numerous other mines and caches throughout the Uintah Mountains.

Wash was in his late eighties when he first began showing me around the mountains. Some of his family claimed he was much older than he professed to be, a strong possibility, inasmuch as he was signer #112 on the Indian lease in 1897. In spite of his age, he was robust, remarkably agile and rugged, well-conditioned from a lifetime in the mountains. The only indication of his age was his wrinkled and character-etched face and slightly stooped shoulders. He got about aided by a walking stick that had been carved by his father, and his twin braids of hoary hair were worn above a print shirt with ever-present wide red suspenders.

Wash's mother died when he was very young; ironically, he could never remember her name. In his youth he lived with his step-mother, his father's widow, Chin-a-witz (called Helen Tecumseh), who was younger than himself, and helped raise his half-brother, Jason Tecumseh, who was deaf and dumb. Chin-a-witz remarried to John Yesto, and died 3 January 1925.

Wash took me to Rhoades Canyon and Rock Creek and showed me a number of things connected to a massacre site. He showed me Spanish symbols carved into the trees, two old rock kilns, and much more. And he told me the story.

Wash explained that when his grandfather, Tabby, was a young man, and Walker was Chief of the Sanpete Utes, the Quatz, or Mexicans, camped in the mountains one summer to mine gold near the headwaters of Rock Creek, and to process the ore into bars for transport by mule train back to Santa Fe. The year was about "two snows" before the Mormons came, i.e. about 1845.

The Utes had only just attacked and destroyed Fort Uintah (Fort Winty) in the Uintah Basin, and they were fired up with a desire to drive the infestation of intruders from their lands. The hated Quatz had chosen a bad time to steal the Ute's gold. A tremendous battle took place at the foot of Rhoades Canyon, where the Mexicans emerged from the mountains, their mules heavily laden with gold. According to Wash, there were about 15 Mexicans and 75 Utes. The Mexicans put up a valiant fight, having the advantage of armor and a 12-pound "grapeshot" cannon, but in the end the Mexican miners were killed to the last man.

Tabby led the assault and afterwards ordered that all traces of the massacre site be obliterated. The Utes dig a pit, drove the Mexican's wagon filled with ore over the hole, then removed the wheels and dropped the wagon into the pit. The bodies of the Mexicans were tossed into the pit and the whole thing covered with dirt. Another pit was dug nearby for the cannon. The Utes raced their horses back and forth across the flat to trample the ground, then set the trees and brush on fire.

The Mexicans had six gold bars in their possession. Tabby turned these over to squaws, who returned the bars to the mountain near the mine from whence the gold had come, and tossed them into a nearby lake.

When Wash was in the fire of his youth, he went into the mountains, to the lake, to attempt to retrieve some of the gold bars. He claimed that the bars had been thrown into the deep end of one of the three Brown Duck Lakes, just above Mirror Lake, which appears on the Caleb Rhoades' "Pine Tree" or "Pine Mine" map.

Wash described the lake as being deep at one end, where it abutted some high ledges, and shallow in the other end, where an outlet traversed a meadow. The deep end of the lake, where the gold bars were submerged, was accessible only during years of drought, because a glacier covered the deep end of the lake during a majority of years.

Wash was able to retrieve one of the gold bars by wading into the lake in chest-deep, icy cold water, and "fishing" with baling wire looped at the end of a ten-foot-long lodgepole. Wash then told a most unusual story. He said he was about to return to the water for another bar when he heard a strange sound emanating from beneath the ledges at the deepest part of the lake. Looking up, he saw a creature swimming toward him, an aquatic creature that resembled a dinosaur. Wash swore it was a spirit guardian of the sacred gold, and it so frightened him that he packed up his camp and hastily departed.

If Wash's incredible story was calculated to

scare away the curious, it did not diminish the truth of his discovery. He had the gold bar in his possession, and I have handled it. It was rectangular in shape, stamped with a Spanish cross, and weighed 84 pounds! According to wash there were a total of six bars, all identical in size and weight, and so each weighed 84 pounds. A single bar, at today's value, would net over half a million dollars!

I also went with Wash to the site of the 1920 gunfight, near Scout Lake in Grandaddy Basin. He told me an interesting account of the battle. The old Ute showed me a trail made in the slide-rock by small stones being piled between large ones, to prevent horses from breaking their legs. The trail had been made by the men of the 1920 expedition. I asked him how he knew. He revealed that he had been one of a band of Utes who had followed the white men, watching them at a distance. He had witnessed the gunfight. After the battle, the Utes took the bodies of the dead white men and covered them with sliderock near the trail. To prove his story, Wash produced the skull of one of the dead gunmen. Above the left eye was a bullet hole, and the back of the skull, where the bullet emerged, had been blown away.

## WAUBIN Q. WANZITZ

Waubin Q. Wanzitz was one of the most interesting characters the reservation ever produced. He knew a great deal about the Ute gold and he was a walking encyclopedia of Ute tribal history.

Wuabin was born in Rock Creek prior to the turn of the last century. His father Wanzitz had been signer #31 on the Rhoades-Hathenbruck Indian lease in 1897. His mother, Elena Trujillo, who was part Mexican, died in childbirth when he was born. Through his mother, Waubin was my relation by marriage. Elena's nephew, Joseph Trujillo, married my aunt Mary Boren. Joe

Trujillo, a descendant of the Mexican miners who once worked the mines during the 19th century, was accidentally killed when his rifle discharged while climbing through a wire fence.

When Waubin was born, his father Wanzitz disowned him, accusing him of being possessed by evil spirits and being the cause of the death of his mother. Wanzitz farmed him out to be raised by old Chief Wanrodes ("Wonrodes", signer #2 of the Rhoades-Hathenbruck lease) whom Waubin called "an ornery old bastard." In fact, Wanrodes was also related, for Waubin's grandmother had been a member of the Wanrodes family.

Until he was eighteen, Waubin was shipped from one school to another, more or less to keep him out of the way. He managed to obtain a good education, even having attended the prestigious Carlisle Indian School in Pennsylvania for a time. When he returned home to Rock Creek at eighteen, he found his father living in one of three cabins belonging to Chief Wanrodes. Waubin had helped to build these cabins because, according to Indian custom, the Wanzitz cabin had been burned following the death of his mother.

But his father still refused to live with him, so Waubin moved in with old Chief Wanrodes. Wanrodes was in old age and had lost most of his eyesight. He spent most of his time propped up on blankets in a corner of his cabin, chanting for hours at a time. He depended on members of his family to look after him and feed him. Even so, said Waubin, the "ornery old bastard" was ungrateful and critical of everything done for him.

On one occasion, the family brought freshly killed rabbits to Waubin and told him to clean them so they could be cooked for the old chieftain. Waubin retrieved a knife and began skinning the rabbits, when he encountered a lump in the throat of one of the dead animals. He cut the lump open and discovered it full of maggots.

Waubin's education had taught him that the

rabbits were diseased, and dozens of Indians had died that summer due to "rabbit fever." Realizing that the rabbits were not safe to eat, he buried them in a hole below a spring, south of the cabin, together with the knife, and piled logs and brush on top and set it afire to kill the germs. The family came storming down on him, saying that now they would have to go hungry and the old chief would starve. He tried to explain the danger to them, but they wouldn't hear it. "They were mad at me," Waubin told me, "and nothing I could say would change their mind. I tried to explain about the disease, but they only thought I was possessed by evil spirits, like my father told them, and it made things worse. I should have first let them eat the damn things, but if I had they all would have died."

Two or three days later, Waubin became ill. He suffered from fever and vomiting and was too weak to stand. Within a week, he lost his eyesight. He realized that he had probably rubbed his eyes after handling the infected rabbits. The family wouldn't help him, other than to string a line from the cabin to the outhouse so he could find his way. He learned to follow the fence line to find the spring for water. The only one who helped him out was Dick Wanrodes, the old Chief's son, with whom Waubin was raised. They were as close as brothers. Waubin overheard his father talking to Dick Wanrodes at night, when they thought he was asleep.

"My dad said I was a big burden to them now, just another mouth to feed," Waubin recalled. "He said that the rabbit thing and my blindness was punishment for killing my mother. Dick knew better than to believe them superstitious old Indians and he felt sorry for me, and helped me out a lot. Then one day, after about six months, I woke up one morning and could see light. I ran outside and the first thing I seen was the sun coming up over the moun-tain. Oh God, what a beautiful sight! I was so happy to be able to see again, I fell down on the ground and said, 'praise, praise, praise'. I never was so happy in my life. All the folks come running out to see what all the commotion was about. Sadie and Dick had big happy smiles on their faces. Then my dad come out. There was no expression on his face at all. He just grunted. I think he must have thought mebbe my punishment was over for killing my mother when I got my eyesight back. But he never said."

Dick Wanrodes was older than Waubin. Waubin called him uncle, and Dick's boy, simply called Wanrodes, who was nearer Waubin's age, he referred to as cousin. But Indian relationships are complex and some-times difficult to understand. For example, Waubin always referred to me as "Ed's boy," and called me his cousin, and my father, Edward Boren, he called "grandfather," even though they were near the same age. Sadie was Dick's wife.

Waubin and Dick's boy, Wanrodes, were very close. My father, who grew up on the reser-vation, spent a lot of time with them. It was during this time that Waubin first saw the gold bars. Waubin tells the story:

"The same year that I got my eyesight back, I was so happy that I could see I went all over the place, just enjoying everything I seen. Dick and my cousin Dick's boy took me everywhere with them that year. They was happy for me that I could see again and Dick said I should see everything. That's when he showed me the boxes with gold bars.

"Me, Dick, and my cousin Dick's boy was up high on Rock Creek when we got caught in a hell of a snowstorm. It was early in the year and we didn't expect it. We headed down to where we lived [on lower Rock Creek] when it was blowing stinging cold. Dick pointed off east and said, 'Come on, right now.' so we followed him.

"Couldn't see much because of the snow, but

just a little bit north of some tall sagebrush, tall as a man, Dick pointed at a hole under this ledge and said, 'Come on in.' Inside he showed us some dirt and rock and he said, 'Dig a little bit here. Many boxes, gold bars. Take some and cover rest back up. Are only a little. Never have to worry. Don't forget where it is.' Dick said this was not the mine, but another place. The mine was a little way off, he said, where there was some trees."

Waubin's cousin Wanrodes went off to serve his country in the First World War. Waubin received a letter from him when he was in France. In the letter he asked, "Did you ever look at those boxes that grandpa told us about?" My father, Edward Boren, served with Wanrodes in the Argonne-Meuse campaign in France. My father was wounded; Wanrodes was killed. "I sure missed him," Waubin told me. "We was close. I had to go with him back up the mountain to look at those boxes, but because my cousin didn't come home, I forgot about it for a long time."

Waubin claimed to have an unusual power, and it all began with the gold mine, before he was shown the gold bars. Dick Wanrodes had often spoken with him about a particularly rich mine without ever describing it or telling him were it was. Also, many of the older Indians used to come by to see old Chief Wanrodes–Mountain Sheep, Shotnick, Unca Sam, Redcap, and others– and Waubin often heard them talk about the gold. "I remember one old lady," Waubin told me, "who used to come over all the way from Whiterocks to talk to Chief Wanrodes about the gold. I never did learn what she had to do with it, but she sure did know a lot. I heard them talk about something buried down near the old fort there at the mouth of Rock Creek, some-where on the west side of the creek. There used to be an old fort there, built by the cavalry, but it's all gone now, unless you know where to look. They used to talk real quiet-like, in whispers, but

sometimes I heard them."

One day, Waubin said, he had been out on the mountain all day and did not return home until late in the evening. He liked to walk more often than ride, so when he arrived home after walking all day, he was exhausted. He plopped down on his four-poster bed and, too tired to even lie down, he just rested his head over the edge of the bed-rail.

"I could feel my spirit leave my body out of the back of my head," Waubin related. "It was the strangest thing I ever experienced, and at first it scared the hell out of me. I looked back at my body hanging there over the edge of the bed, just as clear as anything. My spirit floated away, out of the cabin and up the mountain and in an instant I was there. I could see the mine Dick told me about, and after I looked it over, my spirit floated back down the mountain and entered my body and it revived instantly, like I had been shocked.

"I didn't talk about what happened for a long time. Everybody thought I was kinda crazy anyway. Then I decided to tell Dick about it. I went up to him and said, 'You know that mine you told me about?' 'Yeah,' he said. I described it to him, where it was, what it looked like, and the trees and all. He said, 'Who took you there?' I said nobody, I went there myself. I told him what happened and he just started shaking and run out of the cabin and he wouldn't even come near me for weeks. He never said, but I think he thought that I had evil powers, like my dad always said. I think he got to thinking about it, though, 'cause it wasn't long after that he showed me the boxes of gold bars...

"I was kinda scared of this spirit thing, until I heard that this old Indian over near Ouray had this same kinda power. His name was Colorow. I told him what happened and he just smiled and didn't say nothing. Finally we had quiet talk and he said to me to go home and find a quiet place and think. Don't worry, he told me. Just think and be quiet. I was alone then 'cause the folks had all died—Dick was gone, and Dick's son died in the war, and finally Sadie died, too, so I had a lot of time to think. I began to find all kinds of things after that. I would just sit there and think and then it would come to me. I would go look and then I would find things. That's how I found them other boxes of gold—not the same ones Dick showed me, but some other.

"I never went back to the place Dick showed me until after Dick died. Then I went up there and looked around that old massacre place, and I found this old Cavalry belt buckle. I carried it around for a long time and then somebody walked away with it. I think I know who took it.

"I always had to be careful 'cause there was always somebody watching up there. Old Sheep [Mountain Sheep] was always somewhere around. His log cabin where he lived was right under that round hill where you go down on the west side, and he kept a camp just over the hill to the east and a little south of Sheep Pass. He lived there just to keep people away from the mines. He was a mean old bastard and would just as soon kill an Indian as a white man. I was scared of him and always watched out for him.

"Old Sheep had this log cabin and a little corral next to it. Whenever he went up to check on the mines, he used to bring sacks of gold nuggets and maybe gold bars back with him and bury them in caches all around his corral. There's not much left there anymore, but if you know where it was, you might find something."

# Chapter 23

## THE WAUBIN WANZITZ STORY

[Waubin Q. Wanzitz was an old Ute Indian who was willing
to tell what he knew about the sacred Ute gold. The
following chapter is a continuation of his story.]

"One time this white man named Draper come down to the cabin and asked me to take him up and show him where the boxes were. I don't know how he knew about them, but he did. He looked for the mines all the time. I told him I didn't know where the boxes were, just the area, but he didn't believe me. He just kept coming back and asked me to take him up there, so finally I did. I was tired of being bothered by him.

"We went up. That was in the thirties. I took him to one place and say, 'Maybe it's here.' He would dig some and then I would show him other place and say, 'Maybe it's here.' He would dig some more, and when he got all disgusted, I would take him other place and say, 'Maybe it's here.' After a long time he got really disgusted and so I took him to the right place and he was standing right on top of the damn things and I say, 'Maybe it's here.' He said to me, 'What you think you're doing here? They're not over here. I think they are over by that place where they killed the Mexicans. You take me over there.'

"I took him over there and he dug a lot of holes. I looked around and found a piece of a helmet— that part which they pull down over their face. Draper hollered at me to come up and he showed me this brass compass he found in the hole. It still had the glass in it and some writing on it. I think it was French. It wasn't Spanish, [Waubin spoke fluent Spanish.] I reached to take it out of his hand to look at it and he jerked it back, like I was going to steal it or something. Made me mad. 'I'm getting outta here,' I said. I started down the mountain and he followed me, but I wouldn't talk to him more, he just went away. He didn't bother me anymore. He finally realized that I wasn't going to show him anything."

There was a large rock below Waubin's cabin that had a map carved into it. He had often studied it and wondered what it meant. Then one day he was walking in the sage and cedars just above the old trail that came down from Mountain Sheep Pass ("The old trail, not the one people use today") and found some unusual rocks. They had been placed in a line going up the hill to the east, about a foot or a foot and a half apart.

Waubin began following the rocks which went up the hill, "made quite a few jogs," then turned toward the north. He had an old paper sack and a pencil so he began marking the route of the rocks on paper.

"I kept following them and they came down from the vicinity of the massacre in a line and went west from there. They went down to the creek, then turned south. I followed them until I came back to the some spot where I started at the hill. Right away I saw that the drawing on the paper was the same as the map on the rock below my cabin.

"Old Sheep had been watching me and all of a sudden he come up on me and wanted to know what I was doing with the sack and the pencil. I told him I was just drawing pictures, but I know he didn't believe me 'cause he sat up on the ridge and watched me all day. He never bothered me but he sure did watch...

"Many times I just sit up on the hill and meditate. One day the wind was blowing hard and I went on the south side of the hill and sit in some cedars. I sit there maybe three hours and got thirsty. There was this little old lone tree by a spring down the hill, so I went down and got a drink. I walked north maybe 100 feet and stopped. I looked at the ground. I thought something just had to be buried there. I didn't have nothing to dig with so I pictured the place in my mind and went home.

"I just kept thinking about the place so finally I decided to go back up there. I took this old pick and started dragging it through the sand and rocks on this small flat place and right away CLUNK! I hit something. I dug down eight to ten inches and uncovered this little iron box. I opened it up and there was these gold bars in there. Heavy, heavy, heavy. I was excited, I'll tell you. I drug the pick through the sand some more and there was more clunks, maybe ten or twelve more boxes. But before I could dig them up I had this feeling I was being watched and I got kinda scared. I covered them back up and spread the sand out with my hand to hide everything. Then I walked up to the trees on the hill and just sat there for about an hour and then went down to my place.

"After that I was down on Sadie's Flat looking at the picture on the rock below my place, across the creek. BAM! There was this shot and a bullet whistled past my head and hit the rock. Missed me only by about two feet. You can still see the place on the rock where it hit. I laid right down behind the rock and hid. Pretty soon I heard the clickety-clack of horse's hooves going down the creek out of view.

"Another time I was up on the knoll where the bridge crosses just looking around and BANG! BANG! Two shots hit the dirt right by me. I ran into the cedars and hid. Same thing — clickety clack, clickety clack, somebody riding down the creek hiding their tracks. I know who it was. It was old Shotnick. Trying to scare me off. I never seen him, but I knew it was him.

"A lot of them old Indians was like that. They didn't trust me much, you see. I had been away to school. Just got out of high school in 25 [1925] and come home to see my folks. I came to my uncle's place on Rock Creek. I was a

Indian but I never lived with the Indians before in my life. I asked too many questions and I always disobeyed their laws. I was stubborn too, like my uncle [Dick Wanrodes]. I found them boxes in maybe 28 or 29. A lot of the old Indians was still around then.

"Old Happy Jack was one you had to watch out for. He was a sly one. He always wore his hair in braids and he could speak real good English, but he pretended he couldn't. He graduated from the Colorado School of Mines. I never had any training in geology. Always wanted to. Happy Jack did though.

"One day I was up the creek from my place, over on the east side. I was kneeling down looking at something—I don't remember what— when this rock, about the size of a tin plate, come flying right by my head and landed in the bushes. It scared the hell out of me. I fell down on the ground and listened. Pretty soon I heard a twig snap up above and I jump up and run up there quick. There was old Jack just standing there grinning from ear to ear. He didn't say nothing. Just looked at me and grinned. I was madder than hell and I yelled at him, 'If you ever do anything like that again you'll have a fight on your damn hands.' He just kept on smiling, then turns around and walks to his horse and rode away. All them old boys was trying to scare me off, but it didn't work. But I was more careful after that I can tell you.

"What it did was make me think more about them boxes and getting some of those bars. I decided to go up and bring some of them down. I waited until one night when there was a full moon. I went up past the big hill. On top is where Old Wanrodes is buried. Below him is where my dad is buried and right below him is Dick. Up above there, right at the Stillwaters, this big spring comes out. It's a big spring. It's green and the water is good. There's fish in there. Salmon and trout. It's kind of a funny spring. Up there is the boxes.

"I dug up three of those boxes and took the bars out. I couldn't carry them in the boxes so I buried them again. The boxes was too heavy. I carried the bars down one and two at a time until I got ten bars down. I went straight down the creek and buried them on the west side under some big rocks. The next night I went back up and uncovered them and started taking them down to my place. But next morning I thought to myself, hell, I can't keep them here, so I took them over to this wash and buried them.

"They was really heavy those bars and yellow with markings on them. I just threw them in the sand and they sunk right down. That's where I used to keep my wine bottles to keep them cool. It's right off the old trail that comes down off the top where the Indians used to come over from the east to visit old Wanrodes. Those bars was hid in there for a long time when I thought I would go get one and maybe sell it or something. I dug all around where I thought I hid them but I couldn't find them. Maybe I forgot the right place. Maybe somebody found them, but I don't think so. I think they are still there. Now I am too old and crippled up to go back. Maybe I will go back there when I die. I want to be buried there next to Dick. Not next to my father, though...

"The boxes that Dick showed me... he said there must be hundreds of them, but he didn't how many. These was north of where I found my boxes. Dick used to go up there first thing every spring and a couple times during the summer to check on those places. There are three places pretty close together, all in a line, about a fourth of a mile apart, maybe a little more. That one place they was just an inch or two under the surface and he would go up and kick dirt over the lids. They had just been tossed in there, not flat or stacked or anything like that. Some have corners that stick up out of the dirt. It looked like they was in a hurry to hide them.

"There is stuff buried all over up there. That's where the Indians buried the Mexicans after they massacred them. They dug a pit about six feet deep and eight feet around and just threw them in there. That's right close to the massacre site, but south of where the boxes are. I don't think they buried anything else in that area. Only dead Mexicans. Now them boxes is north of that place. About an eighth of a mile north of the massacre site in a grove of aspen trees. A circle grove. Then you cross this flat place where the tall sagebrush are and come to some cottonwood trees. Just north of there is the spring that comes out. Did I tell you there was fish in there?"

* * *

Waubin Q. Wanzitz had lived an interesting life. In the late 1940's he left the reservation and did not return for thirty years. In the interim he worked on railroads on Arizona and New Mexico and lumber camps in Washington; he traveled overseas and played several bit parts in western movies in Hollywood. But by the late seventies he was a homeless drunk on the mean streets of Los Angeles, a story all too common among displaced Native Americans.

By 1979, Waubin swallowed his pride and returned to the reservation. His health was declining rapidly and he felt the need to be among friends. I first met him when he was staying at the home of his good friend Marshall Colorow of Gusher, Utah. The Colorows were my friends too; I was a blood brother of one of the Colorow family. It bought me instant acceptance by Waubin. Because he knew my father, he considered me to be his "cousin."

Frances Ankerpont was not his true sister, either, but he considered her as such, in the Indian way of relationships. Frances had married one of Waubin's cousins. She worked for the U.B.I.C. and he went to live with her briefly in the little town of Myton while she tried to find some help for him. She eventually placed him in the University Hospital at Salt Lake City to get him medical attention, then found a place for him in the Bonneville Care Center. I interviewed him there several times. The following are paraphrased excerpts from those interviews:

KRB: What does the "Q" stand for in your name?

WQW: It don't really stand for nothing. When I was a boy, my dad called me "Quatz" — that's what The Utes call Mexicans. That's because my mother's people was Mexicans. I didn't like it, so I changed it after I left home. Now I tell people it means "Quentin." Some people still call me that.

KRB: Why did you leave the reservation?

WQW: Oh, there was lots of reasons. Mostly I just didn't belong there anymore. My dad had pretty much convinced all the old superstitious Indians that I was full of evil spirits. I was away at different schools until I was eighteen, and when I came back to Rock Creek in 25 hardly nobody remembered me, except for Dick and a few others. Then my cousin, Dick's boy, was killed in the war. We was real close. Pretty soon old Wanrodes, who I lived with, died, and I lived with Dick and Sadie until Dick was gone. When Dick died the place was supposed to go to me, but Sadie claimed it and that left me out in the cold. I went to the council and complained about it, but they wouldn't do nothing. There was Unca Sam, and Mountain, and old Redcap—until he had to leave the reservation for killing white men—they had all been friends of my father. Happy Jack and Mountain Sheep and old Shotnick didn't like me 'cause I looked for the boxes, so they all voted me out. I was mad as hell. I left Rock Creek and went down to Tabiona. I had an allotment coming and I had my eye on a real nice green piece of land there, about 40 acres I think it was, but the council turned me down cold. They said it was

because I was part Mexican. I told myself to hell with it and just left the country.

KRB: How old are you? You said you were 18 when you came home from school in 1925. That means you were born in 1907. But earlier you told me you used to watch the greyhound dog races in 1907 or 1908 when you were a young boy. You also said you were about the same age as Dick's boy, who died in the war. He was close to my father's age, and my father was born in 1893.

WQW: Hell, I don't know! Indians don't keep track of them things like white people do. I must be older than I thought. Hell, sakes, wouldn't that be something?

KRB: Do you remember Caleb Rhoades or F.W.C. Hathenbruck?

WQW: I remember the Doctor. Caleb Rhoades he died before I knew him, but my dad and all the older Indians used to talk about him all the time. They called him Long Whiskers.

KRB: What do you remember about the Doctor?

WQW: I remember seeing him when I was a boy. He spent a lot of time on the reservation trying to get all the Indians to sign papers so he could work the old mine. He only had one arm, you know. Don't remember which one. Then I went away to school and didn't see him again. I think he died before I came home.

KRB: What did the Indians think of him?

WQW: Oh, all the Indians thought he was a good man— for a white man. He never broke his word and he helped the Indians all the time. I remember my dad telling about one real bad winter when a lot of the Utes were sick and starving, the Doctor sent this whole wagon load of groceries and blankets out to the reservation from Provo. He was always doing stuff like that. That's why they liked him.

KRB: Were there any Indians who didn't like the Doctor?

WQW: Oh, yeah. There was a couple I think. Sometimes the whites would pay some of the Indians to make trouble for him. I remember that old Shotnick refused to sign the Indian lease. The Doctor sent him some presents and things but he was stubborn and still wouldn't sign. Chief Tabby was sick and so he sent old Wanrodes down to talk to Shotnick. Tabby was the main chief, but Wanrodes was another chief, not so big as Tabby. Wanrodes tried to talk Shotnick into signing the paper, but Shotnick was a stubborn old bastard and wouldn't do it. He hated all white men. Didn't matter who they was. I have heard my dad say that while all the other Indians were busy signing papers, old Shotnick sat on his

horse on a big knoll not far off and chanted. I had a few run-ins with old Shotnick. He was about as mean and ornery as old Sheep [Mountain Sheep].

KRB: How many boxes of gold bars do you think are buried up on Rock Creek?

WQW: Well's there was three places that I knew about. The place that Dick showed me, he said there was hundreds of boxes buried there. He took care of them, so he knew what he was talking about. Then there was two other places. One place had maybe 70 or 90 boxes and the last place had maybe 40 or 60. Them's only the places I knew about. There could be lots more. Probably is.

KRB: Do you know where the Rhoades Mine is located?

WQW: [Enigmatic grin] Even if I did know that, you don't think I would tell you, do you? After all, I'm still an Indian.

## *ANCESTRY OF F.W.C. HATHENBRUCK*

Count Heinrich = Machteld of Guelders
"the Rich" of Nassau
(1180-1250)

Otto I (+1289)

Engelbert I = Johanna van Polanen
(1370-1442)

Heinrich II

(1482)
Johann V = Elizabeth of Hesse
Count of Nassau        (1466 - 1523)
(1455 - 1516)

(1531)
William I = (2) Juliana of Stolberg-Wenigerode
"the Rich," Count of Nassau,        widow of Philip II of Hanau-Munzenberg
Vianden & Dietz        (1506 - 1580)
(1489 - 1555)

Gaspard de Coligny

(1583)
William I = (4) Louise de Coligny
"the Silent" William of Orange"        Widow of Charles de Téligny
(1533 - 1584)        (1555 - 1620)

Amelia of Selms-Braunfels = Frederick Henry
(1602 - 1675)        of Orange-Nassau
Prince of Orange
(1584 - 1647)

(1625)
Louise Henriette = Frederick William
(1627 - 1667)        Great Elector of Brandenburg
(1620 - 1688)

THE UTAH GOLD RUSH

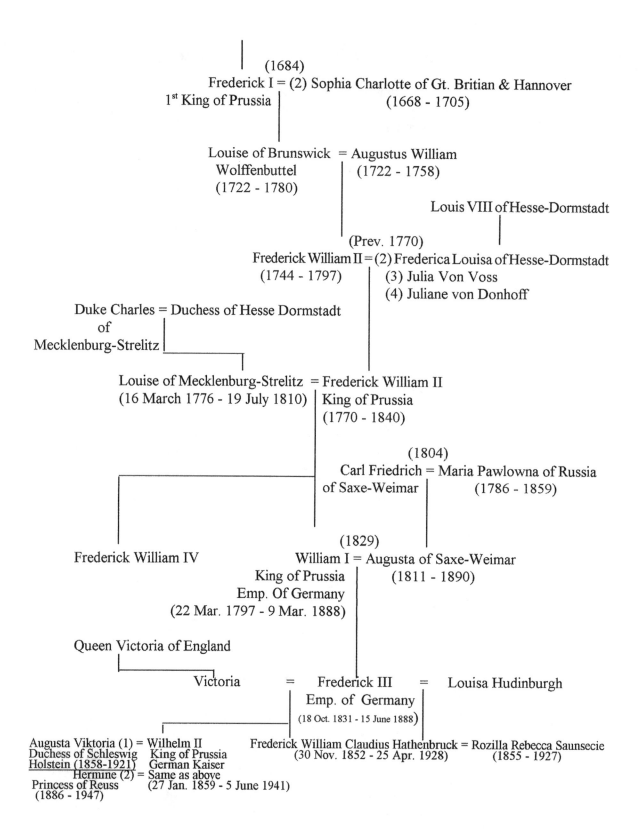

(1684)
Frederick I = (2) Sophia Charlotte of Gt. Britian & Hannover
1ˢᵗ King of Prussia          (1668 - 1705)

Louise of Brunswick = Augustus William
Wolffenbuttel          (1722 - 1758)
(1722 - 1780)

Louis VIII of Hesse-Dormstadt

(Prev. 1770)
Frederick William II = (2) Frederica Louisa of Hesse-Dormstadt
(1744 - 1797)          (3) Julia Von Voss
                       (4) Juliane von Donhoff

Duke Charles = Duchess of Hesse Dormstadt
of
Mecklenburg-Strelitz

Louise of Mecklenburg-Strelitz = Frederick William II
(16 March 1776 - 19 July 1810)   King of Prussia
                                 (1770 - 1840)

(1804)
Carl Friedrich = Maria Pawlowna of Russia
of Saxe-Weimar          (1786 - 1859)

(1829)
Frederick William IV          William I = Augusta of Saxe-Weimar
                              King of Prussia    (1811 - 1890)
                              Emp. Of Germany
                              (22 Mar. 1797 - 9 Mar. 1888)

Queen Victoria of England

Victoria          =          Frederick III          =          Louisa Hudinburgh
                              Emp. of Germany
                              (18 Oct. 1831 - 15 June 1888)

Augusta Viktoria (1) = Wilhelm II          Frederick William Claudius Hathenbruck = Rozilla Rebecca Saunsecie
Duchess of Schleswig   King of Prussia          (30 Nov. 1852 - 25 Apr. 1928)          (1855 - 1927)
Holstein (1858-1921)   German Kaiser
Hermine (2) = Same as above
Princess of Reuss   (27 Jan. 1859 - 5 June 1941)
(1886 - 1947)

## ANCESTRY OF ROZILLA REBECCA SAUNSECIE HATHENBRUCK

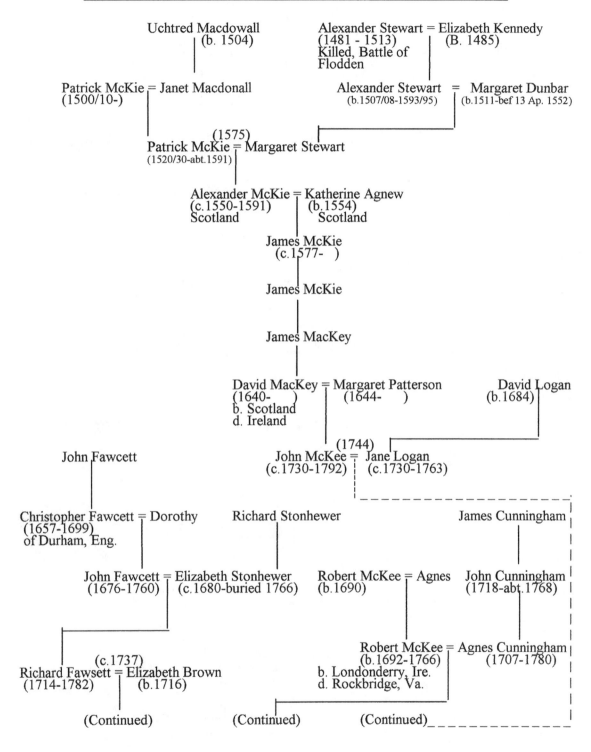

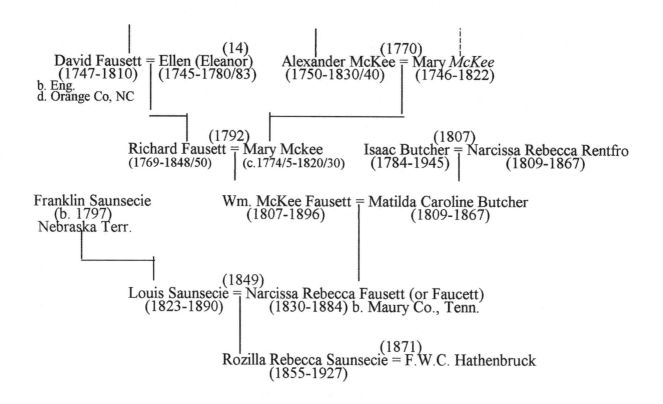

David Fausett = Ellen (Eleanor)    (14)    Alexander McKee = Mary *McKee*
(1747-1810)      (1745-1780/83)            (1750-1830/40)    (1746-1822)
b. Eng.
d. Orange Co, NC

Richard Fausett = Mary Mckee    (1792)    Isaac Butcher = Narcissa Rebecca Rentfro    (1807)
(1769-1848/50)    (c.1774/5-1820/30)      (1784-1945)      (1809-1867)

Franklin Saunsecie    Wm. McKee Fausett = Matilda Caroline Butcher
(b. 1797)              (1807-1896)          (1809-1867)
Nebraska Terr.

Louis Saunsecie = Narcissa Rebecca Fausett (or Faucett)    (1849)
(1823-1890)      (1830-1884) b. Maury Co., Tenn.

Rozilla Rebecca Saunsecie = F.W.C. Hathenbruck    (1871)
(1855-1927)

## *RANDY LEWIS DESCENT FROM F.W.C. HATHENBRUCK*

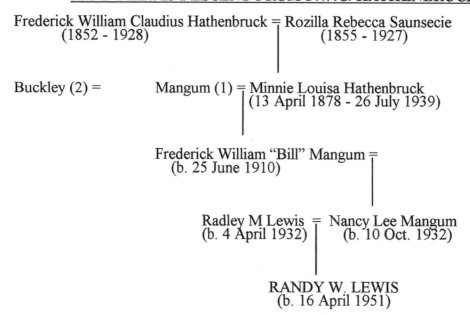

Frederick William Claudius Hathenbruck = Rozilla Rebecca Saunsecie
(1852 - 1928)                             (1855 - 1927)

Buckley (2) =    Mangum (1) = Minnie Louisa Hathenbruck
                            (13 April 1878 - 26 July 1939)

Frederick William "Bill" Mangum =
(b. 25 June 1910)

Radley M Lewis = Nancy Lee Mangum
(b. 4 April 1932)   (b. 10 Oct. 1932)

RANDY W. LEWIS
(b. 16 April 1951)

*A FINAL NOTE*

*THE VALLEY OF GOD*

I am not going to reveal the true name of the Valley of God. It could be a sacred Indian valley. Hathenbruck spoke of the valley with its ancient burial ground and he said that the rich mine is nearby.

I am convinced that the Great Spirit dwells in this Valley. On several occasions I have experienced things there that few people will believe. It usually begins with a bright light, so bright you cannot open your eyes, except to squint, then follows a very peaceful feeling with a calmness beyond description.

The first time this happened I got off my horse to straighten out my legs beneath some quaking aspen. I noticed two small birds sitting in a bush nearby, totally unafraid of me. I reached down and placed my finger in front of one of the birds and it jumped upon my finger. I gently petted its head and returned it to the bush. I thought perhaps it might have been sick, but as I climbed back on my horse and glanced over my shoulder as I rode off, I saw the birds fly away.

Riding farther on I came to a meadow where a huge Bull Elk—a monster, a good six pointer—lay with his antlers spread way back over his butt. I rode toward him to see how close I could approach before I scared the elk away, but as I rode closer and closer, I was surprised to discover that the Bull didn't move. When I was within 20 feet of the Bull I suddenly realized the danger I was in. The Bull could jump up and attack my horse and we would both be history. Yet I noticed that my horse showed no fear and though I was tense I urged him forward to within ten feet of the Bull, which simply laid there looking at me. I left him in peace.

On another occasion I was setting up camp, occupied in laying out the tent, when I looked up to see a young two point buck standing and watching me from about 50 yards away. I continued to set up the tent and when next I looked up the deer was closer by 30 yards.

I was delighted by the attention and so decided to play a little game with him. I went over to the nearest pine tree and hid behind it. The deer circled around to where he could see me. We played this game of hide-and-seek for about half an hour, until the deer had approached to within ten feet of me. I believe I could have reached out and petted him, he was that tame.

I have since thought to myself, was it the animals that were tame, or was it something about the Valley of God?

You decide...

Randy W. Lewis

# APPENDIX A

## LETTERS

### THURMAN TO RAWLINS

*Provo, Utah, Feb. 26th, 1897*
*Hon. J.L. Rawlins, U.S. Senator*
*Washington, D.C.*

*My Dear Sir:*

*I am informed that it is probable that a commission will be appointed to treat with the Indians of the Uncompahgre and Uintah Reservations respecting the lands now occupied by them, and should such commission be appointed and you have any opportunity to suggest the names of persons for said commission, I take pleasure in recommending the name of F. W.C. Hathenbruck, of Provo, as a fit and proper person for said commission.*

*Mr. Hathenbruck is and has been an ardent supporter of yours and was in sympathy with your friends in your election to the Senate, and did what he could to influence members of the Legislature in your favor in the Senatorial contest. Mr. Hathenbruck is peculiarly fitted for that position, as he is a man thoroughly acquainted with the Indians on said Reservations, has always dealt fairly and honestly with them, and has great influence with the Chiefs especially. I have no hesitancy in recommending him to you for this position, and trust you may find it convenient if opportunity is presented, to do what you can to secure his appointment.*

*Yours truly*
*L.R. THURMAN*

### DUSENBERRY TO RAWLINS

*Vernal, Utah, Feb. 27th, 1897*
*Hon. J.L. Rawlins, U.S. Senate*
*Washington, D.C.*

*Dear Sir:*

*On coming into this country some two weeks ago to hold court, I found my old townsman and friend, F.W.C. Hathenbruck here operating in business matters which brought him prominently in company with representative Indian Chief of both the Uintah and Umcompahgre Indian Reservations; and found that his course heretofore have won their as well as the white settlers' confidence.*

*Learning that a commission is likely to be appointed to treat with the Indians of said tribes as to setting apart their lands, I freely and earnestly recommend Mr. Hathenbruck for appointment as one of said commission.*

*I have known Mr. Hathenbruck for more than twenty five years, much of the time connected with him in public affairs that to me tested his ability, honesty and integrity, hence I take pleasure in urging his appointment as one of such commission, believing that the rights of the Indians and the welfare of the Government will ever be maintained by him.*

*Very truly yours,*
*WARREN N. DUSENBERRY*

## BECK TO HATHENBRUCK AND RHOADES

*White Rocks, Utah, August 12, 1897*
*Messers Hathenbruck and Rhoades*
*Vernal, Utah.*

*Gentlemen:*

*I am in receipt of your letter of the 9th instant in which you desire me to set a date upon which to discuss a proposition to be made by you, of considerable importance to the Government, the Indians and the state of Utah.*

*I will be at my office at White Rocks on Monday the 16th instant, and unless something occurs, now unforeseen, also on Tuesday the 17th instant.*

*I will be glad to give your representative all the attention necessary to the full understanding of the proposition which you may have to make.*

*Very respectfully,*
*Win. H. BECK*
*Captain U.S. Army*
*Acting U.S. Indian Agent.*

*White Rocks, Utah, Sept. 14, 1897*
*Messers Hathenbruck and Rhoades*
*Fort Duchesne, Utah.*

*Gentlemen:*

*Your letter of yesterday is received.*

*There is no change in my position in regard to the lease you have consulted with me about making. It is necessary as I have said for you to have the consent of the Indians. The consent to be in open council.*

*There will have to be a carefully drawn lease in somewhat different form than that which you have presented.*

*At any time which you may set for the Indians to meet to vote upon the consent, I will call them together and ascertain if they are in favor of it. Referring to that part of your letter which speaks of Major Peabody I will remark that I never spoke to him upon the subject of your mine at all, until you had seen him at the post prior to his arrival here. I had intended talking to him on the subject; but it was not necessary to introduce it, as he was aware of it when he reached me and spoke to me of your interview. I thought that he might assist you, which he now seems unable to do. I will add that he came here on an entirely different matter.*

*I wish to say that I will be glad to see you at any time, upon this matter, but cannot promise to carry the lease to a successful issue for the reason that I am not at all certain that the Department will approve any mineral lease at this time.*

*As I told you, that if a good income could be obtained for the Indians for such a lease, I would be happy to assist you to get it, as I think it is a good thing for them to receive money benefit from their lands. However I have not time to write further upon the subject as I am very busily engaged in other matters.*

*Very respectfully,*
*Wm. H. BECK*
*Captain U.S. Army*
*Acting Indian Agent.*

## WIGHT TO HATHENBRUCK

*Salt Lake City, Utah, Dec. 15th, 1897*
*F.W.C. Hathenbruck Esq.*
*Fort Duchesne, Utah*

*Dear Sir:*

*I enclose you herewith clipping from the Herald of the 13th inst saying that no lease would be approved on the Uintah Reservation. Is this the account that you predicted would appear in the Tribune? I have seen nothing about it in the Tribune.*

*I also enclose you clipping from the Tribune giving an account of King's bucolic about introducing a bill to open the Uintah etc. which very likely will not cut any figure as regards the lease.*

*I have been unable to learn anything more about the Indian Police I wrote you about on the 13th inst.*

*Hoping to hear from you soon. I remain,*
Respectfully Yours, L.O. WIGHT
Ebbitt House

## BECK TO HATHENBRUCK

*White Rocks, Utah, January 2nd, 1898.*
*Mr. F.W.C. Hathenbruck*
*Provo, Utah*

*My dear Hathenbruck:*

*Your telegram received. I cannot make it out exactly; but what I can I do not understand.*

*I sent you a telegram to Provo some days ago, but received no reply. I told you that your signature was required & to wait until you received leases.*

*I sent you the leases for your signature etc. on Friday morning mail, the 30th, under Cover to the Price Trading Co., with a letter containing full instructions. You should have the leases*

*and etc. today at the farthest.*

*I would be well for you to join forces with my friends at Washington and have my order revoked, as no doubt the leases will come back here for remarks upon some points and if Capt. Cornish is here, he may look at matters differently, as the parties of whom you have some knowledge, are, I understand very courteous to him and he may be mis-led. Cavanaugh had better get to work and I am afraid that he has not been at Washington yet, certainly not very long or I would have heard from his as I have written to him several letters and telegraphed him.*

*See Senators Cannon & Rollins (Rawlins) or have someone else do so, of influence, and have them express themselves as to their desire to have Senator Thurston control appointments in Utah.*

*Let me hear from you at once about the receipt of the leases—by telegraph.*

*With the best wishes of the Season, I am,*
Sincerely Yours,
Wm. H. BECK

## TELEGRAM: BECK TO HATHENBRUCK

*White Rocks, Utah, Jan. 4th/98.*
*F.W.C. Hathenbruck*
*Provo, Utah.*

*Mrs. Bryon (Beck) had better go to Windsor (Washington). Can you arrange Dogma (money)?*

*It will be to advantage of Hugo (Hathenbruck) and Largess (Lease) and will be great help to Cato (Cavanaugh).*

*Imitate Answer.*

Wm. H. Beck

## MRS. BECK TO HATHENBRUCK

*Washington, D.C., Jan. 19th, 1898*
*Mr. F. W.C. Hathenbruck*
*Washington, D.C.*

*My Dear Mr. Hathenbruck,*

*Will you be kind enough to call at the Ebbitt sometime next Monday, as I very much desire to see you about my return to Utah?*
                    *Most Respectfully Yours,*
                    *RACHEL LONGATE BECK*

## CAVANAUGH TO HATHENBRUCK

*National Hotel, Washington, D.C., Feb.. 4, 1898*

*Dear Mr. Hathenbruck,*

*Mrs. Beck desires to see you at once. She leaves today. Please call at the Hotel Ebbitt.*
                    *Yours Very Truly,*
                    *THOS. H. CAVANAUGH*

*(P.S.) I go to Arlington Hotel to meet Mr. McCook of New York, I cannot postpone this meeting.*

*National Hotel, Washington, D.C., Feb.. 8, 1898*

*Mr. Hathenbruck,*

*Will you come and see me at once. I desire to consult about a matter of importance to us both.*
*Send word by messenger.*
                    *Yours Truly,*
                    *THOS. H. CAVANAUGH*

*Grand Hotel, New York City, New York, Feby. 19, 1898*

*My Dear Sir:*

*I have a friend here who hearing of the condition (of) the lease, came to me and made a proposition. He and his friend will go to Washington at their own expense. Will see Secy Bliss and make an effort to have our lease approved at once. If they succeed they want the right to organize a second company and divide the lease with us. We are to have the Rhoades mine and lands 2 X 6 miles, or 1 _ X 8, being 12 square miles. The known deposits of metals are to be divided between the companies alternatively, we take one, they take one, we next they next and so on. They are to pay the Indians 10% and pay to us a royalty not greater than 3%. I have said 5%. The Indian claims are to be divided between us and worked by us for their benefit and profit. They to furnish labor and pay all expenses. Worked under our authority for them, but worked by them.*
*He says he does not want any help from anybody. If he does not succeed he does not want anything. Now I think this a good proposition and Dr. Beatty agrees with me. We take no risk. Unless he succeeds we do nothing. If he does succeed we can afford to do what he asks. Half of that tract of land, with the Rhoades claim to start with is a great deal. Half loaf is better than no bread. Please write me at once.*
                    *Yours truly,*
                    *THOS. M. CAVANAUGH*

*Grand Hotel, New York City, New York,
Feby. 23, 1898.*

*My Dear Sir:*

*I desire to say to you, that for fear you may not have fully comprehended the suggestion in my letter of yesterday. I desire to repeat to you now, that so far as I am concerned, I have no hope of securing that lease except that most unusual influences can be secured to operate with Secy. Bliss. While The Rawlins amendment not included our lease in its terms specifically; yet the Secretary may say, that I look upon that as an expression of legislative will and therefore I will not approve that lease. Mr. McCook and Jones may be strong enough to secure the approval of that lease, but they will not do it for nothing. They will want what the other people do and not offer so favorable terms.*

*If these parties don't get this lease approve, or a positive assurance that it will be at a time certain they do not get a cent, or rather do not get the concession they ask.*

*It has been unfortunate that the complications came up with it, and they were simply barriers and unnecessary ones it seems to me. The situation at this hour, is, we have a lease from the Indians but no prospect of its approval.*

*Very truly Yours,
THOS. H. CAVANAUGH*

*Grand Hotel, New York City, New York, Feby. 28, 1898.
F.W.C. Hathenbruck Esq.
Washington City.*

*My Dear Mr. Hathenbruck:*

*It is quite probable that I shall go to Detroit from here and will be there for possible a week or ten days, may be that I cannot get back to Washington until I have returned West. I have done all that anyone can, under the circumstances for the approval of that lease, and nothing that I can do will change the situation if it is against us, and will not assist much if it is for us. I do not think there is anything to be gained by your remaining in Washington and it may be that you will be required very much at the Reservation, should the Secretary determine to examine into the truth of the charges of McGrew, Myton and Harper.*

*I will write you again soon and tell you the result of my friend's effort with Secy. Bliss. When I know what he found out, and what he thinks of the position and situation of things. Write me here. Grand Hotel.*

*Sincerely Yours,
THOS. H. CAVANAUGH*

*Grand Hotel, New York City, New York,
Mar. 2nd, 1889. 9pm.*

*My Dear Sir:*

*Have had a long talk with Mr. Simmons and his opinion is that himself and his friends can secure the action we desire unless there is some interference by parties who are endeavoring to do the same thing. The matter is to be left in their hands, and no one is to know that anyone is working in our interest at all. As I have insisted all the time it weakens the influence of your friends if every one knows that they are your friends and are interested in your affairs. So my friend, I wish to say to you tell no one that there is any one interested with you in the matter. Do not tell Mr. Payton anything of the new developments.*

*Mr. S (Simmons) says that nothing can be done until the Legislation has been passed. But that our friends will have everything in readiness and when the time comes and matters are propitious they will bring all their influence to bear.*

*So I say to you in Kindness that you cannot be*

of any service down there (Washington). That your presence is a notice that someone is working the Dept. for a purpose and they are opposing your efforts. Dr. Beatty has told me many things since he came, that complicate matters in the Dept and with Secretary, and it is based upon information given by yourself to parties in Salt Lake, Provo and Price. That Berry has repeated things you have told him, about compensating the Indians: There is a whole lot of stuff down there in Washington that came from you to persons whom you confided in, who have either thoughtlessly or purposely repeated there. There is no way for their refutation until the question is raised, and then you should be in communication with the Reservation, and not in Washington. If I knew of anything that you could do to aid the matter I would tell you what it is, and have you do it. You have filed the stipulation Eliminating Gilsonite & etc. Have filed a denial of the charges that you secured the lease by unfair and unlawful means. There remains nothing for you to do, but to spend your money. Everything possible will be done to secure favorable action on the lease and at the proper time I am sure it will succeed. I am trying to secure for you $125.00, if you accept the proposal. I have not the funds on hand, and must get them. I have arranged for the amount on the 15th and will have it for you at that time. I am only speaking for your good and our interests, when I say that you should (stay) at Provo, where you can go into the Reservation upon advices from us. It seems to me the fact of wisdom that you should be where you could reach the ground (reservation) on a telegram from us. You do not want any one in possession of claims asking for subleases when our lease is approved.

The parties do not need my presence down there (in Washington) so I am going to Detroit.
Let me hear from you.

Sincerely Yours,
THOS. H. CAVANAUGH

**BECK TO HATHENBRUCK**
Salt Lake City, Utah, March 13th, 1898
Mr. F.W.C. Hathenbruck
Provo, Utah

My dear Sir:

I have been hoping to hear from you before this, and that you had been successful in obtaining, at least, an indication that you would, finally, have your lease approved.
I will be glad if you will write to me as fully as you can, conveniently, of how the matter stands. At present I am on sick leave of absence and am happy to say that I think my health is improving slowly. I will be here probably about six weeks longer.
There are some points that I would like to discuss with you. When do you think you will be at Provo?
I will be able to go there, if you cannot come here: but I would like very much to hear what you have learned, before I go to Keogh, hence would like to meet you if you will be in the west. As I do not know your present address I will send this to Provo, with the request that it be forwarded.
Hoping to hear from you soon, I am,
Sincerely Yours,
Wm. H. BECK

Salt Lake City, Utah, March 16th, 1898
Mr. F.W.C. Hathenbruck
Washington, D.C.

My dear Sir:

I am in receipt of information that Mr. Simmons will be at Washington, before this reaches you, in the interest of the lease. By an arrangement with Mr. Cavanaugh and Dr. Beatty he is to proceed for certain consideration, agreed to by all parties concerned here. Today a letter from General Clarkson, says that it may be necessary to have the assistance of Mr. Hobart and Mr. Hanna. He (Mr. Clarkson) evidently not being aware of the arrangement with Mr. Simmons. The latter was to obtain the signature of the Secretary within 30 days.

If Mr. S. (Simmons) is not able to obtain the approval in 30 days, he has been or will be instructed to go to General Clarkson and Mr. Simmons by Dr. Beatty. I have written to Mr. Cavanaugh, enclosing this, not knowing your address.

It would be well to see Mr. Simmons and perhaps he can determine in a few days what his chances are of obtaining the desired signature and then he can communicate with General Clarkson, as he may think necessary. Above all agree to any arrangement made with Mr. Simmons and in case of his failure, to General Clarkson's arrangement if approved by Mr. Cavanaugh, Dr. Beatty, Bishop Clawson and myself. You can rest assured it will be the best and all that can be done.

We are anxious to get this thing through, even if we cut our shares pro rata, as the enemies to the measure are strong and unscrupulous.

I hope that you are well and that you will feel that we are all pulling together and that success may crown our efforts.

Yours Very Respectively
RACHEL LONGATE BECK

Salt Lake City, Utah, March 24th, 1898
Mr. F.W.C. Hathenbruck
Washington, D.C.

My Dear Mr. Hathenbruck:

Your letter to my husband was received. We were glad to hear from you. There is one point, in addition to those which I touched upon in my last letter to you, to which I wish to call your attention, as being very important, and which you no doubt are fully acquainted with. It is this. The Secretary of the Interior has the right to lease any and all lands upon the Uintah Reservation the same as upon any other Reservation. The Uncompahgre Reservation has no bearing upon the Uintah. Any promise made by the Secretary to await legislation upon the Uintah lands is unjustifiable. This waiting upon the action of a Member of Congress with the expectation that he is to upset all existing laws, is, to say the least of it, rather peculiar.

Under existing law the Secretary should approve your lease. It will be time enough for him to act otherwise when another law is passed: but it may be properly said that if the heads of Bureaus were to wait for prospective laws, the business of the Government would be paralyzed. Such a position by the Secretary as to leases of Unallotted lands upon Indian Reservations, is untenable and I have no doubt he would change it, if the men who approach him are of weight politically. There is no reason, either, why he should consider the Utah Delegation politically. I mention these points because they are in my opinion, extremely important and might not be mentioned by our friends as pointedly as they should be.

I note what you say to the Captain (Wm. Beck) in your letter, as to the Bonds Etc.. I do so earnestly hope that your party will speedily accomplish our "Dream."

*If you meet Mr. Simmons, let me hear from you about it. We have become anxious concerning this matter, and Dr. B. (Beatty) & T.H.C. (Cavanaugh) have both thought Mr. Simmons could accomplish much.*

*I do not know of any other points to write about and only mention those contained herein, for the reason that in the possession of such men as you indicate you have secured, they will be powerful arguments with the Secretary.*

*I will close now, with an earnest wish for your success.*

*Very Respectfully Yours,*
*RACHEL LONGATE BECK*
*(P.S.) N.B. Leasing law.*


*Act of Congress approved Feb. 28/95*
*Salt Lake City, Utah, April Third, 1898*
*Mr. F. W.C. Hathenbruck*
*Washington, D.C.*

*My Dear Mr. Hathenbruck,*

*Since you last heard (from) me I have been trying to find a moment in which to reply but events so shape themselves so to claim most of my time. First, I will ask, how are you in succeeding with your lease?*

*I suspect you(ve) still found the Washington forces (illegible)...I had hoped to hear that you had met with success and that we might discuss matters. Hope to see you before our departure from Salt Lake for good. The Captain (Wm. Beck) although on sick leave is constantly talking of joining his Troops in the Field and I fear he will end in carrying out his threat. Our daughter Mrs. Walis is with us and her little mrs. Her husband, Capt. P.G. Walis...having gone with the command for Fort (illegible), Nebraska. John has enlisted and Paul is in Denver in news paper work. We are much disintegrated you will (see?) by the War (Spanish American War). Let me hear from you please*

*when convenient ....tell me of your (illegible) with the Department.*

*Captain is looking dreadfully, and I fear the worst. He joins with me with best wishes for your good health and success.*

*Most Cordially Your Friends,*
*RACHEL LONGATE BECK*


## SIMMONS TO HATHENBRUCK

*The Phoenix Oil Company Commercial Cable Building New York City,*
*New York, April 7, 1898. F.W. Hathenbruck, Esq., 1609—13th Street,*
*N.W., Washington, D.C.*

*My Dear Sir:*

*I am pleased to acknowledge the receipt of your favor of April the 6th.*

*It was my intention of being in Washington during the present week, but from certain private information that I received, it was intimated that it would be impossible to accomplish anything with the department while this exciting Cuban proposition was occupying the entire attention of the President and the Cabinet, still I will write to Washington this evening and see if our friends agree with as to the time being favorable to get action on the matter next week. If I get a satisfactory reply, I will wire you what day I will be in Washington. I am to see General Clarkson today, when we shall come to some definite understanding on the line of your letter.*

*Yours very truly,*
*J.A. SIMMONS*

## CAVANAUGH TO HATHENBRUCK

*Detroit, Mich., April 7th, 1898*
*F.W.C. Hathenbruck. Esq.*
*Washington, D.C.*

*My Dear Mr. Hathenbruck,*

*I have your several favors, and have delayed answering them until I could hear from Gen. Clarkson and Mr. Simmons; and hoping also that I could fix the day when I should return.*
*On yesterday I had a letter from C. (Clarkson) and S. (Simmons) and they are now ready to meet Mr. McK (McKay) and agree upon a place of action, in the interest of our lease. General C. (Clarkson) informed me that they had asked McK (McKay) to come to N.Y. (New York) or to fix a time when they could meet in W. (Washington) a. As I understand the plan, it is the intention to arrange terms with that man Harper, if it is possible.*
*My Physician chains me here. He has not yet fixed the day for the operation, saying that I am too nervous and excited. This war business is quite a disturber of my nerves. I have a son at Mobile, they have relieved my son-in-law from duty here, and he will go to the Coast in Torpedo service. All these things are calculated to keep my nervous system unhinged. I expect that he will probably get the thing over by next Wednesday. The I remain in the hands of the nurse for ten days or two weeks. I have written to Mr. Kiey Kendall and explained to him that I wished him to advance you some funds under the arrangement which he made with me when I left. I will hear from him definitely in a few days.*
*You are near M.K. (McKay) and will know what they agree upon long before I will.*
*With best wishes and thanking you for your good wishes,*

*I am Sincerely Yours,*
*THOS. H. CAVANAUGH*

*Detroit, Mich., April 19, 1898*

*My Dear Hathenbruck:*

*Your favor of 15th came to hand today. Do not know where it has been, but it was received here in Detroit on Sunday morning. Now My Dear Sir, your letter and the spirit of it are all right. But the claim is in Washington that we have succeeded in raising in the minds of the officials such a high opinion of the value of the value, as they say 50. to 100. million that it has excited the stupidity of the whole gang, and we have blocked our own interests in that way. So I have been informed by Col. McKay and Mr. Simmons and Gen. C (Clarkson) has written me the same thing, that they have told him so there.*
*I was giving him arguments to use with the gentlemen who think there is such great wealth now lying exposed on the land of the lease.*
*I said that I would prefer to lose my interest, rather than not have lease approved. If it could be approved was what I wanted.*
*I do not desire to lose my interest, I have about lost everything else by this war scare, and I am blue and disheartened. I am sick and cannot get away from the Doctors. In replying to that criticism, I have said that there was no development done on the ground to be leased. That whether there was 25 million or $25,000, we had no way of demonstrating. I also said that I believed it was a valuable lease or I would not labor to have it approved. I also said to Gen. C. (Clarkson) that I had confidence in yourself and Mr. Rhoades and I was satisfied that you were sincere and honest and believed what you stated. But that you had not been able to develop to any such an extent that would warrant any statement, except in belief that there was a million.*
*You will understand that I do not wish to stand in the way of this new deal. I have said to Col. Clarkson, that so far as I am concerned that I*

*authorize him (and speak for some others) to make a new reorganization upon any basis he chose so that he deems it for the best interest of the parties to the lease, and those interested with them. I am obliged for your assurance of desiring to protect my interest in the project. An thankful that I an not forgotten ....*
*With best wishes,*

*Yours truly,*
*THOS. H. CAVANAUGH*

*Mobile, Ala., June 2, 1898*

*My Dear Mr. Hathenbruck:*

*I came here to see my son on very important business of his and mine, and shall return to Washington about the last of next week.*
*I got your last letter, and believe me were it possible I would do all you ask and more to get you back to Salt Lake City. But it is impossible for me as the war has stopped every enterprise in which I am interested and cut off all my supplies of money. Mr. Kiey Kendall has nothing to do with any of my business matters. He was expecting some funds he did not need to use which he was intending to advance to me, but he was disappointed, and could not favor me.*
*I do not go to him with any of my or your troubles, he has enough of his own. You should see Mr. Clarkson or if you do not see him write him at 214 Broadway, N.Y.*
*I hope to see you again soon.*

*Sincerely Yours,*
*THOS. H. CAVANAUGH*

The following four letters were typewritten and bear no visible signature upon them. However, because of their importance, the authors have chosen to include them in this narrative as well. They are:

*Washington, D.C., June 6, 1898.*
*Col. Nathaniel McKay,*
*Washington, D.C.*

*Dear Sir:*

*Having been referred to you by Gen. Clarkson in the matter of securing the approval by the Secretary of the Interior of our mining lease with the Confederated Bands of the Ute Indians; and having been requested by you to submit to you a proposition looking to the settlement of our interest in said lease and the confirmation to be secured, I beg to submit: That for my firm of Hathenbruck and Rhoades we are willing to enter into an obligation to convey or transfer to such person or persons as you and General Clarkson may designate 6/20ths interest in and to a portion of the land embraced in the lease to be 2 X 8 miles in area and selected by us from the lands embraced within the lease and located by a survey of the same. In addition to this 6/20 interest we would further obligate ourselves to transfer and convey to such person or persons as you or General Clarkson might designate every alternate mining claim located upon the leased lands outside of the lands embraced within the said area of 2 X 8 miles. As a further part of the agreement we would require that the persons to whom we assigned the above interest should pay the bonus provided for in the lease with the Indians, to be paid to the Indians upon all products from said alternate locations.*
*We would further provide by the agreement that the persons to whom these interests should be assigned should, upon the confirmation of the lease, reimburse to us the sum of $2000. for expenses we have incurred in the prosecution of our interests since the lease was procured.*
*The consideration for the foregoing assignments by us would be the securing by themselves, or General Clarkson, the confirmation and ratification of our said lease within days.*

*As a condition of the agreement that has here-inbefore been mentioned there would have to be reserved from the general lease heretofore secured by us a tract of land embracing 640 acres on the east fork of the fork which we have heretofore agreed to assign to A. McDonald, a copy of which assignment you have seen.*

*This proposition is not intended to be additional to the agreement heretofore made between my firm and General Clarkson, but in lien thereof and as a suggestion for a new basis upon which the interest of the parties may be determined should you succeed in securing the confirmation of the lease.*

*Very truly yours,*
*(NO SIGNATURE)*


*Washington, D.C., July 13th, 1898.*
*James S. Clarkson, Washington, D.C.*
*Hiram B. Clawson, Esq.,*
*Salt Lake City, Utah.*

*Dear Sirs:*

*On the 10th day of December, 1896, you entered into an agreement with myself and Mr. Rhodes in relation to procuring the approval and ratification of a lease which Mr. Rhodes and myself were attempting to secure from the Uintah Indians of certain mining lands in their reservation. This agreement was modified by a further agreement entered into between us on the 3rd day of November, 1897. We secured the lease from the Uintah Indians on the 18th day of December, 1897, and immediately notified you of such fact. We subsequently delivered into your hands such papers as you required and requested, and have waited until this time to have you secure the ratification and confirmation of said lease as contemplated and required by the agreement between us. More than ninety days have elapsed since we*

*obtained that lease and since you had notice of it and since we delivered to you any paper which you at any time suggested or required.*

*A long time after we had obtained the lease you sent me to Mr. McKay, whom you said would represent you in the transaction, and I had several conferences with that gentleman in relation to the matter, and he informed me finally that he represented interests adverse to those which you had agreed to represent and his refused to render any assistance in the matter.*

*The time within which the agreement between us should have been performed on your part has long expired.*

*My letters to Mr. Clarkson have recently remained unanswered, and I have been absolutely unable to learn from him the status of the lease or what, if any, action has been taken in relation thereto by the Secretary of the Interior.*

*Under these circumstances it does not appear either necessary or proper that any additional time should be extended to you to carry out the terms of the agreements into which we have entered. If, however, you have any claim that any additional time should be given you, or that any practical results will be obtained by the extension of time, I should be pleased to hear from you in that regard.*

*Unless I shall receive a reply to his communication within fifteen (15) days of the date hereof, I shall conclude that you have no further interest in the agreements made between us and that whatever assistance I may need to secure the confirmation of our lease I shall be obliged to obtain elsewhere, if possible.*

*Your very truly,*
*(NO SIGNATURE)[2]*

[2](This letter was most likely drafted by F.W.C. Hathenbruck himself.)

*Washington, D.C., July 16, 1898.*
*Henry C. Henderson, Esq.,*
*100 Broadway, New York City.*

*Dear Mr. Henderson:*

*The Doctor (Hathenbruck) has just returned from an interview with the Secretary of the Interior and brings the important information that his lease has never been before the Secretary of the Interior for consideration nor has the Secretary ever taken any action thereon. The Secretary expressed, so says the Doctor, considerable sympathy for him on account of the treatment that he had received at the hands of his supposed interested friends. He was referred by the Secretary of the Interior to the head of the Indian division of the Interior Department with the statement that he might be able to obtain some information there. The head of the Indian division of the Interior Department told him that he knew nothing about the matter but would look through the correspondence files and see if any communication had been written. In the letter books was found a letter written by Mr. White, chief of division, to the Secretary of the Interior recommending the disapproval of the lease by reason of probable legislation changing the law as to leases. It seems that the matter, this letter, as far as the Interior Department is concerned, went no further than this. The lease had been turned down and recommended for disapproval by the Commissioner of Indian Affairs, who has, from the very inception, been hostile to the lease. As an evidence of this I have among the papers in the case (not on file but private papers) a clipping from a Salt lake City paper, dated December 13, -five days before the lease was signed—giving out a statement that Mr. Tonner, Assistant Commissioner of Indian Affairs, thought the lease would not be approved. It occurs to me that this statement from the official*

*next to the Commissioner of Indian Affairs that the lease would not be approved, before the lease was even made, before they could have known whether it was legal or illegal, or before they knew the terms and conditions of the lease, is highly important in disclosing the animus of the Indian Office to the lease and a determination on their part to block it right or wrong. This will be very valuable information when it comes to a presentation of the question to the Secretary of the Interior.*

*Finn has wired Hooker that the lease has not been presented to the Secretary of the Interior, for him to communicate with Ward, one of whom will doubtless communicate at once with you.*

*I think it highly important that we should confer with reference to what is best to be done, as it appears from the foregoing that the matter is not in nearly so bad a shape as we thought.*

*I will add that the gentleman in charge of the Indian division of the Interior Department stated to the Doctor that no new lease would be approved by the Secretary of the Interior before Congress met; that inasmuch as this lease was secured under the direction and by consent of the former Secretary of the Interior, and inasmuch as the law governing leases remain; in statue that he believed with certain influences enlisted (without stating what influences) that the lease might probably be approved. I would suggest that you get in communication with Ward and Hooker at once and it may be important that you come over to Washington to see us. Aside from the business end of the transaction we will be very glad to see you in our city.*

*Very truly yours,*
*(NO SIGNATURE)*

Washington, D.C., July 22, 1898.
Henry C. Henderson, Esq.,
100 Broadway,
New York City,

Dear Mr. Henderson:

I have just come from the Indian Office; saw Mr. Jones, the Commissioner of Indian Affairs, and also saw the lease which is in his possession and which shows the disapproval of the Secretary of the Interior on the 17th of May; this in direct contradiction to what the Secretary told Mr. Hathenbruck in his interview with him the other day. I am perfectly confident that he told Mr. Hathenbruck that he, the Secretary, had never had the matter before him for consideration; and I am further satisfied that he was perfectly honest in making the statement. I think that the explanation of the matter is that the formal endorsement of the Secretary disapproving the lease was made by him in the course of his official business and without any consideration whatever. The endorsement of disapproval was entered upon the back of the lease by Mr. White, the man who tried to prevent the Indians from making the lease with Hathenbruck and Rhodes and of whom I wrote you a few days ago. My theory is that the matter was presented to the Secretary in the course of the official business of the day and his signature appended without any consideration whatever of the questions involved. This is evidenced by his statement to Hathenbruck that he had not had the matter before him for consideration.

The letter from White to the Secretary that I mentioned in my last communication recommended the disapproval of the lease upon the grounds that legislation was pending in Congress that would doubtless change the existing law; and because the lease provided at the option for the parties for a renewal upon its expiration. The first objection has been removed because Congress failed to change the existing laws. The second objection is frivolous and does not go to the merits of the question at all, because it merely provided at the option of the parties for a renewal of the lease at the expiration of ten years.

I really believe that the case is in a splendid condition for the securing of favorable action by the Secretary of the Interior upon proper presentation.

In my talk with Mr. Jones, the Commissioner of Indian Affairs, he expressed himself as favorable with the leasing of the mineral lands belonging to the Indians but said that the Secretary was not in harmony with him upon this line of policy. If this be true the key to the situation is with the Secretary of the Interior as the objection of the Indian Office would not be serious and I do not believe anything will be done there to hamper the Interior Department in its action should it be determined to be favorable.

The conversation I had with Mr. Jones was entirely voluntary on his part; as I did not care to enter into any discussion with him on the subject, and as he seemed to be just a little curious to know why I wanted to see the lease, I passed the matter off in such a way as to avoid arousing any suspicion on his part as to any further action contemplated. Jones stated that the only objection to the lease was that the agent Beck had permitted the Indians to make the same in opposition to his instructions given at the time. This seems to me to rather raise a question between the Commissioner and the agent than between the leassees and the Department. The Indians had the right, under the law, to make the lease; the consent of the Commissioner was not required, the only person having to give his permission being the agent. The fact that the agent did not comply with the direction of his superior should not, and I do not think can, in the ultimate presentation of the question, affect the rights of the leases.

It occurs to me that the whole matter rests with

*the Secretary of the Interior and involves the policy to be pursued by him with reference to leasing by the Indians of mineral lands. The law expressly sanctions this policy—(see my brief in your hands), and I cannot understand why the Secretary should insist upon a policy for his department that is inharmonious with the law. I do not believe that he will, upon a full and fair presentation of the question, refuse to sanction that for which the law in express terms provides. You may say to our people that the lease is here and all right in the hands of the Commissioner of Indian Affairs and there is absolutely no danger of its destruction or loss. I think it best not to press the Commissioner for leave to make a copy, as he seemed just a little inquiring this morning. The lease is all right, in proper and legal form, and the Commissioner raised no objection to the same upon that score and by way of parenthesis I might say that he stated that if it had not been for the injudiciousness of Beck, the Indian Agent, that the lease might probably have been approved; and also that he believed that such a lease could be approved if held by responsible parties.*

*I wish you would have your people to send F. W.C. Hathenbruck $25. on account of the $100. provided for in the agreement. He is entirely without means, is very blue, and your people must take care of him. Please attend to this at once. His address is No. 1609 13th Street, N.W., Washington, D.C.*

*Very truly yours,*
*(NO SIGNATURE)*

The following letter is incomplete, with one or more pages missing, therefore we are at a loss to know who wrote it, except that the letterhead reads; Grand Union Hotel, Ford & Shaw, Proprietors.

*New York, July 25, 1898.*

*My Dear Peyton:*

*I send herewith—check for the Dr. as suggested. I have just seen Hooker and he has told me of your interview. Will see what if any papers were before the Secretary when the lease was disapproved. I think this most important. We should be able to say without a possibility—if contradicted—that there was writing before him, if that is the fact and if anything was used we should know it ...*

## PEYTON TO HATHENBRUCK
*Bedford City, Va., July 31st, 1898*

*My dear Doctor:*

*I arrived yesterday afternoon at 4 o'clock and found all quite well, and among the first inquiries was as to how you were and why I did not bring you with me—Wish I had thought of it, as you would enjoy the quiet of this country life, after the (illegible) heat of the city.*

*I have just written Henderson to wire me, and you also, if he contemplates coming to Washington this week that I may meet him. I hope they may be able to come in as I think now a most favorable time to reach the Secretary.*

*Hope you are better of your rash. It was delightfully cool here yesterday evening and last night. The breeze was right from the mountains and you can appreciate what the kind of air does for ones comfort. All request me to remember them to you.*

*Please send me the prescription for the Camphor Salve, and will be also obliged if you will send me, or address to Sueih, the Intemezzo of Cazvaleria Reutiema, and the Song Down Upon the Wabash for Winn.*

*Yours,*
*HARRY PEYTON*

*Also send the music to "Coal Black Lady."*[3] *Will pay you for some when I come. Suppose you wire me about Wednesday to come to Washington. I think by that time I will have enough of the country, as after two or three days it gets awful lonesome out here, and I expect to stay till Sunday unless I am called back before that time. Of course if the New York people come before Wednesday I will come in: if not you can wire me that day simply to "Come, parties will be here," and then I will come in Thursday evening, by that time I think I will long for just a little taste of Washington High Life. In the language of the lamented James G. Blaine burn this letter.*

[3] F.W.C. Hathenbruck, according to MEMORIES THAT LIVE by the Daughters of Utah Pioneers, page 99, was a member of the Provo City Silver Band in 1884. Thus, his knowledge of sheet music probably accounts for the above mentioned requests by Harry Peyton.

**FINN TO HENDERSON**

*Department of Justice,*
*Washington, D.C., 7-26-98*

*Dear Henderson:*

*Allow me to trespass upon your most valuable (?) time for a few moments. I requested Hooker to say to you that in my opinion the safest way to get at Bliss was this: Let Sherman go to Jones Comm. of Indian Affairs, who has stated to Peyton that he is in favor of the leasing by the Indians of their mineral rights, and ask him to take the lease from the files in his office & go with Sehrman to Bliss, and then state his notions in regard to the matter. Jones will do this I think as all the favors he expects in this. Congress will go through Sherman (illegible) of the House, "Indian Affairs." This will prevent the lease from going through the usual channels of the Interior Department in which every sucker (is) allied with the other. Clarkson's outfit will see it and he (is) in a position to move against it. Much of our success will depend upon our ability to deprive subordinates of information as to our plans. The majority of these under-strappers, particularly connected with the Interior Dept., are corrupt as hell and are no doubt today & have been working in the interest of the other gang. I am confident that Bliss told the Dr. (Hathenbruck) the truth, when he said the lease had never been before him, and he had never acted upon it. The endorsement of disapproval on the lease is in the hand-writing of one White, a subordinate, whose price is never over $200. You can readily see how Bliss signed their disapproval. At a busy moment this man White placed the paper for him to sign with the statement that his disapproval was necessary & Bliss never examined the paper or asked any questions. This is done every hour in all the Departments and upon the request of some subordinates. These subordinates must be kept ignorant of our plans and movements until we secure the approval.*
*We can win this thing if our first steps are in the right direction. But I am confident you will not take any false steps in the matter. Hooker agreed with me that under all the circumstances the Doctor ought to be willing to make a new deal and let us all stand in, equally share and share alike in the whole lease. Hooker suggested however that Ward was inclined to oppose this on the ground that we made the Dr. a proposition which he accepted. You will however do what you think best in this matter*
*-*

*With Jones and Sherman advising their*

*approval, backed by your own persuasive and convincing arguments we will win.*

*I trust we will succeed for I know it will make us all independent & will afford the Dr. an opportunity to again visit N.Y. You will please accept my sincere thanks for your kindness and generosity during our stay in N.Y. and I hope to be able some day to reciprocate.*

*Yours Sincerely,*
*P.J. FINN*


## HENDERSON TO PEYTON

*New York City, August 4th, 1898.*
*Harry Peyton, Esq.,*
*1609 13th Street N.W.,*
*Washington, D.C.*

*My dear Peyton:*

*On our way over yesterday, it occurred to me that there might be some advantage to us in having the Doctor (Hathenbruck) secure—or attempt to secure—from the Indians a lease of 5000 acres of the Gilsonite deposit in the Uintah Reservation. I learned from the Secretary yesterday that permission had been given to the Babcock interest to negotiate such a lease with the Indians. It occurred to me that if he had given that consent to one party, he could hardly refuse to give like permission to the Doctor, and said permission, if secured, I think would be of great interest to us. It would place the Doctor upon the Indian Reservation, where he would be in constant and direct communication with the Indians and in that way could see what was being done.*

*If we secured the lease we would be in a position, first to compel our opponents to listen to us and perhaps compel their assistance in securing the confirmation of our mining lease, and it occurs to me that if the Babcock interest can afford to spend ten years or thereabouts in efforts to secure such a lease, it must be of great value,*

*and if of value to them I can't see why it shouldn't be of equal value to us. So that it would appear to be worth the effort.*

*These is one other reason why it would be to our advantage to have the Doctor upon the ground when our adversaries are attempting to secure this lease from the Indians which probably suggests itself to you, and of which I will speak to you when I see you again. Again it may be that under the guise of, a lease of Gilsonite lands they might be so surveyed as to take in part of the lands secured to us by our lease, and in that way obtain possession of some of our mining interests. If the Doctor was in communication with the Indians, he could certainly head off this if he did not entirely prevent the granting of any lease to these people and secure one for himself. So much for the project. My notion was for you to- find out what you could concerning these Gilsonite leases of Thornton's and others now controlled by the Babcock interest. Find out the terms and conditions of the leases, and I understand from the Secretary that they are limited to 5000 acres; then see what steps must be taken to secure permission to negotiate with the Indians for such a lease, and I assume that that matter is entirely in the hands of the Secretary. I thought then that I would go to Washington again, say next Wednesday, and go with the Doctor to see the Secretary and make formal application for permission to negotiate with the Indians for this property. It was for the purpose of giving you all the time possible to secure the data which is needed, that I wired you last evening. You see I have nothing at all from which to ascertain the facts which are needed before I approach the Secretary to secure his consent. It is quite apparent that the Doctor should have something to engage his time when he goes West again, and if he is obliged to remain upon the neutral strip and try to find out what is going on upon the Reservation, it is going to be a hard task, while if he can even secure the consent and negotiate with the Indians, his task will be so much lighter, and there will be the possibility of securing something of great value to himself and to us. Won't you take this matter up and let me* hear from you, say next Monday or Tuesday, so that I may determine whether or not I shall go on to Washington in the matter? My engagements are such that I cannot leave here before next Tuesday night and perhaps you will be able to have the brief ready for me to submit to the Secretary when I call upon him. This is not important, however, as I can tell him that it will be ready in a day or two, and I do not suppose that he is over anxious in this matter, for he seems to have put his foot down pretty firmly. These ideas originated with me on our way over yesterday, and I discussed them with the other members of the party and they all acquiesced in the project and thought that it was to our interest to make the efforts suggested.

Yours &c.,
H.C. HENDERSON

**FINN? TO HENDERSON**

Department of Justice,
Washington, D.C., August 19, 1898.
Henry C. Henderson, Esq.,
100 Broadway, New York City.

Dear Mr. Henderson:

I am just in receipt of your telegram and am very much pleased to know that you will be over Tuesday as I have been quite worried by the delay from my inability to hear from you, as I fear that movement is on foot to secure a lease from our Indians. To defeat with absolute certainty will require the doctor's presence among them on where he can reach them. The only new development since writing you is a letter from Mr. Clarkson to the Doctor stating that he desired to see him next Tuesday at the Shoreham; that he believed by the association of new parties the approval of the lease might be secured.

When I take this statement in connection with the attempt on the part of Bishop Clawson' of Salt Lake to induce Rhodes to capitalize the lease proposition and let him in on it I am led to the conclusion that these parties believe that there will be an approval of the lease. From what source they get their information, of course, I do not know.

I believe to carry this matter to a successful termination or rather to facilitate the same (for I believe we will ultimately win), it will be necessary to incorporate with a certain amount of capitol stock, and placate the western opposition by a distribution of this stock. I think it will be well when you come over on Tuesday next to see Clarkson, to have a talk with him; state to him that upon the forfeiture of his contract with H. & R. (Hathenbruck & Rhoades) you took up the proposition with the new contract; that it is your purpose now to do what you can toward the ultimate approval of the lease; that if he can show to you where he can render valuable aid in reaching the desired result that you would be ready and willing to entertain a proposition to let him in. It is going to be necessary to overcome the opposition against us and I know of no other way of doing it than by making some kind of a divide with our opponents. This, in my judgment, will necessitate some of our people going out to Salt Lake and quieting some of the opposition there, especially Dr. Niles of whom I have heretofore written. Also Myton who is now the present agent at White Rock, one of the agencies upon our Indian reservation.

We can talk these matters over when you come but I give you these points for your consideration in the mean time. I think it very important that matters should be delayed as little as possible because if we were to be met with a counter lease while ours stand disapproved there will be no hope for us.

Yours very truly,
(NO SIGNATURE)

## PEYTON TO HENDERSON

September 24, 1898.
Henry C. Henderson, Esq.,
New York City.

Dear Mr. Henderson:

I have received this morning two letters from the Doctor which, with two others I have heretofore received, I enclose. You will note what he has to say in these letters, particularly in the last one with reference to the information that he had from an Indian runner from the reservation. I think the appointment of Myton as Agent for these Indians is for the purpose of getting on the inside track and at some future time securing a lease for the other parties. It is and will be his purpose, evidently, to throw as much cold water upon our lease as possible.

If we could reach this man in some way with a proposition for an interest in the lease or with a suggestion that if he persists in his present course his confirmation would be fought in the Senate, I believe we could bring him to terms. If my information is correct, we can secure evidence to the effect that while negotiations were pending for this lease and while he was acting in the capacity as a Commissioner for the Government for the allotment of the Uncompahgre lands he attempted to secure an interest in the proposed lease and threatened if the interest was not given him that he would defeat the confirmation of the lease when he came to Washington. If this be true and if its truth could be shown to the Indian Committee of the Senate I doubt if a favorable report upon his confirmation would be made. It would show him to be an unfit person to occupy the position to which he has been appointed, and about the best way to put a quietus upon him is to let him know that we have a political influence that will set to work against his confirmation. I would prefer, however, and think the other plan would be better to let him in with an interest and quiet him that way as he doubtless has the Secretary of the Interior behind him in his appointment, and I think it is equally certain that he has parties behind him who want to defeat our lease and secure one for themselves. This is a pretty big game that we are playing and I think the stakes are high and will warrant extreme efforts on our part and those associated with us to defeat the other side and accomplish what we want, and if they will take off their coats and go to work with the influence they have, I believe they can down any combination that comes against them because we have right law and equity on our side.

You will note what the Doctor says about remittances, etc., and I hope that something can be done whereby he will be supplied with such funds as is absolutely necessary for him to attend to his matters at the end of the line. It would be especially valuable if it could be done, if some means could be devised whereby he could get upon the reservation without being subjected to the harassment that these people are going to give him.

I hope very much that we may see some of our New York people at an early date. It is highly probable that I will be in New York in the next ten days or two weeks in which event I will advise you so that you can send word for some of the other parties to meet with us at that time.

Very truly yours,
HARRY PEYTON

## HENDERSON TO HATHENBRUCK

*Chicago, Nov. 13, 1898.*
*Auditorium Hotel.*
*Dr. F.W.C. Hathenbruck,*

*Dear Doctor:*

*Your telegram reached me here last night and I trust that my check reached you before that time. I sent it to Mr. Judd as I understood that you were out of town. In my letter to Mr. Judd I explained the reason why the draft was not accepted. I had my clerk bring my mail up town each evening while I was engaged in White Plains, and he over-looked or did not think the notice from Wells Fargo of any importance. I arrived here last night and intended to leave tonight for Salt Lake City, but a telegram from Ward takes me east at 3:00 this afternoon. I am anxious to see what can be done with Myton and to learn generally of the solution. Mr. Peyton thinks it very important to secure the good will of Myton and also of Mr. Judds who is at present in the West and of course if that is needed we want to do it at once. However I can't go out there at present but may succeed before the end of the year.*
*I will not start again until after December 1st and will let you know if I can go out then.*

*Yours &c,*
*H.C. HENDERSON*

## PEYTON TO HATHENBRUCK

*Department of Justice,*
*Washington, D.C.,*
*December 22, 1898.*
*Dr. F.W.C. Hathenbruck,*
*Provo City, Utah.*

*My dear Doctor:*

*Doubtless you have become very impatient at my silence from this end of the line regarding our business matters, but there has been absolutely nothing of importance for me to write, as I have been awaiting a conference with the New York people. Mr. Henderson was here yesterday and today, going back to New York this afternoon. These people have not by any means given up hopes of securing a confirmation of the lease, but it seems inevitable that the Asphalt people who control the Myton appointment and who seem to have the upper hand in the matter will have to be taken into the deal. I know that our people have done everything that could be done toward the confirmation of our business project. You were in Washington long enough to know by observation that matters of this sort, especially when they are of such possible importance, branch out into many directions before reaching a final and favorable conclusion. Now this question presents this phase:*
*Our lease has been disapproved. These people, the Dick, McKay & Asphalt crowd, have secured the appointment of an Agent for the Indians whom they can control. Mr. Sherman, who is the unquestioned friend of our people, does not believe that we can get Myton away from them because, politically, he belongs to them. With our lease for themselves which they have not yet succeeded in doing, but with their ability to hold you off of the reservation and to let the Indians weaken on our matter by the*

lapse of time, and the seeming want of influence, they unquestionably hope at some time to secure what we now have. Should they be able to do this, we would of course be out.

Mr. Henderson has been in conference with the Asphalt people, who are anxious to secure his good offices with Sherman and other New York influences for the protection of the interests that they already have. He has talked the matter over with them and while they might expect some opposition from the new Secretary of the Interior, who will take office about February the first, and who it is stated, is interested in the St. Louis Asphalt Co. people, in opposition to the Chicago Co., who has the lease, they hope to be able to influence the President through his Ohio friends, Major Dick and others, to order an approval of the lease or through some suggestion from the White House to induce Mr. Bliss to sign it before he goes out of office.

The parties will all be in Washington again early in Jan., for a consultation upon their matters generally, but I believe, and I say this frankly, as you know me to be frank in everything that I do in business matters, that there will have to be a readjustment of interests. We can't get the Asphalt people on a divide of our interests, and they say that your interest, with the lease in its present condition, is not worth half of the business. Their idea is to secure first from the Secretary of the Interior an order rescinding his former order disapproving the lease and then to have an asset, which would be the lease restored, upon which to base a corporate organization. Then to have a distribution of the capitol stock in equitable proportions. I believe the Asphalt people would try to secure a controlling interest, but in this we could oppose them by holding between yourself and your Salt Lake influences and our New York people a controlling interest in the business, thus preventing them from having the same. I feel that it is proper to write you thus fully and frankly because the matter has got to a stage where something will have to be done. I think it would be well for you to see Judd and your Salt

Lake friends at once and submit this letter to them. I know that this is the idea of our New York people, and I will add, as I have hereinbefore stated, that it is also my candid judgment in the matter.

If the proposition is worth anything like the amount that you think it is, to secure an approval upon a readjustment of interests, would, I think, be far better than to take the very probable chances of losing everything. I write this from a point of self-interest because a failure of the lease of course shuts me out from any possible benefits. Let me hear from you at your earliest convenience. Henderson says that he is taking care of your drafts as they come according to contract, and they propose to carry it through as provided in the same. I doubt if any good would have been accomplished by your going with the Indians because I understand they were corralled here by those who had them in charge, and it was almost impossible for anyone to see them. If we can get Myton and his influences in the way I have suggested herein, then we would have every advantage that it seems we can't get otherwise.

Very truly yours,
HARRY PEYTON


P.S. I think it highly probable, after the conference I have mentioned early in January, that it will be necessary for you to come to Washington. In this event our people will, of course, provide for your transportation and expenses.

H.P.

## MACDONALD TO HATHENBRUCK

*Fort Du Chesne, Utah Dec. 24th, 1898.*

*Friend Doc:*

*Yours received upon my return from Price yesterday. I was out after 91 new Cavalry Horses.*

*The Indians are back from Washington, while there they asked the Commissioner of Indian Affairs to annul your contract, lease or agreement made with you.*

*I did not learn what the Comm. did or intends to do.*

*But I believe they are all working against you, and I believe they will accomplish what they are after.*

*I believe the Connels lease went through O.K. I saw Mac. in Price, and while I was there he left to get out his first car load of Elaterite. If I hear anything that would be of use to you, I will write you.*

*Every thing is quiet here. Wishing you a Merry Christmas and a Happy New Year believe me.*

*Yours Truly*
*A. MACDONALD*

## MYTON TO SMITH

*Department of the Interior,*
*U.S, Indian Service,*
*(No Date)*

*Mr. Smith,*

*You must not allow the Indians to bother Mr. Bassant and his party, he has authority from Washington to be on the Reservation. You and Mr. McAndrews must see that they are protected, regardless of what the Indians say,*

*Rspt*
*N.C. MYTON*
*Agent*

## WIGHT TO HATHENBRUCK

*Salt Lake City, Jan. 8th, 1899.*
*F.W.C. Hathenbruck, Esq.*

*Dear Friend:*
*Your favor of the 4th inst at hand and contents noted. In reply, the following is a correct statement of interest sold us:*

*Date Nov 4th 1897 1/40 interest in L.O. Wight*
*Jan 1898 1/40 int. to L.O. Wight & F. Eberhardt*
*• Feby 14th 1898*
*• Mar 24th 1898 1/40 int to Wight, Eberhardt & Turton*
*• June 1st 1898 1/20*

*Total sold to us 6/40 interest in the lease.*
*We have sold at various time, out of our interests, to other parties and some of it recently, as follows:*

*1/200 int to FWC Hathenbruck*
*1/200 int to Wm Turton*
*1/200 int to Jacobs*
*1/100 int to King*
*1/400 int to King*
*1/200 int to Redfield*
*1/1000 int to C.L. Wight*
*1/200 int to Morrison*

*The 1/100 int to Turton and the 1/200 to Jacob's I sold out of my 1/20 of the 4th Nov. 97. We have sold none our of the last 1/20 except to ourselves as it was not to be paid in full until the mines were opened up.*

*The dates on which the payments were made to you and the different amounts you can easily find from my former letters to you and the copies of your letters to me, which I presume you have preserved, as I have preserved your letters and copies of mine to you.*

*Trusting that this will give you the desired information, I remain,*

*Very truly,*
*L.O. WIGHT*

## MACDONALD TO HATHENBRUCK

*Fort Du Chesne, Utah Feb. 1899.*

*Friend Doc:*

*Yours arrived O.K. I had H.H. (initials possibly those of Hooker) read it.*

*Enclosed find agreement between myself and your Company, also copy of same. Please insert the pr. ct. (per cent) from my net profits that I will have to pay your Company.*

*Your Company to pay the Indians their 10 pr. ct. out of what they get from me, that is the 10 pr. ct. due them from the net profits of my ore.*

*Attend to this and return papers to me as soon as possible, as I want to do something that will do you a lot of good, it will also surprise you.*

*Yours Truly,*

*A. MACDONALD.*

*Over.*

*When you return these agreements, if you want to know my scheme before I start in I will let you know it.*

*But I don't think it will be necessary, as you know that I will make no bad breaks, nor compromise your Company in any way.*

*A. M.*

*I simply think that I can do some thing that will put you in a way to get your lease in a very short time, after you hear from me again.*

## HENDERSON TO HATHENBRUCK

*Westchester, N.Y., March 2nd, 1899.*
*Dr. F.W.C. Hathenbruck,*
*Provo City, Utah.*

*Dear Doctor:*

*I am in receipt of your letters, as you doubtless understand.*

*I have considered it unwise to answer either, and do not now propose to go into details in relation to what has been done concerning our matter. I beg to assure you, however, that nothing has been left undone that it has been possible to do. I now content myself by saying that I shall be much disappointed if you are not out on the Reservation developing the mines before the summer passes, and if that is not a fact I will then relate to you everything that has been done, and I believe that you will concur with me that nothing was left undone which would produce the results desired. My experience has taught me that the value of the concessions there are thought to be so great and so many people have heard of them and are so eager to secure rights, that it is unsafe to say a word even to your best friends concerning the matter, for I have found that the least suggestion is carried, repeated and magnified to our disadvantage.*

*If things go as I hope they will, I shall probably join you there or at Salt Lake City early in the Summer, and then I trust and believe you will approve of all that has been done.*

*Yours very truly,*
*H.C. HENDERSON*

## WIGHT TO HATHENBRUCK

*Salt Lake City, March 9th, 1899.*
*F.W.C. Hathenbruck, Esq.,*
*Provo, Utah.*

*Dear Friend:*

*I enclose herewith statement of moneys paid to you and Mr. Rhoades with the dates on which the same were paid. In some of the amounts the dates given are the dates of your checks and in others the dates on which they were paid in Salt Lake. However, your checks are all here and you can easily be satisfied as to the respective amounts any time you are in Salt Lake.*

*The 1/40 that I bought of you and Mr. Rhoades Nov 4/97 you doubtless have a full recollection of.*

*The 1/40 that Mr. Eberhardt and myself bought of you, the statement gives the dates and amounts of payments, and although the last two hundred collars was left optional for us to pay or not before the lease was approved, at your urgent request we paid $100. Mar 31. and $100 Apr 10/98.*

*The 1/40 interest bought of you in Feby 98 was paid for in three drafts mailed to you in Washington as shown in statement.*

*The next 1/40 interest was where the tug of war began. You sent us papers for 1/100 interest and we had three different men and different times all ready to take the 1/100 at $500. and in each case some little thing would knock it out, but you kept right on drawing checks from us to pay just the same, and we paid them. Mr. Rhoades came about that time and you wired me you would make it a 1/40 in place of 1/100 for $500. You had at that time drawn $140. We held a council and Eberhardt, Turton and I decided to take it, and wired you to draw for $360 bal. Very shortly after, we sold a 1/200 int out of my 1/40 to Mr. Jacobs and got $250. on the very day your $360 check*

*came and we put $100. more with the $250. and paid your check. That explains how Wight, Eberhardt & Turton bought the 1/100 which you changed to a 1/40 interest by telegram and letter which we have pinned to the bill of sale.*

*Next about the 1/20: %z or $500 to be paid in cash or payments and $500 when it was taken out of the mines. You first asked me to secure you a loan of $150. Mr. Rhoades came up about that time again (the last of June). We stated the case to Rhoades and to Mr. Dodge and tried to get Mr. Dodge to take the 1/20 on the terms mentioned above and if he did not want all of it to get some of his friends to take it but he declined to do anything. So about the first of July having a prospect-to sell a 1/100 int to Mr. King for $500, the bal of my first 1/40 (now mind you he was the 4th man we had on the string during the 30 days previous, the other three fell down) we decided to take the 1/20 ourselves and if King put up the money, pay off what we borrowed at the bank in Apr and send you the bal of the $500. on account which with the money we had borrowed for you and the Jenkins $100 would make the $500. for first payment for the 1/20 you had already written me that you would credit me with the money we borrowed for you including the Jenkins note. That is how we came to buy this last 1/20 interest.*

*While helping you to funds, which all other parties interested declined to do, I proposed to help myself out of the hole I got into borrowing money at the bank to pay bal on the 1/40 we bought in Apr.*

*Now you must farther recollect that I gave up business and devoted my whole time to raising funds for you from Jany to July and later, besides, I had to give a very liberal commission, in interest in the lease, to Mr. Eberhardt & Turton for helping me get customers and get the deals closed.*

*You of course know that you drew $168 more than was due on the 1/20, and to provide for that and keep my family I have had to sell still* *more of my own interests as shown in statements I mailed you Jany 8th. ——Now if I am claiming one cents worth more interest in the H & R (Hathenbruck and Rhoades) lease than I am honestly and squarely entitled to, I would like to have you explain why. And as to the future you know from past experience that there is not a man who is interested in the lease that will do more to help "put it on its feet" than I will.*

*I have been figuring a little lately, and with the interests sold to Salt Lake people and what you and Mr. R. (Rhoades) told me you had promised with the _ to N.Y. men leaves you and Mr. Rhoades only a small share, and although I am not responsible for that state of affairs, you will find that I am always willing to-do what is right as well as Mr. E. (Eberhardt) and I believe T. (Turton) if approached right, but please don't insinuate that I have betrayed any trust.*

*If you desire to pursue this subject any farther, I would suggest that you can accomplish more in one day by frank and open personal interviews than months at letter writing.*

*Yours truly,*
*L.O. WIGHT*

### KING TO HATHENBRUCK
*Salt Lake City, Utah, Mar. 22nd, 1899.*
*Mr. F.W.C. Hathenbruck*

*Dear Sir:*
*Your letter of 21st. to hand. You refer to the idea of taking up the present contracts and issuing others, I have not seen Redfield for two weeks, he has sickness in his family, and if it can be arranged without I would prefer to say nothing to Morrison about the trouble. If you will continue on the line that you have arranged, i.e. to get all the data by mail from Wight I believe that we can finally adjust the matter without any trouble. I have been acting as referee the past two years in a matter of considerable*

*money and have held together six parties with conflicting interests in entire harmony, and from my experience as a peace make I believe that I can arrange this end amicably when the proper time comes.*

*I have kept tab on W.E. & c. (Wight, Eberhardt & etc.). They saw Mr. Rhoades in conversation with Cavenaugh and two other parties yesterday A-M, but they separated and Mr. R. (Rhoades) was lost in the crowd. The former parties have been watching for him all the while but up to noon to-day have not met him excepting that W. (Wight) met him Monday early for a few moments only. Mr R. (Rhoades) was not to be found at the hotel yesterday, and last night while the parties were waiting for him his wife came out of the hotel together with a young man and a little girl and went to a house on third east near third south streets. So I am informed to-day. The parties are very much worried to learn what is up. Lane told Wight to-day what word you left at his house. Lane found the old gent (Rhoades) late yesterday, and had a promise to come to his house to-day. W. (Wight) was at the corner a few moments ago waiting. Clawson drove to Lane's house the A-M and I presume was hunting for the old gent, as he could not be located in the hotel yesterday and it is presumed that he was there until evening, I draw the conclusion that he was out of sight from the other parties and is keeping away from them. I should judge that he is all right. I would like to meet Mr. R. (Rhoades) after the other parties get him located. I presume that you have not mentioned your visit to me. I go into this detail that your mind may be easy as possible with affairs at this end.*

*Referring to your assay scheme. Of course you know that country far better than I, but judging from all the reports I get from the mining sections you could not accomplish very much at this early time of the year, especially this season. All of the mountains throughout this latitude are* under immense blankets of snow, and I should think that you would be running a great risk in attempting it. Twelve miles up City Creek the snow is ten feet on a level, and these mountains do not compare with the others in altitude.

Another point: I should judge from the Henderson letter and the Clawson stir that the former is running no risk in turning down your drafts, and that something has been or is to be accomplished, if that is the case do you not think it will be wise for you to be on tap? You might be wanted badly and if not where we could find you quick the New York parties might take some undue advantage of the circumstances. They certainly will advise you sometime during April in case they accomplish' their contract, and that is only a little more than a month. In my judgement it will be wise to wait a little longer rather than run too much risk.

My money is all in mining stocks—what is not necessary to handle my business—I have some stocks which I calculate to unload with others on the Boston market, the broker tells me he is advised that some time during April they expect the market to be in condition to unload, which I trust is correct. I was thinking of your scheme after you left, and I believe we can arrange the matter if the New York parties fall down. Should you want, and find it advisable to have someone along to help you, in case there is no risk of giving away your locations, I believe that Redfield would go along, I suggest this thinking that two might accomplish more than double what one could. I will not say anything to Redfield until you say so.

Should I learn of anything of moment I will advise you promptly, and in case Mr. R. (Rhoades) should write you giving details of what has happened to him I would be pleased to learn the substance.

Yours very respectfully,
FRANK L. KING

## MACDONALD TO HATHENBRUCK
Fort Du Chesne, Utah, March 22, 1899.

Friend Doc:
I received all your letters and papers and they are entirely satisfactory.

I think a certain man (you know who I mean) opened your first letter, the result is that I am fired from my home. Myton I think has had me ordered to Arizona, and I leave tomorrow. I mail this at Price.

The Click here is after the mineral, and they thought I might be in the way of their supplanting you. There is some talk of taking Eleven (11) Indians up to Washington, five Uintahs and five White Rivers, to help the click get a lease, but if things do not change wonderfully they will find when they get to Washington that the Indians are in favor of Hathenbruck and Rhodes, and not the people they brought hear to help.

Do all you can in the mean time.

If Henry used the petition here he would not get to go to Washington all the White Rivers want him to go, the Uintahs also. I am going to Fort Huachuca Arizona.

Doc, I hope every thing will turn out as we wish it will. While we are not doing any loud talk we are doing what we can.

If the Indians go to Washington, try and have some of your people at the council.

If they did not get at the letter you sent they found out that I sent you the telegram when the last outfit went.

You will be notified when this outfit leaves here, and as much before that time as is possible.

Keep a stiff upper lip, and do every thing in your power, and you will be rewarded for all time spent.

Burn this up as soon as you get it: for it is got out my position would not be worth much.

Yours sincerely,
A. MACDONALD

## PEYTON TO HATHENBRUCK

*Department of Justice,*
*Washington, D.C.,*
*March 25, 1899.*
*F.W.C. Hathenbruck, Esq.,*
*Provo City, Utah.*

*My dear Doctor:*

*I am in receipt of yours of the 21st instant and also had a letter from you sometime ago which I have not answered because I had nothing whatever to write.*

*Since I last wrote you I have learned absolutely nothing about our business matters and possibly don't know as much about what is going on as you do; I have had no communication with our New York people and do not know whether they have abandoned the enterprise or not. I do not agree with you however, in your surmise that there is a probability that the lease is approved. I am perfectly satisfied that no further action has, as yet, been taken upon the same.*

*As to that part of your letter wherein it is stated that Mr. Cavanaugh had secured any information from me regarding our matters I have to say that there is no warrant whatever for the statement. I do not know Mr. Cavanaugh nor do I recall ever having seen him. The fact of the things is these matters have been so quiet of late I have had nothing to say about it to anybody other than to write to you on one or two occasions.*

*Replying to your request for a statement as to what was done by you while in Washington I can say truthfully that there was nothing left undone by you that you could do in the interest of the lease. I know that you had repeated communications with both Cavanaugh and Clarkson and trusted in them as long as it seemed that your interest would warrant this course. Of course I knew nothing about what was transpiring between you and Clarkson further than what you told me but I do know that you were constantly in communication with him and further what you told me had transpired between you and McKay after having been referred to McKay by Clarkson. It was then my opinion, and is now, that there was nothing left for you to do but form new associations in the interest of your lease as it seemed from what you told me that they had practically abandoned it. The foregoing is concisely what happened while you were here so far as I know from general observation and from what you told me and I have no reason to doubt the truth of it.*

*Should I learn anything of importance I will communicate with you.*

*Very truly yours,*
*HARRY PEYTON*

## WIGHT TO HATHENBRUCK

*Salt Lake City, Utah,*
*March 25th, 1899.*
*F W C Hathenbruck, Esq.*

*Dear Friend:*

*Yours of the 16th at hand in due time and would have been answered before, but learning you were in town Monday I expected I would be able to see you. In reply to your queries will say that my letters of the 9th and 15th are explicit enough on that subject. However if it does not satisfy your enquiring mood I will explain to your entire satisfaction whenever you see fit to see me personally. I will return you the note at the same time.*

*Now I wish to say, if you are not satisfied with the disposition I made of the bills of sale to interests in the lease, I am willing to go over the whole matter with you before Caleb Rhoades as sole judge and jury, and abide by his decision, of course I should expect to go over all your letters and mine as well as your checks which would be the only way to arrive at a just conclusion, I understand Mr. Rhoades is to be here until next Tuesday.*

*I feel confident that if we were to talk this matter over by ourselves, we could come to a satisfactory conclusion in a very short time.*

*I have always upheld you before Mr. R. (Rhoades) and all parties interested when circumstances seemed against you, and I can assure you it is to your interest to see me before making any demonstration such as your letters to Mr. E. and Mr. T. (Eberhardt and Turton) would indicate you contemplated.*

*Yours truly,*
*L.O. WIGHT*

## HENDERSON TO HATHENBRUCK

*Westchester, N.Y.,*
*March 29th, 1899.*
*F.W.C. Hathenbruck, Esq.,*
*Provo City, Utah*

*My dear Doctor:*

*I have your favor of the 21st at hand, and I must say that its contents did not surprise me at all. They turned to you to get an interest in your lease only after they had made application for a permit to go upon the Reservation and negotiate a new one. When they ascertained that this permit would not be granted to them, they took up the only string left.*

*It is extremely unfortunate that that territory out there has such a far-famed reputation for value. It seems as though it were known over the entire country and the scramble for possession is simply terrible. I do not desire to go into details at all, any further than to say that we are not sleeping and that we will ultimately secure possession of the tract of land that we started for something over a year ago. I don't think you need worry about the McKay-Clarkson crowd at all. I believe that they are disposed of at the present moment, but there are other interests which are proving far more troublesome. When the time comes when I feel that I dare tell you just what has been done, I believe that you will say that we have done the very best that could be done under the circumstances.*

*Yours &c.,*
*H.C. HENDERSON. per. M.B.*

*Hotel Manhattan,*
*July 19th, 1899.*
*Dr. F.W.C. Hathenbruck, Esq.*

*Dear Doctor:*

*I have just succeeded in reaching our parties and I send (illegible) check for $100.—I will have a full conference next week where I will urge the commencement of legal proceedings to force the Department to action. The trouble now is with Jones the Indian Commissioner. What has struck him I don't understand. He has always favored leasing as against selling and now that his help would probably control, he balks. I have been awfully busy in my fight with the (illegible) but will win it all right. I don't think you need fear anything out there until new orders are given for no council can be held under present orders and so no lease made.*

*Yours &c.,*
*H.C. HENDERSON*

## JUDD TO HATHENBRUCK

*Office of John W. Judd, Attorney at Law,*
*Nashville, Tenn., July 20, 1899.*
*F.W.C Hathenbruck, Esq.,*
*Provo, Utah.*

*As you will see by this I am located in my office in Nashville Tenn. for business. Your letter was forwarded to me here at this place & I hasten to answer.*

*There are some things concerning our lease that I do not understand at this time but before long I shall go about finding out. I believe that ultimately we shall succeed in the matter & that we will get the benefits of our labor.*

*I shall write to Peyton today or tomorrow & when I hear from him will advise you.*

*Yours Respy,*
*J.W. JUDD*

## HENDERSON TO HATHENBRUCK

*New York, November 14th, 1899.*
*Dr. F.W.C. Hathenbruck,*
*Provo City, Utah.*

*Dear Sir:*

*I am in receipt of your favor of the 28th instant in relation to our Uintah interests.*

*I wrote you in June last that when the new Secretary of the Interior had taken his office an effort would be made to have him assume a favorable attitude toward leasing the minerals on the Uintah Reservation, and a great deal of work has been done in that direction. Up to the time that he went away on his vacation, and in fact at that point, it seemed as though he would certainly decide in favor of the policy of leasing, and up to ten days or two weeks ago everything looked very favorable so far it's the Secretary was concerned. There has been one difficulty in our way, however, and that has been my inability to satisfy the Government that we were of sufficient financial ability to develop the lands embraced within the proposed lease, and the Secretary has consistently and uniformly insisted upon it that no lease should be given for the purpose of speculation, but simply for the purpose of development and the payment of the proceeds for the benefit of the Indians, and if the Secretary had gone so far as to actually decide in favor of leasing it would have been necessary for us then, I think, to have formed a corporation so as to enable us to satisfy the Secretary of our financial standing.*

*About two weeks ago, however, the Secretary took a back track entirely under the influence, as I have every reason to believe, and in fact know, of the Assistant Secretary, Judge Ryan. It now appears that Judge Ryan has been able up to this time to have greater influence with the Secretary in that regard than has Indian Commissioner Jones, who has always favored the leasing of these rights, so at this time it stands—the Secretary undecided, with Ryan on one side opposing the leasing of the mineral lands, and Jones on the other side in favor of leasing, but although the Secretary is undecided as to what policy to adopt, I feel confident that Judge Ryan is going to be able to control the Secretary. I base this conclusion upon the fact that the Secretary's mind was at one time fully made up that leasing the lands was the proper policy, and some of our New York Congressmen went over there to give the Secretary the idea that that was the proper policy. At one interview the Secretary openly stated that he believed that the leasing of the Uintah rights was the proper solution of the question, and since that time he has gone back and now is very much in doubt, and it would appear to me that if Judge Ryan has been able to induce the Secretary to take a back track even to that extent, he is going to be able to prevent him from approving any leases, or even from granting any permits for the negotiation of leases with the Indians.*

*What our friends can do in Congress towards forcing this thing through I don't know. I do know that the Senators from Utah will have some new forces to contend with if they attempt to force their policy through at the next session of Congress. I am not as yet as I was two weeks ago, and yet I am not without hopes that the thing may eventually come our way. How to handle Judge Ryan I don't know. In fact he has taken such a strong position against leasing, that I cannot see how anybody could possible induce him to change his attitude, and unless his influence over the secretary can be shaken in some way, I am afraid that he will prevail. We have had the strongest Congressional influence that we can reach,—including some prominent men from the West—to work upon this matter trying to have the policy of leasing adopted by the Department, and we have been unsuccessful up to this time. We are still at work at it, but with what prospects of success I am absolutely unable to state more fully. Of course if you desire us to continue to work in your interests in the matter, well and good, and if you feel that you have given us all the time that you want to give us and desire to make other arrangements, I cannot ask you to consider us any further in the matter. I must confess that I feel that we are pretty near the end of our rope, and I am at a loss to know where to get additional influence to bring to bear upon the Secretary of the Interior. I am in hopes, however, that Sherman and some more of the people may be able to do something with him when it comes to Congressional matters and appropriations for Indians. We have not given up our efforts by any means but are working still to induce the Secretary to take the step necessary. There is one thing, however, that you must bear in mind, and that is that if the Secretary should change his attitude and conclude to lease the mineral rights there, it would be necessary for us to at once form a corporation so as to show the Secretary of the Interior that we intend to develop and not to sell, for I believe that he is fully determined that such leases if granted shall not be given to people simply as a matter of speculation and not with an honest intent to develop.*

*I wish you would let me hear from you at your earliest opportunity and advise us what you expect us to do.*

*Yours &c.,*
*H.C. HENDERSON.*

*Dictated*
*By M. Benton*

## MOYLE TO HATHENBRUCK

*Salt Lake City, Utah, April 23rd, 1900.*
*F.W.C. Hathenbruck, Esq.,*
*Provo, Utah.*

*Dear Sir:*

*In reply to yours yesterday will say that we can probably do the business necessary by letter as well as otherwise. The proposition which I desire to present to Mr. Cavanaugh is that we all assign our interests in the property in question to one or more trustees to be agreed upon. I am willing that any of the parties interested may select any well known, substantial, reliable business men in Salt Lake City as trustees. Let the trustees hold the property in trust for the corporation to be formed, the officers of the corporation to be agreed upon at the same time that we agree upon the trustees. Then if there are any differences between the claimants of interests in the property by assignment from you and Rhoades or either, and also of anybody else, they can be adjusted later on, and in the meantime a corporation can be formed to do business. If Cavanaugh refuses to join with us, I will then force an acceptance or refusal from Cavanaugh. So*

answer at once. By this method it will not be necessary to determine what our several interests are, and we can thereby avoid a controversy, except between the individuals having conflicting claims, and those can be adjusted without retarding the progress of the enterprise. Please answer by return mail, as Cavanaugh is liable to leave the city at a very early date.

Respectfully yours,
J.H. MOYLE

Salt Lake City, Utah, April 25th, 1900.
F.W.C. Hathenbruck, Esq.,
Provo, Utah.

Dear Sirs

Your favor of the 24th instant just at hand, in reply to which will say that it is useless to talk about adjusting differences before the corporation is formed. My suggestion is that we all convey our interests and those to Trusties and let the trustees organize a corporation, with a board of directors to be agreed upon by all those interested or to be selected by the trustees, and have sufficient treasury stock set aside to pay the expenses of the corporation and working capital and in that way secure action and desired results. I do not know of anyone who will purchase your interest for any such consideration as you suggest and I do not care to talk with Mr. Cavanaugh further about the matter until I am able to make a definite proposition to him. I have seen him but the once and he talks in a general way friendly and I can do no more now until I can make a definite proposition. It will be perfectly agreeable to me if you name one of the trustees and Mr. Rhodes the other, and they two a third, provided you will name a prominent business man in the community. Whether the others will agree to it I do not know,

but that will be a detail that can readily be adjusted when we agree on the main proposition. Please write and state whether or not you will join in the proposed plan without any conditions attached other than those suggested. By that plan you will be protected so far as it is possible from paying out any moneys whatever and your interest in the corporation will be placed in such a condition that you will readily be able to dispose of all or any part of it if the lease is worth anything. Otherwise, we will go on haggling over side issues forever.

Now I am absolutely certain that his proposition is in the interest of all concerned. It is one which I have determined upon myself, after very careful consideration and one which I know is in your interest and in the interest of all concerned and you can certainly agree to it unless you can suggest some better plan, and I am certain none can be suggested that will be satisfactory, if it contemplates a settlement of all disputes and differences between the various parties interested before incorporation.

I hope to have your reply by tomorrow morning's mail as Mr. Cavanaugh is not going to remain here more than this week, and it will take some time to close the matter up, if the general plan is agreed upon.

Trusting that you will reply promptly, I am,

Respectfully yours,
J.H. MOYLE

P.S. If you insist on it I will take one half your interest for protecting the other subject to foregoing plan, but I think it would be foolish for you to do that. I assure you I'm confident my plan will aid you and a serious mistake will be made by its rejection. It will protect the rights of all.

MOYLE

## WIGHT TO HATHENBRUCK
*Salt Lake City, Utah, Apr. 28th, 1900*
*F.W.C. Hathenbruck, Esq.*

*Dear Sir:*

*Your favor of the 24th was just handed me by the postman: In reply will say that H.B. Clawson returned two or three weeks ago. He reports that matters are O.K. in Washington as soon as matters are arranged here. Mr. Rhoades has not been in Salt Lake since last fall, but is expected up as soon as all matters are arranged to sign final papers.*
*There has been several meetings lately the import of which Mr. Moyle has informed you. There is to be another meeting Monday at 4-30 P.M. I would like to see you present, as I am fully satisfied that the business will go through all right this time. The disposition seems to be to "bury the hatchet," come up and "join the procession" with the majority.*

*Yours truly,*
*L.O. WIGHT*

## MOYLE TO HATHENBRUCK
*Salt Lake City, Utah, April 28th, 1900.*
*F.W.C. Hathenbruck, Esq.*
*Provo, Utah.*

*Dear Sir:*

*In reply to yours of the 26th instant will say that fearing that we would not be able to get a greater number of the parties interested together, the interests of Mr. Wight, Cavanaugh, Clarkson, Beattie, Dodge, Rhoades and myself agreed yesterday to organize a corporation for the purpose of advancing the interests of the incorporators in the Indian lease, and convey all our interests as suggested to you, to the trustees, who will, with the board of directors, which has been practically agreed upon, look after the interests of those concerned in the corporation. The arrangement is so made that you can come in and also others who are interested. Each party to produce evidence of his title under the assignments made by you and Rhodes. By this means, I am satisfied, we will be able to accomplish something and if you desire to join your interest with the rest so advise me.*

*Respectfully yours,*
*J.H. MOYLE*

## HATHENBRUCK TO MOYLE
*April 29th, 1900.*
*Hon. James H. Moyle,*
*Salt Lake City, Utah.*

*Dear Sir:*

*From your of the 28th inst. I presume that my opinion on any measures you and your colleagues have contemplated upon, will not be considered of any weight: In consequence I will quietly await results. But with this proviso: "That I authorize no one to act for me-nor will I be bound by any measures adopted unless my consent is first obtained in writing.*
*In conclusion I cannot understand these "high-handed" measures, I being the legal owner of an undivided Seventeen -fortieths interest in and to the Hathenbruck and Rhodes Lease unimpaired and unencumbered.*
*Nevertheless I should be pleased to learn of your future acts in the matter and any aid I am able to render in the matter I will willingly give.*

*Yours truly,*
*F.W.C. Hathenbruck*

## KING TO HATHENBRUCK

*House of Representatives,*
*Washington, D.C., May 7th, 1900.*
*F.W.C. Hathenbruck, Esq.,*
*Provo, Utah.*

*Dear Sir:*

*Yours of the first inst. to hand. I read with great interest your suggestions in regard to the Uncompahgre and Uintah reservations, I concur in most of what you say, and I do not know that I disagree with you in regard to any of your statements. There is unquestionably a syndicate formed for the possession and control of all hydro-carbon deposits in Utah, and there is no question but what the influence of the Interior Department has been for years, against the best interests of the people.*

*You know my views in regard to the matter, as we went over the ground very fully when you were in Washington. I oppose leasing, as I think it would retard public occupancy.*

*However, if the department intends leasing, I shall do all I can to see that Utah men get the preference, and shall be glad to aid you, if necessary against any effort, which may be made, to have your lease canceled in favor of some eastern syndicate.*

*I know you are thoroughly acquainted with the Indians on the reservation, and I will be very glad to aid you in securing Government position, as per your request.*

*Yours very truly,*
*WILLIAM H. KING*

## MOYLE TO HATHENBRUCK

*Salt Lake City, Utah, May 11, 1900.*
*F.W.C. Hathenbruck Esq.*
*Provo, Utah.*

*Doctor,*

*Have just learned facts which I believe it will be to our mutual advantage to consider together. I will pay your expense here if you will come to the City at once. Say Sunday or Monday morning.*

*Yours in haste*
*MOYLE*

## WARD TO HATHENBRUCK

*Washington, D.C., May 1st, 1901*
*F.H. Hathenbruck Esq.,*
*Provo, Utah.*

*Dear Sir:*

*I am informed that you know of the location of a valuable mineral (gold) deposit within the limits of the Uintah Indian Reservation.*

*If my information is correct and if it will not be inconsistent with your own interests, I will thank you, without disclosing the location of said deposit, to advise me whether or not you are satisfied that it is in paying quantities, whether you have had any of the quartz assayed and if so the result thereof, whether a lease of the deposit can be procured and on what terms you will disclose the location of the deposit if a lease thereof could be procured, together with such other information as you may deem proper.*

*Yours truly,*
*GEO. A. WARD*

## MOYLE TO SMOOT

*Salt Lake City, Utah, June 12, 1901.*
*Hon. Reed Smoot,*
*Provo, Utah.*

*Dear Friend:*

*I believe you have the Articles of Incorporation, of the Rhoades Mining Company, which I would be very glad to have at your earliest convenience.*

*The lease has not yet been approved but there seems to be every prospects of its being approved, at an early day.*

*With kind regards, I am,*

*Very respectfully yours,*
*J.H. MOYLE*

## PEYTON TO HATHENBRUCK

*The Attorney General,*
*Department of Justice,*
*Washington, D.C., July 9th 1901.*
*F.W.C. Hathenbruck, Esq.,*
*Provo, Utah.*

*My dear Doctor:*

*I am just in receipt of yours of the 4th inst. I have heard nothing of the approval of the lease, and, candidly, I think the lease is dead beyond resurrection. I do not believe it possible, ever, to get the present lease confirmed by the Secretary: the influences that have been behind it would have long since had a confirmation if that had been possible. I have never heard of either of the parties mentioned in your letter and do not think they have ever had any connection with our New York friends. I met Mr. Henderson here a week or so ago, just for a moment, and do not know if he was on the lease matter or not; but do think that if anything ever comes of the mining matter on the reservation, it will come through them. I think you are holding on to false hopes if you expect ever to realize on the present lease. I believe the best thing to do is to steer clear of the parties who have pretended to have your interests in hand. Your experiences here and afterwards showed what treachery they were capable of if an opportunity affords itself*

*I believe your interests would best be served by sticking to the N.Y. Crowd, and cutting loose and having nothing whatever to do with any other interests. If any thing, in any shape, can be done, they will land it if any one can. It seems this Sec'y, like the last one, has been dead set against mining leases. If any are ever granted, in my judgment, it will be limited to certain area. A blanket lease over a large section, in my opinion, will never be approved. My family are all well—Hope you and yours are—My best wishes,*

*Truly Yours,*
*HARRY PEYTON*

## BOYD TO HATHENBRUCK

*Boston Consolidated Mining Company*
*Bingham Canyon, Utah, August 27, 1901.*
*F.W.C. Hathenbruck Esq.*
*243 East 5th Street*
*North Provo.*

*Dear Sir:*

*I am in receipt of your letter of Aug. 23rd to C.C. Parsons, Jr. I cannot say for certain how much of our original outfit remains in Stockmore. There cannot be much left.*

*What remains I am in need of at present—as Mr. Hanchett is thinking of going for a camping expedition next month and would like the use of anything that I can collect for him. I remain,*

*Yours Truly,*
*W.L. BOYD*

## HATHENBRUCK TO TAYLOR

*Salt Lake, Jan. 20th, 1902.*
*Mr. G. Taylor.*

*Dear Sir:*

*I just learned that you have served papers to vacate—(I just returned from the Los Vegas Desert)—I am surprised at that, and have written (illegible) Smoot to see you at once, far (illegible) to your satisfaction. I am regrettably detained here a few days, hence I ask a few days delay from you.*
*Hoping this will meet your approval, I remain,*

*Respectfully,*
*FWC Hathenbruck*

## SUTHERLAND TO HATHENBRUCK

*House of Representatives,*
*Washington, D.C., January 31st, 1902.*
*F.W.C. Hathenbruck Esq.,*
*Provo City, Utah.*

*My dear Sir:*
*I have your letter of the 22nd inst, enclosing brief in the Reservation lease matter. I am very much obliged to you for the papers.*
*Since I have investigated this subject I have become very strongly opposed to any lease bing granted to any person or corporation. I think it is bad policy and think it would tend to delay the opening of the Reservation. You can, therefore, see that I cannot urge or advise the granting of your lease.*
*We are now working with a view to bring about the opening of the Reservation, and will use every possible exertion to bring it about.*
*I have requested that the documents which you ask for be at once sent for you; If you do not receive them, let me know and we will look after them.*

*Yours very truly,*
*GEO. SUTHERLAND*

## HENDERSON TO HATHENBRUCK

*New York, March 14th, 1902.*
*F.W.C. Hathenbruck, Esq.,*
*243 East 5th. St. N.,*
*Provo, Utah.*

*Dear Doctor:*

*I am in receipt of your letter of the 8th. inst.*
*Yes, I went up on the reservation to represent the Florence Mining Company, and succeeded in negotiating a lease for 640 acres of land. No doubt you have seen the basis of the proposed investigation, which by the way, does not apply specifically to the Florence Company, but I wish it did. The Florence Company has nothing to hide, and I am prepared at any time to go before any Committee and disclose everything in relation to the obtaining of the lease in question and everything in relation to the Company itself. Our Company is urging, and will continue to urge, the investigation, for we think that it ought to be demonstrated that we have not now, and have never had, and relations with the people whose correspondence has been published, but on the contrary, we have been opposed to them and have succeeded in getting what they were trying to get. There are some people in your State of some prominence who have, we think, a good deal more to fear from an investigation than any one else, and it will be our effort to make the investigation as sweeping and as broad as possible, if it is ever undertaken.*
*I understand that subpoenas have been issued for some day in the latter part of this month, or the beginning of April, and that your name in on the list of witnesses to be subpoenaed, and if you come on at that time I will be able to inform you of all that has taken place since I last saw you. I trust you will give yourself no uneasiness whatever concerning the regularity of our proceedings, nor of any facts which could possibly be developed by any investigation, no*

matter how thorough it may be. I probably saw the article which you refer to in the Herald, but I didn't notice that Rhoades was particularly lauded. However, there has been so much published, and much of it containing so little truth, that I haven't examined the matter as closely as I otherwise might. I will see if I can run across a copy of the paper, although I don't think it was the Christmas number, and if so, I will be glad to send it to you. If you are summoned and do not come to Washington, let me know at once where you will stop at Washington, so that I may meet you when I go over. If you are not summoned and do not come to Washington, I will gladly give you such information concerning the matter as I can by mail. Trusting that I may see you before a great while, I am,

Yours &c.,
H.C. HENDERSON

New York, May 7th, 1902.
Mr. F.W.C. Hathenbruck,
Provo City, Utah.

My dear Doctor:

I am in receipt of your favor and note what you say with reference to me in your new undertaking. If inquiries are made I shall render you such assistance as I can. In relation to the other matters mentioned in your letters, I am absolutely unable at this time to give you the information which you request.

Things have not changed very materially from what they were when I was with you two years ago, but as I explained to you then, by reason of so many interests, I am wholly unable to determine what I can accomplish for you. As I said to you then I say to you now, I shall do all I can to help you along but as I am not in a position to control matters, it would be folly for me to say what that bill be.

Very truly yours,
H.C. HENDERSON,
(Dictated by M. Benton.)

New York, May 19th, 1902.
F.W.C. Hathenbruck, Esq.,
Provo City, Utah.

My dear Doctor:

Your letter received to-day. I anticipated that Rhoades will cooperate with us and go to the Reservation if he is physically able to do so. I would like to be in a position to advise my friends here in relation to yourself. Of course, if the matter is adjusted as contemplated by the Bill which has passed Congress and the Indians consent to the arrangement, there will be no difficulty whatever in having you and such other persons as we desire to go upon the Reservation and to investigate as fully as we desire. I would like to know whether or not you will l go with us and give us you best knowledge concerning the location of the valuable metals, and more especially concerning the location of the Rhoades mine upon which you place a great value. I must confess that I have never shared your notion of the value of that particular location, fearing that it was probably a pocket and of no very great substantial value. However, it will be of value to me to know that you are prepared to act with us and to assist us in locating that particular place. I will be much surprised if you do not find something which will prove of a great deal more value than this particular parcel, and your knowledge of that locality may be of considerable assistance in that regard.

There was to have been a meeting in this City on the 24th, to determine what steps should be taken by the Florence Company. I shall try to have the matter postponed until a later date and until I receive some definite information *from you which I may then place before the directors.*

*Kindly let me hear from you as soon as you can and let me know where I may be able to meet you if I go West again. If everything progresses as it now appears, there will be no necessity whatever of any attempt to conceal our movements, but we will be able to act openly and to go upon the territory and examine as fully and as freely as if the matter were entirely open and beyond the control of the Indians.*

*Very truly yours,*
H.C. HENDERSON,

*(Dictated by M. Benton.)*


*New York, May 29th, 1902.*
*F.W.C. Hathenbruck, Esq.,*
*Provo City, Utah.*


*My dear Sir:*

*I am in receipt of your favor of the 23d. instant, but I am unable to determine from the tenor thereof what attitude you expect to take toward the Florence Mining Company. If I read your letter correctly, it is not your intention to render it any assistance whatever in its work of locating the mining claims provided for under the Act which has just received the approval of the President. You must understand that the Florence Company is absolutely distinct, independent of, and has not relations whatever, and never has had, with any other company attempting to secure mining privileges or rights in that territory. It is true that some persons connected with the Company have attempted to secure the approval of the Rhoades-Hathenbruck lease, but were unsuccessful in their efforts. It became manifest that the interests in that lease had become so numerous and conflicting that it was absolutely unsafe and unwise to secure its approval, aside from the determination of the Department in Washington to defeat it. This lease has been disapproved,*

*which action was final and conclusive and no rights exist thereunder, nor will any claim be made by the Florence Company relying in any way whatever upon any matter connected directly or indirectly with that lease. If you are to act with the Florence Company at all it must be without regard to any other interests or purpose. If you cannot do that, I would suggest that you say so frankly and we will know exactly where we stand.*

*I received a telegram from you yesterday asking me to see Moyle at Washington. I have no intention of seeing Moyle or anyone else and he may stir up such parties as he pleases, as far as I am concerned.*

*If I read the Act correctly and understand the situation properly, no one but the Florence Company can locate lands upon this territory before it is returned to the public domain, which is to be in October 1908, and the Florence Company can locate but 640 acres. I don't know what other parties you refer to in your telegram, and consequently fail to see the importance of seeing Mr. Moyle.*

*It would appear from your letter that your are laboring under the impression that it is within the power of the Florence Company to permit other interests than those mentioned in the Bill to prospect and locate mining claims before the property is opened for settlement. This is entirely an error. The statute fixes the parties having such right and it is limited to companies who have received a permit from the Department to negotiate such lease, and this permit obtained prior to the passage of the Act in question, viz; prior to May 28th., the date of the approval of the Bill. The records in the Department will show that the only person having such permit is the Florence Company and it is as impossible for the Florence Company to extend that right to another party as it is for an absolute stranger. If you intend to cling to the Hathenbruck and Rhoades lease and the people associated in that matter, be frank enough to say so, and I will understand the situation thoroughly. If, on the other hand, you intend to give your aid to the Florence Company, I trust you will be equally frank and in that event I will bring the matter to the attention of the parties interested in the Florence Company and do what I can to see that you personally have such recognition and assistance as is consistent with the services which you may render and any rights which you may have, or any consideration to which you may be entitled as a prior discoverer of lands of value. Kindly let me hear four you before the 10th of June, as this matter will come up for consideration and determination at about that time.*

*Yours very truly,*
*H.C. HENDERSON*

*(Dictated by M. Benton)*

*New York, July 21st, 1902.*
*Mr. F.W.C. Hathenbruck,*
*Provo City, Utah.*

*My dear Doctor:*

*Your favor of the 13th. inst. reached me this morning, and I have received your other letters and your telegram.*

*As I explained to you some time ago, it is impossible for me to do anything in relation to your property until I have had the title to it searched; that my possibly have been attended to by this time, but if so I have not received the report in relation to it. I asked a party in Salt Lake City to take the matter up some two or three weeks ago, and I assume that it is being attended to. If the title is right I anticipate no difficulty whatever in sending the money. Your letters to me have been very perplexing and somewhat contradictory, and I apprehend that the reason for it is that your are being approached by Moyle, representing the Rhoades Company out there, basing his facts upon some act of Congress which has been disapproved some right to go upon the reservation and to prospect. I know of the claims in*

*relation to this project, but I have not the slightest idea that any such scheme will ever get through Congress.*

*I have not yet received from you any assurance that you will act with me in this matter and do in relation to it as I say, and in the absence of such assurance, I have got to assume responsibilities which I think it is unfair for you to force upon me. I have got to assure our people that you will so act with me before I have any right to ask them to advance the money which it is necessary for you to have, and if I do upon my own responsibility and in the face of your conflicting and perplexing letters, I am doing a great deal more for you than I really feel that I should. In your last letter it would appear that you are willing to do this very thing, and yet you don't say so in express language.*

*In relation to your copper project, I let our mineralogist have some of the specimens and asked him to. Tell me what his opinion of the was. He said that he hardly thought that this was of any value at this time, as we might visit the ground when we were in the West so that he might examine the situation, and possible secure some specimens which had not been so close to the surface, and it might enable him to judge as to whether the vein was sufficient strength to warrant an attempted development; in fact, he would not pass upon the question even if he analyzed the specimens which he already had, so that matter must stand until I can reach your territory, and I will take it up before I return East.*

*There is no truth whatever in the claim that the Florence Company had done any prospecting on the reservation. My information leads me to believe, however, that there are some people there engaged in prospecting, but they are doing it without authority and it must be under cover. It think it is safe to say that the first outfit representing the Florence Company to enter the reservation for the purpose of prospecting, will be in my charge, if the matter can be brought up and pressed during the next six weeks or two months; after that it is doubtful whether I can take the time to go West. The report which you give me is doubtless the same matter that was referred to when I was in Washington a week ago. It will be impossible for me to take the parties in with me as suggested in one of your letters, viz; your nephews. It is pretty well determined who will comprise the first party to enter, and I can see no room in it for anyone from your place except yourself. It is my desire, of course, to have as much accord with both yourself and Rhoades as possible, and I want you to feel and Rhoades to feel that although the Florence Company has the power to enter the reservation, ignoring any claim of either, yet it has no desire or intention to do so, but that it expects to have both you and Rhoades acting perfect accord with us in this matter if it is possible to have you do so. The Secretary of the Interior has made no effort, as yet, to negotiate with the Indians, and when he will do so I do not know, but we do not need to wait for these negotiations unless we see fit. Of course we are anxious to avoid any appearance of friction either with the Department or with the Indians, hence the delay in acting under the rights which are secured to us by the Act of Congress.*

*Upon the receipt of this letter, let me know definitely just how much money it is going to take to satisfy Reed Smoot, and also definitely state whether you will go into this project, leaving the matter entirely in my hands and giving us your best knowledge and experience in the matters concerning which the company is interested. Of course it would not be proper for me to say to you who the people are in our concern who feel that no confidence should be placed in what you say, and who feel that the value of your services are grossly over-estimated by me. However, you are not the only one who is thought of in the same way by people connected with our enterprise. In fact my greatest difficulty has been in trying to harmonize and keep together the*

*conflicting ideas of the people interested in this project. Each one seems to think that the other is of no value in the undertaking, and I have no doubt that there are a lot of them who feel the same toward me and say so when talking about me in my absence. These are matters which are unpleasant but which cannot seem to be avoided, so we must take them up and do the best we can. However, I do not wish to have the situation aggravated by any appearance of vacillation on your part.*

*Yours &c.,*
H.C. HENDERSON,

(Dictated by M. Benton.)

## HATHENBRUCK TO KING

*Provo City, Utah, May 26th, 1903.*
*Frank S. King Esq -*

Dear Sir,

*Yours of the 25th inst. at hand & contents noted. If Mr. Moyle has a plan by which he will have the necessary funds on hand, to secure the 640 acres of mineral land that I am entitled to, and you all agree to it send plan. My plan is to incorporate my right and sell sufficient stock to get the necessary funds.*

*I want some plan agreed upon by next Saturday the 30th inst: and money paid to start P. (project). Put in whoever you choose except Cavanaugh & Turtan nor anyone who you think will be a drag as before.*

*Something must be done before June 1st and if I don't hear from you by May 30th (Saturday) will look elsewhere to protect my right.*

*Respectfully Yours,*
FWC HATHENBRUCK

## HATHENBRUCK TO HENDERSON

*Provo City, Utah, June 1/03 -*
*H.C. Henderson Esq.*

*Dear Sir,*

*Your telegram just to hand, and while I am not surprised I am, in a measure, pleased to see you free of the F. Mng Co. (Florence Mining Company). I have wanted to write you a number of times with a proposition, but feared to do so. I will now explain, and submit my proposition and hope you see fit to join—I owe you some gratitude and a deep obligation, and desire to repay it.*

*I admit the Lease itself is a dead issue—but the right to negotiate for this lease is recognized as in tact by the U.S. Courts, this is the decision of the best attorney's on mining in this State and under the indefinite wording of this Law opening the Reservation, I possess the right to locate, which I contemplate of exercising at the earliest date possible.*

*In submitting my documentary evidence, the opinions are unanimous, that I come under the law, and can locate previous to the Reservation being opened.*

*There will be no more mysterious buss (business): but at once locate & work the ground. To save controversies that might arise, I will sell this right to a Company for an interest & means to locate & work—the interest in the name of some one I can trust. Should you wish to join and have friends that will help, telegraph me as soon as possible. I will give h interest in the mines—am ready to go at once and start operations. Let me hear from you ....*

Respectfully yours,
*FWC HATHENBRUCK*

## DERN TO BROWN

*Salt Lake City, Utah, August 24, 1903.*
*Mr. Arthur H. Brown,*
*Uintah Indian Reservation.*

*Dear Art:*

*This will introduce to you Mr. F. W.C. Hathenbruck, with whom I have made a business arrangement, regarding certain locations he has the right to make on the reservation, before it is opened. If you can be of any assistance to him, whatever you do will be greatly appreciated by me.*

Yours &c
*G.H. DERN*

## DERN TO HATHENBRUCK

*Consolidated Mercury Gold Mines Company,*
*Salt Lake City, Utah, Sept. 15, 1903.*
*Mr. F.W.C. Hathenbruck,*
*Fort Duchesne, Utah.*

*Dear Sir:*

*Your letter of the 6th inst., has just been received. I note with some surprise your request for additional funds to "see you through," as you put it. Under the terms of our contract with you, you assigned to us an undivided 7/15ths in your right to make locations on the reservation, as well as the same interest in any and all locations which you make may by virtue of said right. These assignments were made in consideration of the money we have paid you, the only further stipulation being that we are to pay the expense or recording the locating notices.*

*The contract is very explicit, and under no construction can its terms call for the payment of additional money by us.*

*We are prepared to live up to our agreements, and shall expect the same of you on your side.*

*I have spoken to the other parties who are interested with me, and the above is their view of the matter, and they do not seem to think that you have any reason to ask us to forward additional funds.*

*Yours very truly,*
*G.H. DERN*

## PEYTON TO HATHENBRUCK

*Washington, D.C., Sept. 19, 1903*
*F.W.C. Hathenbruck, Esq.,*
*Provost City, Utah.*

*My Dear Doctor:*

*I had hoped that before this date you would have realized something of value from your mining proposition on the reservation. I recall the very great interest that you had in the enterprise, and also the extreme sacrifices you have made in attempting to carry out to a successful culmination this enterprise. I have understood that nothing definite has yet come of the proposition. You will remember that I have always endeavored to advise you as to what I thought was best for your interest, and I have not, at this time, lost any of my interest in you.*

*I have been reliably informed very recently that Col. George F. Timms had just returned from the reservation, and contemplates going back within the next few days. I believe that it will be very much to your advantage, unless you are involved with other interests, to get into communication with Colonel Timms before he leaves the railroad for the reservation. I understand that Colonel Timms is going to stop a day or two in Denver at the Brown Palace Hotel, and if you want to get into communication with him a telegram addressed to him there would prob-*

*ably induce him to go to Provost to see you. I believe most earnestly that something greatly to your advantage may yet be secured upon the reservation if properly managed, and if I were you I would at once wire Colonel Timms to meet you to Provost before he leaves the railroad for the reservation. Of course, this letter is prompted solely by my interest in you and is personal.*

*With very best wishes for you happiness and success, I am,*

*Very truly yours,*
*HARRY PEYTON*
*714 Band Building*

## DERN TO HATHENBRUCK

*Salt Lake City, Utah, Sept. 29, 1903.*
*F.W.C. Hathenbruck,*
*White Rock Agency,*
*Uintah Reservation, Utah.*

*Dear Sir:*

*I am in receipt of a letter from you consisting of one page marked "P.S.", dated September 28th, beginning with the following words: "Since writing the foregoing I received your letter of the 15th inst." The "foregoing" you evidently neglected to enclose ....*

*Should you meet Mr. J.C. Dick, Mr. Fred M. Brown, or Arthur H. Brown, each of whom has a surveying party, I wish you would explain the conditions fully, so that they may report to me when they return.*

*If you desire to make an offer to return the $125.00 we have paid you, in order to be released from our agreement, please advise me and I will see my partners in the contract and let you know their decision at once.*

*Yours very truly,*
*G.H. DERN*

## TIMMS & HOOPER TO HATHENBRUCK

Camp, Forks of Duchesne River,
Wasatch County, Utah, October 12, 1903.
Mr. F. W.C. Hathenbruck

Sir:

In behalf of the Florence Mining Company, incorporated in the State of New Jersey, we submit to you the following proposition:

If you will show to us, or either of us, a deposit, node, ledge, or vein of mineral of sufficient value to justify us in selecting and locating therein the quality of contiguous mineral land granted to said Company by Act of Congress approved May 27, 1902 and if we shall select and locate said quality of land on any deposit, lode, ledge or vein so shown us, or either of us, by you we will transfer to you, in such manner as you shall direct, two mining claims on said property, and pay over to you ten thousand dollar ($10,000) worth, par value, of the stock of the said Florence Mining Company as soon as (illegible) after the said stock shall be issued. It being understood that the total length of the two said claims combined shall not exceed three thousand (3000) feet, and the two claims must be contiguous, and both selected and made to extend in the same direction from a line drawn the center of the most valuable part of said deposit, lode, ledge or vein, and at right angles with the strike thereof, should any question arise as to the direction from said centre line the said two claims shall extend, such question shall be decided by lot, unless some other method shall be mutually agreed upon.

GEO. F. TIMMS,
F.C. HOOPER

Gentlemen,

I accept the above proposition in all it tenets and significants.

F.W.C. HATHENBRUCK

executed in duplicate.
Witness to all signatures

HENRY WADE

## SMOOT TO HATHENBRUCK

Provo Commercial & Savings Bank,
Provo, Utah, Oct. 14/03.
Mr. F.W.C. Hathenbruck.

Dear Will,

I received your letter Sept. 26th and have read same carefully and note that you expect to furnish me with the legality of the Indian claims, with treaty rights—&c. You know me well enough to know that I do all I can for any person whose rights are jeopardized. I shall take your letter with me to Washington and any other information you can furnish me and do what I can to secure justice for all parties concerned. With best wishes, I remain,

Yours truly
REED SMOOT

## KEIFER TO HATHENBRUCK

Salt Lake,. U. Oct. 28, 1903.
F. W.C. Hathenbruck,
Provo, Utah.

Dear Sir:

I have taken the matter up just as we talked it over and understood it—They have agreed to all the conditions and will put up the $75$^{00}$ and go on with the contracts.

Now they knew Mr. Dick was coming in and

*they wish to wait until he does, as he ought to be here in the next day or two and get his views on the matter, and then the papers will all be made up as agreed and money sent along.*

*This will throw out some of your fears. Can't you go back with Dick—as you will not be able to do anything until he got back any way.*

*Will push it as soon as he gets here.*

Yours truly
JAMES D. KEIFER
Box 1183

## TIMMS TO HATHENBRUCK

*In Camp, Nov. 2, 1903.*
*Dr. F.W.C. Hathenbruck,*
*Provo, Ut.*

*My dear doctor,*

*Your note of Oct 29 is just handed me by a party who was kind enough to ride out here because he thought the letter urgent, having a special del stamp. All our people and horses are out, but I have arranged for one of the surveyor's men to take this out, and I hope that by this hour tomorrow it will be in your hands.*

*The reason for your not returning with our wagon is placed just where I thought it belonged. Without going into detail I will say that our driver disregarded his instructions. He was to wait for you till you were ready to return, or until you notified him that you had made other arrangements for coming in. I regret for your sake and our own that the delay occurred. But we would not be wise to let these things worry. I am quite confident that all these little delays and hindrances will soon be over, and that we will be right up to the harvest for which we have been sowing for so many years. Please consider yourself fully authorized to make, at our expense, any arrangement you think for coming here at once. If you wish to hire*

*a comfortable vehicle and driver to bring you out, do so; if you care to come back on (illegible) with Mr. Hatch and have us send our wagon back for any freight you may have, do that. Or if you prefer to hire a wagon to bring you and your freight, do that. In short, do not hesitate to pursue any course that will expedite your return and your comfortable transportation. Any and all expense that you may incur I will pay immediately on your arrival here. Please have in mind that I want you to incur the expense in order to hasten your return. I have just two specific requests to make—(1) Make all haste, at any cost, to get here. (2) If you can not return with Mr. Hatch send me specific word by him as to what your plans are, and when I may expect to see you here.*

Very Truly Yours,
GEO. F. TIMMS

## KEIFER TO HATHENBRUCK

*Salt Lake, Utah Jan. 7th, 1904.*
*H.W.C. Hathenbruck,*
*Provo, Utah.*

*Dear Sir:*

*Yours of the 4th to hand, and contents noted and in reply will say I can't see how our interview could have changed the matter. Mr. Hooper confirmed your agreement, just as you told me in Provo. But thought as the Camps were all breaking up we had better have Col. Timms come to Salt Lake or let him name the meeting place. Things have turned out so much different from what you present it, they are in a quandary as to what move to make, and will say none of us are in a hurry to spend our money. They all agreed to the arrangements you had with Col. Timms and don't think they will put in any more money until there is something definite, neither do I think they will get out so easy. You know I have always had a great deal of confidence in it and want an interest, and at the* same time can't afford to be putting up money, as it now stands I have got one fourth of the Dern & Hudson interest. Now let me know what they want and how much money there is in it, and I will take it up with them and either get them out or started on going. But I want my interest now—assessable.

Now what is it you want to do, your friends, &c, let me know.

With best wishes,

Yours Truly,
JAMES D. KEIFER

## SMOOT TO HATHENBRUCK

United States Senate,
Washington, D.C., January 15, 1904.
Mr. F.W.C. Hathenbruck,
Provo City, Utah.

My dear Sir:

I am just in receipt of your letter of January 10, 1904, and have read the same with considerable interest. Col. Timms has not called on me yet, and perhaps it is too early to expect him: as soon as he does, I shall listen to him and give his words serious consideration. From your letter I can hardly judge what he really intends to accomplish, or how it can be accomplished, but of course, he will be able to explain this. I certainly hope that you will be successful in obtaining a good large sum of money from the Florence Mining Company people, for you certainly have worked hard and a long time.

I desire to thank you for the interest you have shown in my behalf, and wish you a successful future.

Yours very truly,
REED SMOOT

## HENDERSON TO HATHENBRUCK

New York City, March 31, 1904.
Dr. F.W.C. Hathenbruck,
243 East 5th Street,
Provo City, Utah.

My dear Doctor:

I am in receipt of your favor of March 21st, 1904, and also other communications and telegrams from you. The report which you desired me to forward to Mr. Ward was forwarded immediately upon its receipt, but I have had no communication from Mr. Ward in relation thereto since that time.

No doubt you learned from Mr. Timms that myself and my advise in relation to the Florence matters have been disregarded and ignored, some wise people believing that they knew more about the matter and the situation out there than I did. Of course, I had no desire to force myself into the matter as I had no wish to spend a summer in the mountains, especially, if nothing was to be accomplished.

You will see that it is impossible for me to become interested in your new company without appearing to be acting in bad faith toward the Florence Company so I must decline to accept any stock on a basis of the money which I have advanced to protect your home. Of course, now that you have gone into a rival concern, I cannot expect the Florence Company to return to me the money which I have expended in protecting your home, and can only look to you for it, and I trust that you will take steps to return it to me at the earliest possible date. You know from Colonel Timms that the Company simply refused to advance the money which I sent to protect you, although, at the time I sent it, I felt that they would eventually do so, and the matter is entirely a personal investment made by me, not with any idea, of course, of making money *out of it, but for the purpose of having your name interested with the Florence people. The purpose of the investment has failed, and I am not going to blame you for taking the position which you have, but, as you can see now, I have to rely entirely upon you and upon the property for the return of the money advanced to you. Kindly take the matter up at your earliest convenience and see if you cannot raise the money, and I will be glad to reconvey the property to Mr. Hathenbruck at anytime that you can send the money to me. Give my very kindest regards to Mrs. Hathenbruck, and her family, and say to her that I have very pleasant recollections of my trip to Provo and of my visit to your home.*

*Very truly yours,*
HENRY C. HENDERSON,
HCK/J.PER J.

## TIMMS TO HATHENBRUCK

*Helper, Utah June 11, 1904.*
*Dr. F.W.C. Hathenbruck,*
*Provo, Utah.*

*Dear Doctor,*

*Yours of May 27 was forwarded from Washington, and has come to my hand. So I am hoping to see both you and judge Hatch in a short time. I shall not make any extended answers to your letter now. I thought I should go right on to Provo, but I missed connection with a party whom I thought to meet in Chicago, and have requested him to stop off here for a day. He is going further on, and as I do now know on what day he will reach here I am unable to fix a day for going to Provo. I shall make it as early as possible, however.*

*Very Truly Yours,*
GEO. F. TIMMS.
c/o R.G.W. Hotel,
Helper, Utah.

## HATHENBRUCK TO KEARNS

*Salt Lake City, Utah, Aug. 27, 1904.*
*Senator Thos. Kearns,*

*Honored Sir:*

*In our conversation this morning we touched upon a point in which I am deeply interested, viz: Uintah Reservation. It appears strange to me, that after complying with the Laws and also the rulings of the Interior Department governing Indian reservations, as regard (to) leasing mineral, agricultural and grazing lands, and receiving encouragements and acknowledgments from the Interior Department and the entire sanction (obtained in open council meeting) by all the, then interested Indians residing upon said Uintah Indian reservation, that I should be treated as a criminal when venturing upon said reservation lands, in any capacity.—To qualify the foregoing, I desire to state that I in 1903 was employed as Topographer & Guide by F. M. Lyman, C. R. having a contract to survey several Townships on the Uintah Reservation, and I was prevented from pursuing my labors with said Mr. Lyman, through certain parties inciting the Indians against me, in jeopardy of my life, caused by one F.C. Timms misrepresenting my intentions toward the aforesaid Indian Tribe,—and again this present year 1904, the same Colonel F.G. Timms claiming to represent the Florence Mining Co., makes public assertions that I am entirely tabooed from the Reservation and in addition, that I neither had nor could get any justice, to repeat his words, "from here to Washington," also that he would get his friends to pass a law, whereby I should be debarred from locating any mineral claims on said reservation, for two years after its opening. All of the foregoing I am prepared to prove both by witnesses and documentary evidence, and submit the for going for your favorable consid-*

eration and advice to establish my rights. I have during the time I was getting my lease, successfully treated the Indians when they were sick, clothed them when they were naked and fed them when they were hungry, besides by a sanction all of the Indians and chiefs, paid to old Tabby, the then acknowledged chief, (and this sanction was obtained in open council meeting) about $500.00, old Tabby stating that on account of his age, he desired this amount to help him now.

Senator Kearns, the foregoing is only the briefest synopsis of some of my experience in my labors on the Reservation, during the last ten years, and if compatible with your duties, should deem it an extreme favor to enlist you in my behalf for justice.

Hoping to hear from you, I remain, Honored Sir,

Respectfully yours,
F.W.C. HATHENBRUCK

## WHITALL TO HATHENBRUCK

Denver, Colorado, March 6, 1905.
Mr. F W C Hathenbruck,
Provo, Utah.

Dear Sir:

Replying to .yours of the first inst. Mr. Morley leaves here tomorrow morning, ultimate destination Provo ....He will go into the whole matter with you very frankly, and I trust that you will treat him in a similar way.

"Misery Loves Company," and if we can get together enough of the company we may throw off the misery and burden it upon the Raven (mining company). We all have had more or less similar experience to yours, and if we can get in a pull together, also sufficient Elaterite off the Reservation to warren tour acting, haven't any doubt but what we can make life miserable for the other crowd. With kindest regards and anticipating great success, believe me.

Yours very truly,
THE HYDRO-CARBON MFG.
CO.W.V.R. WHITALL,
President

# APPENDIX B

## INDIAN LEASE AGREEMENTS AND MINING DEEDS

### AGREEMENT—NOV. 15, 1896

This Agreement, made and entered into this Fifteenth day of November, in the year one thousand, eight hundred and ninety six, by and between F.W.C. Hathenbruck of Provo City, Utah County, and C.B. Rhoades, of Price, Carbon County, in the State of Utah, parties of the first part; and John Beck of Salt Lake City, Gotlieb Beck and Eberhardt Bauer both of Eureka, Juab County, State of Utah, parties of the second part, Witnesseth, That:

Whereas, the parties of the first part have a certain knowledge of the existence and location of certain mines, placer, veins or lodes, bearing precious minerals; on the Uintah Reservation, and desire to enter into a contract or lease, with the tribe of Indians occupying the Uintah Reservation, for the development and working of said, placer, veins or lodes, the contract or lease to be on the terms and of the nature and character of the copy which is attached hereto and made a part of this agreement.

Now Therefor, The parties of the first part, at the request of the parties of the second part, and in consideration for the covenants herein expressed to be performed by the party of the second part, the prompt performance of which being a condition precedent, and time be the essence of said condition, do hereby agree to transfer, set over and convey to the party of the second part a One Twentieth part interest in the aforesaid contract or lease, when the legal title to the same shall have been procured and apportioned, as in the said proposed agreement specified.

And the party of the second part, in consider-ation of the promises, hereby agrees to Pay Three Hundred Dollars in lawful Money of the U. S. of America the Receipt of which is hereby acknowledged and use all diligent means, influence and exertions to consummate and help to bring to a successful issue and termination the execution and fulfillment of said proposed agreement between the parties of the first part and the tribe of Indians occupying the Uintah Reservation, Utah.

And it is further mutually covenanted and agreed, if, in any manner, the parties of the second part to the said proposed agreement shall fail or neglect to procure or help to secure the Lease or title to, and the working of said mines, the parties of the first part herein shall be fully and completely, exonerated and released from the covenants and provisions of this agreement.

IN WITNESS WHEREOF, the said parties have hereunto set their hands and seals, the day and year first above written.

SIGNED, SEALED AND DELIVERED
IN PRESENCE OF,

(Signed) JOHN BECK
GOTTLIEB BECK
EBERHARDT BAUER

### AGREEMENT—NOV. 19, 1896

This Agreement, made and entered into this 19th day of November in the year one thousand, eight hundred and ninety six, by and between F.W.C. Hathenbruck of Provo City, Utah County, and C.B. Rhodes, of Price, Carbon County, in the State of Utah, parties of the first part; and Matthew Thomas of Vernal, Uintah County, in the State of Utah, party of the second part, Witnesseth, That:

Whereas, the parties of the first part have a certain knowledge of the existence and location of certain mines, placer, veins or lodes, bearing precious minerals; on the Uintah Reservation, and desire to enter into a contract or lease, with the tribe of Indians occupying the Uintah Reservation, for the development and working of said placer, veins or lodes, the contract or lease to be on the terms and of the nature and character of the copy which is attached hereto and made a part of this agreement.

Now Therefor, The parties of the first part, at the request of the party of the second part, and in consideration of the covenants herein expressed to be performed by the party of the second part, the prompt performance of which being a condition precedent, and time be the essence of said condition, do hereby agree to transfer, set over and convey to the party of the second part a One Twentieth part interest in the aforesaid contract or lease, when the legal title to the same shall have been procured and apportioned, as in the said proposed agreement specified.

And the party of the second part, in consideration of the promises, hereby agrees to Act as interpreter and help to negotiate with the proper Chiefs and use all diligent means, influence and exertions to consummate and help to bring to a successful issue and termination the execution and fulfillment of said proposed agreement between the parties of the first part and the tribe of Indians occupying the Uintah Reservation, Utah.

And it is further mutually covenanted and agreed, if, in any manner, the party of the second part to the said proposed agreement shall fail or neglect to procure or help to secure the Lease or title to, and the working of said mines, the parties of the first part therein shall be fully and completely, exonerated and released from the covenants and provisions of this agreement.

IN WITNESS WHEREOF, the said parties have hereunto set their hands and seals, the day and year first above written.

SIGNED, SEALED AND DELIVERED
IN THE PRESENCE OF

F.W.C. HATHENBRUCK
J.M. THOMAS
CALEB B. RHOADES
THOS. RHOADES

## DOCUMENT—DEC., 1896

STATE OF UTAH

County of Salt Lake
}
} ss.
}

F.W.C. Hathenbruck being first duly sworn on oath says: That he is a resident of Provo, Utah County, Utah. That while he was passing through the Uintah Indian Reservation in 1894, with C.B. Rhoades of Price. Carbon County, Utah, said Rhoades took me to a mine which he claimed to have located in 1859 on said reservation. That I discovered on said claim the original stone monuments erected thereon, and also the remains of the work done on said mine, and from said examination I am satisfied that said work was performed and said locations made as claimed by said Rhoades and as set forth in his affidavit of even date herewith, and which I understand is to accompany this affidavit.

F.W.C. HATHENBRUCK

Subscribed and sworn to before me this _____ day of December, 1896

_____

Notary Public
Original Attached to Lease.

## AGREEMENT—OCT. 6, 1897

This Agreement, made and entered into this Sixth day of October in the year one thousand, eight hundred and ninety seven, by and between F. W.C. Hathenbruck of Provo City, Utah County, and C.B. Rhodes, of Price, Carbon County, in the State of Utah, parties of the first part; and Paul Beck of White Rock, Uintah Reservation, Utah, party of the second part, Witnesseth, That:

Whereas, the parties of the first part have a certain knowledge of the existence and location of certain mines, placer, veins or lodes, bearing precious minerals; on the Uintah Reservation, and desire to enter into a contract or lease, with the tribe of Indians occupying the Uintah Reservation, for the development and working of said, placer, veins or lodes, the contract or lease to be on the terms and of the nature and character of the copy which is attached hereto and made part of this agreement.

Now Therefore, The parties of the first part, at the request of the party of the second part, and in consideration of the covenants herein expressed to be performed by the party of the second part, the prompt performance of which being a condition precedent, and time be the essence of said condition, do hereby agree to transfer, set over and convey to the party of the second part a One Twentieth part interest in the aforesaid contract or lease, when the legal title to the same shall have been procured and apportioned, as in the said proposed agreement specified.

And the party of the second part, in consideration of the premises, hereby agrees to Help to procure the necessary Signatures of the Confederated tribe of the Ute Nation and use all diligent means, influence and exertions to consummate and help to bring to a successful issue and termination the execution and fulfillment of said proposed agreement between the parties of the first part and the tribe of Indians occupying the Uintah Reservation, Utah.

And it is further mutually covenanted and agreed, if, in any manner, the parties of the second part to the said proposed agreement shall fail or neglect to procure or help to secure the Lease or title to, and the working of said mines, the parties of the first part therein shall be fully and completely, exonerated and released from the covenants and provisions of this agreement.

IN WITNESS WHEREOF, the said parties have hereunto set their hands and seals, the day and year first above written.

SIGNED, SEALED AND DELIVERED
IN THE PRESENCE OF

F.W.C. HATHENBRUCK
W.H. BERRY
C.B. RHOADES
THOS RHOADES

## DOCUMENT—NOV. 3, 1897

WHEREAS, on the Tenth day of December, 1896, F.W.C. Hathenbruck of Provo City, Utah County, and C.B. Rhodes of Price, Carbon County, both in the State of Utah, as parties of the first part; and James S. Clarkson, of Philadelphia, Pennsylvania, and Hyrum B. Clawson, of Salt Lake City, Utah, as parties of the second part, entered into a certain contract for the purpose of procuring a lease of certain mining properties situate, lying and being in the Uintah Indian Reservation, in Wasatch County, State of Utah, the terms of which contract are fully set out in duplicate copies, one held by each of the said parties of the first and second part; And

WHEREAS, the parties have agreed upon certain modifications of that contract, which are as follows:

### First.

Hathenbruck and Rhodes, as said parties of the first part hereby agree to procure the lease from the Indians, on or before the 15th day of December, 1897, or within ninety (90) days thereafter, of which fact, notice shall at once be given to Clarkson and Clawson, the parties of the second part, by the mailing of a registered letter to H.B. Clawson, at Salt Lake City, Utah, or be delivering it to him in person.

### Second.

The parties of the second part do now furnish to the parties of the first part Five hundred ($500.00) dollars and do agree to put to the credit of the first parties, in the Deseret Nation Bank of Salt Lake City, on or before the 15th day of November, 1897, Two hundred & fifty ($250.00) dollars, and in like manner agree to deposit, on or before the 1st day of December, 1897, Two hundred & fifty ($250.00) dollars, which money, or so much thereof as may be necessary, is to be used to pay the expenses incident to procuring the lease from the Indians, as well as to pay off and discharge the obligations already incurred in that behalf; and if at any time prior to the last named date, the Indians should sign said lease; upon notification thereof, to the said second parties, which notice is to be given by registered letter through the United States mails, to H.B. Clawson, at Salt Lake City, Utah, all the balance of said money is to be deposited at once and without further delay, or so much thereof as may be necessary.

It is further stipulated that when a check is drawn upon said fund by Hathenbruck and Rhodes, notice is to be given to H.B. Clawson, at Salt Lake City, of the amount of the check and the purpose for which said money is drawn and to be used.

### Third.

The parties of the second part are to procure the ratification of the lease by the proper officials of the United States at Washington, so as to make it effective, on or before January 15, 1898, or within ninety (90) days thereafter, of which written notice is to be given to the parties of the first part within ten (10) days after such ratification, and also to furnish whatever bonds may be required by the United States Government.

### Fourth.

The parties of the first part agree to convey unto the parties of the second part, nine-twentieths (9/20ths) of the property instead of eight-twentieths (8/20ths), as provided in the original contract, of which these presents is a modification.

If for any reason the Indians should refuse to make said lease on or before said 15th day of December, 1897, or within ninety (90) days thereafter; or if for and reason the proper officers of the United States should refuse to ratify the same within ninety (90) days after the 15th day of January 1898, or within ninety (90) days after the Indians have agreed to the same, so as to make it effective; then the contract between the parties hereto is to be considered null and void, and neither party is bound by any stipulation or obligation with respect thereto; except as hereinafter provided.

If either of the parties hereto shall neglect and fail, or neglect or fail to do and perform the several or any obligations, herein contained and assumed by such party at the time and in the manner as herein stipulated and agreed; then these presents are to be null and void and of no effect at the option of the other party to be expressed by written notification by letter through the United States mail.

It is further agreed that if for any unforeseen reason, or particularly on the account of the objection or contest of any person or persons to the execution of said lease by the Indians or to the approval of the same by the proper Officer of the Government of the United States; then such further and additional time shall be given as in reason the circumstances of the case may require; but which said time shall be agreed to by said parties in writing.

In witness whereof the said parties of the

first part and second part hereto do sign these presents on this the third day of November 1897.

Witness

J.H. MOYLE

F.W.C. HATHENBRUCK

C.B.RHOADES

HIRUM B. CLAWSON

JAMES &CLARKSON

by Hirum B. Clawson

his Atty in fact

## DOCUMENT—NOV. 4, 1897

WE, F.W.C. Hathenbruck and C.B. Rhodes, have required the professional services of J.W. Judd in our contracts with H.B. Clawson and James S. Clarkson, and in our transactions with the Uintah Indians in procuring a lease from them, and we will need and require his services further in said matters, as well as in forming our company to mine the property to be leased from the Indians in the Uintah Reservation in the State of Utah, and to look after the interests of the company when it is formed:

Now, that we may at all times have his services in all said matters whenever needed, we do hereby retain him as our legal advisor and Attorney in all said matters, both for the present and future, for which we will pay to him a reasonable compensation.

Dated this Fourth day of November, 1897.

Witness

(MISS) LEONORA TRENT

F.W.C. HATHENBRUCK

C.B. RHOADES

Signed in duplicate.

## AGREEMENT—NOV. 4, 1897

THIS Agreement, made and entered into this fourth day of November in the year one thousand eight hundred and ninety seven, by and between F.W.C. Hathenbruck of Provo City, Utah County and C.B. Rhoades of Price, Carbon County, in the State of Utah, parties of the first part; and L.O. Wight of Salina, Salina County, in the State of Kansas, party of the second part, that,

WHEREAS, the parties of the first part have certain knowledge of the existence and location of certain mines, placer, veins or lodes, bearing precious metals; on the Uintah Reservation, and desire to enter into a contract or lease, with the tribe of Indians occupying the Uintah Reservation, for the development and working of said, placer, veins, or lodes, the contract or lease to be on the terms and at the nature and character of the copy which is attached hereto and made a part of this agreement.

NOW THEREFORE, the parties of the first part at the request of the party of the second part, and in consideration of the covenants herein expressed, to be performed by the party of the second part, the prompt performance of which being a condition precedent, and time the essence of said condition do hereby agree to transfer, set over and convey to the party of the second part half of one twentieth or one fortieth (1/40) interest in the aforesaid contract or lease when the legal title to the same shall have been procured and apportioned, as in the said agreement specified.

AND the party of the second part, in the consideration of the premises, hereby agrees to pay Five Hundred Dollars in Cash down, and use all diligent means, influences and exertions to consummate and help to bring to a successful issue and termination the execution and fulfillment of said proposed agreement, and superintend all surveys to be made between the parties of the first part and the tribe of Indians occupying the Uintah Reservation, Utah.

AND it is further mutually covenanted and agreed, if, in any manner. the parties of the second part to the said proposed agreement shall fail or neglect to procure or to help to secure the lease or title to and working of said mines, the parties of the first part therein shall be fully and completely, exonerated and released from the covenants and provisions of this agreement.

This contract is signed in duplicate.

Witness:

ELIZABETH A. LANE

L.O. WIGHT

F.W.C. HATHENBRUCK

C.B. RHOADES

Recorded at request of F. Eberhart March 9, 1904 at 1 P.M.

THOMAS S. WATSON, County Recorder

## AGREEMENT—DEC. 6, 1897

This Agreement, made and entered into this sixth day of December in the year One Thousand, eight hundred and ninety seven, by and between F. W.C. Hathenbruck of Provo City, Utah County and C.B. Rhoades of Price, Carbon County, in the State of Utah, parties of the first part and A. MacDonald of Fort Duchesne, Utah, party of the second part:

Witnesseth: That

Whereas the parties of the first part are to obtain a lease or contract for the purchase of the products of a certain portion of the Uintah Indian Reservation, and to work and develop said portion for mining purposes:

Now Therefore:

The parties of the first part at the request of the party of the second part, and in consideration of the covenants herein expressed to be performed by the party of the second part, the prompt performance of which being a condition precedent, and time being the essence of said condition, do hereby agree to sublease a certain tract ....to be described hereafter containing Six hundred and forty acres (640) for mining purposes when the legal title to the same shall have been procured and apportioned by the Indians having the right to lease or sell their products, and sanctioned and endorsed by the proper officers at the seat of the Government:

and

the party of the second part, in considera-

tion of the premises hereby agrees to get the consent and the signatures of the White River branch of the Uintah tribe on the Uintah Reservation, Utah—and use all diligent means, influence and exertions to consummate and help to bring to a successful issue and termination the execution and fulfillment of said proposed agreement between the parties of the first part and the tribe of Indians occupying the Uintah Reservation, Utah.

and

It is further mutually consented and agreed; if, in any manner, the party of the second part to the said proposed agreement shall fail or neglect to procure or help to secure the lease and the working of said sublease the parties of the first part therein shall be fully and completely, exonerated and released from the covenants and provisions of this agreement.

In Witness whereof we have set our hands and seals on the date first above mentioned.

(HATHENBRUCK and

(CALIB B. RHOADES

(A. MACDONALD

Sgd

## AGREEMENT—DEC. 13, 1897

THIS Agreement entered into this thirteenth day of December One Thousand and Eight Hundred and Ninety Seven by and between F.W.C. Hathenbruck of Provo City, Utah County and C.B. Rhoades of Price, Carbon County, State of Utah parties of the first part and L.O. Wight and F. Eberhart both of Salt Lake City, State of Utah parties of the second part.

WITNESSETH: That in consideration of the Moneys to be paid by the parties of the second part, in the following manner and terms, to wit: One Hundred Dollars in hand paid, One hundred Dollars January fifteenth 1898, One Hundred Dollars February Sixth 1898 total

300.00 and Two Hundred Dollars April fifteenth 1898. Payments to be made to the credit of Hathenbruck and Rhoades at the Deseret National Bank Salt Lake City. The parties of the first part, will sell, deed and transfer one fortieth (1/40) part interest to the parties of the second part in the following described Lease to be obtained from the Ute Indians on the Uintah Reservation, Utah and the same approved by the proper Officers in the Department of the Interior Washington D.C. beginning at the intersection of the Uinta base line and Longitude 110 (degrees) 15' thence North to intersection of Latitude 40 (degrees) 45' thence West to Reservation line thence along Uintah Reservation line to the intersection of Uinta base line, thence East along Uinta base line to place of beginning and in case the lease should not be obtained at the time last payment is due the parties of the first part shall have no claim on said Two Hundred Dollars (the last payment in April) but is to be left to the option of the parties of the second part to pay the said sum of Two Hundred Dollars and demand the interest afore-mentioned when Lease is procured. This contract shall be binding on the heirs Administrators and assigns of the parties hereto.

In Witness Whereof we have set our hands and seal on the day first above written. (Executed in duplicate)

HATHENBRUCK AND RHOADES
L.O. WIGHT
F. EBERHART

Recorded at request of F. Eberhart March 9, 1904 at 1 P.M.

THOMAS S. WATSON, County Recorder.

## HATHENBRUCK & RHOADES LEASE— DEC. 18, 1897

THIS Indenture, Made the 18th day of December One Thousand Eight Hundred and Ninety Seven, Between the Uintah And White River Utes, the parties of the first part and Frederick William Hathenbruck of Provo City,

Utah County, and Caleb Baldwin Rhoades of Price, Carbon County, in the State of Utah, the parties of the second part, Witnesseth:

THAT the said parties of the first part for and in consideration of the rents, covenants and agreements hereinafter mentioned and reserved to be paid, kept and performed by these said parties of the second part, their successors and assigns hath remised, leased and let, and by these presents to remise, lease and let unto the said parties of the second part, their successors and assigns all these premises situate, lying and being in the Uintah Reservation, County of Wasatch, State of Utah and particularly described as follows to wit: Beginning at the intersection of Longitude one hundred and ten (110) degrees and fifteen (15) minutes and Latitude forty (40) degrees twenty six (26) minutes twenty seconds, thence North along longitude one hundred and ten (110) degrees fifteen (15) minutes to the intersection of Latitude forty (40) degrees forty five (45) minutes thence West along latitude forty (40) degrees forty five (45) minutes to the intersection of the North-western line of the Uintah Reservation, thence along the Western Reservation line in a southerly direction to the intersection of Latitude forty (40) degrees twenty six (26) minutes and twenty seconds thence East to the intersection of Longitude one hundred and ten (110) degrees fifteen (15) minutes to the place of beginning, a further identification of the boundary of said tract of land is indicated and marked by the lines in blue print map. Attached hereto Market "Exhibit A" and hereby made a part hereof, excepting and excluding therefrom all agricultural lands contained therein and all that portion of said premises which is now surveyed by the United States Government.

THE purpose being to include only the Mountain, Mineral, unsurveyed and broken Non-agricultural land within said boundaries, To have and to hold, the said premises with the appurtenances unto the said party of the second part, their Successors and assigns form the 3 1st day of December, 1897 for and during and until the 31st day of December 1907, and the Said parties of the second part in consideration of the leasing of the premises aforesaid, do covenant and agree with the said parties of the first part, their heirs, executors, administrators and assigns, to pay to the said parties of the first part their heirs, executors, administrators and assigns, rent for the remised premises, in lawful Money of the United States, as follows:

1. Two thousand five hundred ($2500) dollars per Annum payable Semi-annually on the first day of January and July of each and every year.

2. If the net value of the Annual product or output of said premises worked and operated as mines, bearing gold, silver and copper and other minerals and mining products shall exceed twenty-five thousand dollars ($25,000) per year; then ten (10) per cent of such excess payable in like manner and at like times, as above. And it is hereby covenanted and agreed by and between the parties hereto:

1. That the words "Net Value" contained herein shall be construed to mean the selling price of each and every carload or lot of rock or ore bearing precious metals, or other metals on board of cars at the nearest railroad point: or if milled on said property, then at said mill less the actual necessary and proper cost of the mining, reduction and hauling to the mill.

2. That while the design and intent of both parties hereto is to cause said premises to be worked and operated for gold, silver, copper, and other precious metals and minerals. It is expressly agreed and understood that all valuable & merchantable Minerals on said premises, of whatever kind and nature may be utilized and Marketed except Gilsonite, and that the value of all such products shall be considered as the proceeds or output of said premises.

3. It is further stipulated, agreed and understood that the parties of the second part, their Successors and assigns shall have the right to cut and take from said premises all timber necessary and sufficient for the purposes of developing and exploiting for Mining or workings of any kind under this lease, including houses, mills, bridges, roads, and all buildings of whatever kind of character, which may be necessary in carrying on the work.

4. The parties of the second part are to pay all expenses of operating and working said premises and are to buy upon their own account and in their name, all tools, implements, and machinery and upon their own account and in their name to erect mills, smelter and other works, buildings and appurtenances which they may consider necessary and shall own them as Chattles: they shall market, sell, and dispose of all products in their own name and in no way shall the parties of the first part be connected with the business of working or operating said premises, or in disposing of its products or to be held liable for any expense of working or cost of improvements or repairs. It is however, expressly made a condition hereof that this instrument shall not in any way operate to exclude the parties of the first part from said premises for the purpose of ingress, thereon, or aggress therefrom, or for a right of way to or across any portion thereof, and for grazing, hunting, or fishing thereon, such right being hereby reserved to said parties but be exercised in such a way and in such a manner as not to obstruct or conflict with effective operation of the rights herein granted to the parties of the second part.

5. The parties of the second part shall at all times keep full, true and accurate books of account at their office in Salt Lake City, and at their office at or on the said premises showing all transactions connected with the business of working and operating said premises and Said parties of the first part or their authorized agent or agents are at all times to have free access to the Same at the office of the second parties at the end of every month, after the execution of these presents and the parties of the second part shall furnish to the parties of the first part or their authorized representative a full, and true and correct abstract of the said books for the month last past, Showing the amounts of business transacted, Sales Made, account of Money received therefor and expense incurred.

6. And it is further covenanted and agreed between the parties hereto, that at the termina-

tion of this lease, or at the time to which it may extend, the parties of the second part will yield and deliver up the said remised premises to the said parties of the first part in as good order and condition as when the same were entered upon by said parties of the second part, Alterations and changes necessary to carry on and effect the purposes herein before mentioned expected.

7. And it is further expressly understood and agreed by and between the parties aforesaid, that if the rents above received, or any part thereof shall be unpaid on the day when the same is due and payable as aforesaid, and for Sixty days thereafter, or if default be made in any of the terms, covenants and conditions herein contained to be kept by the said parties of the second part or their successors it shall and may be lawful for the said parties of the first part, their heirs, executors, administrators and assigns, agents or Attorneys, the said remised premises and every or any part thereof, either with or without legal process to re-enter and the same again repossess and enjoy as in their first and former estate.

8. And it is further covenanted and agreed by and between the Said parties that the said parties of the second part, or their Successors in interest shall pay and discharge all costs and Attorney's fees and expenses that shall arise from enforcing the covenants of this indenture by the said parties of the first part, and that they shall have a lien upon all unsold products of said premises, and upon all machinery, implements and personal property placed upon, or used in connection with said premises by the said parties of the second part for all sums which may be due them at the termination of this lease by lapse of time or otherwise.

9. It is further stipulated and agreed by the parties of the first part, that all the terms, covenants and conditions of this lease having been kept and performed by the parties of the second part, and the power to lease the aforesaid premises being still inverted with the parties of the first part, that the parties of the second part and their assigns may renew this lease for a period of ten years after its expiration upon the best terms offered therefor by any other responsible party, that is to say, upon the expiration of this lease said parties of the second part and their assigns shall have the refusal of renting said premises upon the best terms offered therefor by any other responsible party, providing of course that the power to so lease is then in said first parties, and providing further that if the first parties are not then authorized to lease said premises for ten years more but are for a shorter period, That said new leases shall be for such term as the first parties are then authorized to lease the same. In Witness Whereof, the said parties have hereto set their hands in triplicate this 26th day of December 1897.

In the presence of

WM. H. BECK
Captain 10th Cavalry Acting U.S.
Indian Agent Uintah & White River Utes.
JAMES A MUSE
HENRY E. HARRIS
Witnesses as to Hathenbruck and Rhoades
J.H. MOYLE
GEO. P. COSTIGAN, JR.
FREDERICK W.C. HATHENBRUCK
CALEB B. RHOADES
(Seal)

Hathenbruck & Rhoades Lease

In Witness Whereof we hereby affix our signatures to the above lease this 18th day of December, Eighteen hundred and Ninety-seven,

| 1. Tabby | his X mark |
| 2. Wonrodes | his X mark |
| 3. Tom | his X mark |
| 4. Happy Jack | his X mark |
| 5. John Duncan | his X mark |
| 6. David Copperfield | his X mark |
| 7. Atwine | his X mark |
| 8. Charley Mack | his X mark |
| 9. Bot Ridley | his X mark |
| 10. Ebenezer | his X mark |

| | | | |
|---|---|---|---|
| 11. Martin Van | his X mark | 54. Moley | his X mark |
| 12. Jim Duncan | his X mark | 55. Atchista | his X mark |
| 13. Warren | his X mark | 56. Tumguitach | his X mark |
| 14. Provo Jim | his X mark | 57. Shoawoo | his X mark |
| 15. Richard Provo | his X mark | 58. Lieutenant | his X mark |
| 16. Rough | his X mark | 59. John Watove | his X mark |
| 17. Tom Yanawads | his X mark | 60. Checora | his X mark |
| 18. Petterson | his X mark | 61. Long | his X mark |
| 19. Gardiner | his X mark | 62. Long Ontion | his X mark |
| 20. Jakey | his X mark | 63. Dick Ebenezer | his X mark |
| 21. Loko | his X mark | 64. Verney Mack | his X mark |
| 22. Kanave | his X mark | 65. John Reed | his X mark |
| 23. Towats | his X mark | 66. Cut Lip Jim | his X mark |
| 24. Snap | his X mark | 67. John Hemp Kodge | his X mark |
| 25. Nephi Lehi | his X mark | 68. Bill | his X mark |
| 26. James B. Reed | his X mark | 69. Amencanutes | his X mark |
| 27. Horace Anthony | his X mark | 70. Black Hawk | his X mark |
| 28. John Copperfield | his X mark | 71. Alec | his X mark |
| 29. Jesse Copperfield | his X mark | 72. Mountain Sheep | his X mark |
| 30. Geo. Wanrodes | his X mark | 73. Towanta | his X mark |
| 31. Wanzitz | his X mark | 74. Bridger Jim | his X mark |
| 32. Shackwitch | his X mark | 75. Aporas | his X mark |
| 33. Chapoose | his X mark | 76. Frank Bannocky | his X mark |
| 34. Quip | his X mark | 77. Frank Parriett | his X mark |
| 35. Apporah | his X mark | 78. Stanley Bullethead | his X mark |
| 36. Wabona | his X mark | 79. George Fuckawana | his X mark |
| 37. Joe Morgan | his X mark | 80. Horner | his X mark |
| 38. Frank Doctor | his X mark | 81. Isaac Mawachean | his X mark |
| 39. Antony | his X mark | 82. John H. Patterson | his X mark |
| 40. Carter Ridley | his X mark | 83. Kurip | his X mark |
| 41. Capt. Joe Douglas | his X mark | 84. Lehi | his X mark |
| 42. Ungastominegets | his X mark | 85. Sungquap | his X mark |
| (Soldier Joe) | his X mark | 86. Mawadhean | his X mark |
| 43. Game | his X mark | (Sorquan) | |
| 44. Paumbitch | his X mark | 87. Messatowana | his X mark |
| 45. Geo. Paumbitch | his X mark | 88. Ned | his X mark |
| 46. Joe Gro | his X mark | 89. Pamckook | his X mark |
| 47. Wm. Taylor | his X mark | 90. Peacheant | his X mark |
| 48. Paul Pegaroose | his X mark | 91. Orin | his X mark |
| 49. Ge-gar-kent | his X mark | 92. Paranhi | his X mark |
| 50. John Nick | his X mark | 93. Nanaitup | his X mark |
| 51. Polonia Monter | his X mark | 94. Jim Provo | his X mark |
| 52. Peacheaut | his X mark | 95. Sam Robinson | his X mark |
| 53. Jim Atwine | his X mark | 96. Sagoose | his X mark |

| | |
|---|---|
| 97. Solomon | his X mark |
| 98. Sockniken | his X mark |
| 99. Skaputz | his X mark |
| 100. Square John | his X mark |
| 101. O Okoo | his X mark |
| 102. Three Finger Jack | his X mark |
| 103. Tonegers | his X mark |
| 104. Tasunk | his X mark |
| 105. Unguska | his X mark |
| 106. Uriah Heeep | his X mark |
| 107. William Nash | his X mark |
| 108. Rabbit | his X mark |
| 109. Ephraim Panawiby | his X mark |
| 110. Undudanwootk | his X mark |
| 111. Andres Ahsri | his X mark |
| 112. Wash | his X mark |
| 113. Unquch | his X mark |
| 114. Yanagup | his X mark |

We Certify that we the undersigned interpreted at the Council held at the Uintah Agency, Utah, December 18th, 1897, and that we explained fully the lease to which this is attached and that the Indians understood the matter thoroughly.

Witness;

(Signed) **HENRY E. HARRIS**

Charles Mack

his X mark

December 24, 1897.Interpreters

Department of the Interior

U.S. Indian Service

Uintah & Ouray Agency

\White Rocks, Utah, Dec. 28, 1897

I certify that Hathenbruck, and Rhoades are suitable persons to reside upon an Indian Reservation; that they a persons of good reputation and in my opinion this lease will be for the best interests of the Indians concerned.

W.H. Beck, Captain U.S. Army

Acting U.S. Indian Agent.

**DOCUMENT—JAN. 5, 1898**

Know all men by these presents, That we Frederick William Hathenbruck, of Provo City, State of Utah, and Caleb Baldwin Rhoades of Price, Carbon County, Utah as principals, and T.B. Beatty and H.B. Clawson, Charles M. Garrison, James H. Moyle, and F.H. Cavanaugh of Salt Lake City, Utah, as sureties, are holden and bound unto the Uintah and White River Utes, two Indian tribes in the Uintah Reservation, Uintah and Wasatch Counties, State of Utah, in the sum of Ten Thousand Dollars, to the payment of which to the said Indians, their heirs, legal representatives, and assigns we hereby jointly and severally bind ourselves, our heirs, executors and administrators.

The condition of the above written bond is such that if the above bounded obligors, said Frederick William Hathenbruck and Caleb B. Rhoades, their heirs, executors, administrators or assigns, shall in all things on their part observe, perform, fulfill, and keep, all and singular, the clauses, the said obligor, their heirs, executors, administrators, and assigns are to be observed, performed, fulfilled, and kept according to a lease in writing bearing date the 18th day of December, A.D., 1897, and expressed to be made between the said Obligors in the one part and the said Obligees, said Indian tribes of the other part; then the above written Obligation shall be void, but otherwise shall remain in full force and effect.

In Witness Whereof the said Parties have hereunto attached their hands and seals in triplicate this fifth day of January 1898.

Witness

GEO. P. COSTIGAN JR.

JERROLD R. LETCHER

FREDERICK WM. HATHENBRUCK

CALEB BALDWIN RHOADES

T.B. BEATTY

(seal)

(seal)

(seal)

State of Utah

County of Salt Lake
}
}ss
}

M.B. CLAWSON
(seal)
CHARLES M. GARRISON
JAMES M. MOYLE
J.H. CAVANAUGH
(seal)
(seal)
(seal)

F.B. Beatty & Chas. M. Garrison and James H. Moyle persons whose names are subscribed as the sureties to the above undertaking, being severally sworn each for himself, says: That he is a resident and freeholder within the State of Utah, and that he is worth the amount specified in and said undertaking as the penalty thereof, over and above all his just debts and liabilities, exclusive of property exempt from execution.

F.B. BEATTY
CHAS. M. GARRISON
JAMES H. MOYLE

Subscribed and sworn to before me this 6th day of January, A.D., 1898.

JERROLD R. LETCHER, Clerk
U.S. District court, Dist. Ut.

United States of America

District of Utah
}
}ss
}

I, Jerrold R. Letcher, Clerk of the United States District Court for the District of Utah, do hereby certify that F.B. Beatty, Charles M. Garrison and James H. Moyle, Sureties on the annexed and foregoing bond of William

Hathenbruck and Caleb B. Rhoades whose names are subscribed to said bond are all inhabitants and freeholders of the State of Utah, and they are each worth over and above all their debts exclusive of the property exempt from execution, the sum of Ten thousand dollars, in which sum they each respectfully justify, and are ample security for the penalty thereof ....

## GENERAL POWER OF ATTORNEY—
### FEB. 8, 1898

Whereas, to-wit, during the month of December 1897, there was executed and delivered by the confederated tribes of the Ute Indians a lease of certain ground situated in the Uintah Reservation of the State of Utah, said ground being more particularly described in said lease to Frederick Wm. C. Hathenbruck, of Provo City, Utah County, and Caleb B. Rhoades of Price, Carbon County in the State of Utah, leasing to the said last named persons the said ground, as, above mentioned, with a view to enable said lessees to take therefrom any and all minerals in said ground contained: and

Whereas, it is now desirable that said lease shall be so modified as to exclude therefrom all wax minerals contained in the ground described in said lease:

Now, Therefore, I, Caleb B. Rhoades, with a view to accomplish the foregoing expressed purposes do hereby make, constitute and appoint Frederick Wm. C. Hathenbruck my true and lawful Attorney for me and in my name to agree to and execute any and all modifications and changes in said lease which may be desirable, with a view to procure the approval of the same, by the Interior Department at Washington, and especially enabling him to execute all modifications and releases so as, to exclude from said lease the said wax minerals aforesaid, hereby, agreeing in advance to be bound by and ratify and confirm any and all acts which may be done and performed by my said attorney in the premises in as full and ample a manner as if done by myself in person.

Given under my hand this the 8th day of February A.D. 1898.

CALEB B. RHOADES

State of Utah

Carbon County
}
}ss
}

On the 10th day of February A.D. 1898, personally appeared before me Caleb B. Rhodes, the signer of the above instrument, who duly acknowledged to me that he executed the same this the day of February A.D. 1898.

J.M. SMITH
Notary Public.

## AGREEMENT—FEB. 8, 1898

This Agreement made this 8th day of February, A.D. 1898, by and between F.W.C. Hathenbruck of Provo, State of Utah, and Thomas H. Cavanaugh of Olympia, State of Washington.

Witnesseth:- That the said party of the first part for and in consideration of a sum of One Thousand ($1,000.) Dollars to be paid by said party of the second part as hereinafter set forth, does grant, bargain, sell and set o r to said second party his heirs, administrators and assigns, one-twentieth interest in a certain mining lease made with said Hathenbruck and Rhoades by the Uintah Indians, for the metals upon certain lands in the Uintah Reservation in the State of Utah, therein described; said lease is now pending in the Department of the Interior for approval.

The terms of payment as agreed upon are as follows:-

Said Cavanaugh pays said Hathenbruck Seventy-five ($75.00) Dollars cash. One Hundred and Seventy-five ($175.00) Dollars

within ten days from the date hereof; Two Hundred and Fifty ($250.00) Dollars on March 15th, 1898, and the balance, Five Hundred ($500.00) Dollars from the proceeds of his share of the lease. Upon the default of any payment herein, this agreement shall be null and void.

In Witness whereof the parties hereto have hereunto set their hands and seals this, the 8th day of February, A.D. 1898.

F.W.C. HATHENBRUCK
THOS. H. CAVANAUGH
(Seal)
(Seal)

Witness
JOHN E. BUCKY

## AGREEMENT—FEB. 14, 1898

This agreement made this 14th day of February, A.D., 1898, by and between F.W.C. Hathenbruck of Provo, State of Utah, and L.O. WIGHT and F. Eberhardt of Salt Lake City, State of Utah.

Witnesseth: That the said party of the first part for and in consideration of the sum of five hundred dollars ($500.00), to be paid by the said party of the second part, as hereinafter set forth, does grant, bargain, sell and set over, to said second party his heirs, administrators, and assigns, one fortieth interest in a certain Mining lease, made with said Hathenbruck and Rhoades by the Uintah Indians, for the metals upon certain lands in the Uintah Reservation, in the State of Utah therein described. Said lease is now pending in the Department of the Interior for approval.

The terms of payment as agreed upon are as follows; said L.O. Wight and F. Eberhardt pays said Hathenbruck five hundred dollars cash, upon the default of said payment this agreement shall be null and void.

In witness whereof the parties hereto have

set their hands and seals this the 14th day of February, A.D. 1898.

F.W.C. HATHENBRUCK
L.O. Wight
F. Eberhart
(Seal)
(Seal)
(Seal)

Witness,

GEORGE S. COLEMAN

Witness as to L.O. Wight and F. Eberhardt

M. SHAEFFER

making interest one fortieth (1/40) L.O. WIGHT WM. TURTON F. EBERHARDT

It is hereby agreed that the interests in the within contract for 1 /40 interest in the H & R mining lease are as follows:- L.O. Wight three fifths. F. Eberhardt one fifth. Wm. Turton one fifth.

L.O. WIGHT
WM. TURTON
F. EBERHARDT

## AGREEMENT—MAR. 24, 1898

This agreement made this 24th day of March A.D. 1898 by and between F.W.C. Hathenbruck of Provo, State of Utah, and L.O. Wight, F. Eberhardt and Wm. Turton, Witnesseth:

That the said part of the first part for and in consideration of the sum of Five Hundred Dollars to be paid by the said party of the second as hereinafter set forth does grant, bargain, sell and set over to said second party, his heirs, administrators and assigns one hundredth (1 / 100) part interest in a certain mining lease made with said Hathenbruck and Rhoades by the Uinta Indians, for the metals upon certain lands in the Uinta Reservation in the State of Utah, therein described. Said lease is now pending in the Department of the Interior for approval.

The terms of payment as agreed upon are as follows; Said Wight, Eberhardt & Turton pays said Hathenbruck by April 15th to be deposited in Deseret Nat. Bank at Sale Lake City Five Hundred Dollars (500°°). Upon default of any payment herein, this agreement shall be null and void. —— In witness whereof the parties hereto have hereunto set their hands and seals this the day first above written.

Witness

HARRY PEYTON

F.W.C. HATHENBRUCK

Accepted in connection with telegram

## AGREEMENT—JUNE 1, 1898

This agreement made this 1st day of June A.D. 1898 by and between F.W.C. Hathenbruck of Provo, State of Utah and L.O. Wight, F. Eberhardt and Wm. Turton, Witnesseth that the party of the first part, for and in consideration of One Thousand Dollars to be paid by the party of the second part as hereinafter set forth, does grant, bargain, sell and set over to the said second parties their heirs, administrators and assigns one twentieth interest in a certain mining lease made with said Hathenbruck and Rhoades by the Uinta Indians, for the metals upon certain lands in the Uinta Reservation in the State of Utah therein described, said lease is now pending in the Department of the Interior for approval. — The terms of payment as agreed upon are as follows: said Wight, Eberhardt and Turton pays said Hathenbruck 250°° cash down, and two Hundred and fifty in 30 days from the date hereof, and $500°° from the first proceeds of their share of the lease, upon default of any payments herein this agreement shall be null and void.

In witness whereof the parties hereto have hereunto set their hands and seal this 18th day of June A.D. 1898.

F.W.C. Hathenbruck & Rhoades
L.O. WIGHT
WM. TURTON
F. EBERHARDT

It is hereby agreed that the interests in the within contract are as follows:—L.O.

Wight 121000. F. Eberhardt 89500. Wm Turton 39500

W-250000E-250000    T-250000

L.O. WIGHT
WM. TURTON
F. EBERHARDT

## INJUNCTION AND RESTRAINING ORDER—JAN. 15, 1900

Complaint and Prayer for an Injunction and Restraining Order in the "Hathenbruck & Rhoades" lease now in the Department of the Interior. Before the Hon. Secretary of the Interior.

Washington, D.C.

F.W.C. Hathenbruck, Plaintiff

VS.

C.B. Rhoades & T.H. Cavanaugh, Defendants.

F.W.C. Hathenbruck complains in this action of C.B Rhoades and T.H. Cavanaugh and for cause of action avers:

That heretofore he has been and now is the duly appointed and an acting Agent for Hathenbruck & Rhoades, a partnership formed to procure the approval of a Lease to Mine Precious Metals on the Uinta Indian Reservation, County of Wasatch, State of Utah, now pending before your Honor.

That the said Plaintiff had the said lease sanctioned, verified and signed in the presence of Capt. W.H. Beck Indian Agent, Henry Harris Government Interpreter and Mr. Reynolds Special Commissioner and Mr. Pardge Chairman of General Indian Commissioners of this District, on the 18th day of December, 1897, in "Open Council Meeting," by the Chiefs, Representative Men, and Interested members of the Ute Indian Tribe, at White Rocks Agency, Utah.

Plaintiff further avers that he has been at all times and still is working to procure the approval of said Lease by the Department of the Interior according to instructions and advise received from the Hon. Gentleman Mr. Bliss Secretary of the Interior and Mr. Thos. Ryan Assistant Sect. of the Interior, and Mr. Jones Commissioner of Indian Affairs in 1898 at Washington, D.C.

Plaintiff further avers that he now is and at all times herein states has been the owner of an undivided One-half interest in said lease. And that through the machinations, misrepresentations and fraudulent practices of defendant T.H. Cavanaugh the Said T.H. Cavanaugh has been and now is secretly alienating and destroying the partnership existing between Hathenbruck & Rhoades, owners of said lease and thereby jeopardizing and injuring the interest of the plaintiff in said lease and disturbing and preventing the carrying out of the instructions received to obtain the approval of said lease above referred to.

The plaintiff further avers, that he is informed and believes and on said information and belief states the facts to be: That the said Thomas H. Cavanaugh, defendant with the consent of defendant C.B. Rhoades obtained by and through fraud and misrepresentations, is now endeavoring to organize a Stock Company for the handling and managing of said lease to the detriment and injury of plaintiff, and claiming that plaintiff made said assignments as Hathenbruck & Rhoades. But plaintiff avers the facts to be that he is still the owner of an undivided One-Half interest and to said lease and in no wise has made such assignments or any assignments of any interest at all in said lease as agent or otherwise or at all, and that said claims of T.H. Cavanaugh are false and without right and are made for the purpose of defrauding and injuring plaintiff and plaintiff is injured and defrauded thereby.

Wherefore plaintiff Prays that the Hon. Secretary of the Interior enjoin & restrain the said defendants, their agents and all persons acting under or for them or by their authority from obtaining an approval of the said Hathenbruck & Rhoades lease, or interfering at all with said lease, until this Cause can be heard upon its merits, and upon said T.H. Cavanaugh. And for such other orders as may be just and right. And your petitioner would ever pray.

F.W.C. HATHENBRUCK

Dated this 15 day of January A.D. 1900.

## DOCUMENT—APRIL 24, 1901

FOR VALUE RECEIVED, I hereby sell, assign, transfer and set over, to Reed Smoot, all my right, title and interest in and to that certain lease between the Indians of the Uintah Indian Reservation, in Utah, and myself and Caleb B. Rhoades; and also all my right, title and interest in and to the capitol stock subscribed by me in the articles of incorporation of the Rhoades Mining & Milling Company, and which articles, with my assignment, have been deposited with H.S. Young, Cashier of the Deseret National Bank, to be used and filed and said company incorporated when the said lease is approved by the Secretary of the Interior of the United States, or prior thereto, if a majority of the parties interested therein so desire.

I hereby authorize the filing of said articles and the substitution of the name of Reed Smoot for my own wherever it appears in said articles, and hereby authorize and direct the officers of said corporation, when formed, to transfer and deliver to said Reed Smoot all stock to which I would have been entitled in said company if I had not made this assignment.

And I hereby authorize the said Reed Smoot, to sign all papers, documents, receipts and released in my name, wherever the same is necessary, to perfect in him the interest hereby assigned by me to him in said lease and in said corporation.

Witness my signature this 24th day of April, A.D.1901.

F.W. C. HATHENBRUCK

Signed in the presence of:
ELIAS A. GEE

## DOCUMENT—APRIL 25, 1902
State of Utah

County of Salt Lake
}
}ss.
}

F.W.C. Hathenbruck, being first duly sworn, says, that he with Caleb B. Rhoades, obtained a lease from the Indians on the Uintah Indian Reservation some years since, which lease is now pending before the Interior Department of the United States. That while said matter was so pending in the year 1899, H.C. Henderson, an attorney of New York City was interested with affiant and his associates in securing the approval of said lease by the Secretary of the Interior of the United States, and said Henderson represented to affiant that Mr. Sherman, Representative from the State of New York and Chairman of the Indian Committee of the House of Representatives, was acting in the interest of affiant's said lease and that said Henderson has secured the services of said Sherman. That affiant met said Henderson, Sherman, Representative Ward of New York and a Mr. Hooker at the Manhattan Hotel in New York City during said year and had an interview with them at said hotel, during which affiant was assured that said Sherman would do all he could to secure the approval of affiant's said lease, and would not let any measure pass the House detrimental to the interests of said lease.

Affiant was introduced to said Sherman first by Nathaniel McKay, who was also acting in the interests of affiant's said lease. That without any notice to affiant or his associates, said parties ceased to act in the interest of affiant's said lease and became interested in the lease subsequently obtained by the Florence Mining Company and are now acting in its interest. That said parties are using the information obtained from affiant and his associates in his said lease to further the interests of said Florence Mining Company through which they hope to secure the Rhoades Mine on said Reservation, and which was located previous to the creation of said Reservation by said Rhoades.

That during the spring or early part of the summer, 1897, affiant met Mr. Myton, now Indian Agent on the said Indian Reservation and then a member of the Allotment Commission of the Uncompahgre Indian Reservation at Fort Duchesne at which time and place said Myton stated to affiant that if affiant would allow said Myton to come in on the ground floor on the said lease of said Rhoades and Hathenbruck, meaning to give him an interest therein, that he would do what he could, and, in fact, secure the approval of the said lease, but that if such was not done, he would see that the lease was not approved.

Affiant said that he would submit the matter to Mr. Rhoades and during the summer and as near as affiant can state, the month of July, 1897, said Myton met affiant and said Rhoades on 2nd South Street between Main and State Streets in Salt Lake City, Utah, at which time said Myton asked affiant if he had spoken to Mr. Rhoades about the proposition he had made relative to said lease, affiant said that he had. Then said Mr. Myton wanted to know what we were going to do about it. Mr. Rhoades said that he would not accept Mr. Myton's proposition, whereupon, Mr. Myton said "you will never get your lease approved."

F.W.C. HATHENBRUCK

Subscribed and sworn to before me this 25th day of April, 1902.

RAY VANLOTT
Notary Public
(Seal)

## AGREEMENT—AUG. 24, 1903

THIS AGREEMENT, made and entered into this 24th day of August, 1903, by and between F.W.C. Hathenbruck, of Provo, Utah County, Utah, and Caleb B. Rhoades, of Price, Carbon County, Utah, parties of the first part, and Chas. E. Hudson and Geo. H. Dern of Salt Lake City, Salt Lake County, Utah, parties of the second part, WITNESSETH: ,

WHEREAS, the said parties of the first part did on the 18th day of December, 1897, duly execute and enter into a lease, whereby the Uintah and White River Utes did remise, lease and let unto the said parties of the first part certain lands in the Uintah Indian Reservation, State of Utah; and

WHEREAS, in consequence of the foregoing conditions, acts and circumstances said parties of the first part have the right and privilege, by virtue of an act of Congress, approved May 27, 1902, entitled "An Act making appropriations for the current and contingent expenses of the Indian Department, and for fulfilling treaty stipulations with various Indian tribes, for the fiscal year ending June 30, 1903, and for other purposes," to enter upon said Uintah Indian Reservation, and to select and locate six hundred forty (640) acres of land under the mineral laws of the United States; and

WHEREAS, the said parties of the first part are in need of funds to defray the necessary expenses of making said locations and selections; and

WHEREAS, the said parties of the second part have paid and advanced to the said parties of the first part the sum of One Hundred Twenty-five Dollars ($125.00), the receipt of which is hereby acknowledged by the said parties of the first part; now

THEREFORE, the said parties of the first part do hereby assign, transfer and set over unto the parties of the second part, or their assigns, an undivided seven fifteenths (7/15) interest in and to all lands and mining claims, together with such water rights as may appertain thereto, which said parties of the first part may select and locate, by virtue of the right hereinbefore described.

It is further agreed that the parties of the first part shall forthwith proceed to locate 640 acres of mineral land, as hereinbefore provided, on said Uintah Indian Reservation, Wasatch County, Utah, containing gold, silver, copper, or other precious metals.

It is further agreed that when said locations are made said parties of the second part are to pay the expenses of recording the same.

It is further agreed that, after the claims have been recorded, and proper title to the same has been duly secured, and duly vested in the parties hereto, as their interests may appear, and said claims shall have been demonstrated to be valuable, an incorporation shall be formed, of the basis of five hundred thousand (500,000) shares, all the expenses of said incorporation to be paid by said parties of the second part.

It is further agreed and understood that the capitol stock of the said proposed incorporation shall be divided into the following proportions, to-wit:

Hathenbruck and Rhoades,    200,000 Shares.
Hudson and Dern,            175,000 Shares.
Treasury Stock,             125,000 Shares.
Total,                      500,000 Shares.

F.W.C. HATHEnBRUCK
CALIB B. RHOADES per
F.W.C.H.
Atty in fact
CHAS E. HUDSON
G.H. DERN

In the presence of
G.W. KEIFER

## GENERAL POWER OF ATTORNEY— OCT. 71, 1903

KNOW ALL MEN BY THESE PRESENT: –
That we, Caleb B. Rhoades, and Sidsie Rhoades, wife of same, of Price, Carbon County, State of Utah, do hereby make, constitute, and appoint John T. Clark, of Provo City, Utah County, State of Utah, our true and lawful attorney in fact for us, and in our name and stead, and as our act and deed, to lease, assign, sell, execute, and deliver deeds of conveyance of other conveyances whatsoever, and to look up any matter whatsoever, and generally to do and perform all things that we ourselves personally could do as to disposing of, leasing assigning, selling and conveying the following described real estate, situated and being in Wasatch County, State of Utah, and known as the "Rhoades" mine about 1895 or 1896 by the Indians on the Uintah Reservation, State of Utah, to Caleb B. Rhoades of Price, Utah, and F.W.C. Hathenbruck, of Provo City, Utah County, Utah, and see to it that the interests of the said Caleb B. Rhoades and Sidsie Rhoades as above, are protected in every way and to take such steps and do such things to accomplish this end as to the said Caleb B. Rhoades and Sidsie as above.

In consideration of the said John T. Clark of Provo City, Utah, doing the acts and attending to our interests as above set forth, we do hereby quit-claim to him the undivided one-half interest in and to all our rights, titles, and interests in and to the said "Rhoades Mine" in Wasatch County, State of Utah, and especially in and to the rights, titles, and interests derived or in any appertaining to or growing out of the above named lease from said Indians on the Uintah Reservation, State of Utah, to the said Caleb B. Rhoades and F.W.C. Hathenbruck.

In Witness whereof we have hereunto set our hands this 17th day of October A.D. 1903.

Signed in the presence of;

MAGGIE JONES
CALEB B. RHOADES
SIDSIE RHOADES

State of Utah

Carbon County

ss

On this 17th day of October A.D. 1903 personally appeared before me Caleb B. Rhoades and Sidsie Rhoades, his wife, who duly acknowledged to me that they executed the above instrument freely and voluntarily and for the purpose therein set forth:

(Seal)

My commission expires Jan. 22, 1905

Recorded at the request of John T. Clark, October 21, 1903 at 13 Noon.

THOMAS S. WATSON
County Recorder

**TRANSFER OF INTEREST—JAN. 26, 1904**

STATE OF UTAH
COUNTY OF WASATCH

SS

KNOW ALL MEN BY THESE PRESENTS: That we, Frederick William Hathenbruck of Provo, Utah, and Caleb B. Rhoades of Price, Utah, the persons named as second parties in a certain lease dated December 18, A.D. 1897 and executed December 26, A.D. 1897, between the Uintah and White River Utes, as parties of the first part and said Hathenbruck and Rhodes as parties of the second part, do hereby, sell, assign, transfer and set over to Abram C. Hatch and John E. Austin, both of Heber City, Wasatch County, State of Utah, for a valuable consideration, all of our and each of our right, title, interest, claim and demand both in law and in equity, of, in and to the said lease, a copy of which is hereto attached, and also all of our

right, title, interest, claim and demand, under the permit from the Secretary of the Interior to obtain said lease from said first parties, including the right to locate 640 acres of Mineral land within the Uintah Indian Reservation within the State of Utah, as provided by the Act of Congress entitled "An Act Making appropriations for the current and contingent expenses of the Indian Department and for fulfilling treaty stipulations with various Indian tribes for the fiscal year ending June 30th, 1903, and for other purposes" Approved May 27th, 1902, and an Act of Congress, entitled "(Public Resolution No. 31.) Joint Resolution Supplementing and modifying certain provisions of the Indian appropriation Act for the year ending June 30th, 1903," Approved June 19th, A.D. 1902. And we do hereby warrant to the said Hatch and Austin and each of them that the said permit to obtain said lease from the said parties of the first part named therein was obtained from the Secretary of the Interior (Cornelius N. Bliss) on the day of September, A.D. 1897, and that no rights exist under the said lease or the said permit except such as are hereby assigned.

Signed and delivered in the presence of,
WM. BUYS, Heber,
Witness to

F.W.C. HATHENBRUCK
A.W. HORSLEY, Price, Utah,
Witness to

C.B. RHOADES

State of Utah

County of Wasatch

ss.

On this the 26th day of January. A.D. 1904, personally appeared before me Frederick William Hathenbruck, one of the signers of the foregoing assignment, who duly acknowledged to me that he executed the same.

WM. BUYS

Notary Public. My commission expires January 14th, A.D. 1905. State of Utah County of Carbon ss.

On this the 29th day of January, A.D. 1904, personally appeared before me Calcb B. Rhodes, one of the signers of the foregoing assignment, who duly acknowledged to me that he executed the same.

A.W. HORSLEY

Notary Public My commission expires Jan. 27th A.D. 1906.

## AGREEMENT—JAN. 30, 1904

Abram C. Hatch and John E. Austin, both of Heber City, Wasatch County, State of Utah, for a part of the consideration of the payment for the transfer to them by Frederick William Hathenbruck of Provo. Utah and Caleb B. Rhoades of Price, Carbon County, Utah, of all of their rights, claims, interests and demands of in and to a certain lease negotiated between the Uintah and White River Utes as parties of the first part and the said Hathenbruck and Rhoades as second parties, to certain mineral lands upon the Uintah Indian Reservation, in Utah, and the permit from the Secretary of the Interior for the said Hathenbruck and Rhoades to negotiate said lease, and their right under said lease and permit to locate 640 acres of Mineral lands within the said Indian Reservation as provided by the acts of Congress heretofore approved, do hereby agree to and with said Hathenbruck and Rhoades to incorporate a company under the laws of the State of Utah, with said rights under the said lease and permit as a basis for the Capital stock of the said corporation, and to deliver to said Hathenbruck and Rhoades each four-fifteenths of the said capital stock of said corporation less eight-fifteenths of the stock reserved and held as

treasury stock as hereinafter set forth. It is further agreed by the said Hatch and Austin that in case said corporation is not organized on or before the first day of July A.D. 1904, that then and in that case they will re-transfer to said Hathenbruck and Rhoades each a four-fifteenths of the said lease and permit and all rights existing thereunder by virtue of acts of Congress or otherwise.

It is further agreed by the said Hatch and Austin that in case of the incorporation of the company as herein above set forth that the same shall by a capital stock of $500,000.00 divided into shares of the face or par value of one dollar each, one-fifth of which shall be reserved as treasury stock to be disposed of for the purpose of prospectus, prospecting and location of claims and development thereof and such other purposes as the board of Directors of such corporation may determine, and that 80,000 shares thereof shall be paid out for legal services performed and being performed under an agreement made by the said Hathenbruck with other parties in the interest of said lease and permit herein above mentioned, said agreement being dated October 16th, A.D. 1903, a copy of which is this day delivered and certified by said Hathenbruck to said Hatch and Austin, and if not so paid under said agreement then one third of said stock shall go to Hatch and Austin, and 2/3 to said Hathenbruck and Rhoades in equal parts.

Witness the hands of the said Hatch and Austin this the 30th day of January, A.D. 1904.

Signed and delivered in the Presence of,

WM. BUYS
A.D. HATCH
JOHN E. AUSTIN

State of Utah

County of Wasatch
}
}ss.

}
On this the 30th day of January, A.D. 1904, personally appeared before me Abram C. Hatch and John E. Austin, the signers of the foregoing agreement who each duly acknowledged to me that he executed the same, in triplicate.

WM. BUYS
Notary Public
My commission Expires Dec. 23, A.D. 1905.

## ARTICLES OF AGREEMENT
## OF
## THE SYLVANITE MINING COMPANY
## MARCH 9, 1904

KNOW ALL MEN BY THESE PRESENTS: That we, the undersigned, whose names and places of residence appear in full herein, for the purpose of forming a corporation under and in pursuance of the laws of the State of Utah, do hereby certify, agree and declare as follows, to-wit:

### ARTICLE I.

That the name of said corporation is and shall be "THE SYLVANITE MINING COMPANY," and it is formed and organized at Heber City, Wasatch County, State of Utah; that said Heber City shall be the place of its general business, but the corporate business may be carried on and branch and transfer offices established elsewhere in the State of Utah, and in the United States, but no such office shall be established or meetings of the Board of Directors held at any place other than the general place of business of the corporation, except by authority of an order of the Board of Directors made and entered and concurred in by a majority of the entire Board at a prior meeting of the Board.

### ARTICLE II.

The time of the duration of this corporation shall be for a period of one hundred years from and after the issuance of the certificate of its incorporation by the Secretary of the State of Utah.

### ARTICLE III.

That the names and places of resident of the parties to this agreement, incorporators, are as follows:

John E. Austin
Heber City, Wasatch County, State of Utah
Abram C. Hatch
Heber City, Wasatch County, State of Utah
Charles S. Carter
Vernal, Uintah County, State of Utah, Provo City,
John E. Booth
Utah County, State of Utah, Provo City, Utah
Dermont H. Roberts
County, State of Utah

### ARTICLE IV.

That the limit of the capital stock of said corporation shall be five hundred thousand ($500,0000 Dollars, divided into five hundred thousand (500,000) shares of the face or par value of One Dollar each ....

### ARTICLE V.

That the purpose for which this corporation is formed, and the business and pursuit agreed upon and to be engaged in, are as follows:

1. To acquire by purchase, all of the rights, privileges, and franchises resulting from, or growing out of a certain mineral lease entered into between the Uintah and White River Tribes of Ute Indians, occupying the Uintah Indian Reservation in the State of Utah, first parties, and Frederick William Hathenbruck, of Provo City, Utah County, and Caleb B. Rhoades, of Price, Carbon County, in the State of Utah, second parties, said lease having been authorized at the Council of said Indian Tribes held at the Uintah Agency, Utah, December 18th, 1897, and executed on the 26th day of December, 1897; which said lease was negotiated with said

Indians under a permit issued by direction of the Secretary of the Interior to William H. Beck, the Agent in charge of such reservation at the time said lease was executed; the originals of said lease being on file in the office of the commissioner of Indian Affairs at Washington D.C., and a copy thereof is of record in the County Recorder's office of Wasatch County, State of Utah, in Book 2 of Miscellaneous Records, at page 42 et seq.

2. To locate, purchase, acquire title to, develop, sell and exchange mining claims within the Uintah Indian Reservation in the State of Utah, and else wherein the States of Utah and Wyoming; PROVIDED, that no mining claim acquired by said corporation shall be sold or exchanged, and no mining claim shall be acquired by the corporation in any way except by location, unless such purchase, sale or exchange is concurred in by three-fourths of the entire Board of Directors.

3. To buy and sell, build and operate mills, smelters and refineries for the treatment of ores of different kinds, and to buy and sell ores, metals and products of mines and mining claims, mills, smelters and refineries.

## ARTICLE VI

That the private property of the stockholders of said corporation shall NOT be liable for the debts or obligations of the corporation.

## ARTICLE VII.

That the subscription to the capital stock of said corporation consist wholly of the interests of the respective subscribers hereto of, in and to that certain mineral lease and permit to negotiate said lease, hereinbefore in Article V hereof mentioned and described, which said property is necessary to the pursuit and business agreed upon in this agreement, and which said property is conveyed to this corporation by deed actually executed, and delivered to Chase Hatch, to be by him delivered to said corporation as soon as the

organization thereof shall be perfected. That the said interests of the subscribers hereto include the whole of the interests of in and to the aforesaid lease and permit to negotiate the same, and that the fair estimated case value thereof is $500,000.00. That each of the parties hereto has subscribed to the capital stock of the said corporation according to their respective interests in said property, after deducting from the interests of Abram C. Hatch and John E. Austin therein one hundred thousand shares to be held by said corporation as treasury stock to be disposed of by order of the Board of Directors, as they may deem necessary, for the purpose only of creating a fund for the payment of the debts and obligations of the corporation, and for carrying on the business and pursuits of the corporation, as set forth in Article V hereof; and the further amount of eighty thousand shares of said capital stock, to be set apart for the express purpose of fulfilling the terms of a contract entered into between F. W.C. Hathenbruck, one of the original owners of said lease, and George F. Timms, dated the 12th of October, 1903, and in accordance with the conditions of an agreement made and entered into between A.C. Hatch and John E. Austin, as first parties, and F.W.C. Hathenbruck and Caleb B. Rhoades, second parties, said contract being dated January 30th, L.D. 1904, a copy of each of said contracts to be placed on file in the office of said corporation ....

## ARTICLE VIII.

That the amount of the subscription to the capital stock of said corporation and the value of the interest of each of the parties hereto in the property herein above described, except the one hundred and eighty thousand shares in the preceding article mentioned, and which said interests have been conveyed to the corporation, as in the preceding article set forth, as and for full payment of his subscription to the capital stock thereof, is as follows:

| Names | Number of Shares | Value |
|---|---|---|
| John E. Austin, | 40,333-1/3 | $40,333.33-1/3 |
| Abram C. Hatch | 40,333-1/3 | $40,333.33-1/3 |
| Charles S. Carter | 25,000 | $25,000.00 |
| John E. Booth | 1,000 | $1,000.00 |
| Dermont H. Roberts | 1,000 | $1,000.00 |
| Abram C. Hatch & John Austin | 212,333-1/3 | $12,333.33-1/3 |
| Treasury stock, as in preceding article mentioned, | 100,000 | $100,000.00 |
| Trust Fund for particular purpose as in preceding article mentioned | 80,000 | $80,000.00 |
| Total | $500,000 | $500,000.00 |

## ARTICLE IX.

That upon the perfecting of said corporation, a certificate or certificates of the stock subscribed by each of the parties hereto, as shown in the preceding article, shall be issued to said parties ....

## ARTICLE X.

The number and kind of officers of said corporation shall be as follows: A Board of five Directors, a President, a Vice-President, a Secretary and a Treasurer. The President and Vice-President shall be Directors. No person shall be a director unless he is the owner, in his own right, as shown by the books of the corporation, of at least one thousand shares of the capital stock ....

## ARTICLE XI

The term of office of the officers of this corporation, except as hereinafter in Article XII provided, shall be for two years, and until their successors shall have been duly elected and shall have duly qualified, and except in case of death, resignation or removal, as hereinafter provided.

## ARTICLE XII

That the following named persons, parties hereto, shall be directors of said corporation from the date hereof until the first Monday in June, A.D. 1905, and until their successors shall have been regularly elected and duly qualified, as hereinafter provided, namely: John E. Austin, Abram C. Hatch, Charles S. Carter, John E. Booth and Dermont H. Roberts: and the said John E. Booth shall be President, and the said Abram C. Hatch shall be Vice-President; the said Dermont H. Roberts shall be Secretary, and the said John E. Austin, Treasurer, for the above named term ....

## ARTICLE XIII

That the annual meeting of the stockholders of this corporation, for the purpose of hearing the reports of its officers as to the condition of its affairs, and for the transaction of such other business as may lawfully come before the meeting, shall be held on the first Monday in June of each and every year at two o'clock P.M. of said day, at the general office of the corporation, in Heber City, Wasatch County, Utah ....

## ARTICLE XIV.

That at the annual stockholder's meeting held on the first Monday of June, 1905, and biennially thereafter, a full Board of Seven Directors shall be elected. The Directors shall be elected by ballot, ....

## ARTICLE XV.

That the President, Vice-President, Secretary and Treasurer, may be removed at any time by a vote of a majority of the entire Board of Directors at any regular meeting of the Board of Directors, or at any special meeting of the Board of Directors duly called and held for that purpose.

## ARTICLE XVI.

That any or either of the Directors or officers may be removed at a stockholders' meeting called and held for the purpose of considering and voting upon such removal, by a two-thirds vote of the outstanding capital stock being represented such meeting....

## ARTICLE XVII.

That a majority of the entire Board of Directors shall form a quorum and be and are hereby authorized to transact the business and exercise the corporate powers of said corporation in all matters, except as provided to the contrary in Articles I, V, and XV of this agreement.

## ARTICLE XVIII.

That if from any cause the Directors shall not be elected at the time hereinbefore provided, said election may be held at a special meeting of the stockholders called and held for that purpose ....

## ARTICLE XIX.

Special meetings of the stockholders of said corporation other than for the purpose of electing Directors, may be called at any time by the President, or in case of his failure to do so, by the Vice-President, by any three Directors, or by stockholders representing not less than one-third of the outstanding capital stock ....

## ARTICLE XX.

That Three-fourths of the entire Board of Directors of said corporation voting therefore, may levy and collect assessments upon all of the outstanding capital stock of said corporation in the manner provided by the laws of the State of Utah for levying and collecting assessments upon the capital stock of the corporation. PROVIDED, that no one assessment shall exceed Five per cent of the outstanding capital stock of the corporation; and provided further, that the sale of the capital stock of the corporation as Treasury stock to be sold by order of the Board of Directors as herein above in Article VII provided, shall not be a necessary prerequisite to the levying and collecting of assessments on the outstanding capital stock.

In Witness Whereof the parties hereto have hereunto set their hands to these Articles of Agreement in six copies, this the Ninth day of March, A.D. 1904.

J.E. BOOTH
ABRAM C. HATCH
CHARLES S. CARTER JOHN E. AUSTIN
DERMONT H. ROBERTS

## REVOCATION OF POWER OF ATTORNEY—JUNE 2, 1904

KNOW ALL MEN BY THESE PRESENTS:

That whereas we, Caleb B. Rhoades and Sidsie Rhoades, of Price, Carbon County, State of Utah, in and by our letter of writing, warrant, or power of Attorney, bearing the date October 17th A.D. 1903 did make, constitute and appoint John T. Clark, of Provo City, Utah County, State of Utah, our true and lawful attorney for the purposes and with the powers therein set forth, as will more fully and at large appear by reference thereto or to the record thereof made of the 21st day of October A.D. 1903, in book "2" of Miscellaneous Records, in the County Recorder's Office of Wasatch County, State of Utah, at pages 34 and 35.

Now therefore, we, Caleb B. Rhoades and Sidsie Rhoades, for divers good causes and considerations as hereunto moving have revoked, countermanded, annulled and made void, and by these presents do revoke, countermand, annul and make void, the said letter, warrant, or power of Attorney, and all power and authority thereby give or intended to be given to the said John T. Clark.

In Witness Whereof we have hereunto set Our hands this the 2nd day of June, A.D. 1904.

Signed in the presence of

L.O. HOFFMAN
CALEB B. RHOADES
SIDSIE RHOADES

State of Utah

County of Carbon
}
}ss
}

On this 2nd day of June A.D. 1904 personally appeared before me Caleb B. Rhoades and Sidsie Rhoades, his wife, the signers of the above instrument, who duly acknowledged to me that they executed the same.

L.O. HOFFMAN
Notary Public
(Seal)

My commission expires January 22 A.D. 1905.

Recorded at request of A. C. Hatch June 3, 1904 at 4 o-clock P.M.

THOMAS S. WATSON,
County Recorder

## QUIT CLAIM—AUG. 8, 1904

Caleb B. Rhoades and Sidsie Rhoades, his wife, Grantors of Price, Carbon County, Utah, hereby bargains, sell, remise, releases and conveys A Quit Claim to John T. Clark of Provo City, Utah County, Utah, Grantee, for the sum of $1.00 (one dollar) and other valuable considerations, an undivided one-half interest of their right, title and interest, estate, claim and demand, both in law and in equity, as well as in possession, expectancy of in or to that certain portion claim and mining right title on precious metals of gold, silver, lead, and copper, situated in the Uintah Range of Mountains, on what is now known as the Uintah Indian Reservation in Wasatch County, State of Utah, and described as follows to wit:—An undivided half interest in that certain Mining Claim known and located as the Rhoades Mine such said claim was located by the Grantor above named Caleb B. Rhoades, On or about the tenth day of July, 1859, and also that certain Mining Claim known as the Pine Mine located by the Grantor above named Caleb B. Rhoades on or about the 10th day of July 1859.

This deed is given for the purpose of making more certain and definite a deed heretofore executed by said Grantors to said Grantee on the 17th day of October, 1903.

Together with all dips, spurs and angles, and also all the Metals, ores, gold and silver bearing quartz, rock and earth therein; And all the right, privileges and franchises, a thereto incident appendant and appurtenances thereto belonging, and the rents, issues and profits thereof; And also all the estate right, title interest, possession, claim and demands, whatever of the said Grantors of in or to the premises and every part and parcel thereof. To Have and to hold all and singular the premises together with the appurtenances and privileges thereto incident, and said Grantors, for themselves and their heirs doth hereby agree and with said Grantee that they have full rights and power to sell and convey the said premises; And that the said premises are now free and clear from all encumbrances, sales or mortgages made or suffered by the Grantors. Witness the hand of said Grantors this 8th day of August, 1904. Signed in the presence of SAMUEL A. KING LEVI N. HARMON

CALEB B. RHOADES
SIDSIE RHOADES

State of Utah
County of Carbon
}
} ss.
}

On this 8th day of August, 1904, personally appeared before me Caleb B. Rhoades and Sidsie Rhoades, his wife, who acknowledged to me that they executed the same. (Seal)

A. W. HORSLEY Notary Public My Commission expires January 27, 1906. Recorded at request of John T. Clark, May 16th, 1905 at 11:30 A.M... (Mining Deeds & Records of Wasatch County -Book 5, pages 305 & 306.)

*Courtesy of Randy W. Lewis*

## F.W.C. Hathenbruck
### Born November 30, 1852

Came to Utah with Johnson's Army as a Topographer and graduated from the Hiedelburg University, received honors in the field of geology and a degree in Medicine. As the son of William the 3rd Kieser of Germany, was fluent in five languages, including Ute. Lived one year with the Ute Indians and took care of Chief Tabby through an illness. Supplied the Indians with blankets and dry goods from his store in Provo, Utah. Hathenbruck also worked for the Denver & Rio Grande Railroad where he served as a Topographer during the building of the railroad over Soldier Summit to Springville to Price. Later he lost his right arm in a sawmill accident in Park City, Utah. Because of this he reverted back to his medical background, and also opened a dry good store in territory of Provo, Utah.

During this time Hathenbruck gained a reputation as a gentle, kind and honest physician and businessman who held no malice against minorities of mankind, whether they be black, yellow, or red and in fact constantly treated and traded with them even though many could not otherwise afford his services. This generous act on his part quickly gained for him his widespread reputation of "The Doctor." He was well-liked, especially by the Ute Indians. Through his constant dealings with them, both on and off the reservation, he gained a thorough knowledge of their customs and their language. Caleb formed a partnership with Mr. Hathenbruck in the Fall of 1894.

## Young F.W.C. Hathenbruck

*Courtesy of Randy W. Lewis*

*Courtesy of Randy W. Lewis*

Top: Hamburg, Toralansicht, Hathenbruck's boyhood home.
Bottom: The Imperial Palace in Berlin where Hathenbruck was raised.

A *Herald* representative had a pleasant interview with Mr. Hathenbruck yesterday. . . According to Mr. Hathenbruck, "The Ledge is well defined, and the pay streak is from 3 inches to 3 feet in width. There is what we call barren rock in the ledge, but even this assays 35 ounces in silver and 4 dollars in gold, while the pay streak goes as high as $150,000 in gold and silver to the ton, the gold contents of the mineral predominating." Mr. Hathenbruck then got his grip and showed the *Herald* man a number of samples of ore from the mine and they were magnificent, the mineral being almost solid tellurium, and was covered and streaked through and through with wire silver and gold that was beautiful to look at. Mr. Hathenbruck also stated that the Caleb Rhoades ledge was full of just such mineral as this, and he produced an assay certificate showing the results obtained from half an ounce of ore, the values of which were 1.800 ounces of silver and $17,000 in gold to the ton. (This was at $32 an ounce for gold.) Mr. Hathenbruck has succeeded in obtaining permission from the Indians to work the old Caleb Rhoades mine, but before he can strike a pick in the development of the property or ship a pound of ore he will be obligated to also secure permission of the government to mine there, and it is this that has brought him to Salt Lake, as with his associates, he has made application to the Department of the Interior for a grant of four miles square in the desired locality, and if he is successful he will inaugurate a mining enterprise on a gigantic scale.

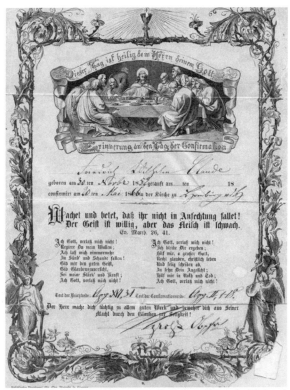

*Courtesy of Randy W. Lewis*

Christening confirmation for F.W.C. Hathenbruck.

*Courtesy of Randy W. Lewis*

Mimmie Louise, daughter of Rozella Hathenbruck and great-grandmother of co-author Randy Lewis, with child Norma Clark.

*Courtesy of Randy W. Lewis*

Mimmie Louise

*Courtesy of Randy W. Lewis*

F.W.C. Hathenbruck as an old man seated in front of his house in Provo.

*Courtesy of Harold and Bette Hathenbruck*

Interior of the "F.W.C. Hathenbruck & Company Store," Provo, Utah, as it appeared about 1900.

*Courtesy of Randy W. Lewis*

Mr. Hathenbruck was forced to hire a bookkeeper
because of his long absences in the Uintahs.

*Courtesy of Randy W. Lewis*

F.W.C. Hathenbruck with his wife Rozilla Rebecca
Saunsesie and four of their children.

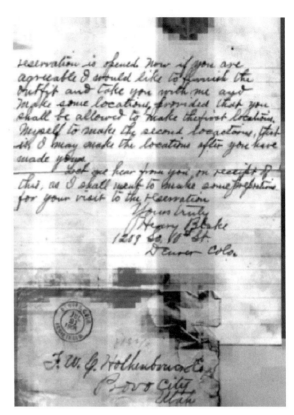

*Courtesy of Randy W. Lewis*

Letter to F.W.C. Hathenbruck

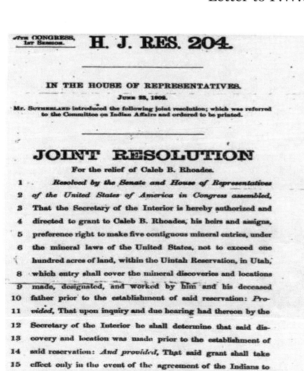

*Courtesy of Randy W. Lewis*

Hathenbruck's attempts with Congress.

Rozilla Rebecca, wife, FWC Hathenbruck, their son Willard Earl Hathenbruck, and his wife, Margaret.

*Courtesy of Harold and Bette Hathenbruck*

Frederick William Claudius Hathenbruck, his wife, Rozilla Rebecca Saunsecie, and their young granddaughter. Photo taken shortly before Mr. Hathenbruck's untimely death.

*Courtesy of Harold and Bette Hathenbruck*

*Courtesy of Randy W. Lewis*

### F.W. (Bill) Mangum

Frank William Mangum of Heber City, Utah took care of his grandfather F.W.C. Hathenbruck in his last days as a boy of 15. Bill was told all the stories and locations of the mines of the Uintahs. He related to me the cabin of Grandaddy and those exciting stories.

*Courtesy of Randy W. Lewis*

Hathenbruck's Gunfighters on a mining trip to the Uintahs. Hathenbruck is third from the right. Matt Warner is on the right with the open vest.

*Courtesy of Randy W. Lewis*

The FWC Hathenbruck Crossing

*Courtesy of Randy W. Lewis*

The F.W.C. Hathenbruck Gunfighters in 1905. In this group is Matt Warner, Elza Lay, Henry "Hen" Lee, Iowa J. Hall, Bob Meeks, and others.

*Courtesy of Randy W. Lewis*

Hathenbruck's body guards-gunfighters, 1905.

Back row, left: Elza Lay, unidentified, Henry "Hen" Lee, Matt Warner, F.W.C. Hathenbruck.

Front row, left: unidentified, Bill Meeks, Iowa G. Hall, last two unidentified.

*Courtesy of Randy W. Lewis*

Hathenbruck Gunfighters with a wrecked wagon in the vicinity of the mine. Butch Cassidy is standing in the center.

*Courtesy of Randy W. Lewis*

Hathenbruck's gunfighters with wrecked wagon; second man from right (standing), Elza Lay.

*Courtesy of Randy W. Lewis*

Hathenbruck wagon.

F.W.C. Hathenbruck with companion on a hunting party.

*Courtesy of Randy W. Lewis*

F.W.C. Hathenbruck camp in the mountains. 1905-1906.

*Courtesy of Randy W. Lewis*

211

*Courtesy of Randy W. Lewis*

Rhoades & Hathenbruck cabin in Grandaddy Basin as it appeared in the 1800s. F.W.C. Hathenbruck is seated at the table in front.

*Courtesy of Randy W. Lewis*

Caleb Baldwin Rhoades

Born 1836        Died 1905

*Courtesy of Randy W. Lewis*

The remains of Hathenbruck's cabin.

*Courtesy of Randy W. Lewis*

Rhoades & Hathenbruck cabin as it looked in the late 1960s.

*Courtesy of the Utah Historical Society*

*Courtesy of Randy W. Lewis*

Happy Jack

Chief Tabby, 105 years old. Chief of the Goshutes for 73 years. While ill and near death, this remarkable man braved the fierce storms of winter to aid F.W.C. Hathenbruck in obtaining his lease.

*Footprints in the Wilderness (Gale Rhoades & Kerry Boren)*

Chief Ouray, Utah Chieftain, and his sub-chiefs; Warets, Shavano, Ankatosh, and Guero.

213

*Courtesy of Randy W. Lewis*

Gale R. Rhoades with his grandfather
James Walter Boren at an old homestead
on the Price River in Carbon County, Utah.

*Courtesy of Randy W. Lewis*

Author Kerry Ross Boren during the
1970s in the High Uintahs.

*Courtesy of the author*

Kerry Ross Boren

*Courtesy of Randy W. Lewis*

*Courtesy of Randy W. Lewis*

Lisa Lee Boren signing books at Planet
Rainbow in Ogden, Utah.

Paul Tabbee, great-grandson of
Chief Tabby at "Picture Rock."

*Courtesy of Randy W. Lewis*

Radley and Nancy Lewis. Nancy is a descendant of F.W.C. Hathenbruck.

*Courtesy of Randy W. Lewis*

Randy W. Lewis mining.

*Courtesy of Randy W. Lewis*

Bill Bleazard

*Courtesy of Randy W. Lewis*

Randy W. Lewis mining at Current Creek.

*Courtesy of Randy W. Lewis*

Randy W. Lewis

*Courtesy of Randy W. Lewis*

Headwaters of the Provo River.
(Timpanogos River)

*Courtesy of Randy W. Lewis*

Mine west of the Placer Mine.

*Courtesy of Randy W. Lewis*

Happy Jack Mine

*Courtesy of Randy W. Lewis*

Location Grant

Indian head rock carving.

*Courtesy of Randy W. Lewis*

*Courtesy of Randy W. Lewis*

Mercury Separator. A tool used to separate mercury from gold. Discovered in the Grandaddy Basin.

*Courtesy of Randy W. Lewis*

Placer Mine in a meadow near Lodgepole Lake in the Grandaddy Basin.

*Courtesy of Randy W. Lewis*

An old mining sluice.

*Courtesy of Randy W. Lewis*

This is Grandaddy Lake Basin at the top of Hades Canyon, near DeFa's Dude Ranch. Caleb Rhoades & F.W.C. Hathenbruck had a cabin between Grandaddy Lake and East of Lodgepole Lake. In 1968, there were two cabins—one by Lodgepole Lake with a metal roof. The Rhoades and Hathenbruck cabin had a dirt roof with a pine tree growing on top of the cabin. The Forest Service claimed that the cabin was blown up and is no longer there.

*Courtesy of Randy W. Lewis*

Grandaddy Hades Basin

*Courtesy of Randy W. Lewis*

Area in the vicinity of the Hathenbruck Mine.

*Courtesy of Gary Christensen*

Roadmap

*Courtesy of Gary Christensen*

Spanish Bridle

*Courtesy of Gary Christensen*

Spanish Armor, found in Utah.

*Courtesy of Gary Christensen*

Spanish Cannon

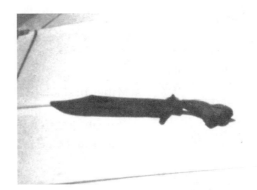

*Courtesy of Gary Christensen*

Spanish Knife

# EXPLANATION OF THE MAPS

When all of the evidence is weighed, it appears that the Lost Rhoades Mine of Caleb B. Rhoades and F.W.C. Hathenbruck is identical with the so-called Lost Josephine Mine discovered by Wes Young. The area of location is the same, the description seems to fit, and the contents are identical. Both accounts confirm the presence of the wooden door, stone steps, blacksmith tools, and the gold and silver bars. In both accounts there is mentioned of an Indian burial ground nearby. There is still another parallel: men have perished in search of both. The history of the Lost Rhoades Mine is written on pages of misery etched in blood.

The written history of the mines (there were many, though we concern ourselves here only with the mine known to Hathenbruck) begins in the year 1540 when Garcia Lopez de Cardenas led an expedition north from Mexico to the rim of the Grand Canyon. Cardenas dispatched a party of seven men, commanded by one "Tomás Blaque," to proceed northward to the land of the Utes in search of the source of their gold.

"Tomás Blaque" was not a Spaniard. He was a Scottish soldier of fortune, son of William and Agnes (Mowat) Blake of Scotland. For twenty years he was the only man of British blood allowed to reside in Mexico, and he became the first known European to enter what is now the State of Utah. With six followers he arrived at an Indian village on the site of present day Vernal, Utah, in about September 1540. They tortured and killed several Indian braves until they were given gold from the mine, but the Indians rebelled at the last, and sent the expedition out of the Uintah Mountain country without the gold or their horses.

Blake's visit is well-documented. A map dated 1564, located in the Archives of Spain at Madrid, is titled: "Mapa de los Indios del Norte de la Rio Tizon en los Provincias Internas de la Nuevo España, de la exactitude de lo referido a Senor Tomás Blaque, acerca de aquel pais, en Julio, 1540." Translation: "Map of the Indians of the North of the River Tizon (Colorado) in the Internal Provinces of New Spain, exactly as referred to by Senor Thomas Blake, who was near this country in July, 1540." [For greater detail, see: *The Gold of Carre-Shinob*, op. cit. at Chapter One; also: *Following the Ark of the Covenant*, Kerry Ross Boren and Lisa Lee Boren, Council Press, Springville, Utah, 2000.]

The Spaniards returned to the region, lured by the lust after gold and silver. They located and worked numerous mines across the length and breadth of the Uintah Mountains and elsewhere. They forced the natives into slave labor and compelled them to work in the mines. Many hundreds of Indians died under the oppressive yoke of their taskmasters.

In 1848, Fran Juan Ortiz told officers of Stephen F. Kearney's American Army at Santa Fe that as early as 1650 there had been a series of Spanish forts as far as five hundred miles up the Green River. In that same year, according to Fray Ortiz, the Indians arose in open rebellion against the Spaniards and burned the forts, killing most of the occupants and driving the remainder of them from the country.

One of the last of these Spanish forts existed as late as 1666 in the Grandaddy Lakes Basin, in the vicinity of the Lost Rhoades Mine. There exists a map dated 1768 titled "Mapa del Camino de los Minos del Yutas" ("Map of the Trail to the Mines of the Utes") that details that, in addition to a number of mines, there existed both a fort and a church in the region, 40 kilometers east of "Laguna de las Yutas" (Utah Lake), and that it was destroyed in 1666.

Nevertheless, the Spaniards continued to return to the region over the years, guided by their maps and journals, and removed much of the gold and silver from the mountains. The Indians frequently attacked them and attempted to keep them away, but they came again and again in spite of it. They came with soldiers in armor; they came with cannon; they came with muskets and in such number that the Indians could not prevail. Often the Spaniards returned to Santa Fe and Mexico with Indian captives whom they sold into slavery, never more to see their happy mountain home. All of this in the name of the golden god.

Tracing only the history of the Lost Rhoades Mine in the Grandaddy Basin, which appears to be synonymous with the Lost Josephine Mine near Hoyt Peak, we make an important discovery. According to the Waybill discovered by Gale Rhoades: "...The Treasure abandoned for fear of death by hostile natives—of 42 comrades 8 survived. This Mine worked (from) year 1782 and covered in 1814, as so written in the journal of work of the expedition by me—Jose Jonqin Garcia, Captain—Mexico City, November Year 1814."

Pan-a-pitch was chief of the San Pete (or Sanpete) Utes. He had been born circa 1752 on the banks of the Seeds-ka-dee (Green River) and when only a boy of three or four years he accompanied his father Uin-pah-quint and other members of his tribe to the land of the Timpanogos, or Lake Shore People (present day Utah Valley). Eventually they settled southward in what became known as the Sanpete Valley.

The Spaniards captured Pan-a-pitch and tortured him to learn the sources of Ute gold, but he would not tell them. They placed him in a monastery in Mexico and chained him to the floor while they attempted to convert him to Christianity by force, hoping that if he converted, he would give the gold to the Catholic Church. They gave him the Christian name "San Pedro" or Saint Peter, which eventually became simply "San Pete." His people called him "Sanpitch."

After several years of captivity, San Pete escaped and returned to his people in Utah. In the year 1814 or 1815 the Spaniards launched an expedition from Santa Fe to convince the obstinate old chieftain to take them to his mines in the mountains. Still he refused. At last the Spaniards turned their cannon on his tepee, blowing it to pieces, together with his favorite wife and at least one of his younger children.

At last, San Pete relented and agreed to escort the Spaniards into the mountains and show them several gold sources. No sooner had he done so, however, than the Spaniards killed him, together with two of his fellow braves, and buried them in rock cairns near the mines. But when the Spaniards came down out of the mountains, their mules loaded with gold, and camped near present day Nephi, Utah, the Indians, led by San Pete's son Moonch, attacked them with a vengeance. A number of Spaniards were killed, but some of them escaped, though compelled to abandon the heavily laden pack animals to the Indians. The Utes returned the gold to the mountains and cut off the mules' hooves after killing them, superstitious that the burros might return in the spirit to aid the Spaniards. Moonch was the father of Chief Walker, and San Pete was Walker's grandfather.

There are many elements to this account that correspond with the account of the Lost Josephine. Both concern themselves with a massacre of the Spaniards, both occurred in about 1814, and both events took place at mines on upper Rock Creek in the Granddaddy Lakes Basin.

* * *

The next event of consequence connected to this elusive mine occurred in 1857 when eight Mexican miners were killed at Chicken Creek, near Levan, Utah. It was originally reported that the Mexicans had been killed by the Indians, who mutilated their bodies, and returned their stolen gold to the mines. According to this account, five days after the massacre, Brigham Young dispatched a detachment of 21 militiamen led by First Lt. Thomas Rhoades to bury the dead Mexicans. Ostensibly, Rhoades discovered several maps in a tin box at the massacre site, maps which showed the location of rich Spanish mines in the high Uintahs. And thus it was, as the story goes, that the rich mine fell into the hands of Thomas Rhoades, and eventually his son Caleb, and became the famous Lost Rhoades Mine.

In recent years, however, research had revealed a somewhat different story, supported by documentary evidence. During the 1850s a Spaniard named Antonio Reinaldo, born near Seville, Spain, in 1820, led mining expeditions from Santa Fe, into the Uintah Mountains in search of gold. He had in his possession a map drawn by one Juan de Meyo, showing the location of a mine or mines along the "Huella de San Pedro"—the San Pedro Trail—which connects it to the 1814 mine whereby Chief San Pete was killed.

Reinaldo and his party had been in the mountains for several years, mining gold during the summer months, and returning to Santa Fe before winter, carrying both gold and Piede Indian slaves for sale in Mexico.

Then in the autumn of 1851, Reinaldo and six of his companions were arrested by none other than Marshal Wm. H. Kimball and others and brought to trial on 24 December 1851 before Judge Snow for trafficking in slave children with Ute war chief Arapene. The names of the Mexicans were as follows: Antonio de Reinaldo, Fernán Santiago, Philip Perez, Juan de Corso, Alvaro de Perón, Pedro de Santa Cruz, and Juan de Meyo. The latter may have been the same who led the 1831 expedition, or a member of his family of the same name. [For a complete record of the Reinaldo story, including excerpts from the trial, see: *The Gold of Carre-Shinob*, op. cit., at chapter two.]

The result of the trial was that Brigham Young expelled the Mexicans from the Territory, with a stern warning never to return upon penalty of death. But Reinaldo did return, in 1853. He recovered a great deal of gold in that year and returned to Santa Fe. Then, in 1857, Reinaldo sent another expedition to Utah in quest of more gold. He did not accompany the eight Mexicans, but sent with them two maps to the mines.

The first map, dated 1851, is simple, showing three mines in one area, an arrow pointing apparently to the only one which they mined that year. On the bottom of this map, Reinaldo wrote: "Explanation—these mines of gold and silver are in the high plateaus, two canyons from the east beyond the headland of the Mountain of the Timpanogos, and are hidden among a great many lakes. Here there is much wire gold and silver in a formation of rock crystal... Antonio de Reinaldo, 1851."

The second map, dated "1851-1853," indicates much more extensive exploration. Reinaldo details rivers, streams, waterholes, peaks, trails, passes, plateaus, and mines, in considerable detail. The most important single detail is the "Huella de San Pedro," connecting the mine with the 1814 "Lost Josephine." While Reinaldo awaited their return in Santa Fe, the eight Mexicans camped with their packloads of gold on Chicken Creek. Mormon V. Selman, a Mormon missionary to the Ute Indians, recorded in his personal journal:

*My father used to tell me of a time in the early days when a pack trail came down the Provo River and camped by his place for a few days to rest up their small pack mules. He said they loaded these animals with a heavy pack load that did not appear to be very large, but it was all those mules could carry. The miners kept an armed guard at their camp and no one was allowed near. He said that they stayed a few days and then went south. A few days later there was a report that some indians had killed those men down on Chicken Creek and had stolen the mules, horses and whatever those animals were carrying in their packs. No one suspected that Indians would steal a pack train, so everybody decided that it was someone who had dressed up as Indians.*

Dimick B. Huntington recovered the two Reinaldo maps and delivered them to Brigham Young. Thus it now appears that Thomas Rhoades obtained the maps from Brigham Young himself, by which he was able to locate a number of the gold mines. In the very next year (1858) Brigham Young and Thomas Rhoades shared equally in a massive private land grant which extended from the Kamas Prairie eastward to the headwaters of the Provo River, encompassing much of the area indicated on the Reinaldo maps. In the same year, Brigham Young dispatched Thomas Rhoades with a company of twenty-five men to establish a permanent settlement in the Kamas Valley. The settlement would constitute the "improvements" needed to legalize their claim to the grant.

During the ensuing years, Thomas Rhoades discovered and worked several of the mines illustrated on Antonio de Reinaldo's maps, all of which were in the Rock Creek-Moon Lake area in the high Uintahs. About 10 July 1859, twenty-three-year-old Caleb Baldwin Rhoades located two of the three mines shown on Reinaldo's 1851 map, which he called the "Pine Mine" and the "Rhoades Mine." Of the thirteen mines shown on Reinaldo's 1851-1853 map, Caleb Rhoades is believed to have located at least four.

At the time of Caleb Rhoades' death in 1905, the Antonio de Reinaldo maps became the property of Caleb's widow, Sidsie Jensen Rhoades, who later relinquished the maps to Caleb's brother, John Joseph Rhoades (whose son married the daughter of Walter Boren, uncle of Kerry Ross Boren), who upon his death on 5 June 1935, passed the maps to his eldest child, Olive Ann Rhoades Westenskow.

By the year 1962 the maps, originally etched and inked on dry buckskin, were in such a deteriorated condition that they were carefully copied and the originals discarded. Mrs. Westenskow died on 14 October 1972, but in 1968, prior to her death, she relinquished the copies of the Reinaldo maps, together with other materials, to her nephew Gale Rhoades and Kerry Ross Boren for their book, *Footprints in the Wilderness* (1971). The maps were withheld from publication at that time, however, due to the authors' ongoing searches in the mountains.

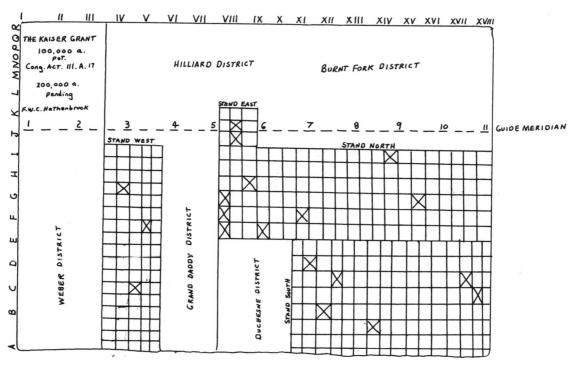

AUTHOR'S RENDITION OF HATHENBRUCK MAP OF KAISER GRANT

Author's rendition of Hathenbruck Map of Kaiser Grant.

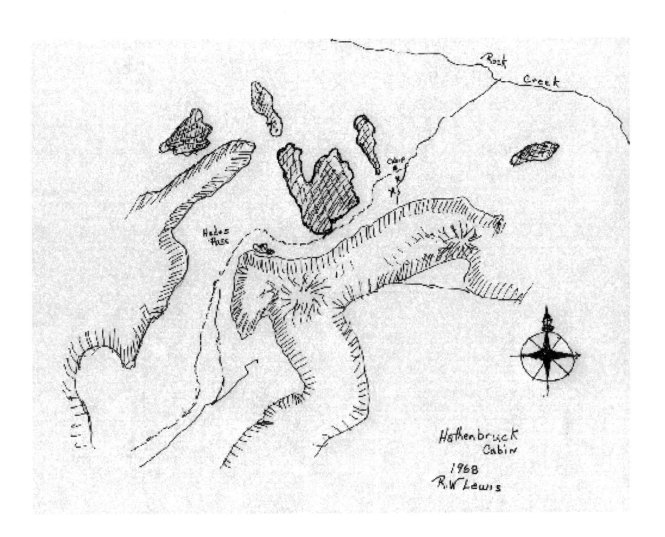

Hathenbruck Cabin Map

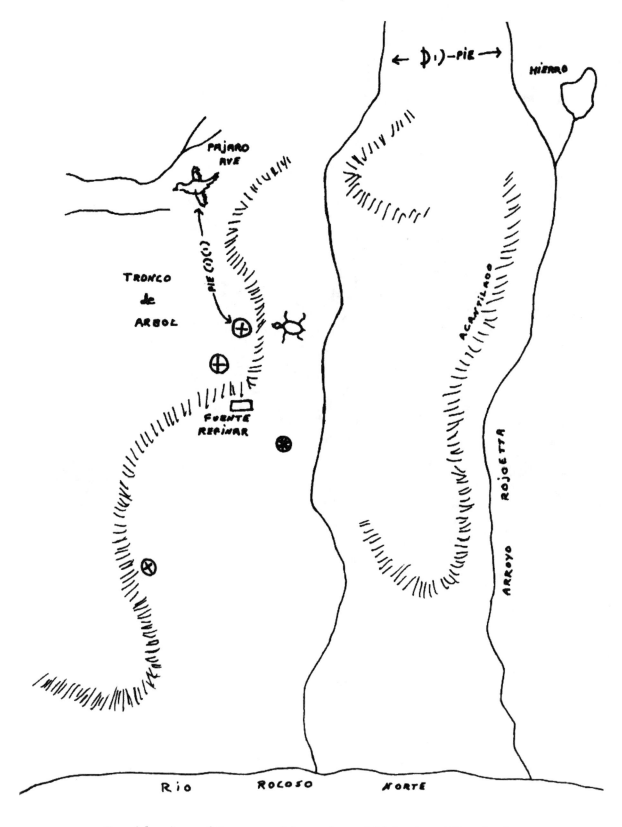

Spanish mines of Soapstone Mountain and Lightning Ridge, in the area of the Lost Stone Staircase Mine.

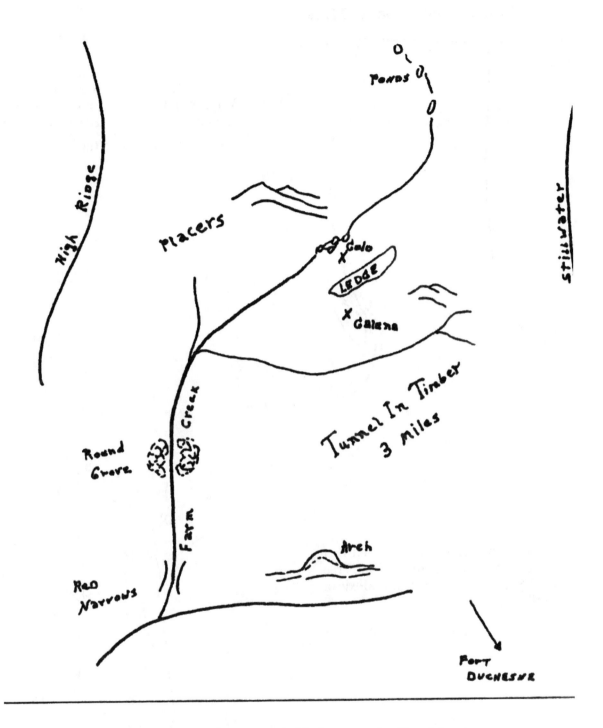

The Tunnel In Timber Map. Gold placers and a Spanish mine in the Farm Creek mountains.

## Map of Lost Rhoades Mine

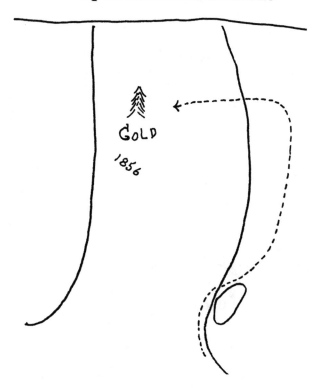

The Thomas Rhoades 1856 Pine Mine Map. What area does it really portray? (Compare it with the 1851 Reinaldo map.)

(Map just as it was on the buckskin.)

The Sulser map that ostensibly led Ben Bullock to the discovery of the "Pine Tree Mine." Supposedly drawn in a Mexican jail cell.

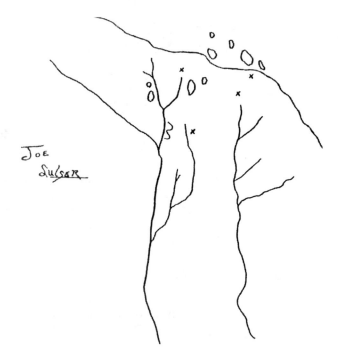

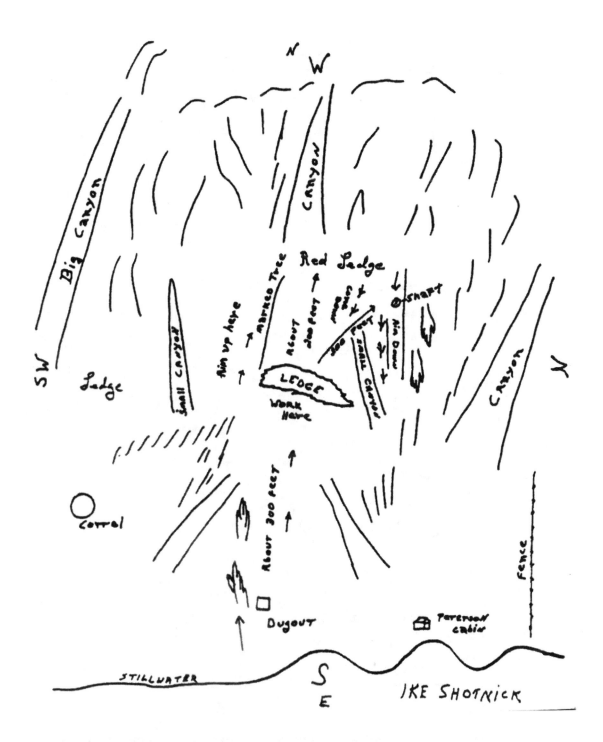

Ike Shotnick's map of his mine along Rock Creek. (Note the confused directional markers.)

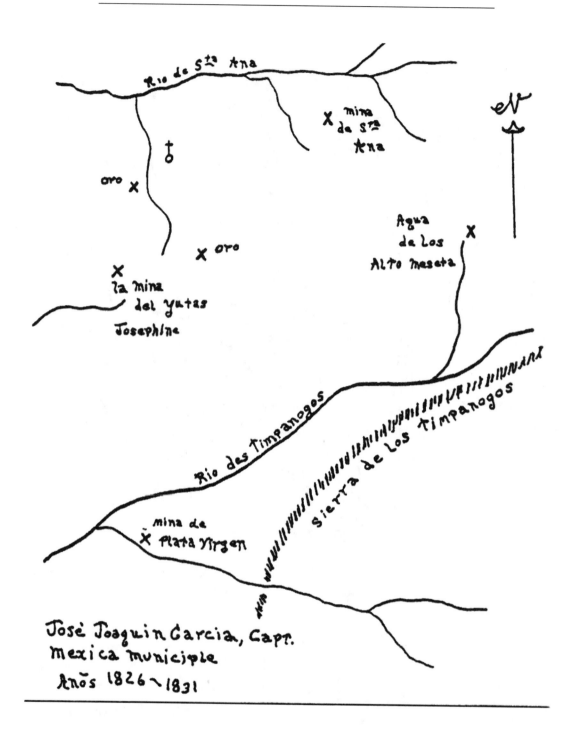

The Jose Joaquin Garcia Map of 1826-1831. Old Spanish mines above Kamas Valley. (Compare with Reinaldo maps.)

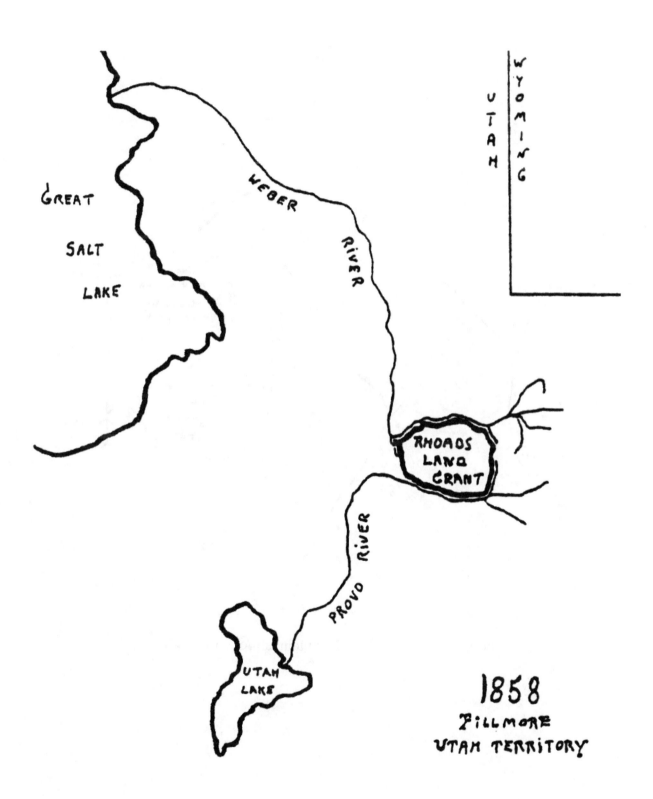

Thomas Rhoades Land Grand map—1858.

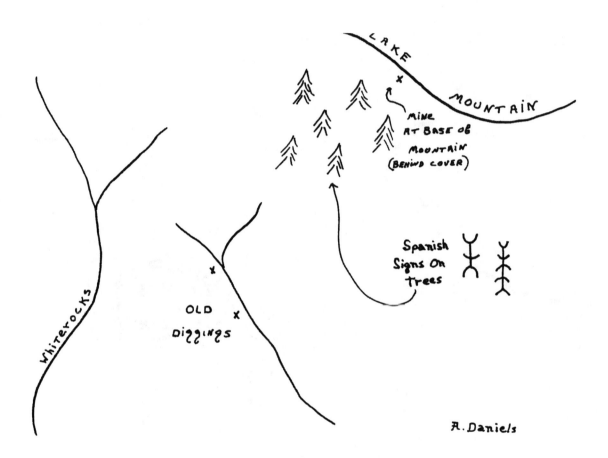

The Spanish mine at Lake Mountain; an Aaron Daniels map.

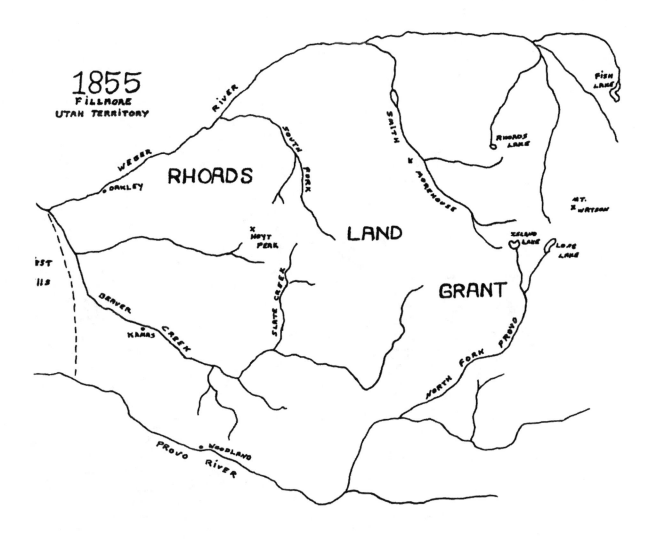

Thomas Rhoades Land Grant Map—1855. The grant contained all of the land between the Provo and Weber rivers to their headlands.

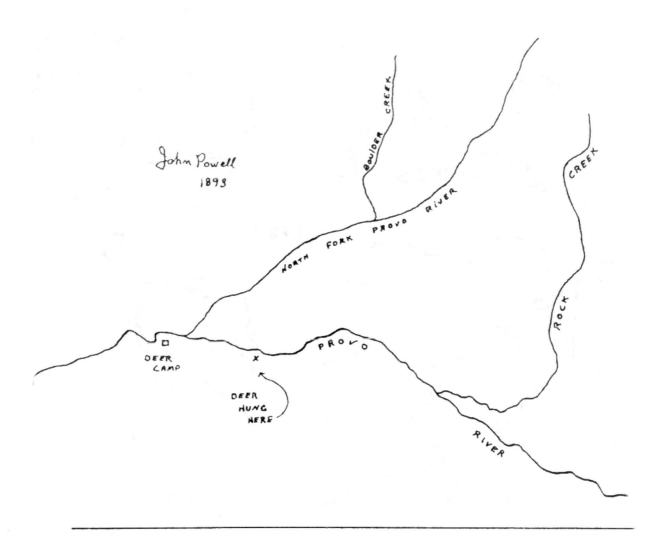

The Powell "Dear Hunt" Map. Caleb Rhoades found gold "not far" from where he hung his deer.

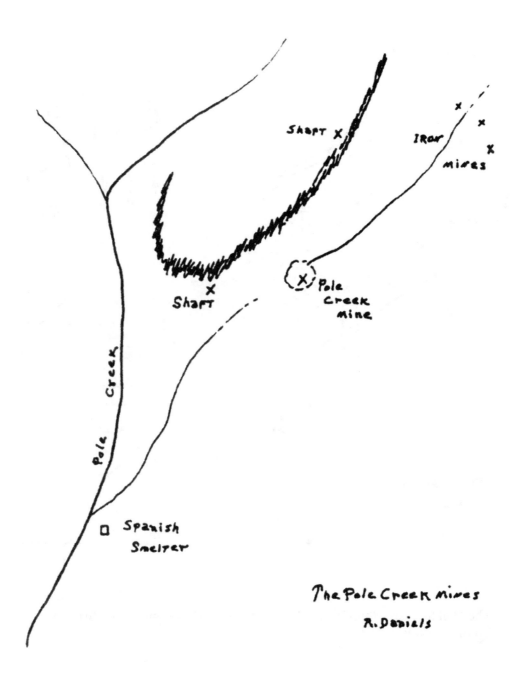

An Aaron Daniels map of the Pole Creek mines. Note the old Spanish smelter.

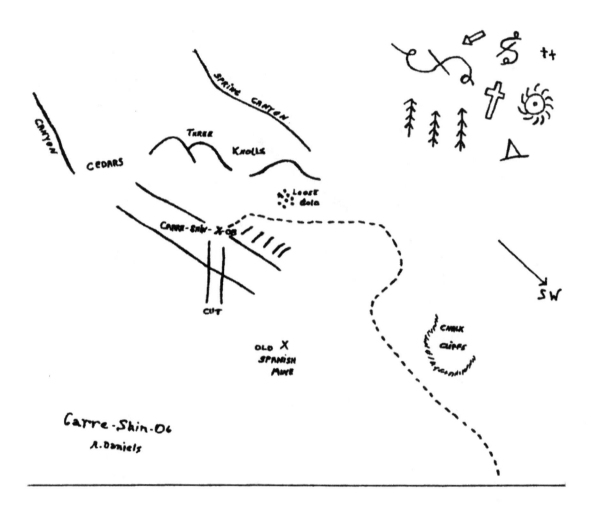

The trail to Carre-Shin-Ob, an Aaron Daniels map of the sacred Brigham Young or Church Mine.

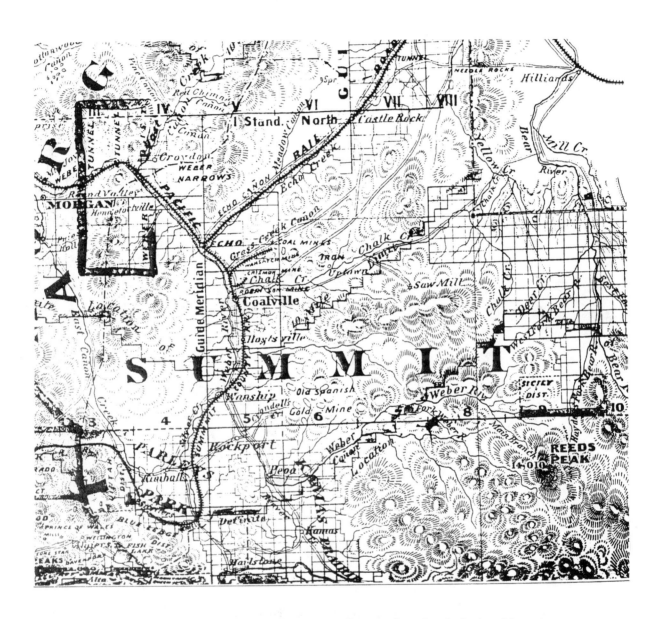

Froiseth's New Section & Mineral Map of Utah, 1878. An old
Spanish gold mine overlooks the Weber River.

THE UTAH GOLD RUSH

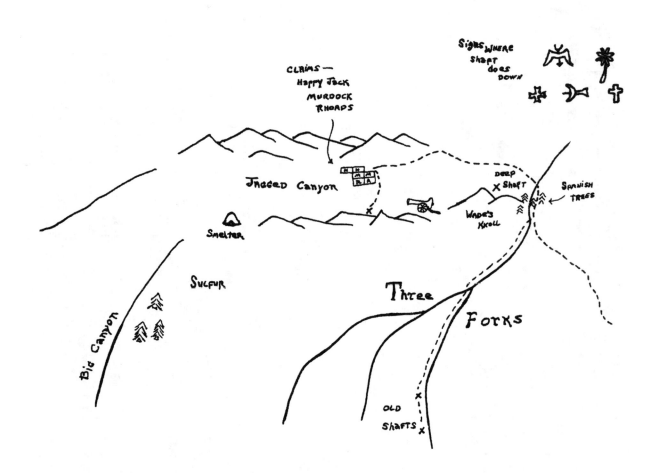

Happy Jack's "Three Forks" Map

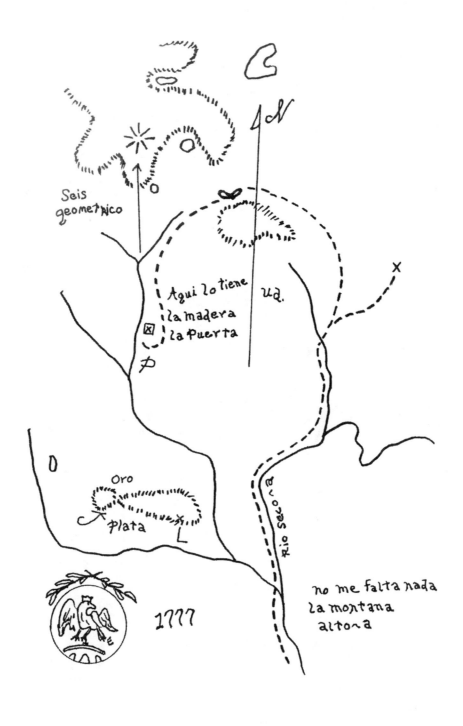

The Dry Fork or Mine of Lost Souls map.

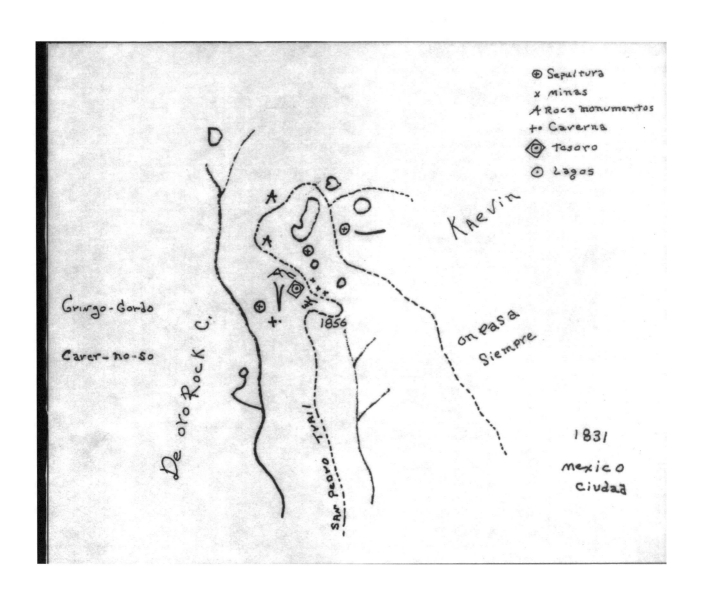

An altered copy of the Gringo-Gordo Map. Compare it with the original. Why was it changed?

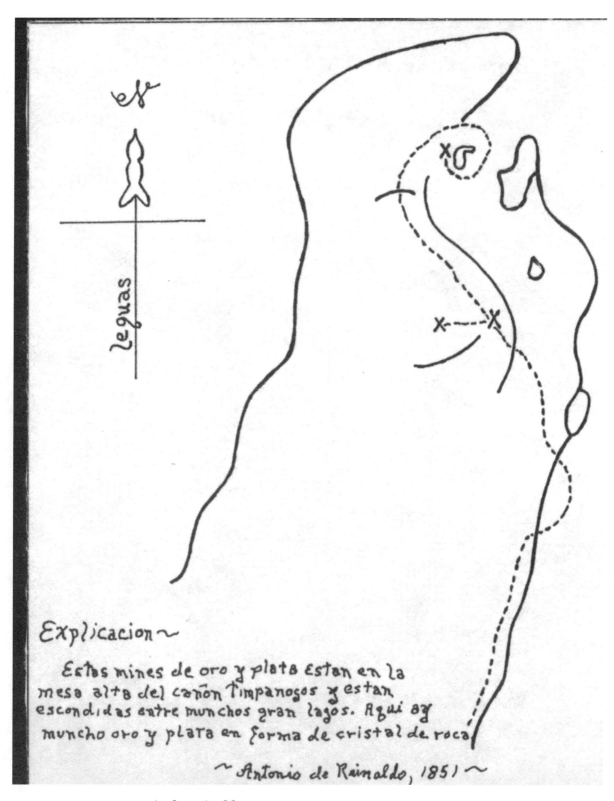

Antonio de Reinaldo Map—1851-1853.
Headwaters of the Provo and Weber rivers, Uintah Mountains.

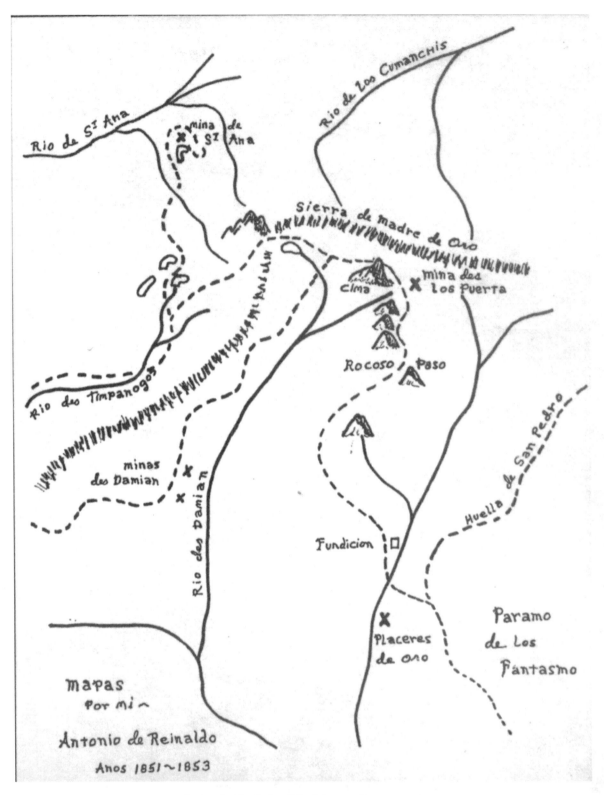

Antonio de Reinaldo Map—1851.
Headwaters of the Provo River.

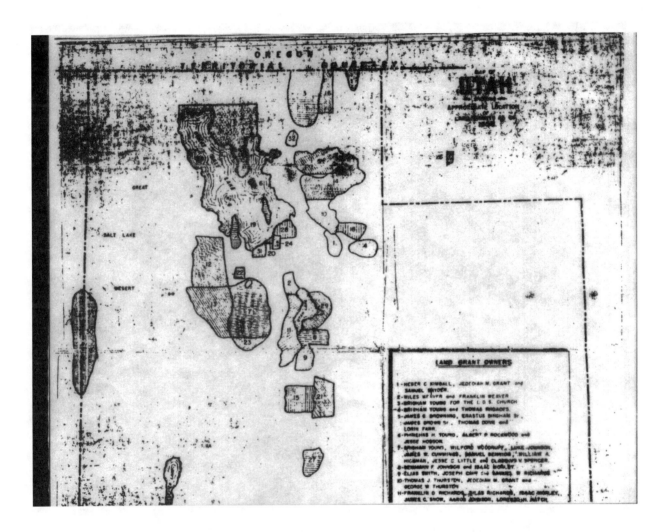

The LDS (Mormon) Church Rhoades Land Grant Map of 1858. The grant includes all the upper Weber River and Provo River area.

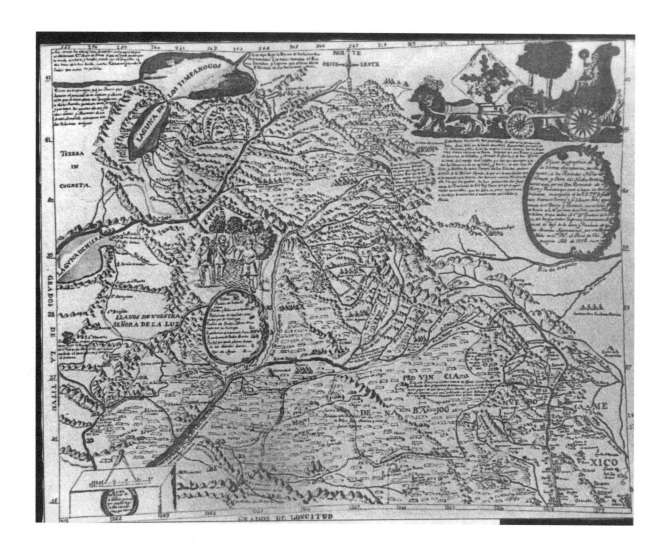

The Don Bernardo Mierra Map of 1776. Laguna De Los Timpanogos at the upper left.

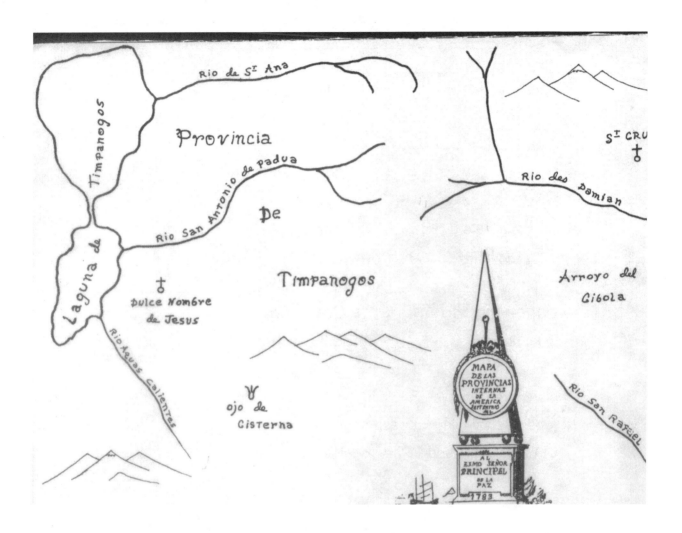

The La Paz Map of 1783: Mapa de los Privincias de la America Septemtrioal, the Province of Timpanogos.

# CEDAR FORT, INCORPORATED
## Order Form

Name:_____

Address: _____

City: _____ State: _____ Zip: _____

Phone: (    ) _____ Daytime phone: (    ) _____

### *The Utah Gold Rush*

Quantity: _____ @ $24.95 each:           _____

Also available by Kerry Ross Boren:

### *The Gold of Carre-Shinob*

Quantity: _____ @ $19.95 each:           _____

### *Following the Ark of the Covenant*

Quantity: _____ @ $19.95 each:           _____

plus $3.49 shipping & handling for the first book:           _____

(add 99¢ shipping for each additional book)

Utah residents add 6.25% for state sales tax:           _____

TOTAL:           _____

Mail this form and payment to:

Cedar Fort, Inc.

925 North Main St.

Springville,  UT  84663

You can also order on our website **www.cedarfort.com**

or e-mail us at sales@cedarfort.com or call 1-800-SKYBOOK

9  26575 76143  9